*The Challenge
of Local Feminisms*

Social Change in Global Perspective

Mark Selden, *Series Editor*

Exploring the relationship between social change and social structures, this series considers the theory, praxis, promise, and pitfalls of movements in global and comparative perspective. The historical and contemporary social movements considered here challenge patterns of hierarchy and inequality of race, gender, nationality, ethnicity, class, and culture. The series will emphasize textbooks and broadly interpretive synthetic works.

The Transformation of Communist Systems: Economic Reform Since the 1950s, BERNARD CHAVANCE

The Challenge of Local Feminisms: Women's Movements in Global Perspective, edited by AMRITA BASU, with the assistance of C. ELIZABETH MCGRORY

FORTHCOMING

African Women: A Modern History, CATHERINE COQUERY-VIDROVITCH

Power Restructuring in China and Russia, MARK LUPHER

Japanese Labor and Labor Movements, KUMAZAWA MAKOTO

THE
CHALLENGE
OF LOCAL
FEMINISMS

Women's Movements

in Global Perspective

edited by **AMRITA BASU**
with the assistance of C. Elizabeth McGrory

Westview Press • *Boulder • San Francisco • Oxford*

Social Change in Global Perspective

Published in 1995 in the United States of America by Westview Press, Inc., 5500 Central Avenue, Boul- der, Colorado 80301-2877, and in the United Kingdom by Westview Press, 12 Hid's Copse Road, Cumnor Hill, Oxford OX2 9JJ

Library of Congress Cataloging-in-Publication Data
The challenge of local feminisms : women's movements in
    global perspective / edited by Amrita Basu, with the assistance
    of C. Elizabeth McGrory.
        p.   cm. — (Social change in global perspective.)
    Studies initiated by the Women's Program Forum of the Ford
Foundation in preparation for the Fourth World Conference on Women,
scheduled for Beijing in 1995.
    Includes bibliographical references and index.
    ISBN 0-8133-2627-3   ISBN 0-8133-2628-1 (pbk.)
    1. Feminism—Cross-cultural studies.   2. Feminism—Developing
countries.   I. Basu, Amrita, 1953– .   II. McGrory, C. Elizabeth.
III. Ford Foundation. Women's Program Forum.   IV. Series: Social
change in global perspective (Boulder, Colo.)
HQ1101.G57   1995
305.42—dc20
                                                                                                95-7664
                                                                                                CIP

Printed and bound in the United States of America

The paper used in this publication meets the requirements
of the American National Standard for Permanence of Paper
for Printed Library Materials Z39.48-1984.

10   9   8   7   6   5   4   3   2   1

For Anna and her children,
Mark and Judy

Contents

Part 3: Latin America

Part 4: Russia, Europe, and the United States

Foreword

The Ford Foundation's programs to improve women's status and opportunities reflect its long-standing mission to provide resources to individuals and organizations working to reduce poverty and injustice, advance human achievement, and strengthen democratic values. Since 1972, when the first grants for women's programs began, the Foundation has supported a wide range of efforts to help women shape better futures for themselves, their families, and their communities.

In 1986, as part of the process of strengthening understanding about gender issues and women's concerns, the Ford Foundation established the Women's Program Forum. The Forum brings together Ford Foundation staff and colleagues from other foundations to explore issues important to women and produces written materials based on discussions held under its sponsorship. To date, the Forum has organized two international meetings and a seminar series on women's issues at the Foundation's headquarters in New York City. Recent forums explored women and violence, the 1992 elections in the United States, women and agricultural institutions in Africa, gender dimensions of school reform, and the relationships among women, population, and the environment.

Members of the Women's Program Forum expect the United Nations Fourth World Conference on Women scheduled for 1995 in Beijing, China, to be an important milestone in the worldwide movement to expand women's opportunities and choices. The world has changed since the close of the U.N. Decade for Women in 1985 was celebrated at the Third World Conference on Women in Nairobi, Kenya. Over the ensuing ten years, feminist activism and scholarship have profoundly altered local politics, national policies, and international debates about our common future.

The 1995 gathering will bring together, among others, some of the dynamic women throughout the world who have struggled for justice and who increasingly help shape the international agenda. Many others who attend the conference or follow its course through the media will not be familiar with the work and struggles that contributed to the present state of affairs. With this in mind, beginning in 1992, staff in a number of the Foundation's offices, with support from the Women's Program Forum, engaged scholar-activists to assess the characteristics, achievements, and current priorities of the women's movements in their countries. The authors were given a general assignment as well as latitude to select the issues and events most relevant to their countries' contexts. Some chose to work singly or in pairs; others assembled groups of colleagues to reflect on the common history, achievements, and ongoing challenges of the movements in which they were deeply involved. Several of these efforts also helped initiate discussion and preparations for the conference in Beijing. The Forum engaged Dr. Amrita Basu to compile these commissioned chapters into a comparative, edited volume and to help shape them for the volume's international audience. This process was facilitated during a meeting of the authors in Amherst, Massachusetts, in January 1994, where they worked together to share ideas and develop a common framework.

This book thus seeks to draw lessons of broader significance while allowing each chapter to explore the distinctive influences of local context and individual effort on the nature and strategies of national women's movements. We are grateful to the authors and to Dr. Basu for so powerfully conveying the richness and complexity of dynamic global movements to advance women's rights and opportunities.

Susan V. Berresford
Executive Vice President
The Ford Foundation

Acknowledgments

A book of this scope and complexity could not have been written without the involvement of many people. Members of the Women's Program Forum at the Ford Foundation have been deeply committed to this project since its inception. I am particularly grateful to Betsy Campbell and Steve Zwerling for steady doses of advice, encouragement, and humor.

It is difficult to adequately convey Liz McGrory's contribution to this project. She read and commented on successive drafts of the chapters and made superb editorial suggestions. She helped coordinate a wide network of communications with faxes, E-mails, phone calls, and mailings to diverse corners of the world. She compiled the bibliography, the list of contributors, and the boxed information that appears at the beginning of each chapter. Her contribution has been substantial and invaluable.

The conference that assembled most of the authors in January 1994 was held at Amherst College. We benefited from the participation of several colleagues who served as discussants: Martha Ackelsburg, Leila Ahmad, Paola Bachetta, Susan Bourque, Joye Bowman, Carlene J. Edie, Kay Ann Johnson, Mary Katzenstein, Hannah Papanek, Stephanie Sandler, and Frances White. Renee Heberlee helped with the conference arrangements.

I have been fortunate to have worked with Susan McEachern, senior editor, and Mark Selden, series editor, at Westview Press. Their appreciation for scholarly rigor and efficiency in meeting very tight deadlines has been invaluable. Jess Dev Lionheart, copy editor, took a difficult assignment in her stride; my thanks to her for her efforts.

I am grateful for support I have received while working on this project from the John D. and Catherine T. MacArthur Foundation.

Many friends and family members contributed in diverse ways. Most important among them is my mother, Rasil: It was her work with the United Nations Branch on the Advancement of Women that first sparked my interest in women cross-nationally. She drafted the U.N. document that served as the basis for the World Plan of Action for Women at the first international women's conference in Mexico City in 1975 and the program for the second half of the decade for the Copenhagen conference in 1980. She made possible my participation in the second international women's conference in Copenhagen in 1980 and the third conference in Nairobi in 1985. My mother taught me a great deal about the challenges and rewards of bringing together global and local concerns. Her passionate commitment to both her work and her family has been a model for me to emulate. My father, Romen, has inspired me with his boundless energy, his own feminist commitments, and his love of writing. Rekha's creativity, courage, and conviction have brought her richly deserved acclaim. Rekha, Rob, Raji, and little Romen radiate the most comforting sense of warmth and well-being.

My husband, Mark, read successive drafts of the Introduction, thought up many titles for the book, and shared in the anxieties and rewards of this ambitious project. Mark, Ishan, and Javed seem to have found just the right balance of making space and making demands. In doing so, they have helped my work in the most profound and sustaining fashion.

Amrita Basu
Amherst

The Challenge
of Local Feminisms

Introduction

AMRITA BASU

FEW SOCIAL MOVEMENTS have flourished in as many parts of the world as *women's movements* have. And yet while these movements share certain broad commonalities, they differ radically along many dimensions. Both feminist scholars and women activists often diverge among themselves and with each other on what feminism is, whether a women's movement exists in a given country, and if so, whether it has been successful. How then should we interpret a term such as *global feminism*? Does it identify a common movement that is spread across many regions or several movements that conveniently but inaccurately share the same name? This is one of the central questions that I address in the pages that follow.

I begin by situating the chapters in this book within the scholarly literature on women's movements and then within the changing global context from which contemporary women's movements emerge. This lays the groundwork for a discussion of some broad themes: how the authors of this book understand feminism and why the concept is so controversial, what the diverse origins are of women's movements cross-nationally, how the issues that women's movements address converge and differ, and how success might be measured. I conclude by exploring the extent to which women's movements should be understood as a product of national or of global influences.

The Scholarly Context

The vast literature on women's movements is characterized by three broad tendencies: It ignores women's movements in the postcolonial world, considers women's movements products of modernization or development, and assumes a sameness in the forms of women's oppression and women's movements cross-nationally. First, the problem of silence and omission: With some important exceptions, most comparative studies of women's movements focus on Western Europe and the United States and ignore women's movements in the postcolonial world.[1] Conversely, studies of women in the non-Western world tend to be preoccupied

1

with the problem of development. Regardless of whether scholars within this tradition consider women as beneficiaries or victims, the scholarly literature on development generally fails to consider women as agents and activists in their own right. *The Challenge of Local Feminisms* seeks to rectify this imbalance by focusing on women's movements in postcolonial nations of Asia, Africa, and Latin America, where such movements are often thought to be absent. Closer examination reveals our ignorance rather than their absence.

The second tendency is to characterize women's movements as products of modernization or development. Thus, sociologists Janet Chafetz, Anthony Dworkin, and Diane Margolis argue that the growth of women's movements is correlated with industrialization and urbanization because they bring into being the middle class, which forms the backbone of women's movements.[2] Expanding educational and job opportunities increase women's capabilities and ambitions and make feminism more attractive to them. Thus, according to this view, women's movements are strongest in the most industrialized nations.

The chapters in this book show that, while women's movements have often been predominantly middle class, poor women have been at the forefront in many places. In India, the women's movement has been radicalized by the activism of poor women, who have not only raised employment and wage demands but have also fought domestic violence.[3] In the United States, Leslie Wolfe and Jennifer Tucker show that poor women, particularly women of color, have redefined the priorities of the women's movement and sustained it amid the challenges it has confronted in the 1990s. In a similar vein, Ethel Klein, in another book, *The Women's Movements of the United States and Western Europe,* finds that black women have been much more receptive than white women to the demands of the women's movement. As recently as 1970, only 37 percent of white women compared to 60 percent of black women believed that feminist activism was necessary; by 1985 the gap had narrowed, but black women were still significantly more supportive than white women of women's rights (78 percent versus 72 percent).[4]

Even more problematic is the assumption of the second approach that feminism is the outcome of a linear process of socioeconomic change. It cannot explain why women's movements are stronger in the Philippines and India, for example, than in the more industrialized nations of Russia and Eastern Europe. As this book demonstrates, a much more important influence on women's movements than the level of development is the extent of state control. Women's movements tend to be weak where state control permeates civil society and strong where state control is or has been relaxed.

An even deeper problem lies in the tautological nature of the argument: By identifying women's movements as middle-class movements, Chafetz and Dworkin define out of existence movements from which the middle class is absent or unimportant. I argue that women's movements comprise a range of struggles by women against gender inequality. These movements may be independently or-

ganized or affiliated with political parties, they may be of short or of long duration, they may rest on a narrow social base or on multiclass coalitions, they may
be local or national. To limit the discussion by excluding any of these forms would
restrict our understanding of a rich and multifaceted phenomenon.

The third tendency assumes a commonality in the forms of women's oppression and activism worldwide.[5] I select by way of example activist and writer Robin
Morgan's *Sisterhood Is Global* because of its seminal importance in reflecting and
shaping the dominant approach to women's movements in the West in the 1980s.
Moreover, the formats of this book and of *Sisterhood Is Global* are parallel: Both
include diverse country studies situated within a common framework.

Morgan's analysis, unlike some, does not suffer from a naive belief in the fruits
of development. Indeed, Morgan criticizes the reigning "integration of women in
development model" of the mid-1980s for its tendency to deflect attention away
from grassroots activism. Women have become a "world political force," Morgan
argues, because "virtually all existing countries are structured by patriarchal mentality." Reflecting the tendencies for which Marxists have been criticized—namely,
inferring from "objective" measures of exploitation assumptions of class consciousness—Morgan argues that "the overlooked—and most important—factor
in the power of women as a world political force is the magnitude of suffering
combined with the magnitude of women: women constitute not an oppressed minority but a majority—of almost all national populations and of the entire human
species." Women share a "common world view," Morgan repeatedly asserts, as a
result of "a common condition."[6]

To what extent was Morgan correct in predicting that the women's movement
would "have an enormous political impact through the end of this century, and
[would] create a transnational transformation in the next century"?[7] Divisions
among women based on nationality, race, class, religion, region, language, and
sexual orientation have proved more divisive to women's movements within and
across nations than Morgan acknowledged or anticipated. Indeed, it was in part
the assumption of sameness, which many assumed reflected an ethnocentric and
middle-class bias, that incurred the resentment of many "Third World" women
and generated deep divisions between women from the First and Third Worlds at
the U.N. conferences on women in Mexico City in 1975 and Copenhagen in 1980.
Better communication between these groups of women at the 1985 Nairobi conference occurred once they abandoned the myth of global sisterhood and acknowledged profound differences in women's lives and in the meanings of feminism
cross-nationally.[8]

One of Morgan's assumptions that has been seriously challenged is the notion
that "women seem, cross-culturally, to be deeply opposed to nationalism."[9] Not
only has nationalism become a more significant political force than many anticipated but also women have been deeply implicated in its growth. To make sense of
the militant activism of women who are agents of right-wing nationalism pro-

foundly challenges assumptions of female solidarity. Indeed, the appeals of women such as Sadvi Rithambara and Uma Bharati, among the most violent leaders of Hindu nationalism in India, rest partially upon projecting themselves as victims of Muslim violence.[10] In doing so, they make the victimized Hindu woman symbolic of the Hindu community and seek to displace their experience of male violence onto Muslim men. A similar expression of women's agency is evident among some women activists in right-wing groups in the United States. Through their public espousal of antifeminist views, right-wing activists Anita Bryant and Phyllis Schlafly have gained access to unusual power and prominence.

In questioning Morgan's analytic approach, I do not mean to minimize the significant contribution she has made to advancing debates in women's studies or to negate the generous spirit in which she writes. Nor do I contest Morgan's claim that women's solidarities have grown in some respects both within and across nations. However, Morgan does not appreciate the extent to which women's movements are locally situated. What activists in one context call a women's movement, activists elsewhere may contest. Women's identities within and across nations are shaped by a complex amalgam of national, racial, religious, ethnic, class, and sexual identities. If these arguments gain readier acceptance among feminists today than they would have a decade earlier when *Sisterhood Is Global* was published, this is partly because of the insights we have gained from changes in the global order, changes in the forms of women's activism, and the complicated, often conflictual interchanges between local and global feminism.

The chapters in this book are testimony to the distance that women's movements have traveled since the early 1970s. Most of the chapters analyze women's movements in the postcolonial world. Moreover, they do so with the confidence that comes of recognizing both women's sufferings and strengths. The authors suggest that feminists have moved beyond a preoccupation with the relationship between First and Third World women into the realm of what actually existing women's movements have achieved and failed to achieve, of the challenges yet to be confronted together and separately.

This book makes several contributions to the scholarly literature on women's movements. Drawing upon their research and accumulated knowledge, the authors provide rich descriptions that should be of interest to a variety of readers, from scholars to activists and policymakers. Sufficiently large numbers of countries are represented within each major region of the world to allow for comparisons both within and across regions. Regional similarities are most evident in Latin America, where women's movements are closely connected to democratization movements against authoritarian states, and in Africa and the Middle East, where women's movements are intertwined with movements of national liberation and state consolidation. There is much greater diversity in the origins and character of women's movements in Asia, Russia, Eastern and Western Europe, and the United States.

Some of the questions that provide the basis for comparative analysis across regions include, How and why do women's movements emerge? What is their relationship to the state and broader social movements? What implications does the social base of women's movements have for the issues that they address? What are the ways in which women's movements have permeated political institutions? And what constitutes success?

The Political Context

In the decade since *Sisterhood Is Global* was published, many nation-states have disintegrated, and new forms of nationalism have emerged. The chapters in this book reflect these changing national configurations: Namibia gained independence in 1990, South Africa's new government was formed in 1994, and preparations for Palestinian authority are under way. The states of the Soviet Union and Eastern Europe have disintegrated, and new ones have been formed. Although the collapse of the Berlin Wall and the formation of the European Union may appear to have eroded older forms of nationalism in Western Europe, new forms of nationalism—based on racism and xenophobia—have taken their place. The forms that nationalism has assumed are diverse, and its implications for women are complex.

A number of countries that have been defining national identities have supported greater equality for women. Women have played important roles in newly formed nation-states such as Namibia, new democracies such as South Africa, and movements for self-determination among Palestinians. The political leadership has reciprocated by attending to some of women's demands, and women have benefited from democratization, for they often bear the brunt of state repression and authoritarianism. But the legacy of these movements is bittersweet and inevitably includes dashed hopes, broken promises, and unfulfilled commitments.

The collapse of communism in the former Soviet Union and Eastern Europe has had mixed implications for women. Although these communist states were inhospitable climates for independent women's movements and often failed to implement the legislation they had introduced, nonetheless they passed labor laws and legalized abortion, promoted women's education and employment, and created public institutions to perform some of women's domestic work. These gains are under attack in the wake of capitalist development. In China, for example, many protections and benefits for women have been dismantled, and private enterprises often refuse to bear the costs of maternity leaves.

The most destructive implications of nationalism for women can be found in places where there has been a growth of xenophobic nationalism. Ethnic and religious nationalisms have sometimes been associated with barbarisms, as in the civil war in the former Yugoslavia and Hindu-Muslim riots in India. Then there is the violence of right-wing racist groups in the United States and Western Europe. Nationalism that seeks inspiration from an imaginary past usually advocates re-domesticating women and gaining control over their sexuality.

Another important development has been the growing integration of nations and sectors of national economies into the global capitalist system. The overall consequences for women have been damaging and sometimes devastating. As Jane Jenson points out, Western European states have been terminating social services for which they were formerly responsible. Here, as in many other places, the burden of privatization often falls upon women. In some cases these measures have been a catalyst to women's activism. In Peru, for example, women responded to the state's austerity measures by taking up the task of providing food to the community. In Poland, women have taken to the streets in an attempt to protect their rights to abortions. In Russia, women's protest was responsible for blocking the passage of legislation that the Russian Parliament considered in 1992 that encouraged women to stay home and perform "socially necessary labor." It would also have required women with children under fourteen to give up full-time jobs in favor of part-time work.

One of the key issues for women's movements is whether economic reforms are accompanied by an increase or a decline in women's employment. Take, for example, the striking contrasts among the communist states that have embarked on economic liberalization. Employment opportunities for women in Russia and Eastern Europe have sharply declined, so that women constitute a large majority of the unemployed. By contrast, economic reforms in China have provided women with new sources of income from farming and home-based cottage industries. The greater strength of the women's movement in China than in Russia and in Eastern Europe may be influenced by these differences in women's labor force participation.

Conceptualizing Feminism

The authors report that women regard feminism with deep skepticism in Chile, Bangladesh, Namibia, Kenya, China, Peru, Russia, and Eastern Europe. It is hardly surprising to learn that feminism is branded immoral by the Catholic church, Islamic leaders, and Hindu authorities or is considered bourgeois by the established Left. But it is more surprising that women who have championed women's rights and empowerment reject feminism. Unraveling why this is so illuminates a great deal about how we might think about national women's movements from an international perspective.

One reason that many women are uncomfortable with the concept of feminism has to do with the widespread belief that its inspiration, origins, and relevance are bourgeois or Western. Although feminists have often attributed such views to those who seek to undermine women's movements, other interpretations are equally plausible. Many women consider feminism to be narrowly associated with a particular ideology, strategy, and approach. Thus, Naihua Zhang notes that Chinese women's studies scholars and many women activists reject the term *nuquan zhuyi*, or "women's rights-ism," for they believe that Chinese women have already attained many of the legal and political rights that feminist movements are still attempting to achieve. Instead, they use the term *nuxing zhuyi*, or "female-ism," to connote women's unique vantage point for rebuilding society. While the former term implies sameness, the latter emphasizes differences between men and women.

One way that women's movements have sought to challenge the notion that feminism derives from bourgeois or Western inspiration is by finding symbols of women's power within the precolonial context. In Kenya, the women's movement finds in women's work groups, songs, and prayers opportunities to share experiences of oppression and give voice to protest. In India, feminists have reinterpreted women's life cycle rituals surrounding menstruation and pregnancy to find evidence of women's resistance. Until the growth of Hindu nationalism rendered problematic the search for empowering female symbols within the Hindu tradition, feminists found in Kali and other goddesses symbols of women's power and strength. In the Philippines, feminists have displaced the patriarchal Christian creation myth that came to the Philippines by way of Spanish colonialism with an indigenous myth that provides support for women's autonomy. Lilia Quindoza Santiago tells the story of *babaye*, which holds that the first woman was born from the nodes of bamboo at the same moment—but separately from—the first man. "As a person born whole and separate from man, the Filipina legitimately owns her own body and her self and can chart her own future and destiny."

Resistance to feminism may reflect a fear that it demands a total transformation of the social order. A popular rendition of this anxiety is the notion that feminists are "man haters." A scholarly rendition, which aptly highlights the radical potential of feminism, suggests that feminism is potentially transformative of all domains of life—from the way women organize their private lives to their roles in the public sphere. Speaking of France, Jane Jenson notes that in the "heady days of political mobilization ... the goal was no less than a complete transformation of gender relations within French society." Contrast this notion of feminism with the possibility, aired in more than one chapter in this book, that feminism may be an incremental, hidden form of subversion enacted to protect families and communities rather than to undermine them.

Thus, in the chapter on Peru Cecilia Blondet shows how women were galvanized into action by a context of economic and political crisis associated with a breakdown of traditional family structures. The crisis mobilized women to take up public and collective responsibilities. Some of these services appear to reinscribe gender-linked identities and roles. But we might counter that there is nothing about an activity such as cooking or providing food that is intrinsically gendered: Its association with the privatized nuclear family, a lack of economic and social recognition for women's labor, and a variety of other conditions make this activity unrewarding or oppressive to women. Conversely, when cooking and feeding are transformed into public domain activities and become the basis of social recognition, they may actually contribute to the transformation, rather than the reinforcement, of gender identities.

Similarly, Islah Jad notes that the women's work committees that Palestinian women formed after 1978 engaged in activities very similar to those of older charitable organizations: for instance, the creation of nurseries, literacy centers, and small-scale cooperatives and the running of training programs in sewing, knitting, and embroidery. But while these activities may have reinscribed women's conventional sex-linked roles, the process of democratic decisionmaking within the committees resulted in women's increased solidarity and self-esteem.

A very different instance of the reach of feminism concerns the ways in which even women's groups that are formally autonomous have often sought to work within institutions. Jane Jenson shows that in France and Italy women's groups worked with the Communist Party and its trade union allies to wage struggles to legalize abortion. She notes that women's movements in Western Europe often seek to increase their strength by forming alliances with political parties and trade unions. The Brazilian women's movement has pursued a similar strategy and in the process generated impassioned debates about the costs of relinquishing autonomy by collaborating with leftist groups.

Appreciating the reach of feminism also entails looking back in history to the early origins of women's movements. Thus, Wilhelmina Oduol and Wanjiku Mukabi Kabira speak of Kenyan women's protest against colonial soil conservation measures in 1948 and the Mau Mau war of independence in 1952. Hussaina Abdullah speaks of women's key role in the Aba women's riot of 1929 and the Egba women's protest of 1947 in Nigeria. Lilia Quindoza Santiago speaks of women's roles in the Katipunan, the armed struggle that achieved independence from Spain and gave birth to the first Philippine republic in 1898. To confine attention to contemporary urban middle-class feminism would restrict our understanding of the reach of women's movements.

The chapters in this book ask us to be more inclusive in our understanding of women's movements. For example, Roushan Jahan includes in her discussion of Bangladesh the activities of some nongovernmental development organizations that have engaged in "conscientization" and solidarity building among the rural poor. Radha Kumar includes a discussion of grassroots rural movements that embrace but are not confined to women's activism around gender inequality. Wilhelmina Oduol and Wanjiku Mukabi Kabira include in their discussion of Kenya writers and artists who disseminate feminist ideas and images but may not be activists themselves.

The Genesis of Women's Movements

Even women's movements that ultimately define themselves as autonomous from male-dominated parties and institutions are often closely intertwined with broader movements for social change. Women's movements are associated with a broad range of struggles: for national liberation, human rights, and the democratization of authoritarian regimes. In the postcolonial world, nationalist movements often provide opportunities for large-scale women's activism. With this opportunity comes the recognition of gender-specific grievances and concerns.

Women have increasingly vocalized their demands in the context of nationalist struggles. Islah Jad provides a fine example of how feminism grew out of the movement for Palestinian self-determination. From questioning the exclusionary and violent practices of the Israeli state with respect to their community, Palestinian women began to challenge the exclusions and violence to which they as women were subjected. Their growing sense that the Palestinian leadership had failed to reward women's contributions by according them political power further contributed to feminist consciousness.

Similarly, women's movements have often been closely connected with working-class struggles. In Chile, for example, women played an important role in struggles against class and gender inequality in nitrate mining towns in the north in the early twentieth century. In Mexico, "popular feminism" emerged when middle-class women, attacked by the Right and the Catholic church, sought alliances with working-class women and became active in industrial workers' unions. In the Philippines, women were active in peasant organizations from the 1930s on and in worker movements in the 1950s and 1960s. These joint actions were instrumental in bringing about some beneficial legislation, such as higher wages, health benefits, longer maternity leaves, and equal pay for equal work.

Women have been a major force in movements opposing state repression and seeking to democratize civil society. In Chile, the rallying cry of the women's movement in the struggle against the Pinochet dictatorship was "Democracy in the country and in the home." This was echoed in the slogan "Democracy without women is no democracy" in the Soviet Union in the early stages of liberalization. The women's movement in the Philippines played an important role in overthrowing the Marcos dictatorship. Although India was never subjected to sustained authoritarian rule, between 1975 and 1977 Prime Minister Indira Gandhi suspended Parliament and declared a state of national emergency. Women's groups formed an important part of the civil liberties movement that resulted. Similarly, the contemporary women's movement in the United States was in important respects a product of the civil rights and New Left movements of the 1960s.

Nations that have been ruled by authoritarian governments frequently create the conditions for women's activism. State violence, like domestic violence, is often a catalyst to women's resistance, in part because of the ways it impinges on families. Furthermore, authoritarian states tend to destroy political parties and other autonomous institutions. Women may be apt to step into the vacuum because of their power within the family and community. Moreover, women's exclusion from established institutions may make them particularly qualified to mobilize resistance through informal networks. Women's mobilization in the movements on behalf of the disappeared in Chile, Argentina, and Brazil during authoritarian rule provides excellent illustrations of this phenomenon.

The chapters in this book thus suggest that some women's struggles form a subset of struggles for civil rights and human rights. What initially motivates many women to organize is not necessarily a belief in the distinctive nature of their problems but rather a sense of shared oppression with other groups that have been denied their rights. Patriarchal domination is no more apt in and of itself to provide a catalyst to women's activism than class exploitation is likely in and of itself to stimulate class struggle.

However, whether women organize on their own or as members of a larger group is not really what determines whether their activism is likely to endure. The more important issue is whether women's activism responds to their own concerns or to those of external actors, such as political parties and the state. Similarly, many middle-class women's movements have failed to mobilize poor women by assuming that class interests can be subordinated to gender interests. In Brazil, Mexico, Chile, and Peru, the economic hardships that poor urban women experienced provided the impetus for their activism.

Several chapters suggest that women's movements are often disabled by the state's attempts to define solutions to women's problems and create organizations that it can control. Although states may appoint commissions, form women's organizations, and pass favorable legislation, they do not usually create movements. Hussaina Abdullah describes the state-sponsored Better Life Programme as "Nigerian state pseudo feminism" and argues that women's movements must become autonomous in order to serve as dynamic forces for social change. Similarly, the Kenyan state has undermined women's activism by co-opting many successful women's programs and cultivating the dependence of women's organizations. In Russia and Eastern Europe, extensive legislation designed to improve the position of women thwarted possibilities for women to organize independently around their own interests. Anastasia Posadskaya argues that most women were so alienated from the Soviet Women's Committee, the official women's organization during the communist period, that they were unresponsive to feminist appeals even after the demise of communism. Islah Jad argues that one benefit of the lack of a

Palestinian state was the space this opened up for grassroots movements to organize.

One country where a state-affiliated women's organization forms the backbone of the women's movement is China. Naihua Zhang argues that the official All-China Women's Federation (ACWF) has acquired a broader base of support among poor rural women than predominantly urban women's groups have achieved. In part this might be attributed to the very different circumstances that surrounded the growth of official and autonomous women's groups. Formed in 1949, the ACWF worked closely with the Chinese Communist Party during the anti-Japanese and the civil wars and thereby gained legitimacy among rural women at the grassroots level for its association with nationalism and communism. With ninety-eight thousand full-time cadres on the state payroll, the ACWF exercises the means to implement state policy. By contrast, independent women's groups were formed only in the late 1980s and lack access to comparable networks and resources.

Feminist Issues

Just as women's movements have organized in multiple arenas, they have addressed a range of issues. These issues cluster around some broad themes: women's legal and political rights, violence against women, reproductive choice and abortion, sexual freedom, employment opportunities and discrimination, and women's political participation and representation. The movements described in this book address these issues in very different ways.

Rather than simply describing each of these issues in turn, I wish instead to identify some broad patterns that help explain why particular movements are drawn to particular issues. While women's movements have sought to politicize the private domain in some contexts, they have concentrated their efforts on the public domain in others. The former approach characterizes the women's movement in the United States, where feminists have focused on such issues as domestic violence, rape, abortion, and sexual orientation. Similarly in India, the most intensive battles that the women's movement has fought have centered on private sphere issues such as dowry deaths, rape, and amniocentesis for purposes of sex selection. By contrast, women's movements in China, Russia, and Eastern Europe tend to be more concerned with public domain questions such as employment, political representation, and social security.[11]

One possible explanation for this difference in focus concerns the varying relationship of the private to the public cross-nationally. In liberal democracies where the public and private are sharply demarcated, women's movements have sought to reveal the "secrets" concealed in the private realm. In communist nations with fewer barriers between public and private spheres, feminists are suspicious of state scrutiny of the private domain. Elzbieta Matynia argues that for Czech women the recovery of dignity entails a retreat into the family because it was traditionally a realm that was relatively protected from state control. Indeed, many women believe that the family shielded them from some of the abuses that men endured in the public realm.

Often women's movements have addressed the same sets of issues in very different ways. One example is the question of violence against women. Although many women's movements have focused on domestic violence, they have often been concerned with the question of state repression, as in the struggles of the Mothers of the Plaza de Mayo in Chile and elsewhere in Latin America during the period of authoritarian rule. In Namibia, Concerned Women Against Violence Against Women has taken up questions not only of sexual violence but also of all violent crimes that affect women. In addressing the question of state repression in Brazil, women's groups have examined the ways in which women were vulnerable to sexual violence. Upon coming to power in 1985, after twenty-one years of military rule, the civilian government responded to feminist demands by creating special police stations to assist women who had been victims of sexual abuse.

The issue of birth control also exemplifies the diversity that surrounds an apparently common set of feminist issues. While in some countries women have fought for freer access to contraception, in other countries their concern with reproductive freedom entails challenging their government's emphasis on population control. In Bangladesh, women's groups have questioned the assumption that population control provides an adequate response to poverty and women's subordination. In China, women's studies scholars are highlighting the connections between the one-child family policy and female infanticide. In the Philippines, women's groups have interpreted reproductive freedom to include the rights of prostitutes, access to a range of contraceptive methods, and education to prevent the spread of acquired immune deficiency syndrome (AIDS).

There are striking differences in the extent to which women's movements have addressed the question of sexuality and the ways in which they have done so. In many places women's movements have concentrated their attention on reforming the institution of marriage to allow women greater freedom within it. This may entail attempts to gain greater freedom for women to choose their spouses, raise the age of marriage, and achieve greater mobility and freedom after marriage. Such attempts at marriage reform address women's sexuality only in passing.

Women's movements also vary significantly in the extent to which they have addressed questions of sexual orientation. In many places, including Bangladesh, China, Eastern Europe, Kenya, and Nigeria, lesbianism is rendered invisible, and the subject of sexual orientation is taboo. In other places lesbians occupy a very prominent place in women's movements. Lesbians have been active not only in battered women's shelters, AIDS activism, and reproductive rights issues but also in challenging feminists to rethink many of their positions. Indeed, one of the important theoretical challenges to feminists concerns the relationship between the rights of women and those of sexual minorities.

Lesbians constitute an important force within the women's movement of the Philippines. They have also organized a gay and lesbian liberation movement, which held its first public lesbian march in 1993. In the 1970s, a number of women's organizations in the United States split over issues of sexual orientation. While lesbian and heterosexual women continue to be active in some different organizations, there has been an expansion of coalitions between lesbian and heterosexual women in the 1980s and 1990s. Among the large national women's groups, the National Organization for Women has supported lesbian rights, the American Association of University Women has recognized a lesbian caucus, and the National Women's Studies Association has encouraged lesbian studies. Lesbians have been active within women's movements and in gay and lesbian organizations in Brazil, Mexico, Russia, South Africa, the United States, and many Western European countries. They have organized conferences at the regional level in Asia, Latin America, and Western Europe and have become an increasingly influential group at international conferences. Witness the shift from the 1975 Mexico City conference that launched the UN Decade for Women, where lesbians were pushed into the background, to the 1985 Nairobi conference that closed the Decade, where they were an important presence.

It is difficult to explain why questions of sexuality are significant in some contexts but not in others. As lesbian organizing in the Philippines, South Africa, Brazil, and Mexico suggests, it is no longer possible to argue, as some did in the past, that questions of sexual identity are "luxuries" that only "bourgeois" feminists in the Western world can afford to address. Along with a host of economic questions, sexual orientation may be a survival issue, for lesbians are often persecuted for their sexual orientation. Just as the absence of women's movements should not be equated with the absence of women's oppression, silences around lesbianism should not be considered synonymous with the absence either of lesbianism or of homophobia. The experiences of women in the countries discussed in this book suggest that the stronger women's movements are, and the less defensive and fearful they are about their survival, the more likely they are to raise questions concerning sexual orientation and welcome lesbian activism.

The Dimensions of Success

The question of whether a women's movement has been successful is extremely complex. Success can be judged relative to a movement's stated goals, or it can be judged according to some more universal standards of social justice. Instead of focusing on the tangible gains that women have achieved, we might explore the more subtle ways in which women's movements have shaped popular consciousness. But none of these standards is unproblematic: Women's consciousness of their gender interests need not translate into feminist activism. Women's movements may precipitate a backlash by right-wing groups. And the life cycle of even the most dynamic movements is quite limited.

In some respects, the criteria of success and failure may be different for women's movements than for other social movements. In *The Women's Movements of the United States and Western Europe,* Mary Katzenstein argues:

> If the health of the women's movement is to be accurately gauged, it is important to appreciate that some of the instruments that plumbed the strengths and weaknesses of other social movements are inappropriate as measures of the well-being of feminism. Membership figures, for instance, that give a reasonable indication of the well-being of trade unions tell little of the story of feminist movements. There are many feminist activists, not to mention supporters, who are neither dues-paying or card-carrying members of any particular organizational unit. Unlike the civil rights movement, moreover, whose strength was measured in large part by its very public protests and demonstrations, the women's movement even at the outset made less use of the "orthodox" tactics of disorder. It has instead pursued its often very radical agenda in less visible ways—through consciousness raising groups, collectives, caucuses, and local organizations.[12]

The chapters in this book concur with Katzenstein that the vitality of the women's movement does not lie primarily in the activities of large national organizations. While they may be the most visible actors, small, local-level activist groups often provide the dynamism behind women's movements. Furthermore, as Katzenstein notes, it is difficult to assess changes in consciousness. Judged by the fact that abortion remains illegal in many countries, pro-choice movements may be deemed a failure. But this conclusion disregards some of the consequences that may flow from struggles around abortion: women's greater understanding of their own bodies, involvement with decisions concerning their health, and confidence in confronting the state.

Women have achieved some significant gains as a result of their participation in recent nationalist struggles. Whereas the Equal Rights Amendment has yet to be ratified in the United States, the Namibian constitution forbids sex discrimination. Furthermore, women's activism seems to have borne greater dividends in contemporary nationalist struggles than in earlier anticolonial movements. For example, the Indian constitution excludes women from affirmative action programs that are designed for untouchables and implicitly sanctions sexual inequality by upholding customary law in matters concerning the family. By contrast, the Namibian constitution authorizes affirmative action for women and recognizes customary law only if it does not violate the constitution.

Women have been extremely active in seeking to extend their rights in the new South Africa. The Women's National Coalition, a broad coalition of women's organizations, drafted a women's charter for effective equality in February 1994. A number of women members of Parliament who drafted the charter now form a powerful official lobby. Similarly, in preparing for Palestinian authority, Palestinian women have drafted a bill of rights and sought legislation protecting women from family violence.

Within older and more established states, feminists have achieved some gains by lobbying for electoral candidates who are sympathetic to their demands. In the Philippines, for example, support from the women's movement was critical to Corazon Aquino's election. The number and influence of women in public office increased significantly while she was in power. Women utilized new democratic processes to achieve such reforms as the Philippine Development Plan for Women. Similarly in the United States, Bill Clinton's stance on abortion, education, and health care reform resulted in women's electoral support, which in turn contributed to Clinton's successful bid for the presidency. Clinton appointed several women to key political posts, and more women were elected to Congress in 1992 than in any previous election. But as Aquino and Clinton bowed to pressures from conservative political and religious groups, their commitment to women's issues diminished.

In reviewing the global situation, we may be struck by how few women serve as heads of state. In many of the countries discussed in this book, including Bangladesh, India, Nigeria, and the Philippines, women come to occupy positions of power through their relationship to male leaders and officials. These women have usually failed to lend support to women's movements. In some cases, as with Khaleda Zia in Bangladesh and Cory Aquino in the Philippines, they are under intense pressure and scrutiny from right-wing groups. In other cases, as with Maryam Babangida, the founder and coordinator of the Better Life Programme and wife of Nigeria's former military president, Ibrahim Babangida, their appointments demand compliance with official dictates. Without strong connections to women's movements, political leaders are unlikely to be responsive to female constituencies.

The women's movements described in this book are at very different stages in their life cycles. In France, Italy, the United States, Chile, and India, the heady days of political mobilization in which everything seemed possible are long past. Does this signal a steady decline in women's movements? Within social movements, periods of active mobilization are often followed by periods of quiescence in which organizations engage in consolidation and rebuilding. Alternatively, they may seek different venues of participation. In several countries women's movements that formerly emphasized direct action outside of formal institutions have increasingly sought to work within state structures.

Several authors in this book assert that women's movements have endured because they have turned to new arenas and forms of activism. Leslie Wolfe and Jennifer Tucker find the sources of longevity within the feminist movement in the United States in its infiltration of mainstream institutions. They note that the

1970s and 1980s witnessed the creation of a feminist establishment in Washington D.C., composed of legal groups, political action committees, and research institutes. This network of organizations played a critical role in mobilizing support among policymakers for feminist causes.

Similarly, the Chilean government created the Servicio Nacional de la Mujer (SERNAM), an administrative organization at the ministerial level, to implement gender-specific public policies. SERNAM drafted several pieces of legislation that expanded women's rights. Although some feminists criticize SERNAM for being overly cautious and conservative, and Alicia Frohmann and Teresa Valdés note that it provides no substitute for the women's movement, they argue that it has done much to advance women's interests. For example, the Plan for Gender Equality that SERNAM proposed in 1994 represented the most comprehensive agenda for women's rights ever developed in Chile.

In Mexico, the government headed by President Carlos Salinas de Gortari that was elected to power in 1988 introduced a number of programs designed to assuage opposition to the previous regime's austerity measures. One of these was the National Solidarity Program. Marta Lamas et al. argue that, while Solidarity created new channels for social involvement, it also enabled the central government to increase control over grassroots movements. Women's groups were confronted with the need to relinquish their autonomy in exchange for access to state resources.

In Brazil, Vera Soares et al. note that the women's movement was deeply divided over whether feminists were being co-opted by participating in a national council for women's rights that the civilian government of José Sarney created in 1985. From their experience of participating in the council between 1985 and 1989, feminists came to see their collaboration with the state as an extremely effective means of combatting gender inequality. However, they also recognized that to constitute an effective presence and avoid co-optation and marginalization, they needed an independent institutional base within the state.

As these examples suggest, women's movements have increasingly sought to influence state policy and increase women's political representation and participation. In Mexico, Brazil, Chile, and the United States, women's movements have moved off the streets and into political institutions. However, the question of how women can best "work the state" is by no means settled. Debates rage about the efficacy of quotas to increase women's political representation, the viability of forming women's political parties, and the emphasis that women's groups should place on organizational and financial autonomy.

Some of the most important gains of women's movements have been located within the cultural domain. Women's studies represent a steadily burgeoning field, and centers for the study of women and gender exist in many parts of the world, including Russia, India, Nigeria, Chile, Brazil, Mexico, the Middle East, Western Europe, and the United States. Feminism has found expression in the arts: Theater, dance, song, photography, and fiction all reflect its influence. Women's journals, newspapers, radio stations, and even television shows, which were once considered revolutionary, are by now well established in many places. Less visible but no less significant are the social spaces that women have carved out in cafés, bookshops, bars, restaurants, clubs, and theaters. Women's social worlds grow out of and in turn energize women's movements.

Although it would be reassuring to end on a positive note, the record is more complicated and more mixed. Women's movements have simply failed to achieve many of their major demands, among them the legalization of abortion in Brazil, the passage of the Equal Rights Amendment in the United States, and the reform of customary laws governing the family in Kenya, India, and Bangladesh. There are a variety of possible explanations for these failures. In some cases, women's movements may capture media attention as a result of their flamboyant or courageous actions, membership by politically prominent and well-connected women, and the importance of the issues they raise but may lack support among the large majority of women.

Even when there is widespread sympathy for feminist demands, the opposition is often better organized and funded. Some of the most serious challenges to women's movements have come from right-wing and religious groups claiming that feminist demands are subversive of family and community. It is unlikely that any single issue has met with the same degree of opposition as abortion—from the Catholic church in Latin America and Eastern Europe and from Christian fundamentalists and right-wing groups in the United States.

Similarly, women's movements in Bangladesh and India have been unable to reform customary law or pressure the government to pass a uniform civil code because of the fierce opposition they have encountered from religious fundamentalists. In many other countries, men have resisted women's attempts to reform customary law for fear that this would challenge the integrity of the patriarchal family. One of the most renowned struggles around this issue took place in Kenya when Wambui Otieno fought a prolonged legal battle to bury her deceased husband on their farm. The court ultimately ruled that in keeping with customary law, her in-laws could bury his body on their ancestral lands.

Not only is the relationship between consciousness and activism difficult to establish, but consciousness itself is neither uniform nor monolithic. Often women's experience of their identities as gendered subjects may not assume a feminist form. Naihua Zhang reports that since the 1980s Chinese women have challenged the androgynous ideals of the past by emphasizing their femininity. In the United States, the growing consciousness that identities are multiple rather than singular has often led women to emphasize race, ethnicity, and sexual orientation as much as gender. As a result, identity politics flourishes at the same time that a unified women's movement has declined.

Finally, the very achievements of women's movements may contribute to a backlash against women and feminism. Many nations are witnessing the emergence or resurgence of xenophobic nationalist movements that emphasize the restoration of idealized forms of women's traditional roles. Some of this seems to be a reaction against women's movements for supposedly contributing to the breakup of families. This is an ironic charge for, as we have seen, women's commitment to their families has often been a catalyst to their activism. But to right-wing groups this may provide a rationale for targeting women's issues. In the United States, antiabortion activism has resulted in the picketing of clinics, harassment of their personnel, and even murder of clinic staff and doctors who perform abortions. If 1992 signified a victory for feminism in the United States elections, 1994 signified backlash and defeat, with many recently elected women and pro-choice candidates losing their seats.

Sisterhood Is Local/Sisterhood Is Global

In a book that appears at the time of the 1995 United Nations Fourth World Conference on Women, it is appropriate to acknowledge how important an influence the United Nations Decade for Women (1975–1985) was for women's movements globally. In declaring a decade for women, the United Nations was undoubtedly responding to the growth of feminism worldwide. But the United Nations also helped strengthen this trend by placing pressure on governments to pay lip-service to women's movements. This in turn galvanized women's groups to organize in preparation for the U.N. conference on women in Mexico City in 1975.

Both at the official U.N. conference and at the nongovernmental forums, women had important opportunities for collective reflection in truly international settings. Initially, this generated a great deal of tension, above all reflecting north-south divisions: Women from postcolonial states worried that feminism represented yet another form of cultural imperialism, while Western women felt that they were the only feminists. By the third international women's conference, in Nairobi in 1985, women's movements had come of age. At the same time that feminism had become a more powerful force, it had also become more dispersed, decentered, and divided. Women's organizations—from both the industrialized and the postcolonial worlds—were less likely to identify with government policies. Nor did they simply embrace global sisterhood.

In the years since Nairobi, networking between women's studies institutes and women's movements cross-nationally has continued. Since financial support for international conferences and organizations comes primarily from the West, many women continue to assume that feminism is Western. Elzbieta Matynia notes that women's studies research in Hungary is often responsive to the concerns of foreign scholars who issue invitations to conferences abroad. In Namibia, Dianne Hubbard and Colette Solomon note, the women's movement has been thrust into the international arena and subjected to pressure by donor agencies before it has developed its own priorities. Roushan Jahan argues that donor agencies in Bangladesh prefer to invest in projects that yield quick results rather than in long-term projects that might eventually affect policy changes at the national level. But international donor agencies have helped mitigate the influence of Islamist parties by providing support for programs that empower women.

However, there are many examples of networking among women across the North-South divide. Certain themes provide the basis for scholarly collaboration across regions: the implications for women of the growth of religious nationalism and fundamentalism, the global assembly line of women workers in multinational corporations, and the implications for women of economic liberalization and structural adjustment policies. Women have also become increasingly active in regional networks. The Encuentros Feministas have created strong bonds among Latin American and Caribbean women's groups. Women have formed similar, if not comparably strong, regional organizations in Asia and Africa. There has also been a growth of issue-specific networks among women around concerns such as reproductive health, human rights, Muslim fundamentalism, and trafficking in women.

My account of women's movements has emphasized their local origins, character, and concerns. Feminists, particularly from the industrialized Western world, have been apt to make sweeping generalizations about commonalities among women across the globe. Such generalizations aggravate tensions not only along north-south lines but also along other lines of cleavage, including class, race, and sexual orientation. Paradoxically, the very attempt to universalize feminism makes it more exclusionary. The equation of feminism with movements organized by women autonomously from male-dominated organizations excludes many forms of activism within the context of democracy, nationalist, and human rights struggles in which women ultimately take up questions of gender inequality even if this was not their initial objective.

However, if my intent was simply to emphasize the local character of women's movements, it would be hard to justify a book on women's movements in global perspective and almost impossible to explain the excitement that surrounds the international conference in Beijing. For even if women approach these international conferences with previously established agendas, they also come together to learn from one another. Thus, it is appropriate to conclude with some thoughts about the interplay between the local and the global in the context of women's movements.

Earlier I noted the widespread resistance to feminism among women. But equally striking is how many women who believe that feminism is bourgeois or Western go on to identify indigenous alternatives to Western-style feminism within their own cultural and political contexts. What better illustration of the productive interplay between global and local feminism is there than debates in which women ultimately define feminism by refusing to associate it with dominant values or groups. Similarly, within many national contexts lesbians, women of color, and religious minorities have productively challenged universalist understandings of feminism and thereby relocated feminism amid marginalized or subordinated groups.

In fighting for what appear to be particularistic goals—finding their voices, setting their own agendas, and creating their own social spaces—women's movements are seeking the most universal objectives. But note that at such moments when the particular and the universal coincide, the subject may no longer be women. Thus, the tensions between local and global feminisms reverberate within the relationship between women's movements and the movements of other oppressed groups. The strengths of women's movements lie in their insights into that which distinguishes them and that which joins them to others who have suffered. And from these encounters come the most exquisite knowledge, vitality, and power.

NOTES

I am fortunate to have received thoughtful comments on an earlier draft of this chapter from Betsy Campbell, Margaret Hunt, Liz McGrory, Mary Katzenstein, Mark Kesselman, Mark Selden, and Steve Zwerling.

1. Examples include Barbara J. Nelson, *American Women and Politics* (New York: Garland Publishers, 1984); Gisela Kaplan, *Contemporary Western European Feminism* (New York: New York University Press, 1992); Mary Katzenstein and Carol Mueller, eds., *The Women's Movements of the United States and Western Europe* (Philadelphia: Temple University Press, 1987); Joni Lovenduski, *Women and European Politics* (Amherst: University of Massachusetts Press, 1986); and Joni Lovenduski and Vicky Randall, *Contemporary Feminist Politics in Britain* (Oxford: Oxford University Press, 1993).

Some important works that focus on the postcolonial context include Jane S. Jaquette, ed., *The Women's Movement in Latin America: Participation and Democracy*, 2d ed. (Boulder: Westview Press, 1994); Kathleen Staudt, *Managing Development: State, Society, and International Contexts* (Newbury Park, Calif.: Sage, 1991); and Valentine M. Moghadam, ed., *Identity Politics and Women: Cultural Reassertion and Feminisms in International Perspective* (Boulder: Westview Press, 1994).

2. Janet Saltzman Chafetz and Anthony Gary Dworkin, *Female Revolt: Women's Movements in World and Historical Perspective* (Totowa, N.J.: Rowman and Allanheld, 1986); Diane Rothbard Margolis, "Women's Movements Around the World: Cross-Cultural Comparisons," *Gender and Society* 7, no. 3 (September 1993):379–399.

3. In studying grassroots activism among "tribal" or aboriginal women from landless households in western India, I found that in the course of organizing around wage demands, these women had taken up a range of questions specific to women, including bat-

tering, rape, and men's alcoholism. Although middle-class feminists later became involved in this struggle, it was initiated by tribal women themselves and sustained for over a decade. See my *Two Faces of Protest: Contrasting Modes of Women's Activism in India* (Berkeley and Los Angeles: University of California Press, 1992).

4. Ethel Klein, "The Diffusion of Consciousness in the United States and Western Europe," in Mary Katzenstein and Carol Mueller, eds., *The Women's Movements of the United States and Western Europe* (Philadelphia: Temple University Press, 1987), p. 27.

5. Some examples of this approach include Chilla Bulbeck, *One World Women's Movement* (London: Pluto Press, 1988); Charlotte Bunch, *Feminism in the 80s: Bringing the Global Home* (Denver: Antelope, 1985); Jill M. Bystydzienski, *Women Transforming Politics: Worldwide Strategies for Empowerment* (Bloomington: Indiana University Press, 1992); Angela R. Miles and Geraldine Finn, *Feminism: From Pressure to Politics* (Montreal: Black Rose Books, 1989); Robin Morgan, *Sisterhood Is Global, The International Women's Movement Anthology* (Garden City, N.Y.: Anchor Books, 1984); and V. Spike Peterson and Anne Sisson Runyan, *Global Gender Issues* (Boulder: Westview Press, 1993).

6. Morgan, *Sisterhood Is Global*, p. 3.

7. Ibid.

8. For a useful summation of the debates at these conferences, see Arvonne S. Fraser, *The U.N. Decade for Women: Documents and Dialogue* (Boulder: Westview Press, 1987); and Nilufer Cagaty, Caren Grown, and Aida Santiago, "The Nairobi Women's Conference: Toward a Global Feminism?" *Feminist Studies* 12 (1986):401–412.

9. Morgan, *Sisterhood Is Global*, p. 23.

10. See the special issue of the *Bulletin of Concerned Asian Scholars* on women and religious nationalism in India (25, no. 4 [1993]).

11. This broad conclusion must be qualified. In the United States, liberal feminists have addressed public sphere issues, particularly concerning women's political representation, in recent years. However, both in the early stage of the women's movement, under the influence of radical feminists, and today, questions of incest, battering, rape, and pornography have stimulated the most vigorous debates and forms of activism.

12. Katzenstein and Mueller, *The Women's Movements*, p. 1.

PART ONE

Asia

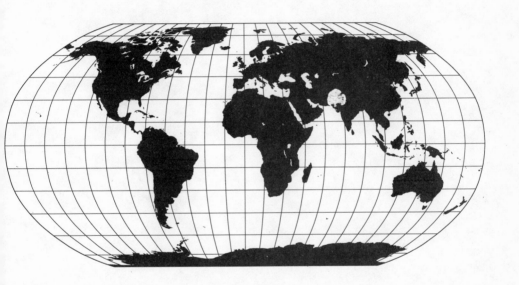

1

Discovering the Positive Within the Negative: The Women's Movement in a Changing China

NAIHUA ZHANG WITH WU XU

THE JANUARY 1988 ISSUE of *Women of China,* the leading Chinese official women's magazine, published a letter written by Li Jing, a woman worker who had lost her position as part of her enterprise's efforts to increase productivity and profit.[1] After losing her position, she earned only 80 percent of her previous salary and no bonus, which affected the living standard of her family, and she felt humiliated after being dismissed as redundant labor. In her letter Li wondered why economic reform had brought bitterness to women like her, making them appear undesirable employees just because they had to shoulder heavier child care and housekeeping burdens. She asked, "Where is my way out, where is equality?" In response to her letter, the magazine initiated a nationwide, year-long discussion entitled "1988: Where Is the Way Out for Women?" It covered topics such as gender equality, female labor force participation, the social welfare system, and women's interests versus the state's interests in economic reform.

This incident took place amid a growing urban women's movement in the People's Republic of China (PRC), highlighting its focus on women's enthusiasm for and frustration with recent economic reform; a reexamination of past experiences, including the legacy of the Chinese Communist Party's (CCP) theory and practice as they relate to women's issues; the awakening awareness of women as an

25

CHINA

GENERAL

type of government: State socialist
major ethnic groups: Han Chinese (94%); 56 other recognized minority groups
language(s): Mandarin; Cantonese; regional languages
religions: Officially atheist; Confucianism; Taoism; Buddhism; Muslim minorities;
   some Christians

DEMOGRAPHICS

population size: 1.151 billion
birth rate (*per 1,000 population*): 22
total fertility (*average number of births per woman*): 2.0
contraceptive prevalence (*married women*): 83%
maternal mortality rate (*per 100,000 live births*): 115

WOMEN'S STATUS

date of women's suffrage: 1949
economically active population: M 87%   F 70%
female employment (*% of total workforce*): 43
life expectancy   M 69   F 72
school enrollment ratio F/100 M)
   primary   86
   secondary   72
   tertiary   42
literacy   M 87%   F 68%

---

independent group; and women's determination and desire to find organized solutions to the problems they face as they continue their struggle.

The current women's movement emerged with China's 1979 economic reforms, which led to a more diversified economy as well as to more relaxed political, social, and intellectual climates that allowed for the expression of a variety of interests, including those of women. Two major factors shaped the development of the new women's movement. The first was a response to the problems women faced. The second was an intellectual effort to understand the position of women in Chinese society. The majority of the participants in this new movement are urban intellectual and professional women from governmental and nongovernmental organizations (NGOs). They have collaborated and clashed in their efforts to define and articulate women's demands and to fight for women's interests. While the movement is deeply rooted in and is part of the national effort to reform the country, women seek a more independent identity for themselves and their movement. It is marked by women's initiative and spontaneity from the bottom up.

In this chapter we aim to provide a snapshot of the movement and to shed light on the development of Chinese feminism. We touch on the relationship between women and a party/state that claims women's liberation as its mandate, and we show how this specific context poses a challenge to the women's movement of combining a top-down and a bottom-up strategy. We want to reveal the complicated legacies of Marxism to and the CCP's impact on the women's movement. As a Chinese woman remarked, "There is something negative within the positive, positive within the negative."[2] It is in addressing issues left from China's traditional and revolutionary past and responding to challenges emerging in the current reform that today's women's movement is shaping a new future for women and for China as well.

We define a women's movement as an active, organized effort by a nation's women to promote gender equality and the advancement of women's interests. It is marked by the basic characteristics of other social movements, such as shared ideology, organizations, and organized activities on a scale that affects not only the individuals involved but also society as a whole. Some Chinese scholars also emphasize that a women's movement should be initiated and led "by women," designed "for women," and result in raising women's consciousness—to distinguish a women's movement from a movement organized by the state, not directly for women per se, that brings about a "liberating effect" on women.[3] Thus, while scholars and women activists agree that China is witnessing a women's movement that started in the 1980s, they disagree about the relationship between today's women's movement and past women's activities as well as the implications of the legacy of the CCP on the "woman question."

History and Legacy

Prerevolutionary China: From the Turn of the Century to 1949

China's first modern women's movement developed alongside the country's political movements.[4] The issue of women was initially brought to public attention by male advocates during the reform movement of the mid-1890s. Women's plight, their ignorance because of their exclusion from education, and their bound feet symbolized a nation weakened by the assault of foreign powers and the traditional rule of the decaying Qing dynasty. While a small number of elite women's organizations had appeared by the turn of the century, recognition of women as a social category, broad attention to women's problems, and large-scale organized women's activities grew out of the 1919 May Fourth Movement.[5] This movement attacked traditional culture and Confucian ideology as well as oppressive family and marital institutions. (Confucian influences, having shaped many social institutions, had also helped define gender relations.) The movement was also patriotic and anti-imperialist, and it signaled the rise of a socialist movement in China.

During the 1920s, an urban-based women's movement appeared, pushed by women students, professionals, leftist women activists, and industrial women workers. During the first national alliance between the Guomindang (GMD) and the CCP (1924–1927), women campaigned to include their organizations at the First National Congress held by the GMD. They also rallied support for the Northern Expedition aimed at destroying warlord power to unify China as a national republic. It was also during this period that rural women were first mobilized amid the rising peasant movement, especially in places the Northern Expedition swept through. Women took off their foot-binding bandages and defied and opposed local customs and clan practices that discriminated against or persecuted women. They were further drawn into political and social activities in the CCP base areas by the party's effort in rural organization after it was forced out of cities in 1927 by the GMD. Urban women activists were mobilized again in the mid-1930s to combat a regressive move to push women back into the family. Anti-Japanese resistance brought another resurgence of women's organizations throughout the country. New coalitions were once more established among women's groups to support the resistance effort and to promote women's interests during the second alliance between the GMD and CCP.

In retrospect, this context encouraged the development of a modern feminism in China that differs from that of the West. Radicalized by the impact of imperialism in China's coastal cities, and particularly by the patriotic explosion associated with the May Fourth Movement, many intellectual women, despite the influence of Western individualism, switched their earlier emphasis on personal autonomy, dignity, and individual liberation to liberation of the collective. These women chose a political, as opposed to a literary, sexual, or individual, path to liberation.[6] Thus, the liberation of women as part of the national struggle for independence was the dominant strategy of the women's movement in pre-1949 China.

The two goals of national independence and gender equality were not the same but could not be separated. In the context of the anti-imperialist, anti-Confucian movement, women's rights became a cause linked with, yet subordinated to and defined by, the interests of the nation.[7] While the notion of female emancipation based on Western feminist ideas was embraced by some elite Chinese women, it did not "survive as [a] viable alternative to the Marxist categories of class-bound liberation" because of the prominent role played by women workers and rural women under the direction of the CCP during its rise to power in 1949.[8] The CCP,

Chinese communists viewed women's liberation as a necessary and inevitable part of socialist revolution. Partisans and members of the People's Liberation Army greet each other in 1949.

gaining legitimation through its leading role in the anti-Japanese resistance, also cast a strong influence on women who were responding to its patriotic messages and built their movement in that context.

Postrevolutionary China: 1949–1978

The CCP's theoretical framework on the woman question is based on Marxist, nationalist, and May Fourth feminist discourse.[9] It links women's oppression to the rise of private ownership and class society and views women's liberation as a necessary and inevitable part of socialist revolution. The CCP's organizational relationship to women is also shaped by its theory and practice of the mass line, a working philosophy and leadership style initiated by Mao Zedong to maximize enthusiasm and participation of the people in the revolution. Mass organizations were established to act as an intermediate structure to connect society to the party/state.

The All-China Women's Federation (ACWF) was set up in 1949 on the foundation of women's associations established in the years 1937–1945 in the anti-Japanese base areas and women's organizations in the GMD-occupied cities that worked closely with the CCP during the anti-Japanese war and the civil war.[10] The ACWF quickly established branches throughout the country as the mass organization designated to mobilize and represent Chinese women. Since there was no

Hsu K'uang-P'in, vice president of the All-China Women's Federation (ACWF), speaking at a meeting in Moscow in November 1949, the year the ACWF was founded.

government department in China in charge of women's affairs, the ACWF had the authority and resources to help interpret and implement state policy on women. As of 1994, it had over ninety-eight thousand full-time cadres on the state payroll. In contrast with government organs, it has no administrative or legislative power, and its functions rely heavily on hundreds of thousands of grassroots activists throughout the five-tier system from the village to the center. This allows the ACWF to reach millions of women. It officially incorporates women into mainstream CCP politics and social structure. Women enter the mainstream political structure as members of a mass group whose biologically based membership makes them a constituency with special concerns and needs. Yet like other mass organizations whose group interests are subordinate to those of the state,[11] the ACWF does not exist only to make special gender-based demands. The gender interests of women are often downplayed when there is a conflict in interests between women and the state.

The ACWF was to act as a bridge, a two-way channel of communication, between women and the party/state and a vehicle for the mobilization of women in the service of party goals. As the new government sought to undermine important elements of the old social order, it attacked aspects of patriarchy associated with the system of marriage. Following the Marriage Law of 1950, the party launched the single most important mobilization campaign directly targeting women's issues as a means to attack what it designated as the feudal elements of former marriage practices, such as forced marriage and bride-price. This was the first in a series of events that significantly improved women's lives and raised their status in society. Consciousness-raising among women was adopted by the ACWF to make women see that they had been oppressed under feudalism and that the new society would bring them liberation and equality with men. The CCP's ideas about women's liberation became the ideology of the women's movement, which subsequently subordinated the independent interests of women to state policy; this marked the beginning of women as a state product.

Women's programs were all state induced from the top down. However, women were not passive recipients. Many, especially young workers and peasants who were the main beneficiaries of state programs on women, embraced party policy, believing that their liberation would come from submitting their interests to those of building socialism in China. The ACWF, at the time a united front organization including non-CCP women advocates and activists groups,[12] pushed for progressive policies for women. It grew rapidly, serving as a space for women's leadership development and political participation.

With the completion of the nationalization of industry and commerce and the collectivization of agriculture in 1956, China declared that the socialist transition was essentially complete. This implied that issues such as the equality of women were essentially resolved. ACWF cadres hotly debated how to view the woman question in this changed social context. CCP leaders did not want to tangle with this theoretical impasse and asserted that continual emphasis on sexual inequality was counter to the revolutionary cause. Unfortunately, the political climate pressed the ACWF to adopt this position, and in 1957 it declared that socialism had brought women's liberation and equality between men and women.

While later official admissions acknowledged that "factual inequality" remained and that women had not been "completely" liberated as a result of inadequate economic development and the fading residues of feudal ideology, official discussion of the need for political struggle for gender inequality ended.[13] During the Great Leap Forward of 1958–1960, striving for women's "complete liberation" became part of the official rhetoric as female labor was mobilized on an unprecedented scale through socialization of domestic labor to contribute to the experiment for rapid economic development and social transformation. In the years that followed, notably during the Cultural Revolution of 1966–1976, women's issues tended to be buried beneath the all-consuming emphasis on class struggle. The Cultural Revolution slogan "What men can do, women can also do" confirmed the ideology of sexual equality at the very time that the ACWF was abolished, leaving no national organization responsible for women's issues in the years 1966–1978.[14] Talk about the interests of any groups except those based on class ceased.

During the 1950s, Chinese women entered diverse sectors of the economy. Lu Yen, left, man-
ager of the Tangshan Power Plant, is shown here in 1954.

Problems

The class-struggle-inspired turmoil of the Cultural Revolution aggravated many
women's problems, frequently shredding families but also delegitimizing attention to women's issues. After the Cultural Revolution, with the introduction of
major economic reforms, the growth of the private sector and the market economy resulted in certain gains for women, such as rising incomes and greater autonomy. It also brought a host of new problems and made some of the previously
existing problems more visible. There were increasing incidents of trafficking in
women, of purchased and forced marriage, of intense pressures on women associated with the rigorous enforcement of birth control, leading to female infanticide
and abuse of rural women who gave birth to daughters. Discrimination against
women in state-sector employment increased as enterprises gained more control
over personnel and hiring. Rural girls dropped out of school to help with family

The Cultural Revolution, which began in 1966, declared "What men can do, women can also do." Red Guard members pledge their support of the Cultural Revolution in a Shanghai rally in 1966.

farming as agriculture once again was organized by households rather than collectives. The number of women holding political positions declined as a result of direct election. Prostitution and pornography became more prominent in areas experiencing the rapid development of a market economy.

These problems shocked women. They realized that women's liberation was far from achieved and that women's interests were not always compatible with or addressed by the state, as they had thought. These problems disturbed the government, too. In 1978, it rehabilitated the ACWF and encouraged it to play an active role in helping solve China's emerging social problems.[15] This gave the ACWF legitimacy to launch a nationwide campaign in the early 1980s for the protection of the rights and interests of women and children. The end of the Cultural Revolution also brought about the "thought liberation movement," which led to a reappraisal of the CCP's policies and practices over the previous thirty years. A more open, liberal, and pluralistic environment characterized by freer expression of individual choice, an inflow of Western thoughts and ideas, a revival of academic studies in all fields, and a greater freedom to form new networks and groups created conditions for the emergence of a new women's movement.

The New Movement

Protecting Women's Rights and Serving Women's Needs

The first activities of the new women's movement were the documentation of inequality and the protection of women's rights and interests. Old concerns—equal rights, employment, women's role in production, and women's participation in politics—were taken up by the ACWF. One legal victory was a new law on the protection of the rights and interests of women that took effect on October 1, 1993. Although further regulations are required to facilitate implementation of the law and China observers debate the power of the legislation, most agree on the law's symbolic significance.[16] The sweeping fifty-seven-article law has consolidated previously fragmentary measures and given new importance to women's issues. It helps women recognize their rights and interests and pursue justice when these are violated. It also commits the state to deal with these violations.[17]

Another achievement was progress made in women's formal political representation. As the result of the ACWF's effort, a coordinating committee on women and children in the State Council was established in 1990. With twenty state agencies on the committee, it has more power and authority than the ACWF to mobilize resources to work for women's benefit.[18] The ACWF and the Women's Committee of the Workers' Trade Union also worked to set up "social reproductive funds" in thirty-eight cities and counties by 1991 to help solve problems women face in employment due to maternity-related issues.[19]

Since the economic reforms of the late 1970s, women have organized and worked in cottage industries such as toy making.

While these efforts addressed long-standing problems women have faced, efforts have also been made to meet the emerging needs of women. For example, since 1989 the ACWF has carried on a literacy and technical training campaign among rural women. With women increasingly taking on the major responsibility for family farming, the ACWF and twelve other government agencies provide training, loans, technical assistance, materials, and other resources.[20]

In cities NGOs have formed to address issues that traditional institutions do not deal with. Beijing, for example, has seen the emergence of marriage and family counseling, a women's hotline, a singles' club (the majority of the members are educated women), and classes for teenage girls (mothers are invited) to discuss the puzzling physical and emotional changes teens experience at this transitional stage. Meanwhile, the expansion of the women's press has played a vital role in documenting gender inequality and providing a forum for women to voice their concerns. Over forty magazines and newspapers are in open circulation. There are also more than twenty journals circulating within the ACWF system.[21] The press has become more and more vocal in exposing gender discrimination and in advocating for women's interests.

Women's Studies

The initiative and efforts of the ACWF and the activities of women scholars have resulted in the growth of women's studies in China. Women's studies have an unusually important place in the development of the contemporary Chinese women's movement, especially in the formation of independent associations and thinking. Establishing women's studies is perceived by women scholars as "a women's movement in itself."[22]

The ACWF set up research units at its headquarters and twenty-seven women's cadre schools at the provincial and municipal levels after its rehabilitation. Associations for the study of women's issues were established nationwide after 1984,[23] coordinated by the local chapters of the ACWF and including academic and professional women.[24]

Within the academic community, initial studies of women's issues focused on marriage and the family. By the mid-1980s, academic women had started forming groups. The Women's Society in Zhengzhou, Henan Province, led by Li Xiaojiang and set up in 1985, was the first NGO of this kind. It grew into the Center for Women's Studies at Zhengzhou University in 1987. Other organizations followed. In 1993, there were four leading women's studies centers in universities nationwide.[25] Courses on women's history, the history of the women's movement, women and law, and feminist theories have been offered at over a dozen universities. Groups studying women's issues have also found their way into nonuniversity settings.[26] These groups organize research projects, publish papers, hold national and international conferences, and promote public awareness of women's issues and *funuxue* (science on women, or women's studies) as a legitimate area of academic inquiry.

Women's studies scholars touch on many sensitive and controversial issues. For example, a scholar pointed out in 1986 that Chinese theoretical studies on women had to overcome three taboo areas: sex (dismissing sex in research), class (equating women's oppression with class oppression), and feminism (excluding feminist thought in studies of women in China).[27] These three taboos have been broken to some degree in the 1990s. ACWF colleagues' discussion between 1987 and 1988 on the federation's work among women examined the structural and operational weaknesses of the ACWF and linked reform of the federation to political and social reform of the entire society.[28] The study of women's history and the women's movement has expanded from documenting the history of the party-led women's movement to focusing on the broader experiences of women. For example, China's first women's museum and the ambitious Twentieth-Century Women's Oral History project will help recover a record of women's past in their own voices.[29]

Women's studies programs in China are focused less on political goals such as agitation for gender equality than were women's studies programs in the United States during the early 1970s. The focus in China has been more on the academic task of what scholars term *discipline building*. The effort is not to emphasize women's studies' critical edge and challenge to the establishment of traditional academic studies, as has happened in the West, but to promote the discipline as a new, "objective," and "scientific" subject readily accepted by the existing academic scholarship in China.[30]

Chinese women's studies and the women's movement are certainly influenced by Western feminism as the result of increased contact between Chinese women and the outside world through both official and unofficial means. However, many Chinese scholars emphasize the "national character" of women's studies in China to distinguish it from Western feminism. Take the translation of the term *feminism* as an example. One scholar argues that feminism is now translated as *nuquan zhuyi* (women's rights-ism) when referring to Western ideas and as *nuxing zhuyi* (female-ism) when referring to Chinese experience because *nuquan* (women's rights) is too political and *nuxing* (female) sounds more academic and better reflects the fact that in China women have already received legal equality and been incorporated into society.[31] Echoing such an opinion, some contend that *nuquan zhuyi* refers to Western women's struggle to wrest their rights from men, while *nuxing zhuyi* describes Chinese women's efforts to express their own desires and points of view, but not through fierce political movements. They say that *nuquan zhuyi* requires women to follow men's standard, while *nuxing zhuyi* builds up a female culture and uses women's points of view and standards to re-mold a society with men in it.[32]

Such a discussion shows Chinese scholars' and activists' efforts in grappling with the changing political and historical themes of Western women's movements and in creating a concept of Chinese feminism at the same time. Given the rich connotation of the English term, no one single translation or explanation would do justice to such a complex phenomenon. The matter is further complicated by the history of Western feminism's contact with the Third World. Despite the disclaimer made by some scholars that the political connotation of feminism is not the reason few Chinese women refer to themselves as feminists,[33] the term has long been associated with a liberal, bourgeois, and radically antisexist ideology seen as divisive to working-class struggles. Many women may still want to maintain a distance. Stressing the differences between women's studies in China and in the West may also be an unconscious strategy for avoiding political suspicion. However, whether conscious or unconscious, such emphasis on differences runs the risk of depoliticizing the feminist struggle and women's studies in China, thereby reducing their critical power and obscuring the common political base shared by women all over the world in their struggle for equality and advancement. Some scholars say they do not call themselves feminists because they do not know the term well. We find there is ambivalence and a lack of clarity about feminism and women's studies in Western countries on the part of Chinese scholars. Thus, more studies about Western feminism need to be conducted, and more exchanges between scholars inside and outside China should be initiated.

Marxist theories remain the dominant framework for women scholars both inside and outside the ACWF. Many scholars have engaged in conscious efforts to reconcile women's studies with Marxist theories. Marxist historical materialism's emphasis on gender difference as a social, rather than a biological, phenomenon and its stress on equality and emancipation for humankind appeal to Chinese scholars, just as they do to not a few Western feminist scholars. Marxism is increasingly viewed less as dogma and more as an intellectual approach. However, the inadequacy of Marxism's analysis of the woman question has not been sufficiently addressed in the PRC, and class analysis remains the dominant theoretical framework in women's studies. The introduction and application of other Western feminist perspectives, especially feminist critiques of male-centered culture and gender analysis in research, are still in the initial stages in women's studies in China. Despite the growing range of perspectives and topics for inquiry, many important issues are underdiscussed. Take the issues of sexual orientation and the politics of sexuality, for example. Homosexuality is still considered taboo by the general public, and there have been few studies of it.[34] Nevertheless, to borrow the words of an overseas scholar from China, "this scientific, ungendered, and Marxist Chinese *funuxue* does give the involved people legitimacy, and even some prestige, which they need to carry out researches on women and to form organizational networks."[35]

As China entered the 1990s, women's studies expanded more rapidly and took a more critical edge. This was demonstrated by new studies on gender issues presented at a two-week seminar at Tianjin Normal University in 1993. It was at this seminar that the gender perspective introduced by Chinese scholars from the United States (they were paired up with mainland scholars to discuss Western feminist studies on similar gender issues) became the focus of discussion. Many participants found the concept of gender useful and enlightening and expressed a strong desire to learn feminist theories and methodology more systematically.[36] Further exchanges and collaboration in research between scholars inside and outside China have been carried out and planned since then. We are confident that the 1990s will be an important decade for creating new discourses on women. A large number of professional and intellectual women have gathered under the banner of women's studies, successfully using it as a strategy for change. This discipline is a source of dynamism for the women's movement and is in the process of creating a new ideology for the movement.

Women's Self-Perception and Consciousness

The rise of women's subjectivity and their consciousness of themselves as a social category and an independent group is both an objective and a consequence of the current women's movement. A thriving Chinese women's literature that describes women's spiritual and material frustrations and their aspiration reflects such an awakening. The development of women's self-consciousness has partially been achieved, ironically, by emphasizing gender differentiation and stereotypes. There was a revival of femininity after the Cultural Revolution as seen in women's pursuit of fashion and makeup and media coverage and promotion of homemaking.[37] Some Chinese women scholars have actively promoted these tendencies.[38] They seem to reflect Chinese women's aversion to previous state control over individual choice and inattention to women's family lives. These trends also reject the androgynous Cultural Revolution concept of equality, which desexualized women. Rejecting androgyny and state control is a necessary step in women's search for a new collective identity as gendered beings, and it has had a liberating effect during the initial stage of the new women's movement. At the same time, a strong essentialist tendency among some scholars, a new focus on women's nurturing nature and domestic and reproductive role, and an emerging commercialization and objectification of women also present new challenges for the women's movement as it seeks to construct a new identity.

Chinese women realize that equality on paper cannot automatically mean actual equality. Thus, women learn to rely on themselves for their emancipation. There is also a concern about the "poor quality"[39] of Chinese women shared by women from academia and the ACWF. Some scholars argue that the CCP's top-down approach has resulted in women's dependence on society for the delivery of rights and benefits.[40] It is interesting to observe that, while some Western scholars focus their criticism on the CCP's approach to the woman question as creating a "public patriarchy,"[41] Chinese criticism is on women themselves. The ACWF developed a "four-self" slogan (self-respect, self-confidence, self-reliance, and self-improvement) based on the assumption that women's own weaknesses prevent them from becoming full members of society. While recognizing the importance of education for women, the emphasis on poor quality and on self-improvement could direct Chinese women to seek individual solutions to problems rather than searching for organized means for structural change. This is a real danger in the current women's movement. However, the focus on women's self-determination and self-empowerment also represents a break with the collective definition of goals that characterized the earlier women's movement.

Both young and middle-aged women struggle over defining the proper role and image of women in society. The contradiction between work and the family remains an unsolved issue central to women's lives. So does the issue of the ideal image for women. The competing images of the modern woman—on the one hand, a woman with her own career and social recognition as an equal partner and, on the other hand, a woman with a happy home, satisfied about herself as a woman—become increasingly equally attractive to today's women. During the Cultural Revolution, the first model, depicted as "iron girls," was the dominant norm. Today the superwoman who is capable of performing three roles well— worker, wife, and mother—is still promoted by the majority of Chinese women scholars as the ideal model for women's development.[42] But there is also concern that the model women who sacrificed family to achieve success in work lack a certain *nuren wei,* "womanliness."[43] It is clear that the issues presented in a 1986 na-

Concepts of beauty and femininity that were taboo in the Mao era have made a comeback under post-Mao reform. In 1984, the Oriental Fashion Modelling Team recruited professional fashion models in Beijing.

tional discussion carried out in *Women of China* entitled "Women's Ideal and the Ideal Women" are far from being solved.

This indicates that the search for the new woman that began with the May Fourth Movement is still going on but being carried out on different fronts. Today's women's movement has been able to address with some success the legal, economic, and political barriers to equality, yet restrictive views about gender relations and gender identity remain a big problem. Women are now also searching their inner worlds, exploring issues of psychological and cultural emancipation, just as women in other socialist states are doing. A Yugoslav feminist has used the term *neofeminist* to describe the struggle for feminist goals in a society in which many of the political and economic issues relevant to women have been legally addressed by state socialism but many of the social, sexual, and psychological dimensions of women's emancipation remain essentially unexplored within formal channels.[44] While China is moving rapidly toward a market economy, the legacy of its socialist rule remains in many aspects of people's lives. This adds another dimension to women's struggles and means that intellectual/professional women are bound to play a leading role in this new movement. This, however, also shows that there is a dichotomy within the women's movement. While these concerns are important for urban professional and intellectual women and are being addressed, they are not the primary concerns of rural women.[45] Rural women's experience and voice have not been well articulated. This is a weakness of the current urban-based women's movement.

Women's Organizations

The development in women's organizations is an important achievement of the current women's movement. In the reform era, the ACWF, undergoing changes and recruiting many young and educated women, has become more independent and militant in representing women's interests. For example, it firmly and openly rejected a 1980 proposal to send women home as a way of reducing employment redundancies. The ACWF is also a strong advocate of women's participation in politics, including establishing quotas to guarantee a certain proportion of women in the National People's Congress.[46] Increased local autonomy of the ACWF branches also brings new dynamics to the organization.[47] The federation's advantages are its resources and legitimate position, which allow it to advocate the formation of policies and measures to advance women's interests. Its penetrating network, which is often referred to as having "legs," and its ability to organize grassroots women in the rural areas are additional strengths.

However, the growth of new women's organizations since the early 1980s has broken the monopoly of the ACWF. Emerging first were women's professional and occupational organizations. Such groups signaled a break from the prereform era when vertical structures of connection confined a person's social life to her work unit. Around 1986, a second type of new organization—salons in universities and interdisciplinary, cross-occupational research organizations—was also initiated by women intellectuals and professionals. Despite better than average social and economic positions, these women also experience gender discrimination and face the double burden of work and family. They encourage other women to think about gender issues, and their theoretical research brings new impetus to the women's movement. Many of them are also actively involved in projects and activities for protecting women's interests and serving women's needs. These organizations are not completely autonomous because each is required by law to have a formal link with a state agency that supervises its activities. However, they are initiated by individual women and are referred to as nonofficial organizations (*minjian zuzhi*) in China. These groups (the research-based women's organizations in particular) and the ACWF are the two major forces in the women's movement.

Tensions between these two forces emerged, especially when the research-based organizations began to develop.[48] These tensions have been largely attributed to some conservative leaders of the ACWF. However, cooperation and collaboration between women inside and outside the ACWF have continued, especially at the local level and on an individual basis. Such cooperation has further expanded since the early 1990s.[49] But despite such cooperation, even as recently as the 1993

National Congress on Women, the ACWF's rhetoric unfortunately remains focused on identifying itself as the organized women's movement without acknowledging the importance of autonomous groups, treating them on equal terms, or mentioning plans for the development of more such organizations.[50] The relationships between different groups within the women's movement need to be worked out further.

Whether from the governmental or the nongovernmental sector, the driving force of the current women's movement is women themselves. Their discussions on women's issues are no longer confined within parameters set by the state. They are defining new issues for the women's movement. One example is the new research on women's reproduction and health. This research has touched on the very sensitive issue of China's family planning program, including the very skewed sex ratio,[51] which reminds us of the pressing population problem and how this, too, is a women's issue. Western scholars have written extensively on the negative effect on women associated with the family planning program—the extraordinary pressures on women, forced abortion, female infanticide—and the urgency and serious implication of the growing sexual imbalance to the Chinese people and society; Chinese scholars have remained relatively silent on these issues. The ACWF has been one of the key agencies responsible for implementing China's family planning program. Traditionally, discussion among the ACWF and scholars emphasized the importance of the family planning program for the country. Activities focused on changing people's attitudes and developing more effective means to carry out the program. Recently, some scholars have begun to explore some more controversial issues, including conflicts between the family planning program and women's health care, the negative effects of certain contraceptive methods, and abortion abuse.[52] Some have also suggested revisions in population policy to address these concerns.[53] Although still tentative, these initiatives have begun generating awareness of the implications of the family planning program for women's reproductive health and position and have generated a demand for more critical research in these areas and greater input from women in formulating population policy and programs.

The Course of the Chinese Women's Movement: Past and Future

The Past of the Women's Movement: Route and Legacies

Chinese women scholars and activists have different opinions about the relationship among the current women's movement, women's collective activities historically, and the forty-year legacy of the CCP. One controversial issue is the assessment of the period from 1949 to 1956. Some believe that this era was characterized by the CCP's top-down approach to the woman question, in which women were not the conscious subject of the movement. Therefore, activities during this period cannot be characterized as a women's movement as much as women being moved; not women's liberation, which requires the active intervention of women themselves, but the attempt to liberate women in ways defined by the state. In this view, Chinese women's liberation was "bestowed from above" or "given" (*enci*) and "premature" (*chaoqian*) because Chinese women did not achieve emancipation through their own separate struggles. The benefits women received, including high employment for urban women, were based on an underdeveloped economy. Thus, the employment setbacks suffered by some women workers during the reform reflected a natural adjustment.[54]

Other scholars contend that the top-down approach to women's issues was perfectly compatible with a thriving women's movement since women assumed leadership, women's interests were represented, and women were the subject. Women's interests and will were represented through the ACWF, which had the social position and power to pass women's perspectives from the bottom to the top.[55] This view emphasizes that women's liberation and the inclusion of women's liberation on the state agenda were "earned" by women through their hard struggle and sacrifice during the revolution.

While the first position points out the importance of autonomy and women's self-awareness for the development of a women's movement, we disagree with its assessment of the period, especially its assertion that Chinese women's liberation was given and premature.[56] First, the argument ignores the fact that Chinese women have been the subject of the women's movement as well as agents for change. They remained active after the revolution. There is a dialectical relationship between the state and women, and women are not always opposed to or completely separate from the state. Women's impact on the making of state policy has varied. Some women were (are) located in the state hierarchy and expressed (express) gender concerns.[57] The role these women played, their impact on the formation of state policy in different periods, and their effect on the women's movement need further study. Women's history is not only about subjection; it is also about subjectivity.

Second, the premature argument lacks historical perspective about the process and development of the Chinese women's movement. In China's case, both the initial integration of the women's movement into the larger revolutionary agenda and the current search for more independent identities reflect contextualized choices and realities. The course of the Chinese women's movement can be traced to the turn of the century. Every step made, including the setbacks the women's movement suffered, should be viewed as part of the long process of consciousness-raising for women. There is nothing premature about the actual course or about social justice preceding economic development. Moreover, the Chinese women's movement should not be measured by Western models. Women develop their strategies and agenda as they go along.

The road Chinese women have taken is not unique. Nanette Funk suggests that there are two models for women's movements.[58] One is characterized by a change in the totality through the transformation of the particular—as has taken place in the second wave of the U.S. women's movement, where the movements of women, blacks, and gays transformed society. In contrast, in Eastern and Central Europe and the former USSR, it was the transformation of the totality that created the possibility for a transformation of the particular. This is similar to the debate on whether women's interests are better served by explicit feminist activism, as has occurred in the West, or by subordination to a larger revolutionary movement whose stated goals include liberation and equality for everyone, as has taken place in China.[59] It seems to us, however, that the focus should not be on making value judgments about which approach is better but rather on recognizing that there are different routes to and models for women's movements and, to borrow from a Russian woman, that "it is possible that the paths of western and Russian [read Chinese] women will come closer at some point in the future, to which both sides will arrive changed."[60] For Chinese women in the reform era, the transformation of the particular also greatly affects the totality. The current wave of the women's movement, with women's points of view and voices much stronger than ever before in modern Chinese history, casts its own influence on people's values and behaviors and on the reorganization of China.

Despite Chinese scholars' differing opinions on the women's movement in the 1950s, most agree that what the current women's movement in China is experiencing is very much conditioned by the state policy on women developed in the 1950s. We think that, while Chinese women's full emancipation cannot be achieved from above, governmental ideology created expectations for gender equality that became a source of consciousness-raising for women and that motivated them to pressure the government to deliver what it had promised. The generation of middle-aged educated women who were born or grew up in post-1949 China are the products of the CCP. They have internalized their rights to work and equality and are idealistic, independent, and full of self-confidence about themselves as women. They are the main force of the current movement.

Chinese women have made great progress since 1949. Their *condition*—the material state women find themselves in—has improved tremendously compared to their condition in pre-1949 China. Yet they have not gained full equality in their *position*—women's social and economic standing relative to men in society and in the family has not kept pace with their condition. To emphasize the improvement of women's condition by downplaying the existing gender gap, as the CCP has done, is to paint an incomplete picture. To focus on the failure of socialism to liberate Chinese women as if women are faring worse under communist rule than before is also inaccurate. Rather, the impact of the CCP's approach to women's issues is a mixed legacy.[61] The complications of the CCP model in terms of theory, practice, and organization need to be fully recognized.

The staff of World Women's Vision, *a new magazine exemplifying the emerging independent women's movement. The magazine publishes an array of articles seeking to bring Chinese women in contact with women and ideas from other parts of the world.*

The Future of the Women's Movement: Challenges and Directions

When talking about the future of the women's movement, Chinese women scholars and activists, like their sisters in the past, look beyond gender issues. They are concerned about the success of economic reform because they feel that the fate of women is bound up with that of the nation and society. One leading scholar, after declaring that the main characteristic of the women's movement in the new era has been to "separate," says that "the leading trend of the women's movement is now to be re-integrated into society." She urges women not to "take equality between men and women as the eternal criterion" but instead to do what they can to contribute to society and to "find and create women's own space in a changed world."[62]

This strong emphasis on the interconnectedness between women's interests and those of the country is based on the perceived importance of reform to Chinese people, including women. Economic reform, representing new problems and challenges for women, also brings new opportunities, greater freedom of individual choice and self-control, and improvements in people's lives. The positive impact of rural reform on women is one such example. Reform has provided opportunities for women to work in growing rural industries; to turn the products of their domestic labor, such as embroidery and poultry raising, into commodities and thus gain productive and managerial skills and improved status in the family; and to seek job opportunities in cities and see the erosion of patrilocal marriage. Reform has also brought increased income to peasant families. This is very important to Chinese women, who, like women in other Third World countries, define survival as a women's issue.[63] The current women's movement is also the result of the more liberalized political atmosphere that started to appear with economic reform. Whether this movement can continue to develop is dependent on the success of broader economic, political, and social transformation processes. Concerns about larger societal interests reflect the traditions of the women's movement. However, emphasis on reincorporation, with women focusing on self-improvement and gaining social recognition through their own contributions, may be indicative of a "second sex" mentality. It may also be indicative of wishful thinking that women's interests will be taken care of automatically when subsumed under larger social interests.

Among the formidable tasks facing women today is reducing the negative impact of economic reform on women.[64] They have demanded the inclusion of women's development as an important index in state planning and the adoption of development models that are favorable to women.[65] Still others warn that as China moves toward a full market economy, women's welfare and benefits in the state sector will erode further. They fear that China's socialist tradition will not protect women from suffering the negative effects of modernization experienced by other Third World women.[66] There has been a revival of traditional views of women and an objectification of women's bodies. These problems are especially apparent in places with a more developed market economy where beauty and femininity, not ability, are regarded as the most valued assets of young women.

There are still other unfinished tasks and difficulties facing the women's movement. For example, the discipline of women's studies, which has emerged with great vigor in recent years, is still in its initial stages of development. It needs expansion and further development but lacks funds to support research, especially theoretical studies, and lacks places to publish research. The urban-based women's movement also needs to reach out more to the broad masses of rural women. Some women leaders are conscious of this and have been actively working to make these connections. For example, Xie Lihua, an editor of *Chinese Women's News*, has started a magazine for rural women, and a number of scholars are conducting applied research on the structural problems rural women face in contemporary China.[67] Breakthroughs in theory may emerge out of these efforts to develop an understanding of and solutions to these problems.

农家女百事通

这本小小的杂志每月从北京寄来 还告诉她 生活种种新知识 1993·第9期

阿香
她的家离城市很远很远
但，因为有了《农家女 百事通》
城里的事 天下的事 她都早知道
这本小小的杂志每月从北京寄来
不光告诉她每月每天的社会新闻和
爱情 法律 美容 时装 生活种种新知识
还告诉她
致富的办法

Magazines such as Farming Women Know It All *have proliferated since the late 1970s, promising to keep women in the remote countryside up to date on current developments in matters of love, the law, beauty, news, and everyday life.*

Another "blind spot" that the women's movement needs to address is women working "outside the system"—in the growing rural industries, privately run enterprises, and businesses with foreign investment. Labor unions are nonexistent in the great majority of these places, and there are serious violations of state regulations on labor protection for women workers in some of these businesses. The large number of young rural women coming to cities to provide domestic services to urban residents have not been incorporated into the ACWF or any other organizations. The situation and position of these women have aroused the concern of some scholars and organizations.[68]

So far the relationship between the state and women's studies/the women's movement has not been very contentious. Many women scholars perceive no major clash between them so far. When the transition to the market economy runs deeper and if the retrenchment of women's benefits and interests continues and is not addressed, women will be prompted to make new demands and to take more contentious actions. Some scholars have predicted a quieter period in the immediate future before the women's movement resurfaces during a new political, social, cultural, or economic crisis. Some perceive new difficulties for women in the stepped-up economic reform since 1992 as development and profit overshadow concerns for social equity and equality. Some women activists also complain about diminishing state support for the ACWF and women's issues. The recent CCP policy of encouraging mass organizations to run economic enterprises so they do not have to rely on entrenched state finance is seen by some women as evidence of reduced state support.

However, the implication and impact of these changes are far from simple and clear. While some ACWF cadres worry about reduced funding from the state, some ACWF branches running successful business have acquired greater power and autonomy from increased revenues and social influence. The newly revised constitution of the ACWF states that, besides receiving funds from the state, the federation at all levels can set up economic enterprises to promote the causes of women and children. For the first time, the ACWF's assets and the enterprises it runs are considered the property of the federation.[69] This can be seen as a desire to make the organization a more independent entity, enhance its economic power, and prepare for the changes on the way. In the process of transformation, the ACWF might lose some of the benefits of official status, but it could also gain more autonomy and make itself an organization first and foremost for women. While it is difficult to predict, these changes will clearly have important implications for the future of the women's movement in China.

There are other factors that work favorably for the further development of the women's movement. For one, the forthcoming United Nations Fourth World Conference on Women, which convenes in Beijing in 1995, has already begun to legitimate greater attention to women's issues. This has created new space for the development of university-based women's studies and the discussion of women's issues. The conference will provide a unique opportunity for Chinese women to contact feminists from around the world to compare notes and exchange experiences. Chinese women scholars and activists are already on the move, taking this opportunity to push for women's issues. Since the second half of 1993, more women's groups have been formed to work on newly defined tasks.

Perhaps the most important factors guaranteeing the further development of the women's movement in China are Chinese women themselves and their raised self-awareness. Chinese women have come a long way since the turn of the century. They rose as a formidable force for social transformation during the Chinese Revolution, and in today's women's movement they have acquired new consciousness of themselves as women and are waging a more independent movement to advance their own interests. The route of liberation they have traveled is unique. It is characterized by an interconnectedness between the women's movement and the national movements for independence, social progress, equality, and reform; by a close and sometimes uneasy relationship between women and the CCP and the challenge of combining top-down and bottom-up strategies in women's struggle; and by the leading role women's studies have played in the new movement. Women draw strength from their antifeudal, anti-imperialist, and socialist past, yet the new movement also grew out of a reexamination and critique of past legacies. Chinese women are carrying out the unfinished tasks on political and economic fronts left from previous struggles, adding to the agenda of their movement the goals of cultural, psychological, and individual liberation not adequately addressed in China's socialist revolution and facing bravely the challenges in the uncharted water of China's transition to a market economy. No matter what is ahead, Chinese women will continue their struggle to create a new future for themselves and for China and make their contribution to the development of feminism in the world as well.

NOTES

We are indebted to Li Xiaojiang, Chen Yiyun, Liu Xiaocong, Xie Lihua, Du Fangqin, Jin Yihong, Gao Xiaoxian, Sun Xiaomei, Tao Chunfang, Min Dongchao, Wu Qing, and numerous other Chinese women for their contribution of ideas; to Mary Ann Burris and Zhang Ye at the Ford Foundation for their support in the writing of this chapter and in the collection of data; to Amrita Basu, Kay Ann Johnson, Mark Selden, Susan McEachern, Lynn Paine, Rita Gallin, Xiaolan Bao, and Wang Zheng for their thoughtful comments; and to Susan Joel and Elizabeth McGrory for their careful reading and editing of the drafts.

1. This chapter is based on a summary and critical evaluation of the different opinions on the women's movement in contemporary China. While writing this chapter, we solicited some Chinese scholars' opinions on the subject through two small roundtable discussions in Beijing and Tianjin in July 1993 and personal communication and interviews with other Chinese scholars. This chapter tries to capture the spirit of scholarship and activism in China but also represents our own thinking about the topic, which is deeply rooted in

where we are from. We see ourselves as participants in the contemporary Chinese women's movement.

Yet our thinking is also shaped by our contact with Western feminism in the United States and a reflection on what came out of this encounter. Both of us are members of the Chinese Society for Women's Studies in the United States, a group of overseas Chinese students and scholars advocating studies of women, especially women in China. We wish to take this opportunity to introduce the Chinese women's movement to the outside world and promote further discussion of and dialogue around the many important issues related to this topic.

2. Xie Lihua, speech at a roundtable discussion, Beijing, July 1993.

3. Li Dun, "Dangdai zhongguo funu yanjiu de xianzhuang, wenti, lilun kuangjia yu zhidu beijing" (State of art, issues, theoretical framework, and system background in women's studies in contemporary China), in Center for Women's Studies at Tianjin University, ed., *Zhongguo funu yu fazhan: Diwei, jiankang, jiuye* (Chinese women and development: Status, health, and employment) (Zhengzhou: Henan People's Press, 1994), pp. 34–61.

4. All-China Women's Federation, *Zhongguo funu yundongshi* (History of the Chinese women's movement) (Beijing: Chunqiu Press, 1989); Lu Meiyi and Zheng Yongfu, *Zhongguo funu yundong, 1840–1921* (Chinese women's movement, 1840–1921) (Zhengzhou: Henan People's Press, 1988); Elizabeth Croll, *Feminism and Socialism in China* (London: Routledge and Kegan Paul, 1978); Delia Davin, *Woman-Work: Women and the Party in Revolutionary China* (Oxford: Clarendon Press, 1976).

5. The movement was named after a student demonstration on May 4, 1919, protesting the bartering of Chinese territory by imperialist powers at the Paris peace conferences.

6. Roxane Witke, "Women as Politicians in China of the 1920s," in Marilyn B. Young, ed., *Women in China: Studies in Social Change and Feminism* (Ann Arbor: Center of Chinese Studies, the University of Michigan, 1973), pp. 33–45. According to Roxane Witke, the transformation from individualism to collectivism "radically narrowed the meaning of liberation in subsequent decades" ("Transformation of Attitudes Towards Women During the May Fourth Era of Modern China [Ph.D. diss., University of California, Berkeley, 1970], p. 333). The emphasis on women's political emancipation left cultural and psychological emancipation unfinished goals to be taken up later. In her opinion, even the sex-neutral, independent, and less feminine image of the modern new woman was the product of the May Fourth era.

7. Charlotte L. Beahan, "Feminism and Nationalism in the Chinese Women's Press, 1902–1911," *Modern China* 1, no. 4 (1974):379–416.

8. Witke, "Transformation of Attitudes," p. 335.

9. Christina Gilmartin, "Gender in the Formation of a Communist Body Politics," *Modern China* 19, no. 3 (July 1993):299–329.

10. The ACWF was originally called the All-China Democratic Women's Federation. It changed to its present name in 1957.

11. The other two major mass organizations are the All-China Workers' Trade Union and the Communist Youth League.

12. These groups included the Women's Christian Temperance Union, the Women's Friendship Association, and the Young Women's Christian Association. The first two stopped functioning after 1958.

13. While the ACWF returned to women's "complete liberation" as a principal organizational goal in its constitution in 1978, it did not take on gender equality again until its 1988 constitution. Conflicts between women and men in a socialist society were perceived as contradictions among the people to be dealt with through education and persuasion but not struggle. This perception connected gender inequality to feudal and capitalist systems and prevented women from seeing other structural causes perpetuating gender inequality in socialist China and the need to struggle for change.

14. Local branches of the ACWF were restored around 1973 but did not play an active role. An effort to restore the central ACWF during this period failed.

15. After the restoration of the three major mass organizations, a CCP leader called on the mass organizations to "take the initiative to work vigorously, conscientiously and independently" to represent and safeguard the interests of their constituencies (Fuguanyan, ed., *Zhongguo funu yundong wenxian ziliao huibian* [Collection of documents and data on Chinese women's movement] [Beijing: Chinese Women's Press, 1989], vol. 2, p. 488). Some party leaders suggested that if a women's organization could not help solve women's problems, what was its use? (Interview of an ACWF official, Beijing, November 1992).

16. Judy Polumbaum, "China's New 'Iron Girls,'" *Boston Globe Magazine*, June 1993, p. 16.

17. Many Chinese women activists are making plans to help women find ways to use the law as a weapon to protect themselves, including publicizing the law as part of the consciousness-raising effort among women. Wu Qing, an assistant professor of English at Beijing Foreign Studies University and an elected deputy to the Beijing Municipal People's Congress, predicts that in the future "the people in China that are most conscious of and knowledgeable about laws will be women because they need the protection of the law most" (Wu Qing, personal communication, January 1994).

18. The coordinating committee became the Working Committee of the State Council on Women and Children in 1994. It will coordinate the implementation of the law protecting women's rights and interests.

19. Zhang Mo, "Nuzhigong shengyu baozhang wenti de yanjiu he shijian" (Research and practice on reproductive security of women workers), in Xiong Yumei, Liu Xiaocong, and Qu Wen, eds., *Zhongguo funu lilun yanjiu shinian* (Women's theoretic studies in China from 1981 to 1990) (Beijing: Chinese Women's Press, 1992), pp. 497–507.

20. By September 1993, 120 million rural women had participated in these activities; 90 million had received training in various applicable techniques; and 410,000 had earned the title of agronomists. Qicao Huang, "Quanguo funu tuanjie qilai, wei jianshe you zhongguo tese shehui zhuyi nuli fendou" (All Chinese women unite and strive for building socialism with Chinese characters), *Chinese Women's Movement* (October 1993):12–19.

21. Xu Chunting, "Xinshiqi funu baokan fazhan gaikuang" (Survey of development of the women's press in the new era), in Li Xiaojiang, Tan Shen et al., eds., *Funu yanjiu zai zhongguo* (Women's studies in China) (Zhengzhou: Henan People's Press, 1991), pp. 139–149.

22. Tong Shaosu, "Speech at the Workshop on Chinese Women and Development held at Tianjin Normal University," in Center for Women's Studies at Tianjin University, ed., *Zhongguo funu yu fazhan: Diwei, jiankang, jiuye* (Chinese women and development: Status, health, and employment) (Zhengzhou: Henan People's Press, 1994), pp. 13–15.

23. In 1984, the First National Conference on Theoretical Research on Women, organized by the ACWF, was convened.

24. Among them, there are male scholars. They are interested and active in studying women's issues and are organizationally incorporated into these groupings. Their role in the making of the discourse on women is a complicated issue requiring separate study.

25. The other three are in Beijing University, Tianjin Normal University, and Hangzhou University. There are also groups for studies of women's issues at other universities. According to Naihua Zhang's personal communication with Xiaolan Bao, by May 1994 there were twenty-four such organizations in universities throughout the nation.

26. For a more detailed discussion on organizations studying women's issues within and outside the ACWF, see Li Jingzhi, "Fulian xitong lilun yanjiu jigou" (Research units within the system of the federation), in Xiong Yumei, Liu Xiaocong, and Qu Wen, eds., *Zhongguo funu lilun yanjiu shinian* (Women's theoretic studies in China from 1981 to 1990) (Beijing: Chinese Women's Press, 1992), pp. 567–579; Liu Jinxiu, "Minjian funu xueshu tuanti yilan" (Survey of nongovernmental academic organizations), in Xiong Yumei, Liu Xiaocong, and Qu Wen, eds., *Zhongguo funu lilun yanjiu shinian* (Women's theoretic studies in China from 1981 to 1990) (Beijing: Chinese Women's Press, 1992), pp. 580–584; Vera Fennel and Lyn Jeffry, *To Increase the Quality of Women: A Preliminary Assessment of Women's Studies in Beijing* (Beijing: Ford Foundation, 1992); Wang Zheng, "Research on Women in the Contemporary China—Problems and Prospects" (Paper presented at the American Historical Association, January 9, 1994).

27. Li Xiaojiang, *Xiawa de tansuo* (Eve's exploration) (Zhengzhou: Henan People's Press, 1988); Tao Tiezhu, "Bashi niandai funu lilun yantaohui shuping" (Survey of conferences in the 1980s on theoretical studies of women), in Li Xiaojiang, Tan Shen et al., eds., *Funu yanjiu zai zhongguo* (Women's studies in China) (Zhengzhou: Henan People's Press, 1991), pp. 183–204.

28. The discussion was carried out in *Funu gongzuo* (Woman work), a journal produced by the central ACWF. The journal changed its name to *Zhengguo fu yun* (Chinese women's movement) in 1993. Such a discussion also appeared in *Women of China*.

29. Both projects were initiated by Professor Li Xiaojiang at the Center for Women's Studies of Zhengzhou University. The Preparatory Committee of the Women's Museum was set up in 1991 and has collected a large number of artifacts on women's lives. The most unique collection among them is "women's script," a language used exclusively by women in Jiangyong County, southern Hunan Province. The Twentieth-Century Women's Oral History Project was started in 1993. The personal stories of women of various ages, nationalities, and occupations gathered by the project participants will be published in nine books. The first three books, on women's lives in the pre-1949 era, are scheduled to be out in 1995 (see "Women reporting women," a newsletter by the International Women's College, Zhengzhou University).

30. This can be seen from the way *funuxue* is defined and discussed in China. See Zheng, "Research on Women"; and Xiaojing Li and Xiaodan Zhang, "Creating a Space for Women: Women's Studies in China in the 1980s," *Signs* 20, no. 1 (1994):137–151. There seems to be a haste to pronounce Chinese *funuxue* as an established independent field of study encompassing many humanities and social science disciplines. A summary of the development of women's studies in China from 1981 to 1990 boasts a list of newly developed areas and disci-

plines with the word *science* as part of the names of many study areas. See *Zhongguo funu lilun yanjiu shinian.*

31. Li Xiaojiang, "Funu yanjiu zai zhongguo de fazhan jiqi qianjing zhanwang" (Development of Women's Studies in China and its prospect), in Li Xiaojiang, Tan Shen et al., eds., *Funu yanjiu zai zhongguo* (Women's studies in China) (Zhengzhou: Henan People's Press, 1991), pp. 3–22.

32. Sharon Hom, "On the Translation of Special Terms of Women's Studies," in Center for Women's Studies at Tianjin University, ed., *Zhongguo funu yu fazhan: Diwei, jiankang, jiuye* (Chinese women and development: Status, health, and employment) (Zhengzhou: Henan People's Press, 1994) pp. 68–70.

33. Xiaojiang, "Funu yanjiu zai zhongguo de fazhan jiqi qianjing zhanwang"; Li and Zhang, "Creating a Space for Women."

34. Some initial studies have begun, however. Li Yinhe and Wang Xiaopo have published a book on male homosexuality entitled *Tamen de shijie: Zhongguo nan tongxing lian qunluo toushi* (Their world: A look at male homosexual groups in China) (Taiyuan: Shanxi People's Press, 1988). The two authors are also studying female homosexuality in China. For the few studies on this topic in English, see Fang-fu Ruan and Vern Bullough, "Lesbianism in China," *Archives of Sexual Behavior* 21, no. 2 (1992):217–226; and Fang-fu Ruan and Yungmei Tsai, "Male Homosexuality in Contemporary Mainland China," *Archives of Sexual Behavior* 17, no. 2 (1988):189–199.

35. Zheng, "Research on Women."

36. For more details about the seminar, which was attended by about one hundred women (and a few men) from all over China, see Center for Women's Studies, ed., *Zhongguo funu yu fazhan;* and Zheng, "Research on Women."

37. Emily Honig and Gail Hershatter, *Personal Voices: Chinese Women in the 1980s* (Stanford, Calif.: Stanford University Press, 1988); Marilyn B. Young, "Chicken Little in China: Women After the Cultural Revolution," in Sonia Kruks, Rayna Rapp, and Marilyn B. Young, eds., *Promissory Notes: Women in the Transition to Socialism* (New York: Monthly Review Press, 1989), pp. 233–247.

38. For example, some scholars promote the teaching of home economics and talk about women's new interest in femininity in terms of women raising consciousness of themselves as females.

39. This is a direct translation of the Chinese term *suzhi cha.* It is used widely to refer to a range of shortcomings commonly associated with women—poor education, psychological weakness, dependence, narrow-mindedness, etc.

40. Li Xiaojiang, *Nuren de chulu* (Women's way out) (Shenyang: Liaoning People's Press, 1989).

41. Judith Stacey, *Patriarchy and Socialist Revolution in China* (Berkeley and Los Angeles: University of California Press, 1983).

42. For an example of such a model, see Li Xiaojiang, Liang Jun, and Wang Hong, *Nuzi yu Jiazheng* (Women and home economics) (Zhengzhou: Henan People's Press, 1986).

43. Xie Lihua, "Shiye, jiating, nuren wei" (Career, the family, and womanliness), *Nongjianu baishi tong* (Farming women know it all), no. 7 (1993):2–3.

44. Ann Ferguson, *Sexual Democracy* (Boulder: Westview Press, 1991).

45. There is a great variation in women's conditions and positions due to regional, residential, ethnic, generational, and social class differences. The urban-rural disparity is especially great. For the majority of rural women in China, economic well-being is still their major concern. Other major obstacles, such as lack of employment and educational opportunities and the existing marriage and inheritance customs that discriminate against women, are especially serious for rural women. Take family planning, for example. This can be very much seen as a women's issue, yet urban women and rural women often have difference stances toward it because of the cultural and material contexts in which they live. Zou Yu, "Guanyu 'zhonghua renmin gonghe guo funu quanyi baozhang fa (cao an)' de shuoming" (Explanation on the law of the People's Republic of China on the protection of the rights and interests of women [draft]), in Drafting Committee of the Law on the Protection of the Rights and Interests of Women, ed., *Funu quanyi baozhang fa jiben zhishi* (Basic knowledge of the law on the protection of the rights and interests of women) (Beijing: Chinese Women's Press, 1992), Appendix.

46. At the time when the law was drafted, the percentage of women delegates in the Seventh National People's Congress was 21.3 percent. It was stipulated in the draft of the law that the percentage should reach 25 percent. See Rosemary Santana Cooney, Jin Wei, and Mary G. Powers, "The One Child Certificate in Hebei Province, China: Acceptance and Consequence, 1979–1988," *Population Research and Policy Review*, no. 2 (1991):137–155. In the final version of the law passed by the Congress, the actual figure was dropped; this version stated only that the percentage of women delegates at all levels of the Congress should be gradually increased. In the Eighth People's Congress convened in 1993, the percentage of women delegates was 21.03.

47. A huge top-down hierarchy like the ACWF leaves room for local autonomy. Such autonomy has been expanded during the reform era as a result of the decentralization process.

48. For example, pressure from some top leaders of the ACWF was exerted on some scholars to conform to official ideological and organizational lines.

49. For example, there are over one hundred people on the editorial board in the oral history project alone, including women inside and outside the federation and from over a dozen provinces and municipalities. Women are continually forming new groups to accomplish new tasks.

50. In the Seventh National Congress on Women held in September 1993, a top leader of the ACWF talked about the "development of a unified, representative and authoritative women's organization as an important organizational guarantee for the development of the women's movement" (Qicao, "Quanguo funu tuanjie qilai, wei jianshe you zhongguo tese shehu zhuyi nuli fendou," p. 15).

51. The sex ratio of infants at birth has been rising over the years, from 107.6 (girls = 100) in 1982 to 109.2 in 1987 (Quanguo Fulian Yanjiusuo and Shaanxi Fulian Yanjiusuo, *Zhongguo funu tongji zilao, 1949–1989* [Statistics on Chinese women, 1949–1989] [Beijing: China Statistical Publishing House, 1991]) and 111.7 in 1990 (Population Census Office, *Zhongguo 1990 renkou pucha 10% chuoyang ziliao* [10 percent sampling population on the 1990 population census of the People's Republic of China] [Beijing: China Statistical Publishing House, 1991]). Scholars have calculated that this implies that 500,000+ female infants (just over 2 percent of all births) are missing annually, raising serious political and so-

cial issues for Chinese families and society. See Terence H. Hull, "Recent Trends in Sex Ratios at Birth in China," in *Population and Development Review* (March 1990):63–83; and Sten Johasson and Ola Hygren, "The Missing Girls of China: A New Demographic Account," *Population and Development Review* (March 1991):35–51.

52. Liang Jun, "Some Aspects Influencing Chinese Women's Child Bearing and Their Health," *First International Conference on Women's Studies* (Beijing: Women's Studies Center, Beijing University, 1992); Cai Wenmei and Jiang Leiwen, "Effects of Family Planning on Women's Reproductive Health," *First International Conference on Women's Studies (Beijing: Women's Studies Center, Beijing University,* 1992), pp. 176–186; Women's Research Institute of the ACWF, "Funu shengyu jiankang xiangmu jieshao" (An introduction to projects of women's reproduction and health conducted by the ACWF), in Center for Women's Studies at Tianjin University, ed., *Zhongguo funu yu fazhan: Diwei, jiankang, jiuye* (Chinese women and development: Status, health, and employment) (Zhengzhou: Henan People's Press, 1994), pp. 283–288.

53. Wenmei and Leiwen, "Effects of Family Planning."

54. Li Xiaojiang, "My Opinion on Women's Studies and Women's Movement in the New Era," pp. 17–33 in Center for Women's Studies at Tianjin University, ed., *Zhongguo funu yu fazhan: Diwei, jiankang, jiuye* (Chinese women and development: Status, health, and employment (Zhengzhou: Henan People's Press, 1994); Xiaojiang, *Nuren de chulu;* Xiaojiang, *Xiawa de tansuo.*

55. Liu Xiaocong, speech at a roundtable discussion in Beijing, July 1993.

56. We think that the 1949–1957 period was certainly different from the rest of the prereform era, either viewed from the breadth and depth of women's active participation, the impact it had on women's lives (progress made and women's positive assessment of the period), or women's influence on state policy. It is true that the CCP had practical considerations when making its policy and was not consistent in all its programs on women. Nevertheless, we think the period was one of the high points of the women's movement in postrevolutionary China. More empirical studies will improve our understanding.

57. This is more so when there is space for women's input, such as during the early 1950s and in the reform era. In the early 1950s, for example, Deng Yingchao, then vice president of the ACWF and a feminist turned socialist, and two non-CCP women leaders, Shi Liang, then minister of justice, and Li Dequan, minister of health, were among the women who actively pushed for the implementation of the new Marriage Law and women's health programs.

58. Nanette Funk, "Introduction: Women and Post-Communism," in Nanette Funk and Magda Mueller, eds., *Gender Politics and Post-Communism* (New York: Routledge, 1993), pp. 1–14.

59. Jane Callels Record and Wilson Record, "Totalist and Pluralist Views of Women's Liberation: Some Reflections on the Chinese and American Settings," *Social Problems* 23, no. 4 (April 1979):402–414.

60. Larissa Lissyutkina, "Soviet Women at the Crossroads of Perestroika," in Nanette Funk and Magda Mueller, eds., *Gender Politics and Post-Communism* (New York: Routledge, 1993), p. 286.

61. Given the limited space and the complexity of the matter, we cannot give an adequate assessment of the achievements and limitations of the CCP's approach to women in the

past four decades. In general, there has been advancement for women in the following areas: law and legislation that provide equality for women, better access to education and health care, employment opportunities coupled with benefits, increased participation in social labor and public affairs, social acceptance of the ideology of gender equality, and improvement in women's general living conditions and life chances. This progress is not the sole result of the CCP's policy on women but is a part of the outcome of the socialist transformation of basic institutions in China. In general, urban women have benefited much more than rural women. Women in more economically developed areas on the east coast have fared much better than women in poorer areas in the west and remote border provinces, where more ethnic minority women live.

On the other hand, there have been limitations and failures. Chinese women continue to face common problems encountered by their counterparts in other parts of the world: deeply rooted patriarchal relations, discrimination in employment and work, the double burden of working in and outside the home, fewer opportunities than men in higher education and professional and managerial positions, lack of power and representation in higher decisionmaking bodies in the government and the party, and incidents of serious violations of women's rights and interests. Moreover, there are also the rural-urban disparity among women in their condition and position; the powerful grip of traditional values, especially in the countryside; less progress in gender relations within the family than in the public sphere; and lack of institutional support for women's cultural and psychological empowerment and individual actualization. Although these problems are not uniquely Chinese, they are shaped by and are often associated with the same socialist transformation process that brought improvement for women in China. For example, the collectivization of agriculture into communes and the establishment of residential registration in cities tied peasants to the land, restricted rural women's individual mobility to cities, and perpetuated patrilocal marriages. The CCP's major concern with stabilizing the family keeps it from taking stronger measures to break the patrilineal heritage and the patrilocal marriage patterns prevalent in rural areas. Some official practice and propaganda that intended to promote good family relations have been criticized as perpetuating traditional views of marriage and the family that are oppressive to women. (See "Socialist Spiritual Civilization or Feudal Ignorance," *Chinese Women's News*, September 1, 1986–March 20, 1987, on the experiences of six "model" women.) The dominant theoretical framework of the CCP, which regards women's subordination as the result of class oppression, greatly narrows the meaning of women's liberation. For a range of assessment and criticism by Western scholars of the CCP's legacy for the women's movement, see Davin, *Woman-Work;* Croll, *Feminism and Socialism in China;* Stacey, *Patriarchy and Socialist Revolution in China;* Margery Wolf, *Revolution Postponed: Women in Contemporary China* (Stanford: Stanford University Press, 1985); and Young, "Chicken Little in China."

62. Xiaojiang, "Speech."

63. For a discussion of the positive and negative effects of reform on rural women see Gao Xiaoxian, "Zhongguo xiandaihua yu nongcun funfu diwie bianqian" (Modernization in China and the change in women's status in the countryside), *First International Conference on Women's Studies* (Beijing: Women's Studies Center, Beijing University, 1992), pp. 54–69.

64. Again, take the experience of rural women as an example. The negative effects of the reform include an increased sexual division of labor and growing stratification among people. Development does not affect women and men in the same manner. There are growing gaps between women and men in income, education, and status. See Xiaoxian, "Zhongguo xiandaihua yu nongcun funfu diwie bianqian."

65. Ibid.

66. Min Dongchao, personal communication, 1993.

67. That magazine is *Nongjianu baishi tong* (Farming women know it all), started in 1993. These scholars include Gao Xiaoxian of the Shaanxi Women's Federation and Ji Yihong of the Academy of Social Sciences of Jiangsu Province. For samples of their works, see Gao Xiaoxian and Cui Zhiwei, "Shaanxi guanzhong diqu baihu nongfu zhuangkuang diaocha" (Investigation of conditions of women in a hundred households in Guanzhong region, Shaanxi Province), in Li Xiaojiang, Tan Shen et al., eds., *Zhongguo funu fenceng yanjiu* (Multilayered studies of Chinese women) (Zhengzhou: Henan People's Press, 1991), pp. 56–60; Xiaoxian, "Zhongguo xiandaihua yu nongcun funfu diwie bianqian"; Jin Yihong, "Jingji gaige zhong nongcun funu de xianzhuan yu chulu" (Current condition and prospect of rural women in economic reform), in Li Xiaojiang, Tan Shen et al., eds., *Zhongguo funu fenceng yanjiu (Multilayered studies of Chinese women),* (Zhengzhou: Henan People's Press, 1991), pp. 32–41.

68. Xiaojiang, "Speech."

69. ACWF, "Constitution of the All-China Women's Federation," *Chinese Women's Movement* (October 1993):20–21.

2

From Chipko to Sati: The Contemporary Indian Women's Movement

RADHA KUMAR

IN THIS CHAPTER I OFFER a selective description of the contemporary Indian women's movement. I am selective partly because space is limited, partly because I want to cover a range of campaigns from urban to rural and radical to reformist, and partly because I describe key moments in the development of the movement since the early 1970s. Inevitably, my discussion is partial.

The phrase *the contemporary Indian women's movement* is itself debated in India. Many would argue that the campaigns described here do not fall under the rubric of one movement and indeed that the women who engaged in some of these campaigns did not regard themselves as part of an overarching women's movement. There is some truth in this criticism, and it is not my intention to misappropriate activity. Nevertheless, social theory would be that much poorer—and so, for that matter, would we—if we were always to restrict our definitions to those offered by the social actors. My justification here for using the article *the* (women's movement) to describe a sum of campaigns around issues of importance to women is that the campaigns fed into a network of women's groups and were part of a process of change and development in feminist thinking: As far as the public impact of women's campaigns is concerned, awareness of women's problems and rights has accumulated through these campaigns.

I have tried to find a concise way of describing this process by dividing the chapter into four sections. The first provides the context in which contemporary

INDIA

GENERAL

type of government: Democratic Republic
major ethnic groups: Indo-Aryan (72%); Dravidian (25%); other tribal minorities
language(s): Hindi and English (official); 14 others recognized by government; more
    than 1,000 others
religions: Hindu (80%); Muslim (14%); Christian (3%); Buddhist; Sikh; Jain
date of independence: 1947; republic declared 1950
former colonial power: Britain

DEMOGRAPHICS

population size: 886 million
birth rate (*per 1,000 population*): 30
total fertility (*average number of births per woman*): 3.7
contraceptive prevalence (*married women*): 43%
maternal mortality rate (*per 100,000 live births*): 340

WOMEN'S STATUS

date of women's suffrage: 1950
economically active population: M 84%   F 29%
female employment (*% of total workforce*): 25
life expectancy   M 57   F 58
school enrollment ratio (*F/100 M*)
    primary   71
    secondary   55
    tertiary   37
literacy   M 64%   F 39%

---

feminist ideas developed. The second describes the early feminist campaigns, which were largely city based. The third describes the period of growth and maturing when a host of movements and campaigns, both historical and contemporary, fed into Indian feminism. And the fourth deals with the years in which feminists faced a series of attacks and challenges.

Muslim women of Peshawar, Northwest Frontier Province (now part of Pakistan), gather in 1947 to exercise their right to vote.

The Context

After India gained independence in 1947, the Congress (ruling party) government made partial attempts to fulfill the promises it had made to women by declaring in the constitution the equality of men and women, setting up various administrative bodies for the creation of opportunities for women, and inducting a number of feminists into the government. In the 1950s and 1960s, therefore, there was a lull in feminist campaigning. The movement that started in the 1970s was very different from its predecessors, for it grew out of a number of radical movements of the time.

In the early 1970s, the Indian Left fractured, and some factions began to question their earlier analysis of revolution. New leftist ideas and movements developed, albeit on a smaller scale. Among these the most interesting movements for feminists were the Shahada and anti–price rise agitations in Maharashtra and the Self-Employed Women's Association (SEWA) and Nav Nirman (New Light) in Gujarat. The Shahada movement, in Dhulia district of Maharashtra, was a Bhil tribal landless laborers' movement against the exploitative practices of nontribal local landowners. Drought and famine in Maharashtra during this period exacerbated the poverty already created by invidious rates of sharecropping, land alien-

Urban women of Gujarat in western India organize consumer protest against the price rise of 1973. From Radha Kumar, The History of Doing *(New Delhi: Kali for Women, 1993), p. 102.*

ation, and extortionate moneylending charges, and these conditions contributed to rising militancy among the Bhils. The Shahada movement began as a folk protest (through radical devotional song clubs) in the late 1960s. It took on a more militant campaigning thrust when the New Left joined the movement in the early 1970s and helped the Bhils form an organization, the Sharmik Sangathana (Toilers' Organizations), in 1972. Accounts of the Shahada movement say that women were more active than men and that as their militancy grew, they began to take direct action on issues specific to them as women, such as the physical violence associated with alcoholism.[1] Groups of women began to go from village to village to storm liquor dens and destroy liquor pots. If any woman reported that her husband had beaten her, other women would assemble, beat him, and force him to apologize to his wife in public.

Meanwhile in Gujarat, what was probably the first attempt at forming a women's trade union was made in Ahmedabad by Gandhian socialists attached to the Textile Labour Association (TLA). Formed in 1972 at the initiative of Ela Bhatt, who worked in the women's wing of the TLA, the Self-Employed Women's Association was an organization of women who worked in different trades in the informal sector but shared a common experience of extremely low earnings, very poor working conditions (most of them either performed piecework in their homes or toiled on the streets as vendors or hawkers), harassment from those in authority (the contractor for homeworkers and the police for vendors), and lack of recognition of their work as socially useful labor. The aims of SEWA were to improve these working conditions through training, technical aid, and collective bargaining and to "introduce the members to the values of honesty, dignity and simplicity of lifegoals reflecting the Gandhian ideals to which TLA and SEWA leaders subscribe."[2]

Conditions of drought and famine in the rural areas of Maharashtra in the early 1970s led to a sharp rise in prices in the urban areas. In 1973, Mrinal Gore of the Socialist Party and Ahilya Ranganekar of the Communist Party of India—Marxist (CPI—M), together with many others, formed the United Women's Anti Price Rise Front, "to mobilize women of the city against inflation just as women ... of the rural poor had been mobilized in the famine agitations."[3] The campaign rapidly became a mass women's movement for consumer protection and its members demanded that the government fix prices and distribute essential commodities. So many housewives were involved that a new form of protest was invented: At appointed times housebound women would express their support for demonstrators by beating *thalis* (metal plates) with *lathis* (rolling pins). The demonstrations themselves were huge, comprising between ten and twenty thousand women. Commonly, demonstrators would protest rising prices and hoarding by going to the offices of government officials, members of Parliament (MPs), and merchants, surrounding them, and offering them bangles as a token of their emasculation or by going to warehouses where goods were being hoarded and raiding them.

Soon after, the movement spread to Gujarat, where it was known as the Nav Nirman movement of 1974. Nav Nirman, originally a students' movement against soaring prices, corruption, and black marketeering, became a massive middle-class movement joined by thousands of women. In its course the movement shifted from protesting these issues to mounting an all-out criticism of the Indian state. The methods of protest ranged from mass hunger strikes to mock courts passing judgment on corrupt state officials and politicians, mock funerals celebrating the death of those condemned by their courts, and *prabhat pheris,* or processions, to greet the dawn of a new era. Women also "rang the death knell of the Legislative Assembly with rolling pins and thalis." It took the police some three months to subdue the Nav Nirman movement, and between ninety and one hundred people were killed.[4]

In the same year as the Nav Nirman movement developed and was subdued, the first women's group associated with the contemporary feminist movement was formed in Hyderabad. Comprising women from the Maoist movement, the Progressive Organization of Women (POW) exemplified rethinking within the Left. As in the Shahada movement, Maoist women were beginning to stress the existence of gender oppression and to organize women against it; but whereas in the former the question came up through the single issue of wife beating, the POW attempted an overarching analysis of gender oppression in its manifesto, which was largely influenced by Friedrich Engels and Isaac Babel.[5]

The year 1975 saw the sudden development of a whole spate of feminist activities in Maharashtra. This has been seen by some feminists as the result of the United Nations' declaration of 1975 as International Women's Year. Perhaps the declaration did provide a focus for activities centering on women. But it seems likely that these activities would have taken place even without the declaration, for an interest in women's problems had been developing in Maharashtra since the early 1970s, as we have seen through the Shahada and anti–price rise agitations. Influenced by the POW, Maoist women in Pune formed the Purogami Stree Sangathana (Progressive Women's Organization), and Maoist women in Bombay formed the Stree Mukti Sangathana (Women's Liberation Organization). March 8, International Women's Day, was celebrated for the first time in India by both party-based and autonomous organizations in Maharashtra; the Lal Nishan (Red Flag) Party commemorated it with a special issue of the party paper. In August, the Marathi socialist magazine *Sadhana* (Contentment) brought out a special women's issue; in September *dalits* (untouchables) and socialists organized a conference of *devadasis* (literally, servants of the gods; or temple prostitutes); and in October a number of organizations that had developed out of the Maoist movement, such as the Lal Nishan Party and the Shramik Sangathana, organized a "United Women's Liberation Struggle" conference in Pune. It was attended by women from all over Maharashtra, including some from left-wing political parties such as the CPI—M, the Socialists, and the Republicans.[6]

Especially interesting was the connection now being made between the anticaste *dalit* movement and feminism. The *dalits,* classified as untouchable under the Hindu caste system for their association with such polluting tasks as curing leather or clearing excreta, had a long history of anticaste protest in Maharashtra. In the late nineteenth century, under the leadership of Jyotiba Phule, *dalits* had also espoused women's rights to education, against purdah, and for widow remarriage. *Janwedana* (Distress of the People), a *dalit* Marathi newspaper, brought out a special women's issue entitled "In the Third World Women Hold Up Half the Sky," a slogan borrowed from the Chinese Revolution to make clear its departure from First World feminism; some months later women from the *dalit* movement formed an intriguing new group called the Mahila Samta Sainik Dal (League of Women Soldiers for Equality). The name itself, which stressed equality and conjured up images of a women's crusade, drew on the Black movement in the United States, and the Dal's manifesto claimed African-American activist Angela Davis as a sister. Both the Dal and POW emphasized women's oppression; the Dal additionally emphasized the oppressive character of religion and the caste system.[7]

The declaration of a state of emergency in 1975 by Prime Minister Indira Gandhi interrupted the development of the fledgling women's movement. Many political organizations were driven underground, thousands of activists were arrested, and most who remained at liberty focused on civil rights, such as freedom of speech and association, the right to protest, and the rights of political prisoners. The lifting of the emergency in 1977 and the formation of the Janata government in 1978 led to a renewal of some of the earlier movements. Women's groups were formed all over the country but mainly in the major cities.

Early Feminist Campaigns

The distinguishing features of the new women's groups were that they declared themselves to be "feminist" despite the fact that most of their members were drawn from the Left, which saw feminism as bourgeois and divisive; that they insisted on being autonomous even though most of their members were affiliated to other political groups, generally of the far Left; and that they rapidly built networks among one another, ideological differences notwithstanding. All three features were, however, defined and in certain ways limited by the history of these groups, whose first years were spent mainly in attempts at self-definition. The fact that most of their members were drawn from the far Left and belonged to the urban educated middle class influenced the feminist movement of the late 1970s and early 1980s in complex ways. For example, one of the main questions that feminists raised in the late 1970s was, How could women be organized and represented? While there was a general agreement that it was not the role of feminist groups to organize or represent women, there was considerable disagreement on why this was so. For some, feminist groups were in essence urban and middle class and so could neither represent Indian women as a whole nor organize them; others believed that, although autonomy was necessary for the development of feminist theory, in practice it would divide existing organizations and movements. The role of feminist groups, therefore, was to raise feminist issues in mass organizations such as trade unions or *kisan samitis* (peasant committees), which would then be in a position to organize and represent women as well as men. Yet others believed that once a women's movement began, it would naturally spread and grow in multiple ways, creating its own organizations and representatives, and so it was superfluous for feminist groups to debate whether they should organize and represent women.

Many groups opted for autonomy, which they defined as separate, women-only groups without any party affiliation or conventional organizational structure, for they considered this hierarchical, self-interested, and competitive. By contrast, the women's groups that were formed in the late 1970s were loosely organized and without formal structures or funds. The only party-based women's organization to be formed in the late 1970s was the Mahila Dakshata Samiti (MDS; Women's Self-Development Organisation), which was founded in 1977 by socialist women in the coalition Janata Party.

While there was therefore a feminist critique of party politics, the terms of criticism varied widely: Some feminists were critical of party practices but believed that parties could enact valuable reform and fulfill feminist aims; others were critical of entrenched political parties, and yet others argued that political parties, even of the Left, were so centralized that they would never fulfill feminist aims. Meanwhile, the influence of feminist ideas was growing. Though the feminist campaigns in the late 1970s and early 1980s were dominated by the new city-based groups, a similar growth of feminist consciousness had taken place in certain rural movements. The 1950s sharecroppers' movement in the Telengana area of Andhra Pradesh was again renewed in the late 1970s, and the area was declared a "disturbed zone" by the government. In Telengana's Karimnagar district, where women had been especially active in the landless laborers' movement from the 1960s on, the new wave of agitation began with a campaign against the kidnapping of a woman called Devamma, and the murder of her husband, by a local landlord. According to the Stree Shakti Sanghatana (Women's Struggle Organization) formed in the late 1970s in Hyderabad (the capital of Andhra Pradesh), the demand for independent women's organizations came from the women themselves, who raised the issues of wife beating and landlord rape through the *mahila sanghams* (women's committees).[8]

At around the same time, in the Bodhgaya district of Bihar feminist issues were raised by women in the socialist students' organization, the Chhatra Yuva Sangharsh Vahini (Young Students' Struggle Organization), which was involved in an agricultural laborers' movement for land reclamation from the temple priest who owned most of the land in the area. As in the Shahada and Telengana movements, women were active in the struggle, and in 1979 a women's camp in Bodhgaya decided that Vahini campaigns to reclaim plots of land would demand that plots be registered in the names of men and women.

The Movement Against Dowry

The first campaigns of the contemporary Indian feminist movement were against dowry and rape. Protests against dowry were first organized by the Progressive Organization of Women in Hyderabad in 1975.[9] Although some of the demonstrations numbered as many as two thousand people, the protests did not grow into a full-fledged campaign because of the imposition of the emergency, which drove most activists underground. After the lifting of the emergency, a new movement against dowry started in Delhi. This time it was against violence inflicted upon women for dowries, especially against murder and abetment to suicide. There have since been protests against dowry harassment and murder in several parts of

A poster created by the Women's Liberation Group marks International Women's Day in Bombay in 1982. It reads in part, "We will only rest after having broken this prison." From Radha Kumar, The History of Doing *(New Delhi: Kali for Women, 1993), p. 107.*

India, but Delhi has remained the site of sustained agitation against dowry and dowry-related crimes, largely because it seems to have the highest number of murders of women for dowry in the country.

Although the MDS was the first women's organization in Delhi's contemporary feminist movement to take up the issue of dowry and dowry harassment, it was Stri Sangharsh, a fledgling feminist group founded in 1979, that drew public attention to dowry-related crimes. On June 1, 1979, Stri Sangharsh organized a demonstration against the death of Tarvinder Karu, a young woman from Delhi who had left a deathbed statement saying that her in-laws had killed her because her parents could not fulfill the in-laws' ever-increasing demands. The demonstration was widely reported by the national press, and in the next few weeks there was a spate of demonstrations against dowry deaths, one of the biggest ones led by the Nari Raksha Samiti (Women's Rescue Committee) on June 12 through the alleys of old Delhi. Each demonstration was headline news, and a public debate on dowry and dowry-related crimes began.

Until this time women's deaths by fire (women doused with kerosene and set on fire, often by the in-laws and husband) had been termed suicide, and even these suicides were rarely seen as being due to dowry harassment. No one (including the police) had ever bothered to investigate them or even categorize them. And mostly they had been passed off as private affairs that took place within the family and were of no concern to the state. Within weeks, however, feminists reversed the indifference of decades, linking death by fire with dowry harassment and showing that many official suicides were in fact murders. Feminists recorded the last words of the dying woman, took family testimony, and encouraged friends and neighbors to come forward with their evidence. As a result, many families began to lodge complaints with the police against the harassment of their daughters by the in-laws for more dowry.

Campaigns against dowry deaths now began to be taken up by neighborhood groups, teachers' associations, and trade unions. Within feminist groups a series of strategies was devised to enhance public awareness of the problems associated with dowry: Stri Sangharsh produced a street play, *Om Swaha* (priests' incantation around the ritual wedding fire), that attracted large crowds all over the city and continues to be performed by different groups today; *Manushi,* a Delhi-based feminist magazine, organized a series of public meetings at which people pledged neither to take nor give dowry.

In 1980, a year after the antidowry agitation began, the government passed a law against dowry-related crimes that recognized abetment to suicide because of dowry demands as a special crime and made mandatory a police investigation into the death of any woman within five years of marriage. However, the law was a considerable disappointment to feminists. Although it acknowledged that dowry harassment could be construed as abetment, it did not specify the kinds of evidence that could be used to prove harassment, nor did it make abetment a cognizable offense. And though the law was passed in 1980, the first positive judgment under it did not occur until 1982, when a Delhi Sessions Court magistrate found two people guilty of dowry murder and sentenced them to death. The judgment was reversed by the Delhi High Court in early 1983. Women's groups from the party-affiliated Left and autonomous groups protested and were held for contempt of court. In 1985, the Supreme Court upheld the verdict but converted the sentence to life imprisonment. Moreover, the storm that women's groups raised in 1983 had some indirect effect: In December 1983 the Criminal Law (Second Amendment) Act was passed, which made cruelty to a wife a cognizable, nonbailable offense punishable by up to three years' imprisonment and a fine; the act also redefined cruelty to include mental as well as physical harassment. In addition, Section 113-A of the Evidence Act was amended so that the court could draw an inference of abetment to suicide. Technically this shifted the burden of proof and thus lessened the burden upon the complainant. Finally, the act amended Section 174 of the Criminal Procedure Code, requiring a postmortem examination of the body of a woman who died within seven years of marriage.

In practice most of these amendments do not make it much easier to secure convictions for dowry death. Hearsay evidence has to be overwhelming for an Indian court to convict, as people will say anything to gain a point, even before a court of law. Traditionally most women are raised with the belief that after marriage they have no source of support—including livelihood—other than their in-laws. So the women themselves are loath to bring charges of harassment. Similarly, postmortem examinations do not necessarily give evidence of murder. As most dowry deaths are the result of burns, generally with kerosene, it is difficult to prove that they resulted from murder, which is why so many dowry deaths were put down to stove accidents before women's groups began to argue otherwise.

Overall the agitation against dowry-related crimes led feminists to varying conclusions. On the one hand, they discovered they could get massive public support for campaigns against certain kinds of crimes against women, such as dowry-related murder. On the other hand, they found how difficult it was to work with the law against such crimes. This latter experience was repeated in regard to rape.

The Agitation Against Rape

Beginning just a few months after the campaign against dowry-related crimes, the agitation against rape started with campaigns against police rape. The scale and frequency of police rape are quite startling in India: Police records themselves show that the number of rapes by government servants in rural and tribal areas exceeds one a day.[10] This figure vastly understates the actual number of such rapes, for it does not cover incidents of mass rape by the police (i.e., the rape of groups of women by groups of policemen, generally as a reprisal to underclass movements for redress in rural areas); even in the case of individual or gang rape,

Women protest the tradition of dowry at a demonstration in New Delhi in 1980.

the figure cannot cover unreported incidents, which are likely to be at least as numerous as reported ones.

When the new feminist groups were formed in the late 1970s, they were already familiar with the categories of police and landlord rape, for both, especially the former, had been addressed by the Maoist movement. Moreover, the issue of police rape achieved new significance in 1978, just as feminist groups were in the process of formation, through an incident in Hyderabad where a woman called Rameeza Bee was raped by several policemen, and her husband, a rickshaw puller, was murdered when he protested his wife's rape. A popular uprising ensued: Twenty-two thousand people went to the police station, laid the man's dead body in the station veranda, set up roadblocks, cut the telephone wires, stoned the building, and set fire to some bicycles in the compound. The army had to be called in, and the uprising was quieted only after the state government had been dismissed and a commission of inquiry into the rape and the murder had been appointed.[11]

In 1979, there were women's demonstrations against incidents of police and landlord/employer rape in many parts of the country. Campaigns against these incidents, however, remained isolated from each other until 1980, when an open letter by four senior lawyers against a judgment in a case of police rape in Maharashtra sparked off a campaign by feminist groups. Known as the Mathura rape case, the incident had occurred several years earlier, when a sixteen- or seventeen-

*A poster created by the Ahmedabad Women's
Action Group protests violence against women.
Courtesy Ahmedabad Women's Action Group.
From Radha Kumar,* The History of Doing
(New Delhi: Kali for Women, 1993), p. 154.

year-old girl, Mathura, was raped by local policemen. Under pressure from her
family and the villagers, a case was registered against the policemen, who were ac-
quitted at the Sessions Court, convicted on appeal at the High Court, and later ac-
quitted by the Supreme Court. The defense argument for the policemen was that
Mathura had a boyfriend and was thus a loose woman who could not by definition be raped. The open letter was in protest at the Supreme Court's acceptance of
this argument.

The campaign against rape marked a new stage in the development of feminism
in India. The networks that had begun to form in 1978–1979 were now consolidated and expanded and used to coordinate action. Finding this letter in the left-
wing journal *Mainstream,* the Bombay feminist group Forum Against Rape (FAR,
which is now called the Forum Against Oppression of Women) decided in February 1980 to campaign for the reopening of the case and wrote to feminist groups
across the country to propose that demonstrations be held on International
Women's Day (March 8) to demand a retrial. In effect, this was the first time that
feminist groups coordinated a national campaign. Groups in seven cities responded to the FAR letter and organized demonstrations on March 8 demanding
a retrial of the Mathura case, the implementation of relevant sections of the In-

dian Penal Code, and changes in the rape law. In both Bombay and Delhi, joint action committees were formed of feminist groups and Socialist and Communist Party affiliates to coordinate the campaign.

Meanwhile, protests against police rape were reported from all over the country, only some of which were organized by feminists. As in the agitation against dowry, the first protests against police rape sparked off a series of protests by neighborhood and trade union–based groups in different parts of the country. The kind of press coverage that was now given to incidents of police rape and protests against them encouraged national parties to use the issue as a political lever against their rivals. When in June 1980 policemen arrested a woman called Maya Tyagi in the small town of Baghpat in Haryana state, stripped her naked, raped her, and paraded her through the streets, the incident aroused such furor from women's organizations and political parties that Home Minister Zail Singh went to Baghpat with ten women MPs and ordered a judicial inquiry into the incident. While they were in Baghpat, the Lok Dal, an opposition political party, staged a noisy demonstration (according to the newspapers) against the incident, claiming it underlined Congress misrule. Roughly a week later, Parliament debated the large-scale increase in the incidents of rape and atrocities against women, and several MPs used the issue to demand the resignation of the home minister and suggested that the death penalty be introduced to punish rapists.

Within months of the agitation, the government introduced a bill defining the categories of custodial rape and specifying a mandatory punishment of ten years' imprisonment, in camera trials, and a shift of the onus of proof onto the accused. The clause over which controversy raged was the burden of proof clause, which said that if the women could prove intercourse with the accused at the time and place she alleged, and if it had been forced upon her, then the accused would be presumed guilty until he could prove otherwise. Immediately there arose the cry that this violated the legal principle that a man was innocent until proved guilty, and the papers were full of articles vehemently protesting the clause, some of which exclaimed that this paved the way for every revengeful woman to frame innocent men.

The government had taken the wind out of feminists' sails by responding to their demands with such a radical piece of legislation. But this was only one of the reasons the agitation faded so rapidly. The highly publicized nature of the campaign and the speed with which rape was used by mainstream political parties in a welter of accusation and counteraccusation placed feminists in the invidious position of having to rescue the issue from political opportunists. Moreover, the nature of the issue, the kind of social sanction accorded to rape, and the problem of acquiring medical evidence to prove it in a country where only the big cities are technically equipped to provide such evidence constituted formidable obstacles.

Indeed, a 1988 Supreme Court judgment in another case of custodial rape, the Suman Rani case, showed how clauses in the law that were intended to ensure fairness allowed scope for interpretations that ran contrary to the purpose of the law. The sentence against Suman Rani's rapists was reduced because of the supposed conduct of the victim—in this case the fact that she had had a lover was held to militate against the crime of the rapist. This issue of conduct was especially important given the circumstances under which much urban custodial rape takes place. In Delhi, for example, the People's Union of Democratic Rights discovered that in several cases the victims had run way from home with the men they loved against their families' wishes; then the police had tracked them down in cities to which they had fled and used their "runaway" status as a reason to separate them from their partners and rape them.[12]

The Supreme Court judgment was a staggering setback for the feminist movement, which in 1980 had appeared to have at least partially gained its point that character and conduct should be deemed irrelevant. Feminists reacted with a storm of protest. The National Front government responded promptly with the promise of yet another amendment of the rape law, this time concerning the rules of evidence. But the key question, of implementation and interpretation of the law, remained open.

However, the judgment also led to a renewed debate on the definition of rape in which feminists stressed that the technical definition of rape obscured the fact that it was an act of violence because the definition treated forcible penetration by anything other than a penis as "molestation" and applied a similar distinction to forcible penetration of any organ other than the vagina (except for anal rape, which it deemed an "unnatural act"). Molestation, in fact, was much more common than rape, according to police reports, but was generally regarded benignly as "Eve-teasing" and rarely punished.

These early years of the contemporary Indian women's movement taught women's groups a series of lessons, of which the foremost was that there was considerable public support—from men as well as women— for campaigns against gender oppression. In effect, a handful of feminists discovered that they could garner public support and influence policy even though their numbers were small and their groups weak. However, this discovery did not bring unmixed pleasure, for it also entailed having to deal with the political exploitation of feminist campaigns, as in the movement against rape.

Growth and Maturing of the Movement

The mixed experiences of the campaigns against rape and dowry led many feminists to question their methods and tactics. The discovery that there was little and faulty connection between the enactment and the implementation of laws left many feeling rather bitter that the government had easily sidetracked their demands by enacting legislation. This gave rise to further questions about the efficacy of basing campaigns around demands for changes in the law and, by extension, around demands for action from the state. On the one hand, this questioning strengthened decisions to take up individual cases and follow them through the intricacies of the courts, no matter how long it took. On the other hand, feminists began to move away from their earlier methods of agitation, such as public campaigns, demonstrations, and street theater, feeling that these had limited meaning unless accompanied by attempts to develop structures to aid and support individual women. In the early 1980s, women's centers were formed in several cities. These centers provided a mixture of legal aid, health care, and counseling; one or two of them also tried to provide employment, but they foundered for lack of sufficient resources.

Though centers to provide women with aid, counseling, health care, and employment had existed from the early twentieth century on, these new centers were different in several important ways. First, most of the earlier centers had concentrated on one or two issues, whereas the new ones attempted to provide help on a range of interrelated issues. Second, the earlier centers had had a social welfare ideology, whereas the new ones were explicitly feminist. For example, earlier centers providing health care had concentrated on maternity and child welfare alone. The new centers, in contrast, took a more holistic view, looking at how women treated their own bodies.

Third, the new centers represented an effort to put feminist concepts of sisterhood into practice as well as to redefine these concepts by basing them on traditionally accepted structures of friendship among women. In both Delhi and Kanpur, for example, the names of the centers symbolized moves to locate notions of sisterhood in a specifically Indian context. Both chose to focus on and thereby reinterpret the traditional concept of a girlfriend; in Delhi, the name chosen was Saheli (Female Friend) and in Kanpur, Sakhi Kendra (Center for Women Friends). Saheli, with its association of playfulness, was chosen by the Delhi feminists who set up the center to signify that they were concerned not only with helping women in distress but also with sharing moments of play and pleasure. The center's founders wished to give due to the positive aspects of women's lives, particularly their forms of celebration and creativity. This led Saheli to host a 1983 workshop for feminists from all over India at which there were sessions on song, dance, drama, and painting.

Attempts to appropriate symbols of women's power grew in the 1980s through reinterpreting myths, epics, and folktales and unearthing historical forms of women's resistance in India. To some extent an interest in tradition had been present in the Indian feminist movement since the 1970s. The street plays *Om Swaha* (against dowry deaths, first put together in Delhi in 1979 and performed all over the city and in several parts of northern India) and *Mulgi Zali Ho* (A Girl Is Born, performed in Bombay in 1979–1980) had both used traditional songs and dances; many exhibitions mounted by feminists had similarly used traditional images. At

Baiyeja, *a magazine for working-class women, was one of the first feminist magazines in India. From Radha Kumar,* The History of Doing *(New Delhi: Kali for Women, 1993), p. 154.*

this stage, however, the main effort was to detail traditional forms of women's subordination in India, from birth to puberty, marriage, maternity, work, old age, and death. In the 1980s, the emphasis changed to looking for traditional sources of women's strength rather than simply suffering. For some, this consisted of identifying images of women warriors to be used as a battle cry for latter-day women and to appreciate and recast Kali, the all-powerful mother goddess, in a feminist mold.

If the interest in tradition led some feminists to reinterpret images, others were more interested in defining the ways in which ordinary women used the spaces traditionally accorded them to negotiate with their husbands, families, and communities. Special attention was now paid, for example, to the way in which women appropriated specific religious practices such as spirit possession, simulating possession by the *devi* (goddess), particularly during pregnancy, to wrest concessions from their husband or families that would otherwise have been impossible. Accounts now began to circulate of women who had simulated possession to reform alcoholic husbands or get money for household expenses, and this tactic began to be highlighted as a means of gaining power.

The search for historical examples of women's resistance led feminists to scrutinize the distant and immediate past, to look at the role women played in broader movements for social transformation, and to reclaim some of the movements predating contemporary feminism. One example was the Chipko movement against deforestation in the northern Indian mountain tracts. Beginning in the mid-1970s, Chipko (literally, cling to) was a movement to prevent forest destruction by timber contractors and was carried forward largely by women, who were traditionally responsible for fuel, food, and water in the family. There was little or no discussion of it as a women's movement until the early 1980s, when feminists began to celebrate it as a mass women's movement and theories of women's special relation to their environment began to be advanced.[13] A new awareness of women's role and problems developed within the movement, and the hitherto defunct government-sponsored village- and district-level *mahila mandals* were revitalized.

By the early 1980s, feminism had branched into a series of activities ranging from the production of literature and audiovisual material to slum-improvement work, employment-generating schemes, health education, and trade unions. New attempts to organize women workers' unions were made. Interestingly, these attempts focused largely on the unorganized sector, as SEWA had done; unlike SEWA, however, they grew out of campaigns for an improvement in living conditions. By this stage the feminist movement had diversified from issue-based groups into distinct organizational identities. The first professions to feel the influence of feminism were journalism, academia, and medicine. Soon after the feminist movement began, most of the major English-language dailies had deputed one or more women journalists to write exclusively on feminist issues, and a network of women journalists evolved. In Bombay, this network was formalized into a women journalists' group in the mid-1980s, with the purpose of lobbying for better reporting on women's issues, such as dowry, rape, and widow immolation. Feminism thus had a much wider audience than before.

Women's studies took off in the 1980s, initially under the aegis of independent research institutes such as the Centre for Women's Development Studies (CWDS) in Delhi, though an attempt to fund research at the university level was made by the S. N. Damodar Thackersay (SNDT) Women's University in Bombay, which set up a women's research unit. The SNDT and CWDS began to jointly host annual national women's studies conferences, and interest in women's studies grew so rapidly that today the University Grants Commission, a central government body, plans to set up women's studies courses at the college level.

While the influence of feminism in medicine has been less effective than in journalism or academics, the connection between theory and activity has been closer here than in the other two. For example, radical medical organizations such as the Voluntary Health Association of India and the Medico Friends' Circle have worked closely with women's organizations in campaigns against harmful pregnancy testing and contraceptive drugs such as Net-en and Depo-Provera, which transnationals have dumped in developing countries such as India. Because of this close cooperation, feminists have been able to generate much more detailed information on issues of health (such as the effects of Net-en and Depo-Provera and the alternatives to them) than on most other issues. And though feminists have been unable to eliminate some of the more glaring abuses of medicine, such as the use of amniocentesis to abort female fetuses, the connection between radical doctors and feminist groups has allowed them to use a wider range of tactics than in other campaigns. For example, in the campaign against the widespread use of abortifacient drugs for pregnancy testing, doctors' groups and women's groups were able to jointly argue their case before the government-appointed drug controller in 1986–1987 and to pressure him into holding hearings about these drugs all over the country. They were also able to produce lists of doctors and medical centers that prescribed these drugs without warning patients of the side effects, which include damage to the fetus.

During the same period, the far Right began to organize its own bases among women. The Maharashtra-based Hindu chauvinist Shiv Sena (Shiva's Army) activated its women's wing to engage in anti-Muslim propaganda. Interestingly, its main argument was one advanced in the nineteenth century that had had enduring success in India: that the Muslim rate of reproduction is so prolific that it will outstrip that of Hindus. The time when it does so, of course, never comes.

An even more worrying development took place between 1982 and 1983 in Delhi, Rajasthan, and parts of Bengal, where attempts were made to revive sati, the practice of immolating widows on their husbands' funeral pyres. Under the aegis of the Rani Sati Sarva Sangh (an organization to promote sati), feminist discourse was used to propagate a cult of widow immolation. Women's demonstrations were organized in various parts of the country to demand women's "right" to commit sati. In Delhi, feminists decided to hold a counterdemonstration along the route of a pro-sati procession. This was the first time that feminists were forced to confront a group of hostile women, which was in itself so distressing that it took the heart out of the counterdemonstration. Most distressing of all, however, was the way in which the processionists appropriated the language of rights, stating that they should have the right, as Hindus and as women, to commit, worship, and propagate sati. At the same time, they also appropriated feminist slogans on women's militancy, for example, *"Hum Bharat ki nari hain, phool nahin, chingari hain"* (We, the women of India, are not flowers but fiery sparks). The feminists who attended that demonstration experienced a humiliating sense of loss on discovering that their own words could be so readily used against them.[14]

The early 1980s witnessed a series of countermovements against feminist ideas by sections of traditionalist society. The rise of these countermovements was partly related to the spread of feminism and the influence it was beginning to have on women's attitudes, especially within the family. The kind of support that women's centers gave women who were being harassed for dowry or forced into arranged marriages, for example, provoked a considerable degree of public and private hostility, and feminists began to face attacks from irate families in person and through the police and the courts. However, where earlier such attacks would have led to a wave of sympathy for the feminists, from the mid-1980s on they were accompanied by a public, and increasingly sophisticated, critique of feminism. Much of this criticism took place in a context of growing communalism.

Challenges to the Movement

The issue of personal, or religion-based and -differentiated family, law became especially controversial for feminists in 1985 in what is now referred to as the Shah Bano case. In India, personal law falls under the purview of religion, though individuals can choose secular alternatives. This choice is, however, circumscribed: A woman married under Muslim or Hindu law, for example, cannot seek divorce or alimony under secular law; she has to abide by what is offered by the religious laws by which she was married. Neither Muslim nor Hindu personal law entitles a woman to alimony. Under Muslim law she is entitled to the return of her engagement gift *(iddat);* under Hindu law she is theoretically entitled to the gifts that went with her at marriage *(stridhan)*. Finding an abnormal number of destitute divorced women in India, the British colonial government passed a law under the Criminal Procedure Code (Section 125) entitling destitute divorced women to maintenance by their husbands. It was Section 125, which remains in Indian criminal law, that was at issue in the Shah Bano case.

Shah Bano was a seventy-five-year-old woman who had been abandoned by her husband and had filed for maintenance under Section 125. While her claim was being considered, her husband divorced her, using the triple *talaq*.[15] The Supreme Court, in its judgment, upheld Shah Bano's right to maintenance from her husband under both Section 125 and Muslim personal law.[16] It asserted that Section 125 transcended personal law. The court was critical of the way women had traditionally been subjected to unjust treatment, citing statements by both Manu, the Hindu lawmaker, and the Prophet as examples of traditional injustice. And the court urged the government to frame a common civil code because the constitutional promise of a common or uniform civil code would be realized only at the government's initiative.

The judgment was widely criticized by feminists,[17] liberals, and secularists as well as by Muslim religious leaders for what were held to be unduly weighted critical comments of Muslim personal law. The ulema (scholar-priests) issued a *fatwa* (proclamation) that the judgment violated the teachings of Islam. Wide publicity was given to the *fatwa*, and within a few months the whole issue took the form of a communal agitation claiming that Islam was in danger. One hundred thousand people demonstrated against the judgment in Bombay and at least as many in Bhopal, both cities with large Muslim populations. Supporters of the judgment were threatened, stoned, and beaten up.

Demands began for legislative action against Section 125. In August 1985, a Muslim League MP, G. M. Banatwala, offered a bill in Parliament seeking to exclude Muslim women from the purview of Section 125. Though the ruling Congress Party opposed the bill, as Muslim public protest against the Shah Bano judgment mounted, the party began to backtrack. To understand why the issue became so heated, one has to look at the context. In October 1984, the Vishwa Hindu Parishad (World Hindu Organization) launched an agitation demanding that a shrine in the precincts of Muslim mosque, the Babri Masjid, in the northern Indian town of Ayodhya be declared the birthplace of the god Ram and a temple be built on the spot. Parishad led demonstrations all over the country between 1984 and 1985, drawing as many as two hundred thousand people. The Babri Masjid issue and the Shah Bano case began to be linked as representing a Hindu communal onslaught on Muslims. The threat of Hindu communalism appeared especially strong in the wake of the November 1984 riots against Sikhs following the assassination of Indira Gandhi.[18]

In the 1985 state elections, the Congress lost in a number of Muslim constituencies. Alarmed by this, it announced that the government would consider a bill along the lines of Banatwala's bill, and in 1986 the Muslim Women's (Protection of Rights on Divorce) Bill was enacted. At the same time, they let a local magistrate's judgment that the shrine in the Babri Masjid be given over to Hindus go unchallenged.

For feminists, the agitation around Muslim women's rights to maintenance consisted of a series of bitter lessons. Discovering the ease with which a "community in danger" resorts to fundamentalist assertions, among which control over women is one of the first, feminists also confronted the ease with which the Indian state chose to accommodate communalism (by taking no action against the Vishwa Hindu Parishad agitation) and balance this by a concession to fundamentalism (allowing personal law to cut into the application of uniform laws such as Section 125).

At the same time, the agitation posed certain issues that were to become increasingly important for feminists in the years to follow. There were the questions of secularism; its definition and practice, particularly by the state; and its relation to religious freedom. By and large, opponents of the Muslim Women's Bill espoused a classic liberal democratic view of secularism as a system that separated religion from politics, that disallowed religious definition of the rights of the individual, and that allowed freedom of religious practice only insofar as it did not curb the rights of the individual. A 1986 petition against the bill jointly organized by feminists, social reformers, and Far Left groups, for example, argued that all personal laws "have meant inequality and subordinate status for women in relation to men" and that therefore religion "should only govern the relationship between a human being and god, and should not govern the relationship between man and man or man and woman."

As against this, the government definition of secularism appeared to be radically different. According to Prime Minister Rajiv Gandhi, "secularism is the right of every religion to co-exist with another religion. We acknowledge this by allowing every religion to have its own secular laws."[19] This statement seemed to imply that personal laws were defined as secular—presumably on the grounds that as religion in this instance defined the relationships between human beings rather than between humans and god, it was on "secular" terrain. Religion, then, could formulate secularism. Another implication of this statement was that all religions had the right to representation within the law and the right to make their own laws. While to a certain extent these rights were not new, the supremacy they accorded to personal law reaffirmed the colonial codification of religion-based family laws and ran counter to the constitutional promises of offering alternatives to personal laws and moving toward uniform rights.

So much pressure was put on Shah Bano that she gave up the right she had long fought for, abjuring the maintenance the court had accorded her. As in the agitation against rape, the problems and needs of women were soon submerged by the discourse of "community." Even worse, in this agitation, setting a trend for others to follow, the individual woman was smothered by a newly constructed symbol of woman, the "real woman" who followed men in demonstrations organized by Muslim religious leaders, who signed petitions against Shah Bano, who abhorred claims for maintenance because they were against her religion, and who saw feminists as unnatural creatures attempting to wrest her identity from her. This positing of the real woman in opposition to the feminist began to be widely made for the first time in the history of the contemporary women's movement in the mid-1980s, and it is revealing that this symbol arose in the course of communal-fundamentalist self-assertion. In the 1987–1988 agitation around sati that followed on the heels of the Muslim Women's Bill agitation, the issues of secularism, religious representation, the Indian nation-state, and the symbol of the real woman were expanded even further.

In September 1987, an incident of sati in the village of Deorala in Rajasthan sparked off a campaign that gave rise to a furious debate that spanned not only the rights and wrongs of Hindu women but also questions of religious identity, communal autonomy, and the role of the law and the state in a society as complex and

The women's group Saheli produced a poster to protest fundamentalist oppression of women during a 1985 campaign against religious personal law.

as diverse as India. Within a couple of weeks of the incident of sati, several articles appeared that engaged in a polemic against Indian feminists, accusing them of being agents of modernity who were attempting to impose crass, selfish, market-dominated views on a society that had once given noble, spiritual women the respect they deserved.[20] These market-dominated views of equality and liberty were portrayed as being drawn from the West, so Indian feminists stood accused of being Westernists, colonialists, cultural imperialists, and, indirectly, supporters of capitalist ideology.

Given that there has been, on average, only one reported sati a year in postindependence India, the extraordinary debate that the 1987 sati incident aroused was puzzling. In a way it can be understood only as part of a process of political reorganization in which the death of Roop Kanwar, the girl who was immolated, became the symbol of Rajput identity politics. In contrast to some of the other areas in which sati had been attempted, Deorala was a relatively highly developed village. The family was well off. Roop Kanwar's father-in-law was headmaster of a district school, while she herself was a graduate. A Rajput family, the Kanwars had links with influential Rajputs and mainstream state-level politicians.

Roop Kanwar had been married only a short while before her husband died. When her marital family decided that she would become a sati, the event was announced in advance because sati is always a public spectacle. Yet her natal family was not informed. Evidence pointed to murder: Some of her neighbors said that she had run away and tried to hide in a barn before the ceremony but was dragged out, drugged, dressed in her bridal finery, and put on the pyre, with logs and coconuts heaped upon her. The pyre itself was lit by her brother-in-law.[21] Reports indicated that the local authorities knew of the planned sati, yet their only action was to dispatch a police jeep, which was overturned on its way to the site. Following this debacle, three more days elapsed before a government representative visited Deorala.[22]

Immediately after the immolation, the site became a popular pilgrimage spot, and a number of stalls sprang up spelling auspicious offerings, mementos, and audiocassettes of devotional songs. Her father-in-law, prominent men from the village, and members of a newly formed organization, the Sati Dharm Raksha Samiti (Organization for the Defense of the Religious-Ethical Ideal of Sati), together formed a trust to run the site and collect donations. Within some three weeks the trust had collected around Rs 50 lakhs (close to $200,000).[23] The leaders of the Samiti were urban professionals or businessmen from landowning families whose sphere of influence extended over both rural and urban areas. Their propaganda was illuminating. Policymakers and the intelligentsia argued that a representative state should recognize and legitimate Rajputs' claim that sati was a fundamental part of their traditions; a refusal to legitimize sati, they said, was a deliberate attempt to marginalize the Rajputs. The women's groups, for example, were represented as using the issue as a means to attack Rajputs. In the 1990 state elections, several leaders of the Samiti won seats in the state legislature.

As the pro-sati campaign developed, the argument about Rajputs was extended to Hindu identity. The head priests of the major Hindu temples in such centers as Benares and Puri issued statements that sati represented one of the most noble elements not only of Rajput culture but also of Hinduism and claimed that issues such as sati should be placed under their purview as arbiters of Hindu personal law and not that of the state. At the same time, they also raised the bogey of "Hinduism in danger" from the opponents of sati.

The Hinduism in danger cry was echoed by far Right Hindu nationalists, spearheaded by the Shiv Sena, which organized a series of pro-sati demonstrations and argued that the Indian state was particularly biased against the Hindus, for it was willing to accede to the demands of minority communities for representation but was unwilling to do the same for the majority. The particular point of reference here was the Muslim Women's Bill, and, as in the Muslim Women's Bill agitation, the pro-sati agitation also posited real women against feminists.

The pro-sati agitators mobilized considerable numbers of women in their support. This allowed them to claim that they represented the "true" desires of Hindu women and to accuse the feminists of being unrepresentative. So the feminists were placed in the anomalous position of appearing to speak in the interest of women whom they could not claim to represent and who defined their interests differently.

The tradition versus modernity argument further isolated feminists. The bogey of modernism was so successful that it masked the fact that sati was being used to create a "tradition," despite feminist efforts to emphasize this. Tradition was defined so ahistorically and so self-righteously that it obscured the fact that the pro-sati campaign was run on "modern" lines, with modern arguments, and for modern purposes, such as the reformation of electoral blocs and identity-based community representation within the state.

However, a closer look at the nature of women's support for the pro-sati agitation revealed that this was ambiguous and at many points consisted of firmly differentiating between the worship and the actual practice of sati. An examination of the women who were mobilized for the pro-sati demonstration made clear that they were not, in fact, the women who were most directly affected by the issue. Widows were conspicuously absent.

For most feminists, the campaign around sati revealed the growing opposition to feminism and spelled a considerable setback for the movement. Yet the challenges it posed to feminist self-definitions yielded some valuable insights: a more complex understanding of the ways in which different groups and communities saw themselves and a recognition that it is not helpful, especially at moments of crisis, to view the state as a monolithic entity, for it is important to assert that women have the right to a voice in the administration of their society. Representation consisted not merely of a show of numbers but also in the encouragement of a plethora of voices, which was to some extent taking place through the feminist and associated movements. Opposition to sati came from a variety of sources: Both the right-wing Hindu reformist tradition and maverick left-wing Hindu reformers such as Swami Agnivesh of the Arya Samaj (community of Aryans) opposed it. In fact, Swami Agnivesh challenged the head priests of the Puri and Benares temples to a debate on the scriptural "sanction" of sati. His challenge was declined. Opposition also came from sections of the Gandhians and from the anticaste movement. Within Rajasthan, considerable opposition to both sati and state inaction on Roop Kanwar's death was voiced by huge numbers of women, largely rural, who joined demonstrations to protest against the glorification of her death.

Conclusion

The contemporary Indian women's movement is a complex, variously placed, and fertile undertaking. It is perhaps the only movement today that encompasses and links such issues as work, wages, environment, ecology, civil rights, sex, violence, representation, caste, class, allocation of basic resources, consumer rights, health, religion, community, and individual and social relationships. It is also one of the rare networks that encompasses party-based, professional, and independent groups and is flexible enough to bring old enemies, such as the orthodox Left and the Maoists, onto a campaign platform and allow traditional rivals among the socialists and the communists to forge a common alliance against the politically uninformed autonomous groups. An index of the movement's influence is the extraordinarily large participation of women in most radical campaigns, particularly in urban areas. One of the most notable examples of the radicalization of women is that of the Bhopal gas victims. Following the tragic explosion of MIC gas from the Union Carbide plant in Bhopal in 1984, the one organization of gas victims that emerged as strong and sustained was the Bhopal Gas Peedit Mahila Udyog Sangathana (Bhopal Gas-Affected Women Workers' Organization). Though the organization is not feminist (indeed, it is headed by a man), a number of feminist groups work with it, and it is linked to the women's movement.

Structurally the women's movement has a vertical as well as horizontal reach: From a horizontal network of autonomous feminist groups, issue- and occupation-based women's organizations, development groups, radical professional associations, and party-affiliated organizations, it reached upward to administrative institutions, state functionaries, members of Parliament, and political leaders. Feminists are now invited to lecture at the Indian Administrative Services Academy, the training school for Indian government servants; they provide courses for the police, who have considerably expanded their employment of women; and many state governments have invited them to organize women's development programs. In many ways it is the horizontal reach of the women's movement that has allowed it to have policy influence; in particular, the combination of the networking capacities of the autonomous groups and the mobilizing capacities of the Left party-affiliated organizations has often given women's campaigns a cutting edge.

These strengths are yet to be fully recognized. The attacks of the 1980s and the rise of communal women's organizations such as Rashtra Sevika Samiti (Women Nation Servers' Organization) and the women's wing of the far Right Hindu Rashtra Swayam Sevak Sangh (National Self-Help Organization) have overshadowed the often quiet work being done locally and regionally and have brought political divisions to the fore. Relationships between Left party-affiliated organizations and autonomous women's groups are frequently strained by differing organizational interests, and each is wary of making concessions to the other. Moreover, the spread and diversity of the movement have coincided with a period of growing atomization, so that campaigns can sometimes be dissipated by the existence of numerous overlapping but separate lobbies.

Acutely as these problems are felt, they are minor. Of the roughly three thousand women who attended the all-India women's liberation conference in 1990 in Kerala, some 60 percent were rural women, in groups ranging from development to church to leftist. In many areas women are pioneering literacy campaigns. Increasing numbers of women are taking advantage of cooperative credit facilities. New avenues for women's political participation have opened at village and district levels. It may be that in the next few years national-level feminist campaigns will lie relatively fallow but that work at the institutional level will be locally and regionally strengthened.

Another development to watch with interest is the diasporic links among Indian women's groups. Both Britain and the United States already have fairly active Indian women's groups, with strong relationships to women's groups in India. South Africa is even more interesting, for feminists of Indian origin are integrated not only in women's groups but also in politics overall.[24] This diasporic network is unusual and could become an important source of mobilization against communal identity politics.

NOTES

1. Maria Mies, "The Shahada Movement: A Peasant Movement in Maharshtra, Its Development, and Its Perspective," *Journal of Peasant Studies* 3, no. 4 (July 1976):478.

2. Devaki Jain, "The Self-Employed Women's Association, Ahmedabad," *How* 3, no. 2 (February 1980):14.

3. Gail Omvedt, "Women and Rural Revolt in India," *Journal of Peasant Studies*.

4. Vibhuti Patel, *Reaching for Half the Sky* (Bombay: Antar Rashtriya Prakashan Bawda, 1985), pp. 8–10.

5. Gail Omvedt, *We Will Smash This Prison* (London: Zed Books, 1980), Appendix II.

6. Omvedt, "Women and Rural Revolt."

7. Omvedt, *We Will Smash This Prison,* p. 174.

8. Stree Shakti Sangathana, "The War Against Rape," in Miranda Davies, ed., *Third World, Second Sex* (London: Zed Books, 1984), p. 201.

9. Dowry is the sum of money as well as other items (jewelry, furniture, car, other consumer durables) given by the bride's family to the groom's family at the time of marriage. Dowry is practiced mainly by Hindus of all classes but has increased most significantly in recent years among the urban middle classes. At the same time, the size of dowries has increased, and the groom's family has demanded additional dowry after the marriage.

10. Figures of reported rapes in India, year by year, are provided by the Bureau of Police Research and Development in Delhi. Evidence for the statements made here is in the bureau's report in the *Times of India, Statesman, Indian Express,* and *Patriot,* April 2–12, 1978.

11. This account compiled from reports in the *Times of India, Statesman, Indian Express,* and *Patriot,* April 2–12, 1978.

12. People's Union for Democratic Rights, *Custodial Rape* (Delhi: People's Union for Democratic Rights, March 1990).

13. A classic example is Vandana Shiva, *Staying Alive: Women, Ecology, and Survival in India* (Delhi: Kali for Women, 1988).

14. This experience was recounted to me by Nandita Haksar and Sheba Chhachi, December 1983.

15. One of several methods of divorce permitted by Islam, the triple *talaq* is the easiest, requiring only that one party say "I divorce you" thrice.

16. In upholding her right to maintenance under Muslim personal law, the Supreme Court referred to two verses from the Koran that had been cited by Shah Bano's counsel, Daniel Latifi:

Ayat 241	*English Version*
Wali'l motallaqatay	*For divorced women*
Mata un	*Maintenance (should be provided)*
Bil maroofay	*On a reasonable (scale)*
Haqqhan	*This is a duty*
Alal muttaqeena	*On the righteous*

Ayat 242	
Kazaleki yuba Iyyanullaho	*Thus doth God*
Lakum ayatehee la Allakum	*Make clear His Signs*
Taqeloon	*To you: in order that you may understand*

17. See, for example, Madhu Kishwar, "Pro-Women or Anti-Muslim?: The Shah Bano Controversy," *Manushi* 6, no. 2 (January-February 1986).

18. See "The Muslims: A Community in Turmoil," *India Today,* January 31, 1986.

19. Gandhi is quoted in a brochure for the film *In Secular India,* by Mediastorm.

20. These articles appeared first in the Delhi-based Hindi- and English-language national dailies *Jan Satta* ("Banwari, September 29, 1987), *Indian Express* (Ashis Nandy, May 10, 1987), and *Statesman* (Patrick D. Harrigan, May 22, 1987).

21. *Statesman,* September 18–20, 1987.

22. *Times of India,* September 17, 1987.

23. Ibid.

24. To cite but one of the most notable examples: Frene Ginwala, a South African ANC feminist of Parsi origin, is now a leader of the House in Mandela's government.

3

Men in Seclusion, Women in Public: Rokeya's Dream and Women's Struggles in Bangladesh

ROUSHAN JAHAN

ONE OF THE IMPORTANT visible changes occurring in Bangladesh since the early 1970s has been the increased participation of women in the public arena. In 1975, International Women's Year, although there was a growing awareness among women about women's problems, no concrete programs or organizational leadership had emerged.[1] In 1994, in contrast, women headed the two major centrist political parties in the country, and a woman served as prime minister. Another Bangladeshi woman, Taslima Nasreen, was generating international attention and inciting major protest within the country based on her controversial writings strongly condemning sexism and communalism in Bangladesh.[2] Five hundred women's organizations are registered with the Women's Ministry, in addition to thousands of other nongovernmental organizations (NGOs) that have programs focused on women. They undertake a wide range of activities, including organization of local women's groups, provision of credit, training, conscientization, research, advocacy, and lobbying.

Whether these varied activities constitute a women's movement is a matter of perception and definition. Some have argued that the "fragmented, issue-based and primarily conciliatory" nature of these activities lacks the "theoretical construct and socio-political strategy which should characterize a movement" in the strict sense of the term.[3] If a movement is defined as "an organized attempt by group/s to bring about either partial or total change in society through collective mobilization based on an ideology," then a women's movement certainly exists in

BANGLADESH

GENERAL

type of government: Parliamentary Democracy
major ethnic groups: Bengali (98%); Bihari; tribespeople
language(s): Bengali (official); also Chakma; Magh; English
religions: Muslim (83%); Hindu (16%)
date of independence: 1971
former colonial power: Britain, Pakistan

DEMOGRAPHICS

population size: 119 million
birth rate (*per 1,000 population*): 36
total fertility (*average number of births per woman*): 4.0
contraceptive prevalence (*married women*): 40%
maternal mortality rate (*per 100,000 live births*): 600

WOMEN'S STATUS

date of women's suffrage: 1947
economically active population: M 87%   F 7%
female employment (*% of total workforce*): 8
life expectancy   M 55   F 54
school enrollment ratio (*F/100 M*)
   primary   81
   secondary   49
   tertiary   26
literacy   M 47%   F 22%

Bangladesh. A broad definition would include all the organized activities that question the legitimacy of the basic tenets of Bangladeshi social structure that support male domination and female subordination; that protest the values, customs, practices, laws, and institutions designed to impose, maintain, and perpetuate patriarchal attitudes and existing gender relations in the family, community, workplace, society, and the state; and that engage in collective action to change societal values and attitudes to realize a gender-just society. This definition emphasizes awareness of the systemic nature of oppressive unequal gender relations, a readiness to act collectively for social transformation, and a holistic view of both the process and the goal. The organizations that are the major actors are thus specified by both membership and purpose. In Bangladesh at present there are three major strands of the women's movement: women's rights activist groups, which raise women's issues at the national policy level; women's research and advocacy organizations, which raise public awareness; and nongovernmental organizations, which work to raise women's awareness and mobilize women at the grassroots level.

Such a definition of the women's movement, though quite broad, does not include, for example, groups that focus on social welfare or charity or those that only provide services such as credit or health care. However, in Bangladesh many development NGOs combine conventional programs with conscientization and group formation among the rural poor. These groups not only meet women's immediate survival needs, which, in view of the crushing burden of poverty, is essential. Through legal literacy, legal aid, functional education, and involvement in participatory planning, these programs also serve to heighten women's awareness of their strategic gender interests. In this role these NGOs serve as valuable allies of the women's movement.

In this chapter I trace the dynamic evolution of the women's movement since the early 1970s, emphasizing the broader social forces that have shaped its development and agenda. I describe how the authoritarian nature of the state, the failure of centrist political parties to develop a sustainable and viable vision based on secular ideology, the resurgence of religious extremism, and the global upsurge of women's movements have affected the context within which the Bangladesh women's movement has developed, sometimes constricting the space and sometimes enlarging it. I briefly look at women's organizations' strategies to address violence against women and population and reproductive rights so as to highlight the points of divergence and convergence within the movement. Finally, I examine the women's movement's evolving relationships with the state and political parties and the challenges it faces in the future.[4]

Women's Situation and Position in Bangladesh

In Bangladesh, a resource-limited, overpopulated, dependent, capitalist country, society is highly stratified, with access to and control over social resources, services, and opportunities determined by gender, class, and location. The constitution guarantees all citizens equal rights, which is also reflected in national policies and plan documents. However, in reality statistics show glaring disparities between men and women, rich and poor, and urban and rural dwellers in access to the development process both as agents and as beneficiaries.

The ideological basis and mechanisms that legitimize, maintain, and perpetuate sexism are deeply embedded in the Bangladeshi social structure. Male domination and women's subordination are basic tenets of social relations in Bangladesh. Women's biological role of reproduction and nurturing is paramount.
Gender discrimination starts at birth and continues through life. Traditionally the
birth of a child is announced by giving *azan,* the call for prayer. For a male child,
the azan is given loudly and clearly, whereas it is whispered in the ears of a female
child.[5] From early childhood, asymmetrical allocation of food, health care, and
social opportunities prepares a female child for playing a subservient and dependent role.[6] Since sexuality in Islam is permitted only within marriage, there is
great pressure to marry daughters at an early age. Women are perceived as vulnerable and in need of male protection. In many areas, men mediate between women
and the world outside, and married women have little contact with anything outside their homes and families. This is reinforced by women's economic dependence on men, who typically control all of the household income. Religious personal laws discriminate in family matters, granting men double the share in
inheritance and unilateral rights to divorce, polygamy, and guardianship over wife
and children, including the right to chastise their wives for "disobedience."

Contrary to the global norm, women's life expectancy is shorter than men's.
This bias is also reflected in women's lower nutritional status, literacy rates, school
enrollment figures, and average wage. Political participation is insignificant; seats
reserved for women in Parliament (10 percent) and local government bodies (25
percent) are filled through nomination by male colleagues. Yet historically
Bangladeshi women have demonstrated great resilience and courage in facing crises—natural, social, economic, political—and considerable ability in leading and
participating in struggles for advancing their civil and political rights as well as in
organized activities for integrating gender concerns into the national agenda.

The Women's Movement: Historical Context and Changing Pattern

Emergence of the "Woman Question" in Muslim Bengal, 1900–1947

Women's organized activities can be divided historically into three phases, each
with its own focus and level of gender awareness. The first phase started in the
context of a postcolonial crisis of identity brought about by the loss of political
power and economic resources that resulted from the sweeping fiscal, agricultural, and educational policy reforms of the British.[7] Muslim social leaders and intellectuals were divided on the question of strategy, with modernists advocating
adaptation of customs, while traditionalists advocated revival of older practices
and norms.

Women's issues were first raised in the public debate by Rokeya Sakhawat Hossain (1880–1932). The organized activities initiated by Rokeya and her associates, all women from urban, educated modernist families, illustrate their class bias. They worked for women's right to education and increased mobility and engaged in charity and relief work for destitute women in the slums. Neither the modernists nor the traditionalists supported Hossain's challenge of the "divine" ordination of male supremacy. Ironically, the modernists supported her demand for women's access to formal education as a necessary qualification for a good housewife and mother in a "modern" household.

Extreme purdah, or seclusion of women, was prevalent at the time. Many modernists also supported the relaxation of this custom, maintaining that the original instructions regarding purdah concerned modesty of behavior in mixed-sex situations rather than this extreme seclusion and that relaxing this practice and increasing women's mobility were necessary for their participation in public life.[8] The modernists were greatly encouraged by the examples of other Muslim countries, such as Turkey, that were experimenting with modernization. Women's appearance and participation in the public arena, often including the adoption of Western dress, became a significant symbol. Women's dress and visibility continue as a symbolic identifier in Muslim societies even today.[9]

Pakistan Period, 1947–1970

The state of Pakistan was born out of religious separatism, emphasizing the religious and political affiliation of the Hindu and Muslim communities in South Asia. During the early years, the modernists were firmly in control in Pakistan, and there was no visible attempt to Islamize at the state level.[10] Muslim women participated in public life, and upper-class women engaged in social welfare, were members of the women's wings of political parties, and even participated in political protest, mostly as students. Like earlier women's efforts, both the focus of these activities and their membership were limited and urban based. Gender issues were subsumed under larger national political concerns of autonomy for East Pakistan, later Bangladesh. The limited mobility of urban women meant that they were seldom exposed to the realities of rural women's lives, and issues of concern to the majority of women who lived in rural areas and engaged in agriculture remained invisible. Women's organizations engaged in welfare activities included the All Pakistan Women's Association, a state-sponsored national organization led by the wives of government officials, and small urban-based neighborhood clubs called *samities* led by educated urban women.

These organizations joined forces to demand reform of Muslim family laws that adversely affected all Muslim women's position and rights within the family. The Family Laws Ordinance of 1961 set a minimum age for marriage and curtailed men's unilateral rights in both polygamy and divorce. While this may have been

Civil war erupted in March 1971 when Bengalis sought independence from Pakistan. The war ended in December 1971 with Bangladesh an independent nation. Many women activists were first politicized working with the poor and displaced to rebuild the country.

based on the militaristic regime's desire to project a modernist image rather than on a true recognition of women's demands,[11] passage of this law and the alliance among women that brought it about demonstrated two important lessons. First, even in an Islamic country under an authoritarian militaristic regime, launching an effective movement for reforming religious personal laws was possible. Second, broad-based alliance among women could be forged around issues of gender oppression and violence that affected all women.

Solidarity among these women was particularly remarkable given the different political and cultural orientation and allegiances between the West and East Pakistanis. Protest against the repressive measures undertaken by the militaristic regime intensified. Women, especially students, played a significant part, particularly through nonviolent acts of defiance. A delegation of leaders of women's organizations also pressured the combined opposition parties to drop women's seclusion from the platform demanded by the fundamentalist Nezam-e-Islam party.[12]

In 1966, the Awami League, the strongest opposition party, started agitating for autonomy for East Pakistan. Hundreds of political leaders and workers were held in prison without trial, students were shot, and protest intensified in 1969–1970. A

Seven Bengali students killed by police in 1952 during the nationalist Tagore language movement are commemorated by demonstrators years later.

group of young women activists, most of whom were associated with leftist parties, approached prominent women, including senior members of the Awami League Women's Wing. They proposed forming a joint women's action committee to persuade the wives and mothers of political prisoners to advocate for the prisoners' release. This led to the formation of Mahila Parishad, which by the 1980s had become the country's largest women's organization, with over thirty thousand members.

The Awami League won a landslide victory in 1970, but the central government of Pakistan would not allow the leader to form a government, causing a massive nonviolent, noncooperation movement in East Pakistan. On March 25, 1971, military action against civilians set the East Pakistanis on a war for liberation. Thou-

The majority of Bangladeshi women live in poverty in rural areas. Since the 1971 war for independence, their concerns have been increasingly placed at the center of the women's movement.

sands fled the country; others stayed amid danger and the constant threat of losing friends, family, property, life, and security. Thousands of young men and women joined the freedom fighters and a clandestine network supplying information, hastening victory of the joint Indian-Bangladesh armed forces. Bangladesh was liberated on December 16, 1971.

Bangladesh Period, 1972–1990

Heightening Gender Sensitivity Among Women: War and Women, 1972–1974.
In the thrill of victory anything seemed possible. Establishing a new republic based on the "four pillars" of democracy, secularism, socialism, and nationalism held the promise of forming a just society based on equitable distribution of resources. Political parties, such as Jamaat-e-Islami, using religion for political gains and supportive of the Pakistani army were banned. The constitution granted women equal rights in the public sphere. To meet the enormous challenge of rebuilding the national economy, the government appealed to its citizens and to the international community; the response from both was immediate and generous. International donors provided funds, technical assistance, and commodity grants. Social services were augmented by new nongovernmental citizens' groups that en-

gaged in relief and rehabilitation in the rural areas. Many women active in student protests joined this effort with enthusiasm.

Personal interviews reveal that many of the present leaders of women's organizations became aware of gender discrimination during the war and its aftermath. Despite their significant role in the independence struggle, women were soon marginalized by the new government. For example, the First Five-Year Plan identified women's development needs only in terms of motherhood. More critical was the government's inadequate response to thirty thousand female victims of mass rape by the Pakistani army and their local supporters, which had been used to publicize the cruelty of the Pakistani army to gain worldwide attention.[13] Interestingly, the nascent women's movement did not work actively to mobilize support for these rape victims either. In reflecting on the reasons for this, women leaders offer a variety of perspectives. Many groups and individuals were still hesitant to challenge the society's strong patriarchal traditions and feared that doing so would invite a backlash that could hurt the victims more. The groups were very new, with limited scope and membership, and as such still quite vulnerable. Even some organizations such as Mahila Parishad that later vocally and successfully challenged the government's stand on gender violence did not articulate a position on rape at this time.[14]

In 1973, a group of young women, mostly academics and professionals, organized an informal study group to discuss and analyze the vulnerable and marginalized position of women in Bangladesh. This group, Women for Women, became the first autonomous women's research organization in Bangladesh. By 1975, the group had published its first "Situation of Women" report. This provided the basis for many women's organizations, and development NGOs, to advocate for strong women-in-development policies, which they continue to do.

Diversity and Broadening of the Agenda. As the 1970s progressed, a series of crises in the national political and economic arena had particularly adverse effects on women, especially poor women, and forced women's organizations to be more assertive, broaden the scope of their activities, and increase membership and geographic coverage. At the same time, policies initiated at the national and international levels facilitated women's emergence as legitimate actors in the public discourse.

The state adopted a growth-oriented development policy that emphasized generating agricultural surplus through mechanization and high-yield crops, export-oriented and labor-intensive light industrialization, and rapid reduction of population growth through the use of contraceptives. Neglect of distributional and ecological considerations exacerbated class and gender inequalities, resulting in impoverishment, an erosion of traditional kinship support, a devaluation of women's contribution to the household, an introduction of dowry, and an increase in wife battering.[15] Prostitution and trafficking in women and children be-

Nongovernmental development organizations are important partners of the women's movement. Many of their programs extend credit to poor rural women to start enterprises like poultry rearing, thereby increasing their economic productivity and independence.

came economic survival strategies. Depletion of fuelwood, water, and fodder; escalating deforestation; and eviction of poor female heads of households had a profound impact on rural women's livelihoods. Many migrated to urban areas in search of jobs in domestic service or garment factories, which, while providing income, also subjected many women to a double load of work, threat of sexual harassment, and no protection under labor laws.[16] The population policy and pro-

Many women's organizations encourage women to shed the seclusion of purdah. Learning such skills as riding a bicycle, driving a car, or running farm machinery can become an act of independence.

grams focused solely on women as targets for contraception, with little attention to providing adequate information or meeting their other health needs.

At the same time, the civil and political rights of all citizens were eroded through a military coup in 1975 and a return to an authoritarian regime. By the 1980s, a breakdown of law and order, an acceleration of violence,[17] and a violation of basic human rights had sensitized women to join the struggle for democratization. The importance of these efforts escalated when the ban on extremist religious political parties was lifted. In a search for legitimacy, the military regime formed an alliance with the Islamist party Jamaat-e-Islam, which reestablished itself in the formal political arena. This alliance, strengthened by aid from oil-rich Muslim countries, led to a constitutional amendment in 1977 that substituted secularism, a basic principle on which the country had been founded, with "an absolute trust in Allah." Forewarned by the drastic curtailment of women's rights in Iran and Pakistan that had accompanied the political ascendancy of Islamists in those countries,[18] Bangladeshi women sought to build public opinion in favor of secular politics.

The threat of Islamization at the national level was offset by positive developments internationally that prompted the state to undertake affirmative actions. The United Nations' declaration of 1975 as International Women's Year and the subsequent Decade for Women (1975–1985) resulted in a series of intergovernmental agreements designed to prompt states to change discriminatory policies and promote gender equity. The conferences and parallel NGO forums provided women from many countries with an opportunity to meet, share views, and exchange information. Women's organizations in Bangladesh were invited by the government to advise in the preparation of the official reports, offering an excellent opportunity to articulate and reflect on their positions. Research groups held national conferences to prepare NGO position papers, which were circulated by activists among grassroots women. Human rights groups and development NGOs also joined in the process by critiquing the gaps between public pronouncements and the implementation of policies and programs. This facilitated both horizontal and vertical dialogue among women and led to the formation of loose coalitions between organizations to address specific issues.

Women's Organizing: Issues and Strategies for Empowerment

The adverse gender impact of national economic and political processes and exposure to the reality of rural and urban poor women led the leaders of women's organizations to embrace a holistic concept of development. In personal interviews and focus group discussions, the leaders, staffs, and members of diverse women's groups agree that over time there has been a shift in the women's movement's priorities and orientation in leadership, scope of activities, and nature of alliance. Experiences during the war of 1971 increased many middle-class women's sensitivity to the challenges brought by crises and the courage with which rural women met them. Addressing these women's problems by organizing and supporting community groups became an urgent and growing priority for many activists. Researchers were similarly motivated by the marginalization of women in national development after the war. A lack of gender-disaggregated data, a dis-

NGOs and women's groups are increasingly advocating the importance of girls' education for women's empowerment and national development.

torted reflection of women's labor force participation, a lack of recognition of women's work, and an awareness of the systemic nature of gender oppression spurred them to generate and disseminate information about women. Research programs for advocacy generated new data and inspired interest among mainstream academics to take up gender issues in theoretical and analytical research. The researchers' professed nonpolitical stance and professional style also made them acceptable spokespersons to the policy planners of an authoritarian regime, most of whom belonged to the same social class.

Activists and researchers found frequent consultation and dialogue to be both enriching and strategic. Visible efforts continue to be made by women's groups to forge links with other organizations, including government and nongovernment

agencies. Given the reluctance of many women's organizations to partisan political affiliation and the general indifference of political parties to women's issues,
linkage with other women's groups has offered the most promising means of alliance building. In spite of different approaches, the groups share many goals, and
while unity has remained elusive, loose coalition has proven to be an effective
strategy in facing common opponents.

The women's movement learned the benefits of coalition building early during
successful campaigns against violence against women. In the late 1970s, violence
against women became a highly visible issue in Bangladesh. This was partly due to
the growing awareness of women's issues resulting from the U.N. Decade for
Women and partly to the publicity given by the media and women's organizations
to the increasing incidence of dowry murders in which a young woman was killed
when her family failed to meet the dowry demands of her husband. These dramatic events raised the curtain of secrecy behind which various manifestations of
violence against women—wife abuse, rape, abduction, molestation—were hidden inside and outside the home. Researchers documented the extent of violence
against women and explored and analyzed the factors that perpetuated it, while
activists and local development groups started intervention programs. Mahila
Parishad spearheaded a signature campaign for an antidowry law that collected
seventeen thousand signatures, and vigorous lobbying by women members of
Parliament resulted in the Prohibition of Dowry Act of 1980. Women's organizations kept the pressure on the government to enact stringent laws providing deterrent punishment, and the Cruelty to Women (Deterrent Punishment) Ordinance
was promulgated in 1983.

Encouraged by this success, women continued to exert pressure to establish
family courts and to change religious personal law relating to inheritance. In 1985,
the streets of metropolitan Dhaka echoed with slogans advocating women's rights
raised by women from all walks of life—politicians, lawyers, teachers, members of
voluntary organizations, students. Most surprising was the participation of many
wives of businessmen and civil servants who had never before joined in any protest movement. However, at the height of this activity, the momentum abruptly
stopped. Through police intervention and threats, the government succeeded in
diffusing the gathering momentum of this militant movement. This led some
women's organizations to join the broader movement for democracy rather than
focusing on women's issues specifically. As the former secretary general of Mahila
Parishad noted, "I became convinced that authoritarian governments will never
let us have the space necessary for effective social action. Therefore, joining the
movement for democratization seemed as important as running the campaign for
violence against women."[19] Other women cited this approach as evidence of the
group's placing priority on socialist transformation, thereby preventing it from
giving women's oppression due importance.[20] However, Mahila Parishad's continued and vigorous campaign against gender violence, combining other activities

and strategies with agitation, seems to demonstrate a revision of tactics based on situation analysis rather than a fundamental difference in ideology.

More recently, women's health and reproductive rights have emerged as areas with the potential to foster dialogue among women's groups. But these issues also have the potential to polarize those groups. When a family planning program was first introduced in the 1960s in East Pakistan, as a senior leader of the women's movement recalled, "we were really happy because we thought that this was a 'god-sent' opportunity which would release the rural poor women from the cycle of repeated pregnancy, hazardous child-birth and the risk of ill-health and fatality which often resulted. Many of our generation worked with a missionary zeal to motivate rural women to accept contraceptive methods."[21] In view of the high maternal mortality rate and the rapid rate of population growth publicized by the government, their enthusiasm was understandable.

However, as women researchers and activists worked in the rural areas, they observed the implementation of the program. The abuse of contraceptives, serious gaps in service delivery, lack of information about side effects, and little choice of method alarmed them. Many critiqued the government's priority on population as an effort to deflect public attention from the more crucial issues relating to poverty, particularly the gross inequity in the distribution and allocation of resources. They also suspected donor organizations of being motivated primarily by the need to promote and protect the commercial interests of their own countries. Local administrations were blamed for blatant neglect of work, ethical breaches, corruption, and lack of concern for women targeted by the program.[22] A serious and often contentious debate is emerging as to whether women's groups should work with and attempt to improve the existing family planning program or whether by its very nature such a population program is coercive and exploits women.

These two examples demonstrate that, as in other countries, women activists are divided in their approach to empowering women. In Bangladesh, these differences can be broadly drawn in two categories. One group has advocated working on broader issues while seeking to more fully integrate women into the development process. This follows the assumptions that broader social change, such as democratization, is necessary to improve the status of women and that increasing the number of women working within the system at all levels will improve gender sensitivity and women's status. The second approach posits that the existing system is inherently exploitative and oppressive to women and not amenable to reform and therefore advocates the development of an alternate economic and political paradigm first. While the clear ideological differences in these approaches have led to some acrimonious splits, the sheer urgency for immediate and concerted action necessitated by the crises of political legitimacy, increasing threat of male violence, and hostilities by Islamists have so far fostered cooperation and limited the scope and time for an extensive debate.

The Women's Movement and the State

While the constitution guarantees women equal rights and even provides for special affirmative measures to promote equality, no comprehensive policy on women's development and gender equity has been instituted in the more than twenty years since independence. Any efforts appear to have been prompted less by a genuine commitment to closing the gender gap than by a desire to project a modernist image.[23] Many are perceived as reactions to the demands of Bangladeshi women's groups and donor organizations. Regardless of the motivation, the lack of priority accorded to women is reflected in the allocation to the Ministry of Women's Affairs, only 0.3 percent of the total budget.

The rhetoric in policy documents has improved progressively under pressure from Western donor agencies. Considerable publicity has also been given to "success" in family planning efforts, highlighting it as the most relevant aspect of poverty alleviation and national development. The state's other claims in furthering women's rights are in the legal area. As noted earlier, in the late 1970s vigorous advocacy succeeded in publicizing the increasing incidence of dowry murders; the government responded by enacting the Prohibition of Dowry Act in 1980 and an ordinance providing deterrent punishment for gender violence in 1983 and by establishing family courts in 1985. To increase girls' access to education, scholarships were reserved for them, and other incentives such as uniforms and books were made available to encourage poor girls to go to school. Food-for-work programs and a series of other development programs aimed at vulnerable groups were undertaken to support destitute rural women. However, none of these measures was adequately implemented, and few had more than limited impact.

While public pronouncements in favor of "integrating women" in national development are common, and women's participation at all levels has increased, no serious effort has been made to change social structures and institutions perpetuating gender inequality. Discriminatory religious personal laws still govern women's rights in the family. When the Bangladesh government ratified the U.N. Convention on the Elimination of All Forms of Discrimination Against Women, it maintained reservations on all articles calling for women's equal rights in the family. To Bangladeshi women activists, this undermined the meaning of ratification. The government's continuous alliance with fundamentalist Jamaat and the growing influence of other Islamic countries have brought about initiatives to emphasize women's modesty in public.

Any review of the many public policy commitments made by the government demonstrates that the basic attitude remains instrumentalist, patriarchal, and urban middle class biased. The inclusion of women is still full of tokenism and symbolic gestures without substance. Why is there so much apparent contradiction and inconsistency in the state's policy regarding women? What has the impact been on the women's movement?

There are several factors that contribute to this apparent contradiction. As discussed earlier, the underlying concern of the male-dominated state apparatus was (and is) to preserve the existing patriarchal social order and gender relations. The authoritarian, militaristic nature of the government reinforced this desire to preserve social stability. Any effort to change the underlying principles for distributing social resources and power, as the women's movement demanded, was perceived as subversive by the regime. Therefore, the government sought to contain the discourse in narrow development channels, emphasizing women's "needs" while leaving the traditional notions of womanhood intact. This was further reinforced by alliances with Islamist parties, whose ideology emphasized confining women to the home and stringently controlling their mobility and sexuality. This Islamist stance was reinforced by funding provided by other Muslim countries.

On the other hand, since the mid-1970s, especially after the declaration of the U.N. Decade for Women, there has been growing pressure on the state to undertake affirmative action. The national women's movement, strengthened by funds from international donors and external pressure on the government to incorporate women in development policy, had to be appeased. Caught between the two emerging political forces with diametrically opposing goals—the women's movement and Islamists—the state was compelled to balance policies that at once appeared to encourage as well as negate women's emancipation.

The impact on the women's movement has on the whole been salutary. Women in the movement have matured in their outlook, especially in their expectations of the state. This more realistic appraisal has contributed to the change in strategies and tactics discussed earlier. The movement has become more sophisticated about the pitfalls of the development model and the potentially co-optive and divisive tactics used by the state and still awaits convincing demonstration of a strong commitment by the state to women's concerns.

In the final analysis, it is incumbent on women to demonstrate to the state their importance as a constituency. This assumes, however, a democratic and accountable government. The experience of living under an authoritarian system lacking transparency and accountability has led many in the Bangladeshi women's movement to more actively engage in the struggle for full democratization. Such a system is a necessary precondition to enabling women to exercise their rights, enjoy full entitlements as citizens, participate in decisionmaking, and share power equally with men.

The Women's Movement and Political Parties

Bangladeshi women have had a curious relationship with political parties. After winning voting rights in 1935, long before Bangladesh became an independent state, women were incorporated into political parties primarily to mobilize women voters. Despite this long legacy, they have not succeeded in securing top positions in significant numbers or persuading party leaders to endorse women's issues. Even when women do occupy top positions in the parties, as they do now in the two centrist parties, they rarely show a strong commitment to women's issues for fear of alienating traditional male constituents. For example, none of the 1991 election platforms showed any strong commitment to women's issues.[24] While there is a quota of thirty, or 10 percent, women's seats in Parliament, they are filled by women nominated by the ruling party; these women become accountable to their male party colleagues rather than women. Women have protested against this system of indirect election, proposing that each district elect a woman member of Parliament through direct vote. Before the 1991 election, women's organizations urged all the parties to include women's issues in their platforms and to reserve 10 percent of the candidature for women. However, none of the party platforms strongly addressed women's issues.

Ironically, the only political party with an explicit policy on gender issues is Jamaat, the major Islamist party. The goals, attitude, and social vision of Jamaat and those of the women's movement are diametrically opposite. Jamaat is an extremist political party that aims to seize state power, if necessary through violent means, to impose a monolithic vision of society. It believes that gender roles are biologically determined and that male supremacy is divinely ordained, as legitimized through religious tradition and laws.[25] In this view, men and women were created unequal by God, so any attempt to bring equality is heretical. Jamaat's support of the Pakistani army in the war for liberation eroded its legitimacy in mainstream popular discourse in Bangladesh. Therefore, it rests its claim of legitimacy in politics to *vox Dei* as the true upholder of Islamic politics and way of life.

In contrast, the women's movement is a nonpartisan political movement whose demand for empowerment and social transformation rests on a vision of a pluralistic and egalitarian society, where power and resources are shared through equal participation. This view holds that gender roles and gender relations are culturally conditioned. The movement aims to persuade society through nonviolent protest, dialogue, and conscientization to adopt this vision and create a gender-just society. The movement's legitimacy rests on visible and significant participation in the war for liberation in 1971 and the movement for democratization in the 1980s.

How these opposing forces will play out depends on a host of internal (national) and external (international) factors, some of which have been discussed. There is no doubt that for the women's movement, facing the challenge posed by Jamaat in the coming years will be critical. To counter Jamaat, an important strategy for women will be to pressure other political parties to actively support women and women's concerns. This is particularly important because only political parties have the resources and power to recruit cadres, organize and mobilize popular support, and formulate an ideology to effectively counter Jamaat's influence. However, political parties are reluctant to raise issues related to religion and patriarchal values, especially in the family, because of their fear of losing male voters. This is reinforced by the conventional wisdom that women voters cast their vote according to the advice of the men in the family. However, field experience demonstrates that women, particularly those organized by grassroots NGOs, make their own ballot decisions. It is critical to make political parties aware of this important change to increase the legitimacy of women as a powerful constituency.

Current Social Context and Women's Situation 1990–Present

In 1990, women played a visible and significant role in the popular protest movement against the authoritarian regime of President Hussain M. Ershad. A strong motivation for women to join this movement for democratization was the hope that an elected government with a strong popular mandate would not be compelled to court alliance with extremist groups. When parliamentary government was restored in 1991 and Khaleda Zia, the female chair of the Bangladesh Nationalist Party (BNP), became prime minister, women were hopeful. However, rivalry between the two centrist political parties, the Awami League and the BNP, and the narrow margin of the BNP's victory led the ruling party to seek the support of Jamaat. This consolidated Jamaat's national position, despite its winning only eighteen of three hundred parliamentary seats.

Jamaat's influence has been extended in a variety of ways. For example, it has encouraged local elites and interest groups such as rural moneylenders to harass women and men involved with development NGOs. The success of development programs, particularly in credit, has empowered rural poor women and decreased their dependence on local moneylenders. In some areas, secular schools have drawn a significant number of children away from Islamic religious schools, threatening loss of influence and income of the local elites and religious leaders. They have become increasingly hostile to staff and beneficiaries of NGOs. Jamaat is fomenting this animosity in the name of protecting social values and curbing what it regards as the pernicious influence of the agents of Western Jewish and Christian donors and Indian Hindus.[26]

This tenuous situation was further exacerbated by communal riots in India following the destruction of the Babri mosque in December 1991. Both Hindus and Muslims consider this a holy site, and growing religious animosity in South Asia resulted in Hindus attempting to destroy the Muslim mosque. Riots also broke out in several places in Bangladesh but were quickly quelled by the alert peacekeeping efforts of citizens and members of human rights groups and NGOs. However, Jamaat's interest in fomenting communal violence remains a grave concern.

On the positive side, the close networking among women's groups begun in the 1980s has continued, and the support base of women's organizations has been broadened. The nonpartisan anti-Islamist movement initiated in 1991 by prominent personalities in the literary-cultural arena and supported by the liberal-progressive section of society, including the Awami League and leftist parties, is a very positive development on the sociopolitical scene. The crude tactics employed by Jamaat and other Islamist groups to intimidate vocal spokespersons (among whom Taslima Nasreen was one), which included accusing them of heresy and/or starting legal action on charges of engaging in "subsersive activities" and "hurting the sentiments of Muslims," have strengthened popular support for this movement. The movement lent strong support to the women's movement in its protest against the recent harassment of poor and powerless women and local-level development NGO workers through issuance of a *fatwa* (religious decree).

In response to the Fourth World Conference on Women to be convened by the United Nations in 1995, the government has reiterated its commitment to women. Two women's organizations, Women for Women and Naripokkho, have been invited to participate as members of the official committee preparing the government's report on the status of women to be presented in Beijing. A national preparatory committee for the Beijing NGO Forum, including representatives from all the major women's organizations, is preparing a platform of action and organizing regional workshops. Bangladeshi women are organizing regional workshops to reflect grassroots women's views both at regional and international forums. Finally, networks continue to be formed with regional and international groups, enriching the Bangladeshi women's movement by reinforcing the commonality and global nature of women's subordination and struggles for gender equity.

Challenges for the Future

The Bangladeshi women's movement currently faces an array of challenges. These can be grouped roughly into those deriving from the movement's own limitations and those arising from the wider social, political, and economic context. In the broader social and economic context, Bangladeshi women remain marginalized at national and international decisionmaking levels. Changing deeply entrenched gender ideology is a long-term process, particularly in the face of resistance and hostility from conservative and extremist groups using religion to legitimize a bid for social and political control.

Institutionally, many women's organizations are challenged to balance the urgent needs of their members with the strategic interests of the ideological and political empowerment of women. This has led to internal struggles over priorities: building the capacity of members, staffs, and program participants; providing services; recruiting members at the grass roots; focusing and streamlining activities;

and determining ways to generate local resources to support programs. Women's organizations are also facing the need to form and strengthen alliances with other similar groups in spite of their diverse interests. Given the many political sensitivities around such alliances, they can be formed strategically, recognizing that alliance does not imply convergence on all issues or tactics.

Relationships with donors is a paradoxical issue for women's organizations. While the Bangladeshi women's movement in many ways has been strengthened by the money and ideas these organizations provide, the issues of dependence and competition are emerging more sharply. With an emphasis on short-term results, many donors are unable or unwilling to invest in the long-term strategic and political work that is needed to effect policy change at the national level and have diverted the attention of women's organizations to other concerns.[27]

A number of women leaders place priority on creating an ideology of gender equity and an alternate vision of development that will lead to a society based on justice and equality. So far little has been done by women in this regard. There are other important areas that have not yet been adequately addressed by women researchers and activists. These include in-depth and sustained analysis of the gender impact of economic policies, especially structural adjustment programs. Questions regarding secularism, its meaning, and its manifestation in the Bangladeshi context and tradition must be raised and analyzed. There is little discussion of women's sexuality, including freedom of choice and homosexuality. These remain controversial within the women's movement; many consider them private and personal issues and so controversial that raising either increases the risk of backlash against the women's movement.

Conclusion

The women's movement has come a long way since 1905, when Rokeya Hossain dreamed of empowering women in her feminist utopian short story by a simple reversal of gender roles, putting men in seclusion and letting women take charge of the public sphere.[28] For the inheritors of Rokeya's dream of women's empowerment, the task is complex and difficult. They have to create an alternate paradigm of development based on participatory politics, egalitarian distribution of social resources and opportunities, free expression of pluralistic culture, and nonhierarchical gender relations in the family, community, and state. The male-dominated social structures are reluctant to forego privileges enjoyed so far on the basis of gender. Bringing about attitudinal changes, involving a radical change in the process of socialization in the family through which gender ideology is transmitted and perpetuated, is especially difficult. In a country with limited resources, inadequate infrastructure, acute poverty, slow rate of industrialization and economic growth, large population, underemployment, rising religious extremism, and class and gender violence, it is a tremendous challenge to go against the current.

However, the women's movement has gained in strength and solidarity over time. The leadership, though still made up of urban educated women, has acquired a broader vision through greater and longer exposure to social realities and closer contact with rural and urban poor women as well as regional and international networks. Issues that were once regarded as women's issues, such as domestic violence, rape, sexual harassment, women's rights at the workplace, and access to social resources and services, are now being addressed as social issues, articulated in public forums and mass media by citizens' groups concerned with social and legal reform and human rights. Even political parties have started to recognize women's legitimate role in public discourse. Whether or not their demands are met, women's articulation of these demands and the struggle to achieve them have made an impact on Bangladeshi social consciousness and women's own identity and self-image. The prevailing mood of the women's movement at present is one of cautious optimism. As one rural woman declared, "We have come this far ... because our cause is just. We shall neither give up nor give in."[29]

NOTES

1. Rounaq Jahan, *Women in Bangladesh* (Dhaka: Women for Women, 1975).

2. I use the term *Bangladeshi* to refer to Bangladeshi Muslims unless specified otherwise. I use this term in this way for several reasons. Bangladesh is an overwhelmingly Muslim country; 85 percent of the population is Muslim. Though women of other religions also have problems and constraints, especially in relation to their being governed by religious personal laws, they enjoy equal civil, political, and economic rights.

3. Rehnuma Ahmed, "Women's Movement in Bangladesh and the Left's Understanding of Women's Question," *Journal of Social Studies,* no. 30 (October 1985).

4. I draw in this chapter on sixty interviews: Fifty were with women in the movement, and ten were with representatives of NGOs with women-focused programs. The interviews were open-ended, based on a list of core questions about the characteristics of leadership, membership, objectives, strategies, obstacles, and successes. I also conducted six local-level focus group discussions and one focus group discussion (five participants) with each of the following major political parties: Awami League and Bangladesh National Party (Center), Five-Party Alliance (Left), and Jamaat-e-Islami (Far Right). Research assistants collected most of the secondary data, conducted six focus group discussions at local levels, and interviewed representatives of local-level structures, journalists, and columnists of selected newspapers.

5. K.M.A. Aziz and Clarence E. Maloney, *Life Stages, Gender, and Fertility in Bangladesh* (Dhaka: International Center for Diarrheal Disease Research, 1985).

6. Lincoln C. Chen et al., "Sex Bias in the Family Allocation of Food and Health Care in Rural Bangladesh," *Population and Development Review* (March 1981).

7. Michael Edwardes, *Raj: The Glory of British India* (London: Pan Books, 1969).

8. Roushan Jahan, ed., *Sultana's Dream and Selections from the Secluded Ones* (New York: Feminist Press, 1988).

9. Haleh Afsar, "Behind the Veil: The Public and Private Faces of Khomeini's Policies on Iranian Women," in Bina Agarwal, ed., *Structures of Patriarchy* (New Delhi: Kali for Women, 1988).

10. Hamza Alavi, "Pakistan and Islam: Ethnicity and Ideology," in F. Halliday and H. Alavi, eds., *State and Ideology in the Middle East and Pakistan* (London: Macmillan, 1988).

11. Ahmed, "Women's Movement in Bangladesh"; Neelam Hussain, "Military Rule, Fundamentalism, and Women's Movement in Pakistan," *Alternatives: Women's Vision and Movements* 2 (1991).

12. Ahmed, "Women's Movement in Bangladesh."

13. Susan Brownmiller, *Against Our Will: Men, Women, and Rape* (New York: Bantam Books, 1975).

14. Roushan Jahan, "Women's Movement in Bangladesh: Concerns and Challenges," *Alternatives: Women's Vision and Movements* 2 (1991).

15. Roushan Jahan, "Hidden Wounds, Visible Scars," in Bina Agarwal, ed., *Structures of Patriarchy* (New Delhi: Kali for Women, 1988).

16. Hameeda Hossain et al., *No Better Option? Industrial Women Workers in Bangladesh* (Dhaka: UPL, 1990).

17. Anthony Mascarenhas, *Bangladesh: A Legacy of Blood* (London: Hodder and Stoughton, 1986).

18. Afsar, "Behind the Veil"; Hussain, "Military Rule."

19. Interview with Maleka Begum, former general secretary of Bangladesh Mahila Parishad, Dhaka, December 27, 1993.

20. Naila Kabeer, "The Quest for National Identity: Women, Islam, and the State of Bangladesh," *IDS Bulletin* (October 1989).

21. Interview with Dr. Neelima Ibrahim, chairperson of Bangladesh Mahila Samity, Dhaka, November 11, 1993.

22. Nilufar Ahmad, "Reproductive Rights and Population Program in Bangladesh," in Rousan Jahn et al., eds., *Reproductive Rights and Women's Health* (Dhaka: Women for Women, 1994); UBINIG/FINRRAGE, *Genetic Engineering and Women's Health* (Dhaka: UBINIG, 1989).

23. Rounaq Jahan, "Public Policies, Women, and Development," in Rounaq Jahan and H. Papanek, eds., *Women and Development: Perspectives from South and South-East Asia* (Dhaka: BILIA, 1979).

24. United Nations Development Program, "Human Development Report" (Dhaka: UNDP, 1994).

25. Riffat Hassan, "Feminist Theology: An Islamic Perspective," *Harvard Divinity School Bulletin* (Spring 1987).

26. The daily *Inkilab*, founded and funded by a prominent Jamaat leader, ran a series of editorials and columns against the activities of agents of Indian Hindus and Western Jews and Christians from March to July 1994.

27. Sarah C. White, *Arguing with the Crocodile: Gender and Class in Bangladesh* (London: Zed Books, 1992).

28. Jahan, *Sultana's Dream.*

29. Focus group discussion, October 12, 1993.

4

Rebirthing Babaye: *The Women's Movement in the Philippines*

LILIA QUINDOZA SANTIAGO

THE FIRST WOMAN IN THE world, Filipino indigenes believe, was born simultaneously with the first man. She emerged from nodes of the bamboo as *Babaye,* a whole person, separate from, yet born together with *Lalake.*[1] This indigenous myth of creation is common among the various ethnolinguistic communities in the country and has continued to be retold in folktales.[2] The simultaneous, yet separate births of woman and man distinguish early Philippine civilization from predominantly Christian societies, where the belief system is based on woman's derivation from man.

Filipina feminists have used this myth as a cultural norm to distinguish Filipinas' heritage from that of other women. The fundamental difference between indigenous Filipinas and those in the Hispanic/Christian tradition thus arises not out of color or race but out of a cultural belief in patriarchy, which "existed only legally after the Spanish conquest."[3] As a person born whole and separate from man, the Filipina legitimately owns her body and her self and can chart her own future and destiny.

The story of the women's movement in the Philippines comes full circle in this story of *Babaye.* Rebirthing *Babaye* in the postcolonial Philippines means reinventing Filipinas in multiethnic, multiracial, multireligious, and socially diverse identities. This is crucial to ending the predominantly colonial, Christian, urban, elitist, and Western definitions imposed on Filipinas by hundreds of years of local feudal and colonial patriarchy. Filipinas are retracing, retrieving, and recovering

PHILIPPINES

GENERAL

type of government: Democratic Republic
major ethnic groups: Christian Malay (91.5%); Muslim Malay (4%); Chinese (1.5%);
    Negritos and Dumagats (indigenous)
language(s): Pilipino (national language); English; Spanish; 70 indigenous languages
religions: Roman Catholicism (83%); Protestant (9%); Muslim (5%)
date of independence: 1946
former colonial powers: Spain, United States, Japan

DEMOGRAPHICS

population size: 67 million
birth rate (*per 1,000 population*) : 62
total fertility (*average number of births per woman*): 4.1
contraceptive prevalence (*married women*): 40%
maternal mortality rate (*per 100,000 live births*): 74

WOMEN'S STATUS

date of women's suffrage: 1937
economically active population: M 81%   F 36%
female employment (*% of total workforce*): 31
life expectancy   M 62   F 68
school enrollment ratio (*F/100 M*)

primary	94
secondary	99
tertiary	119

literacy   M 90%   F 89%

---

the qualities of their foremothers—poets, artists, and cultural leaders—who were cast early for public life. Rebirthing *Babaye* underscores the importance of reclaiming this culture in the valuation of women in history and society.

Reconstructing the status and activism of women at various stages of Philippine history will help explain the continuing militancy and relevance of the Philippine women's movement. The women's movement is defined here as any action undertaken by institutions, groups, organizations, or individuals that results in social change favorable to women as a whole. The participants in this movement, and others for social justice, derive enormous strength from the stories of their foremothers' struggles as they engage in their own—for religious freedom of choice and self-determination among minority women; for employment, fair wages, and reproductive rights; for human rights. In the Philippines, the women's movement remains always acutely aware of its social, political, cultural, and historical context.

In this chapter I explore the historical evolution of the movement for women's empowerment in the Philippines and its changing relations with other movements for social change. During some periods, women worked within broader social movements to promote their rights and issues. At other times, women found it necessary to develop independent organizations and positions in order to avoid women's issues being subsumed within the cause for national liberation. The continuing legacy of these tensions for the present is also described. I begin with a brief overview of Philippine political history to provide a context for the story of the Filipina and the women's movement in the past and today.

Philippine Political History: An Overview

Filipinas are the product of the numerous demographic, socioeconomic, and political characteristics of their country. The Philippine archipelago comprises seven thousand one hundred islands, of which approximately two thousand are inhabited by peoples of Malay, Chinese, Hispanic, and indigenous racial groupings. The archipelagic nature of the country contributed to uneven and socially diverse development for many different ethnolinguistic communities, and Philippine indigenous societies varied widely. While thriving communities were linked by a sophisticated trading system and loose political compacts, political unity has always been somewhat fragile and unpredictable.[4]

After several decades of contact, fighting, and trade, Spanish colonial conquest occurred in 1565 and lasted for more than three hundred years. The legacy of Spanish colonization is evident in many aspects of Philippine political and social culture. A relatively small number of Filipinos benefited greatly by cooperating with the Spanish, and a similarly small elite continue to control much of the country's economic and political power. More than 80 percent of the Philippine population is Roman Catholic, and another 9 percent belongs to other Christian denominations, making the Philippines the only Christian country in Asia. The Catholic church continues to exert considerable conservative influence over social policy and politics.

A significant Islamic minority is concentrated mostly in the south. Islamization began as early as the twelfth century and eroded many of the characteristics of the traditional, indigenous societies. However, in the Philippines Islamization is widely considered a gradual result of migration and settlement or an offshoot of trade and marketing agreements. In general, its effects were therefore less devastating to local communities than the forcible Christianization process.

Throughout the long Spanish colonial period, Filipinos waged brave protests and uprisings, which finally led to independence from Spain in 1898–1899. The United States almost immediately replaced Spain as colonial power. While the cultural legacy of the United States has been far less significant, the United States has exerted considerable influence over the Philippine political and military systems. The United States supported the notorious dictator Ferdinand Marcos for the twenty years of his military regime, despite his amassing enormous personal wealth and engaging in extreme political repression, especially after declaring martial law in 1972. The presence of enormous U.S. military bases on Philippine soil until 1992 was long a symbol of U.S. imperialism and a focus of protest for Philippine nationalists.

Since the fall of Ferdinand Marcos in the "peaceful revolution" of 1986, the Philippine government and Philippine people have continued to exert their cultural and political autonomy. Economically, the country has recently shown some signs of recovery, but the benefits are not evenly distributed. A majority of Filipinos remain economically marginalized as plantation workers, fishers, farmers, and workers in the informal economy. A great number of both men and women are compelled to seek work as migrant laborers around the world. Female workers outnumber males in migrant labor and are thus said to be the major export in an export-driven economy.

The women's movement was central in the coalition of political and social movements that helped precipitate the end of the Marcos regime. In the more open political climate that has followed, the women's movement has played an increasingly important and visible role in redefining Philippine policy, culture, and politics.

Women in Protohistory

While historians and anthropologists doubt the existence of a true matriarchy in the early social formations of the archipelago, many concede to traces of a matrilineal society where women enjoyed high status and played important public roles. For example, there was no sexual bias in determining lineage; in the tracing of kinship the mother's side was taken into account equally with the father's.[5] Many communities tolerated premarital sex, divorce, and abortion. Daughters had equal rights to inheritance with sons, and there was no special demand for male children.[6] Women were also responsible for naming children. Perhaps the most significant evidence of these gender-fair systems is imprinted in all indigenous Philippine languages, which do not have sexual bifurcation in the third person pronoun: There is no hierarchical demarcation between he and she. The presence of gender-neutral terms for brother/sister, son/daughter, and poet/poetess, who can be male, female, or gay, reinforces this cultural particularity. Women were empowered to lead spiritual ceremonies in honor of deities; to become healers, poets, and bards; and to imagine and create cultural and political heroes in chants of the epics.[7] Women were thus responsible for preserving, interpreting, and recounting history. These important social roles underscore the relatively higher status of Philippine women in ancient times compared to women in much of the rest of Asia and the world.

Women and Resistance in the
Spanish Colonial Era

The process of Hispanization/Christianization that began in the fourteenth century affected women in the archipelago in different ways. Women of the elite and the principalia were most affected as they had the most contact with settlers, administrators, traders, and priests. Sister Mary John Mananzan, in explaining how these Filipinas came to be subjugated, cites the far-reaching influence of misogynist theologians in the Iberian Peninsula in prescribing a code of conduct for indigenous women.[8] These codes of conduct were recorded in numerous manuals for young women that proscribed behavior aimed at urbanizing and Hispanizing them. The most popular of these was by Father Modesto Castro.[9] Mananzan also speculates that many "orphans" sheltered in schools run by religions orders were in fact fathered by the friars themselves.

In contrast, women in the northern highlands as well as Muslim women and others in many areas of Mindanao in the south were never really acculturated through Spanish conquest.[10] Even in areas where Catholicism did take hold, women were critical to preserving local traditions and to resisting and undermining Spanish influence. Building on their traditional roles as priestesses and bards, they creatively maintained many of their own beliefs and forms of worship. For example, a Father Pedro Chirino recounts how an anonymous *babaylan* mobilized men and women and established her own cult in defiance of Catholicism, complete with a golden idol of the chief priestess, which was kept concealed through "connivance with the Devil."[11]

The enterprising and resourceful imagination of many of these women helped incorporate folk beliefs and customs within Catholicism, thereby preserving their own culture and undermining the influence of Catholicism. Some *babaylanes* joined in parish fiestas, after which they would return to the uplands to continue with their own forms of worship. One study revealed how the natives on the southern island of Mindanao used occasions such as these fiestas to display a "feigned" obedience to the Catholic hierarchy. Finally, chanting of the *Passion* (retelling of the story of Christ) was initiated and led by *cantoras,* who preserved much of traditional history and values by incorporating existing epics into the *Passion.* According to Reynaldo Ileto, such creative use of the *Passion* played a crucial part in forging a revolutionary consciousness among the masses.[12] These examples, and others, challenge many preconceived notions of the colonized Hispanized Filipina as submissive, passive, and weak.

Resistance to the Spanish inspired a number of heroic women. In the seventeenth century, Gabriela Silang waged a brilliant military strategy against the Spaniards after a rebellion led by her husband failed. Leona Florentina, a poet and writer, protested against patriarchy by defying the authority of her husband. Her poems, printed in Madame Andzia Wolska's *Bibliotheque internationale de ouvres de femme* in 1889, remain a poignant and poetic expression of artistic freedom for feminist writers. It is clear from these two life stories, and countless others, that colonization failed to transform many women into total subjects of the Spanish empire.

Three events in the late nineteenth century were particularly significant in contributing to the birth of the Philippine feminist movement. These were the informal, yet socially significant movements of women workers, especially in Manila; the women of Malolos demanding establishment of a Spanish academy for women; and the direct involvement of women in the Katipunan independence movement and the revolution of 1896.

After Manila opened to world trade in the late nineteenth century, factories in the area proliferated. The labor demands of these factories drew increasing numbers of both male and female workers to the city. Certain industries, such as garments and tobacco, employed more women than men. Women also worked as domestic servants in cottage industries and as entertainers, where they were usually classified together as vagrants or prostitutes. While there are no records of outright union organizing among women workers at the time, their substandard living and working conditions led many women to engage in organized protest. These complaints were significant enough that they were registered officially as disturbances with the local authorities.

Women in the factories were also exposed to new technologies for which they needed additional skills and training. However, the educational system was both inadequate and male biased. Lack of skills, inadequate education, and increasing demands in the workplace were among the multiple burdens women faced in transforming economy and society. This stimulated women to seek reform, first in the educational system and later in the more complete overhaul of colonial society.

One of the more significant events for women during this period occurred in the town of Malolos in 1889. Seeking training and education to meet the increasing demands placed on women by changing material conditions, some twenty women, many of them from landed families, petitioned the parish priest to conduct night classes in Spanish for women. Spanish had rapidly become the language of education, commerce, and government, and without knowledge of Spanish, women were unable to participate in public life. The parish priest refused their request. The women then collectively raised the issue to higher authorities, writing a petition to the Spanish governor general, in effect defying the powerful parish priest.[13] This defiant movement for equal education can be interpreted as a way of retrieving the status of women in early Philippine society as preachers and cultural leaders. Having been deprived of education, these women wished to become involved in the growing discourse on reforms, assimilation, independence, and nationhood, as equal members of the emerging nation.

Historians consider the independence group now known as the Katipunan as the movement that founded the Filipino nation.[14] The Katipunan initiated the armed liberation struggle that led to the downfall of the Spanish empire in the Philippines and gave birth to the first Philippine republic in 1898. Women's important role in the Katipunan has been largely obscured by the historical record of the time. The autobiography of Gregoria de Jesus, possibly the most important woman in the organization of the Katipunan and revolution of 1896, was first published as a simple appendix to the biography of her second husband, Julio Nakpil.[15] Gregoria de Jesus' autobiography reveals a number of significant details about the involvement of women in the Katipunan, some of which challenge commonly held assertions. For example, Teodoro Agoncillo and Milagros Guerrera, in the *History of the Filipino People,* describe the women's chapter of the Katipunan as follows:

> Bonifacio's [the leader of the Katipunan] idea of expanding the membership of the Katipunan led him ... to the formation of the Women's Chapter ... in the middle of 1893. ... He opened the door of the society to patriotic and scrupulous women who had the virtue to keep their tongues in place. To be sure that no woman of dubious character could penetrate the deep secrets of the society, Bonifacio limited the membership to the wives, daughters and sisters of the male members. It was their duty to take in new members, male and female, and, more important from the point of view of security, to see to it that meetings of male members were not disturbed by surprise raids of the authorities. Thus, while the men were holding their meeting in the backroom, the women, in order to draw away the suspicion of the authorities, danced and sang in full view of the passersby. It was thus that the women members acted as front for the clandestine goings on of the Katipuneros.[16]

There are several points worth mentioning about this narration. It was Bonifacio, the leader of the Katipunan, who initiated the formation of the women's chapter, and female members were limited to wives, daughters, and sisters of male members. These women had to have the virtue of "keeping their tongues in place"; at the same time they took charge of security arrangements for the meetings of the Katipunan. The requirement that women keep their tongues in place is

sexist in implying that only women could divulge the revolution's important secrets and reinforces the popularly held historical distortion that a woman's confession to a priest betrayed the Katipunan. However, this can now be considered
an excuse to blame women for a fait accompli—the Katipunan's existence was already known to the authorities, and it was only a matter of time before the group
would be raided.[17] These assertions also lack internal consistency. If the society
was apprehensive of women, why would they be assigned such a delicate task as
security?

Gregoria de Jesus' version of the formation of the Katipunan women's wing also
challenges both the claim that it was Bonifacio who initiated the formation of a
woman's chapter and the assertion that only wives, daughters, and sisters of
Katipunan members could join the women's wing. Many of the women leaders
were not in fact related to the Katipuneros. It seems likely that membership in the
women's wing was instead based initially on membership in an existing Masonic
lodge for women, many of whose members became active in the revolution.[18]

Like Gregoria de Jesus, the critical actions of many of the women in the revolution have been overshadowed and remembered only as afterthoughts. For example, Gregoria Montoya was "the only Katipunera known to have led her troops in
several engagements against the Spaniards,"[19] including leading the victory of the
Katipuneros in the famous battle of Calero in Cavite on November 10, 1896. Although Montoya has been characterized as the "greatest woman" who fought in
the revolution, because she was the wife of an unknown farmer with no social status, her heroism has not been fully appreciated.

There are many other such women, and their contributions to the revolution
that formed the Filipino nation have never been fully uncovered. There are no stories that tell of Rosa Sevilla Alvero and Florentina Arellano, the two women writers on the staff of *La Independencia,* the newspaper of the revolution.[20] Few accounts have told of the courage of five Iloko women noted for fighting for national
liberation by supervising the supply lines of the Katipunan who were imprisoned
in February 1901.[21] Although Tandang Sora is remembered as a "mother" who
provided shelter and food, an activity absolutely vital to the maintenance of revolutionary forces, her actions seem to be regarded more as a virtue of motherhood
than of a revolutionary.

The problem in depicting women's contribution to the revolution is a basically
male-dominated, urban-biased, and elitist history writing and historiography.
Exclusion of women from historical recognition also derives from the use of a language inappropriate to Filipino culture and history. When the documents and
texts of the Katipunan were translated into English from Tagalog, many of the native qualities and characteristics of a social movement with roots in indigenous
traditions were lost. For example, the ceremony *sanduguan* was translated as a
"blood compact," where blood was used to sign the names of new members. However, *sanduguan* has a host of other cultural implications. It describes kinship ties

between parties and a relationship untranslatable in English because the term is gender neutral and encompasses more than "comradeship" or "brotherhood." This is perhaps most powerfully illustrated in the translation of the name itself when the Katipunan became Most Supreme, Most Esteemed Society of the *Sons* of the People.[22] The use of the terms *sons of the people* and the Spanish male *Katipunero* blurred the reality of women's leadership, membership, and participation in the Katipunan and the revolution.

The Suffragist Movement and the Struggle for Political Equality

The first two formal women's organizations in the country were formed in the early 1900s and both carried the name *feministas.* Thus, feminist, or *feminista,* had an early functional and material use in the Philippine women's movement and cannot be dismissed as a "borrowed" Western concept or term. Feminist consciousness can be found in the speeches and writings of pioneer feminist Concepción Feliz, the founding president of the Asosación Feminista Filipina:

> If indeed we aim for equality among citizens, if our goal is for the people to have real freedom, to have the right to decide for themselves on issues involving the country's welfare, and for them to know the consequences of their actions and not simply believe in nonsense, in "miracles" or magic, then there is no other recourse but to prepare the women, whether single or married, through full education. However high that education must be, women should be equally entitled and it should not be the exclusive right of the men alone.[23]

Concepción Feliz put these words into action as she campaigned publicly for women's rights. In her personal life she challenged her husband for chair of a corporate board and won. Thus, as early as 1904 public debate about equality between the sexes and segregation of roles based on gender had already started. The Asosación Feminista Filipina also campaigned to appoint women to municipal and provincial electorates and committees, initial moves toward achieving political equality in public governance. Its work also encompassed social welfare initiatives such as institutional reforms in prisons, schools, and factories; campaigns against prostitution, drinking, and gambling; and the establishment of recreational facilities. Several other organizations were also formed around this time to do this kind of charity and welfare work.

In 1909, a feminist magazine, *Filipina,* was founded, with Constancia Poblete as editor. Part of its objectives were "to revindicate the rights of women," an indication that Mary Wollstonecraft's *A Vindication of the Rights of Woman* had found its way into the discourse of early Philippine feminists.[24] Links with women's movements outside the country were also evident in the visit of two suffragists, Carrie Chapman Catt of the United States and Dr. Aleta Jacobs of Holland, to the Philippines in 1912. This resulted in the founding of the Society for the Advancement of Women, which joined the Asosación Feminista Ilonga (founded in 1906 and the first feminist association to set women's suffrage as its ultimate goal). A number of other groups soon joined in this quest.

These suffragist pioneers campaigned in the Philippine Assembly, in media, in schools, and in public and private gatherings to advocate women's right to vote. They studied hard, traveled extensively, and debated men, especially during the constitutional convention of 1935. The suffragists' goal took almost three decades to achieve. In a plebiscite held on May 14, 1937, women's right to suffrage was finally affirmed,[25] making Filipinas the first women in Asia with this right.

Some feminists later criticized the suffragist movement as a middle-class-led cause that enjoyed the blessing of the American colonial government and was used as an instrument of political consolidation of American rule in the islands.[26] Nevertheless, the suffrage movement achieved a great deal for women and for Philippine society as a whole. The right to vote also meant the right to hold public office and participate in public governance. Women's suffrage was the Filipinas' first victory toward political empowerment. The suffragist movement also made the first connections between the women's movement in the Philippines and the international women's movement. This started the globalization of both the discourse and the organization of the Philippine feminist movement, which were to become such an important part of the movement in the following decades.

Immersion in Social Movements and Civic Affairs, 1937–1970

Political equality as envisioned by the early feminists meant empowerment for women at all levels of public life. It also signified the presence of women and women's perspectives in all movements promoting social change. In the victory of the suffragists in 1937, the war of national liberation against Japanese aggression in World War II, and the peasant and workers' movements of the 1950s and 1960s, political equality became a subdued battle cry of women activists involved in social movements. Women generally accepted that involvement in movements for social change would automatically bring about women's emancipation and improve women's lives. Thus, women immersed themselves in various civic, sociopolitical, and cultural events, most of which were led and dominated by men.

However, women's experience in the peasant and workers' movements were disappointing. In the workers' movement, women participated as members of many key organizations promoting workers' rights, just wages, and collective bargaining for workers' welfare. Similarly, peasant women launched campaigns for equitable distribution of land and agrarian reform beginning as early as the 1930s. Salud Generala Algabre, a woman visionary and leader, was a central figure in

Sakdal, a prominent peasant organization. Women also made up much of the membership of the Organization of Philippine Peasants as well as the armed peasant organizations that fought during World War II.

Many women enlisted as guerrillas and soldiers in the resistance to Japanese aggression during World War II and fought alongside men against the Japanese invasion from 1941 to 1945. A number of women who rendered sexual services as "comfort women" to the Japanese Imperial Army during this time are now telling their stories and seeking recompense. These sexual services were usually appropriated by force and coercion, yet there is evidence that women also performed them to conceal espionage activities for the Philippine liberation movement.

Despite their critical participation, women in both the peasant and workers' movements were segregated, discriminated against, and occasionally subjected to sexual harassment. Segregation of work based on gender and the sexual division of labor marginalized women in the workers' movement. Few companies ever recognized the need for equal pay for work of equal value, and women continued to suffer from both gender-based segregation and discrimination. Similarly, the peasant movement was slow in recognizing equality between men and women in landownership and social status, land tenure, and benefits accruing from land and agrarian reforms.

Despite this discrimination, from the 1950s through the 1970s most women continued to believe that these broader social movements were instrumental in promoting women's liberation. Women believed that social change and national liberation would bring about women's equality. Toward this end, women engaged in various civic, political, and social service activities, among them food distribution, rehabilitation, and community development work. The early nongovernmental organizations (NGOs) developed from this work. Women's associations, clubs, and auxiliary services became involved in civic affairs and promoted a wide range of social programs. While some addressed women's concerns, few of these activities and advocacy campaigns organized women on gender-sensitive issues.

The Feminist Movement, 1970s–1990s

The upsurge in the nationalist movement of the 1960s and 1970s culminated in what activists have termed the First Quarter Storm. From January to March 1970, massive student demonstrations were organized to protest the policies of the Marcos and U.S. governments. During this time, women members of several of the key organizations formed the Malayang Kilusan ng Bagong Kababaihan (MAKIBAKA), or "Free Movement of New Women," which paved the way for a vigorous ideological debate on the "woman question" within various sectors of the national democratic movement. MAKIBAKA first challenged the assumptions of Marxist discourse on women's issues by questioning whether women's liberation was secondary to national liberation. This was demonstrated in MAKIBAKA's picketing of the national beauty contest in May 1970, symbolizing a shift in the debate from Marxian terms of productive relations to feminist terms of social imagery and the right of women to control their bodies and destinies.

When the entire country was placed under martial law by President Ferdinand Marcos on September 21, 1972, it not only validated dictatorship and one-man rule but also threatened to produce a militarized citizenry and to entrench authority, hierarchy, and patriarchy in Filipino culture. MAKIBAKA and other progressive feminist groups reintegrated their demands within the entire front waging war against the Marcos dictatorship. Thus, the militant sections of the women's movement became an integral part of the anti-imperialist, antifeudal, anticapitalist, and antifascist movement advocating for the end of the U.S.-supported Marcos dictatorship. Maria Lorena Barros, founding chair of MAKIBAKA, was killed by government forces in 1976.

Within the workers' movement, as discussion of women's issues intensified during the 1970s, the impact of "development" was contextualized and given a gender-sensitive perspective by working women in the Philippines. Women workers from factories, allied with nuns working with urban poor communities, initially organized around workers' issues and vigorously participated in the first strike, in 1975, after the institution of martial law. When export processing zones were established in the 1970s and early 1980s, organized women workers mobilized other women to protest gender-based segregation of work. Migration of women workers also increased during this period, meaning that more and more Filipino women were exposed to exploitation and harassment in other countries. Trafficking in women intensified as more women became enmeshed in the sex trade. Through networking with other Third World women, women workers and victims of sex trafficking successfully exposed issues of sexual harassment and violence, including organized sex trafficking.

Following MAKIBAKA's initial efforts at inserting a feminist perspective and agenda in the broad framework for national liberation, similar issues continued to be raised by some other women's groups, among them Kilusan ng Kababaihang Pilipina (PILIPINA) founded in 1981, and the Katipunan ng Kalayaan para sa Kababaihang (KALAYAAN) founded in 1983. These groups advocated for a separate but not necessarily separatist women's movement. They argued that separation from the overall organizational framework of the national liberation movement was essential to give women the opportunity to articulate their interests without patriarchal intervention through male Marxist discourse.

PILIPINA insisted that dictates from leftist male leaders had debilitating effects on women and women's movements. KALAYAAN, while not hostile to national democratic discourse, insisted on its independence and pushed for use of the term *feminist*, despite charges that it was a Western and middle-class concept. The organizational experiences of these and other women's groups demonstrated to the

Philippine women's movement that women's issues were not and could not be subordinate or secondary relative to national liberation, but rather that women's issues had to be put forth alongside issues of national and social liberation.

Marcos's attempts to soften his image by pronouncing the institution of a "constitutional authoritarian" government and his supposed lifting of martial law in 1981 became farcical as social reforms were postponed and activists continued to be detained, tortured, and assassinated. The assassination of opposition leader Benigno Aquino on August 21, 1983, exposed the highly militarized mind-set and culture of Philippine society and began the rapid decline of Marcos's political machinery. Aquino's assassination catalyzed the pent-up social rage against two decades of repression, violation of human rights, and martial law; rallies and demonstrations exploded on major streets of Manila and in many other urban areas of the country.

In this context of growing social protest, the women's movement demonstrated its resilience in pushing the frontiers of struggle from the underground into more public arenas. Notable among these efforts was the founding in 1984 of a feminist political party and a broad-based feminist coalition. Women for the Motherland promoted and supported the electoral candidacy of women on a feminist agenda. The General Assembly Binding Women for Reforms, Integrity, Equality, Leadership, and Action (GABRIELA) derived its inspiration from the heroism of resistance leader Gabriela Silang. Its founding members represented a coalition of groups from various sectors, classes, and political perspectives integrated within the movement for national and social liberation but with relative autonomy on women's issues. Feminist groups such as PILIPINA and KALAYAAN played pivotal roles in the founding of GABRIELA. GABRIELA rallied women and organized campaigns against violations of women's human rights, sexual harassment in the home and the workplace, commodification of sex, sex trafficking, and the distorted imaging of women in media and culture.

Soon after, in 1985, Marcos called for snap elections, and Corazon Cojuangco Aquino, the widow of Benigno Aquino, was put forward as an opposition candidate. During the campaign, Marcos repeatedly raised the issue of Aquino being a woman and questioned her ability to lead. In doing so, he both initiated the downfall of his military rule and laid the groundwork for the emergence of a stronger, more vigilant, and more comprehensive women's movement.

The ascendance of Corazon Aquino as the first woman president of the Philippines is often interpreted as the result a sympathetic response to her husband's martyrdom. It can also be regarded as one of the major victories of the women's movement in the country. Women's organizations were central to the alliance that challenged the election results declaring a Marcos victory. This alliance waged a "peaceful revolution" that, in February 1986, toppled the Marcos dictatorship and affirmed Aquino as president. On March 8, International Women's Day, some ten

Corazon Aquino acknowledges a crowd in February 1986, after Ferdinand Marcos declared that he had won the presidential election. Later that month a nonviolent popular movement overthrew the Marcos dictatorship, and Aquino became president. Her presidency made some headway in legitimizing women's issues but did not effectively address them or execute reforms to enfranchise the poor.

thousand women marched in Manila to affirm her victory as a victory for the women's movement in the Philippines.

While Aquino was clearly not a feminist, her victory over several military uprisings during her term prevented a return to military dictatorship. This was critical to demonstrating that a woman could be a resolute leader and to creating a more open political climate in which the women's movement could flourish. This is evidenced in the enormous number of women's organizations that either started or were reinvigorated during the 1980s. The floodgates were opened for discussion of more women's and feminist issues, led by an invigorated, tested, and more militant women's movement. During this time, women's groups took advantage of the new democratic processes and new leaders to push for reforms in public policy in a range of areas. Over the course of Aquino's presidency, some headway in legislation, policy, and plan formulation was made. For example, a Philippine development plan for women was developed for the first time. The number and influence of women in public office increased dramatically, among them high-profile feminists such as Senator Leticia Ramos Shahani and Representative Nikki Coseteng, who have paved the way for more gender-sensitive legislation and continue to be involved in programs for women.

However, the unity between Aquino and the women's movement gradually eroded, especially after she continued the brutal military policies aimed at eradicating the political and military struggles of leftist guerrillas and Islamic separatists. This resulted in political repression as well as in more women becoming victims of a brutal and more devious form of militarization. In addition, Aquino acquiesced to powerful political forces among landowners and failed to implement the highly publicized Comprehensive Agrarian Reform Program, a centerpiece of her administration intended to enfranchise many of the Philippines' desperately poor rural citizens. This both broke an important political compact and resulted in even greater marginalization of women peasants and farmworkers. Finally, Aquino's deep alliance with conservative forces in the Catholic church prevented her from exerting leadership or even permitting open debate on a range of issues critical to the women's movement, most notably in the areas of health and reproductive rights.

The women's movement campaign for women's reproductive rights has been a significant achievement. While a deep schism exists within women's groups on issues of population policy, contraceptive choice, and abortion, there has been considerable progress in articulating positions and in giving women more control over their reproductive options. The women's movement has largely succeeded in defining the issues of reproductive health and choice broadly, thereby bringing many other often very controversial issues relevant to women's health into public debate. This has included the concerns of prostituted women, such as their right to know the hazards of the sex trade, the decriminalization of prostitution, and intensive information campaigns on preventing human immunodeficiency virus/acquired immune deficiency syndrome (HIV/AIDS) and other sexually transmitted diseases. Such health campaigns and information drives initiated by the women's movement have effectively influenced formal policies, leading the government to institute programs on informed contraceptive choice and HIV/AIDS information, for example. These campaigns have also opened discussion on sexuality and sexual orientation, which precipitated the coming out of the gay and lesbian liberation movements in the Philippines, symbolized by the first lesbian march held in 1993. Filipinas have emerged among the leaders placing issues of lesbian women on the agenda of human rights groups and the Asian and international women's movements.

The Philippine women's movement since the late 1980s has been rocked by contradictions and contention from several sectors. As a whole it has developed along two general tracks. A number of groups, including GABRIELA, have assented to working with men within a broader framework and have been criticized as subservient to the broader forces advocating for national liberation. While GABRIELA has remained highly visible and is the largest feminist organization in the country, the issue of working with men on broader matters has caused dissension, splintering, and disunity within its "umbrella coalition." The other stream, exemplified by

In the face of severely constrained economic options, many poor and unskilled women in the Philippines work in the sex industry in nightclubs like this one in Manila. Women's groups have initiated educational and empowerment programs with sex workers, especially since the onset of the HIV/AIDS pandemic has made their work more hazardous.

KALAYAAN and PILIPINA, has continued to lean toward absolute autonomy for the women's movement. Challenged as unrepresentative and middle class, and deeply concerned with the plight of the majority of Philippine women who live under conditions of extreme poverty, many women's groups intensified efforts at organizing women in various sectors. These initiatives included teachers and professionals but focused on working with grassroots women, the urban poor, peasants, workers and fishers, and indigenous peoples. While there have been many instances when these different approaches and interests have not been reconcilable, the women's movement has remained deeply united on a wide range of issues, including exposing and eradicating violence against women, dismantling the U.S. military bases, and asserting women's reproductive rights.

After rapidly expanding in the 1980s, the women's movement showed signs in the early 1990s of developing and growing in new ways in its capacity to organize multisectoral, multiethnic, multiclass campaigns. While not being subsumed within other social movements, alliances have broken new ground in a number of areas. In the peasant movement, women have been able to assert co-ownership of land between husband and wife with legislation requiring all conjugal farmlands to be titled in the name of both spouses. Women farmers have also contributed to redefining farmwork to include women's work such as nurturing seeds, planting, sowing, harvesting, and marketing farm produce. Alliances between the women's and workers' movements have been instrumental in bringing about legislation

Dismantling of U.S. military bases was central to the women's movement's commitment to national sovereignty and addressing the exploitative sex industry. These women protest outside the American Embassy in 1988.

beneficial to working women, such as higher wages, health benefits, longer maternity leaves, and equal pay for equal work. Unions and workers' organizations have also become more active forums for discussion of violence against women. In the 1990s, the women's movement has also spearheaded the struggle for the termination of the U.S. military bases in the country. The women's movement continues to advocate for final closure to issues associated with the U.S. bases, including removal of toxic wastes and indemnification of Asian-American children left by American servicemen on the bases.

Through these efforts and others, the Philippine women's movement has gathered strength and diversity. It is an increasingly vocal and influential participant in the global women's movement, where its perspectives have been critical to shaping discourse and advancing issues such as women's human rights, national sovereignty, and reproductive rights. According to one prominent activist, the women's movement in the 1990s has actually ceased to be simply "the other half" but has "broken new ground and reached new heights."[27] Ceasing to be an other half, read culturally, can only mean that *Babaye,* the original Filipina feminist and foremother, has taken hold of the Philippine women's movement. Her free spirit and independence will guide the movement from here on.

NOTES

This chapter benefited from the editorial comments, suggestions, and insights of Anna Leah Sarabia, Fe Mangahas, and Jurgette Honcolada.

1. These are the terms usually found to refer to woman and man. *Babaye* and *lalake* are early spellings; *civaye, babae, babai,* or *bai* have also been recorded in various texts to mean "woman."

2. See F. Landa Jocano, *The Philippines at the Spanish Contact* (Quezon City: MCS Enterprises, 1975). This volume reproduces accounts of early Philippine culture by Miguel de Loarca from 1582 (pp. 81–107); Pedro Chirino from 1604 (pp. 125–146); and Francisco Colin from 1663 (pp. 147–187).

3. Dolores Feria, "The Patriarchy and the Filipina as Writer," in *The Long Stag Party* (Manila: Babaylan Women's Publishing Collective, 1991), p. 53.

4. See Mauro Garcia, ed., *Readings in Philippine Prehistory* (Manila: Filipiniana Book Guild, 1979), p. 264; and Daniel B. Schirmer and Stephen Rossamin Shalom, eds., *The Philippines Reader* (Boston: South End Press, 1987).

5. Robert Fox, "The Philippines in Pre-Historic Times," *Journal of Philippine History* (March–December 1963).

6. Teresita Infante, *The Woman in Early Philippines and Among the Cultural Minorities* (Manila: University of Sto. Tomas, 1975). See also Priscelina Patajo Legasto, "The Image of Women in Philippine Epics" (M.A. thesis, University of the Philippines, 1972).

7. These women were known variously as *babaylanes* (Visayan); *catalonas* (Tagalog); *anitera* (Gaddang); and *doronakit* (Itneg).

8. Mary John Mananzan, "The Filipino Woman Before and After the Spanish Conquest of the Philippines," in Mary John Mananzan, ed., *Essays on Women* (Manila: Women's Studies Program, St. Scholastica's College, 1987), pp. 7–36.

9. This volume was called *Ang Pagsusulatan nang Dalawang Binibini na si Urbana at Felisa at Nagtuturo ng Mabuting Kaugalian* (1864).

10. Muslim women's history and various tribal, lumad formations need more elaboration, which is not within the scope of this chapter.

11. See F. Landa Jocano, *The Philippines at the Spanish Contact* (Quezon City: MCS Enterprises, 1975), pp. 137–138.

12. Reynaldo Clemena Ileto, *Pasyon and Revolution* (Quezon City: Ateneo de Manila University Press, 1979).

13. Romeo Cruz, "Ang Pilipina sa Panahon ng Himagsikan at Digmaang Pilipino-Amerikano," in *Women's Role in Philippine History* (Quezon City: Center for Women's Studies, University of the Philippines, Diliman), pp. 59–62.

14. The full name of the Katipunan was Kataas-taasan, Kagalang-galang na Katipunan ng mga Anak ng Bayan (Most Supreme, Most Esteemed Society of the Children of the People).

15. Encarnacion Alzona, *Julio Nakpil and the Philippine Revolution* (Manila: Carmelo and Bauerman, 1964).

16. Teodoro Agoncillo and Milagros Guerrero, *A History of the Filipino People* (Manila: R. P. Garcia, 1973), pp. 183–184.

17. This is affirmed in the memoirs of Santiago Alvarez, *Ang Katipunan at Paghihimagsik* (The Katipunan and the revolution), translated to English by Paula Carolina Malay (Que-

zon City: Ateneo de Manila University Press, 1992). Alvarez's memoirs even emphasize the role of women as security force.

18. The Katipunan, according to Agoncillo, was one of two groups of the La Liga Filipina, which disbanded after the arrest of José Rizal (the "father of Philippine independence") and his subsequent deportation to Dapitan in July 1892. The other faction, named Cuerpo de Compromisarios, chose reform as a means of struggle in contrast to the Katipunan's call for armed struggle. The members of the La Liga Filipina had been Masons.

19. Alfredo Saulo, "Gregoria Montoya," *The Philippines Free Press,* October 9, 1971, p. 26.

20. Rosa Sevilla Alvero was a mentor of Concepción Feliz, the founding president of the Asosación Feminista Filipina (1905), and provided a link between the Katipunan and the feminist groups/suffragists of the early twentieth century.

21. Arnold Molina Azurin, *Reinventing the Filipino* (Quezon City: CSSP Publications and University of the Philippines Press, 1993), p. 151.

22. All translations of the Katipunan by historians used "sons" for the words *Anak ng Bayan,* which more accurately meant "Children of the People." The tag *A n B* was very important as it signified membership in society and was an acronym for Anak ng Bayan, meaning that membership was not exclusively male but was open to both men and women and even to children.

23. These compiled letters of Concepción Feliz and other women on topics such as the *tapis* and Filipino women were republished in book form in Lope K. Santos, *Ang Babae at Karunungan* (Manila: 1934), pp. 8–9.

24. Tarrosa F. Subido, *The Feminist Movement in the Philippines* (Manila: National Federation of Women's Clubs, 1955), p. 18.

25. Ibid.

26. Aida F. Santos Maranan, "Do Women Really Hold Up Half the Sky?", in Mary John Mananzan, ed., *Essays on Women* (Manila: Women's Studies Program, St. Scholastica's College, 1987), p. 45.

27. See Adora Faye de Vera, "The Women's Movement in the Nineties: Problems and Promises" (Paper presented at the Group of Ten Second National Congress, Los Banos, Laguna, Philippines, May 1993), pp. 1, 4.

PART TWO
Africa and the
Middle East

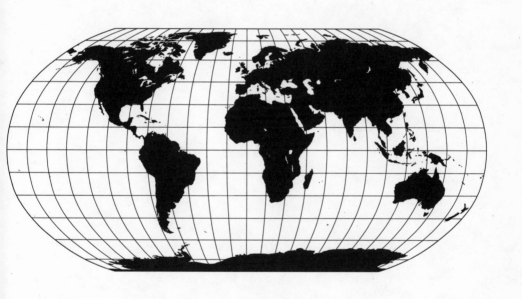

5

The Dawn of a New Day: Redefining South African Feminism

AMANDA KEMP, NOZIZWE MADLALA,

ASHA MOODLEY, & ELAINE SALO

IN FEBRUARY 1990 THE apartheid regime in South Africa reversed the orders banning liberation organizations and their leaders,[1] thus fundamentally altering the face of South African politics. In response, antiapartheid groups assessed the new situation, reorganized their structures, and mobilized their membership. The difficulties subsequently encountered by previously banned organizations, such as the African National Congress (ANC), the Pan Africanist Congress (PAC), and the South African Communist Party, were foreseeable. What could not have been predicted, however, was the extent to which the unbanning and the political negotiations that followed this watershed event would fuel the convergence of progressive women's movements and enable a surprisingly successful campaign to put gender on the nation's political agenda.

The growth of gender consciousness in South Africa in the years since 1990 has been phenomenal, so much so that it is quite common to hear these days of a "burgeoning" women's movement. This by no means implies the growth of a monolithic, homogeneous movement; rather, it encapsulates the sense of the increasing numbers of women throughout the country who are organizing and mobilizing in their various sectors around issues that affect them and in ways that challenge many patriarchal assumptions. Black women have been able to include in the predominantly race/class debates formerly prioritized by the national liber-

SOUTH AFRICA

GENERAL

type of government: Democratic Republic
major ethnic groups: Black (75%); White (14%); Colored (8%); Asian (3%)
language(s): 11 official languages, including: Afrikaans, English, Ndebele, Pedi,
    Sotho, Swati, Tsonga, Tsawa, Venda, Xhosa, Zulu
religions: Christian; Hindu; Muslim; Jewish
date of independence: 1961; majority government 1994
former colonial power: Holland, England

DEMOGRAPHICS

population size: 41.7 million
birth rate (*per 1,000 population*): 35
total fertility (*average number of births per woman*): 4.1
contraceptive prevalence (*married women*): 50%
maternal mortality rate (*per 100,000 live births*): 83

WOMEN'S STATUS

date of women's suffrage: 1930 (White); 1983 (Asian and Coiored); 1994 (Black)
economically active population: M 75%   F 40%
female employment (*% of total workforce*): 36
life expectancy   M 57.5   F 63.5
school enrollment ratio (*F/100 M*)

primary	97
secondary	115
tertiary	*not available*

literacy   M 57%   F 57%

---

ation struggle the very specific articulation of women's rights; unbanning has created the space for Black women to address gender issues without being called self-
indulgent.[2]

Since the unbanning, many progressive women's groups have converged to
make demands that could not be effectively advanced through individual political
party affiliations or through the efforts of individual lobbying groups. Major figures in political parties, especially in the ANC Women's League (ANCWL), early

on projected the need for the creation of an interest group made up of a broad co-alition of women's groups to which political parties and public structures would have to be accountable. Not surprisingly, this convergence and the subsequent articulation of "women's interests" remain fragile, as organizations and individuals clash over perceived interests and very real differences. The lack of unity among South African women and our apparent failure to identify and struggle together against a single patriarchy have led to a perception that South African women's struggles lack a feminist consciousness. This particular view, however, presents only one perspective of an ongoing debate on what constitutes South African feminism.

The challenge, especially for Black feminists, has been to shape South African feminism based on three central assumptions. First, our identities as women are shaped by race, class, and gender, and these identities have molded our particular experiences of gender oppression. Second, our struggles as feminists encompass the struggle for national liberation from a brutal white state.[3] Furthermore, the liberation of Black people as a whole is a feminist issue. Third, we have to challenge and transform Black patriarchies even though Black men have been our allies in the fight for national liberation. These three concerns are of equal importance and are often so inextricably linked that a theoretical perspective that insists on isolating certain issues as feminist and others as not is alienating.

Chandra Mohanty writes that "to define feminism purely in gendered terms assumes our consciousness (or identity) of being 'women' has nothing to do with race, class, nation, or sexuality, just gender. But no-one becomes a woman purely because she is female. Ideologies of womanhood have as much to do with class and race as they have to do with sex."[4] Under apartheid, Black women in South Africa came to understand, for instance, that it was the white state, not the family unit, that was the primary locus of their oppression: The establishment and maintenance of a family unit that included fathers and sons at home were, in fact, one of the rights for which Black women had to fight.

In this chapter we examine the new South African feminism that we see emerging in the space created by national liberation. Framing our discussion historically, we argue that this new feminism differs from conventional South African–adopted Western feminisms in that it is based on Black women's experience of multiple oppressions and includes issues, such as access to clean water and housing, that have not been traditionally defined as feminist. We offer the Rural Women's Movement (RWM), a network of forty-five rural women's groups in the Transvaal region of South Africa, as a case study of contending feminisms and an example of the conceptual shift advanced by the new South African feminists. We analyze the founding, objectives, and performance of the Women's National Coalition (WNC). This coalition, which includes party-political, legal, business and professional, urban, rural, and service organizations, illustrates the problematic nature of forging unity within a constituency of differing interests and experiences. These two very different but characteristic organizations demonstrate the fluidity of the transition years between unbanning and achieving national liberation as well as the increasingly distinct and unapologetic articulation of a new South African feminism. Finally, we look at the unresolved questions and issues, the dilemmas and challenges that obtain for South African women in the current period.

This chapter is the collective effort of four women, three South African and one African American. In order to draw on the experiences and perspectives of a range of women activists, former activists, and/or scholars, we drafted a one-page questionnaire asking for feedback on women's movements in South Africa. Of 400 copies distributed, we received 54 completed questionnaires in return. We also conducted three regional focus groups to engage in a dialogue with women about broad issues in the women's movement and about what they wanted to communicate to an international readership. Approximately thirty women, including local activists, national organizers, and academics, generously shared their time and experiences in these focus groups.

The chapter also draws on interviews conducted with representatives of national women's organizations as well as with staff of the women's desks of nongovernmental organizations (NGOs) and political parties. We have added first-person accounts by the chapter's three South African authors to the other women's voices in our narrative. While our research and discussions have informed our analysis, this chapter ultimately reflects the views of its four authors. It is not a compilation of the views of all South African women but rather the perspective of a team of diverse Black women who care very deeply about the issues we confront here and who are committed to continuing the dialogue and dealing with the challenges that we present to our readers.

The Legacy of Apartheid

South Africa's colonial history began when European traders first established a staging post for seamen at the southern tip of the country in 1652. The conquest of local Khoisan-speaking people's valuable grazing land for the post initiated a long history of dispossession as the expropriation of land from Africans became the hallmark of colonial conquest. British colonialists were enthusiastic practitioners of racism and carried out brutal military campaigns to capture and extend control over African-held lands. Though the Afrikaner nationalist state, which came to power in 1948, did not initiate racial separation or Black male disenfranchisement, the Afrikan-dominated National Party continued this expropriation and legislated the policy of rigid racial separation known as apartheid.

As a legacy of apartheid, most African women in South Africa today remain marginalized in geographic areas, some of which are still commonly referred to as

Bantustans, or homelands, which are isolated from economic, social, and other resources. This marginalization is largely a result of the impact of influx control legislation, which, through pass laws targeted specifically at Africans, legally enforced the breakup of African families by specifying that people qualify for permission to remain in urban areas on an individual basis, not as a family member.[5] Recent data show that, while 95 percent of Asian women and 81 percent of coloured women reside in urban areas, only 32 percent of African women reside in urban areas; 9.6 million African women live in rural areas, making up over 90 percent of all women there. There are more African female pensioners in rural areas than any other sector of the population and more African children in rural than in urban areas, meaning that the burden of raising children and retaining family links falls squarely on the shoulders of rural women.[6] In most poor African families, women de facto maintain an extended matriarchal family from which Black males are isolated, a situation exacerbated through male out-migration and teenage pregnancy.[7]

Given the history of neglect in the rural areas of the country, especially the Bantustans, African women's access to resources such as clean running water, health services, schools, and jobs is limited. The sight of African women carrying loads of firewood or water on their heads as they walk long distances to their homes is common. It was estimated in 1989 that 80 percent of all African households did not have access to electricity; enormous amounts of physical energy and household financial resources are spent obtaining water. In the Transkei, for example, the average household spent three hours every day fetching and carrying water. In rural KwaZulu, where three out of five women over the age of thirty suffer from a severe, crippling form of arthritis, 60 percent of households spent one hour per day collecting water. For those too disabled to collect it, water cost twenty-eight times more than it did for urban families.[8]

The stresses on family life resulting from migrant labor, forced removals, influx control, and poverty have taken their toll on the health of Black women. Women have only limited access to health facilities, which are completely inadequate in Black areas. In addition, state violence against women has historically been particularly sinister in the area of reproduction. The old South African state emphasized the distribution of often unsafe methods of birth control, particularly among African and coloured women, while at the same time neglecting to stem the high incidence of cervical cancer, especially among African women.[9] Furthermore, abortion is still illegal in South Africa, except under very restricted conditions, such as statutory rape or narrowly defined medical circumstances. Wealthier women have been able to afford the cost of obtaining safe abortions abroad, but many impoverished women have had recourse only to unhygienic, unskilled abortionists.[10]

Even while Black women have been victims of structural racial and economic oppression, they, like all women, have been victims of rape and battery, most cases of which go unreported.[11] South African law as well as customary law protects men's right to beat their spouses, and the police are ill-equipped and reluctant to deal with rape and battery, preferring to define the latter as a private family affair. Women's economic dependence on their male partners continues to prevent them from taking legal action in cases of battery and marital rape. In addition, decades of poor education for Black youth have resulted in the denigration of a culture of learning and contributed to the development of a strong, urban, Black youth sub-culture in which male chauvinism and immediate material gratification are emphasized and in which women are sexually objectified.

Approximately 52 percent of African women and 65 percent of all rural women remain illiterate. The illiteracy level for coloured women is estimated to be 32 percent, compared with 13 percent for Asian women and 0.6 percent for white women. Women's multiple contributions to the economy continue to be ignored, especially those of Black working-class women. Most women still work at home as unpaid invisible workers or as low-paid wage earners. The vast majority of domestic workers are African women (86.3 percent), followed by coloured women (9.4 percent). Fewer Black women than men are formally employed; most semi-professional Black women still work in such traditional occupations as nursing, teaching, social work, or clerical work. The South African economy is under-pinned by the labor of large marginalized sectors of women domestic workers and farm laborers, who are the least unionized workers and thus do not enjoy the benefits given to unionized workers and have to subsist on meager wages.

Women's Resistance

Women in South Africa have always been involved in the struggle for national liberation. The organized resistance of Black women in the twentieth century dates back to the 1908 protests of African women in East London against high rents and threats of arrest.[12] This short-lived, local resistance was followed by a broader-based and more sophisticated campaign in 1912 and 1913 against the pass laws that required African and coloured women to carry passes and purchase permits to move outside designated Black areas. While the women's antipass campaign used the tactics of the newly formed South African Natives National Congress (SANNC),[13] including petitions to the Ministry for Native Affairs, the campaign also ventured into mass actions, such as refusal to carry passes and attempts to block arrest of its members. Black women eventually formed their own autonomous organization, the Native and Coloured Women's Association, to fund-raise and build support for jailed women activists. The women's antipass campaign was suspended at the outbreak of World War I, as was the SANNC's.[14]

A national antipass campaign was reactivated in the 1950s when the white state decided to implement influx control legislation fully by extending pass laws to African women and to their children and other dependents. Despite the discourage-

The Federation of South African Women (FEDSAW) actively resisted apartheid until the banning of its leaders forced the organization to cease functioning. FEDSAW was revived in 1987 during this meeting in Johannesburg.

ment of male comrades, the ANCWL and the Federation of South African Women (FEDSAW) led this campaign, utilizing mass action techniques, including the historic march of twenty thousand women on the Union Building in Pretoria to present their demands. This is an extraordinary number considering the lack of transportation infrastructure, the repression of the state, and the resistance women faced at home.[15] FEDSAW's leaders were banned, forcing the organization to cease functioning; the ANCWL, as a part of the ANC, was banned in 1960 along with other opposition parties. National protest activities came to a halt until the Black Consciousness Movement, which viewed both race and class as fundamental, began to spread in the 1970s.

Although many adult women continued to play the traditional role of supplying material and psychological support to a predominantly male leadership, women did help shape the ideologies of the Black Consciousness Movement, which was founded by a group of university students and focused on Black self-reliance and pride. By their very presence women challenged unequal gender relations in the organization. However, the immediacy of the state's attack on Black people and the constant bannings and detention of Black Consciousness activists meant that the debate over issues of gender and women's oppressions could not be sustained in any meaningful way. As Asha Moodley remembers, "When I look back, I think the concept of gender was always on the periphery of one's consciousness—inchoate and ephemeral. To put it bluntly, no one was making any audible noises around gender issues—if they were, they must have been whispering."

In an attempt to address Black women's unique experience of oppression, the Black Women's Federation was formed in 1975. The organization was weakened, however, when its leaders were detained, thus reaffirming Black women's understanding that the white state was at this point their primary enemy. Asha Moodley remembers these events as follows:

> Whatever we read supported the race and class aspects of our struggle. Internationally it appeared that all Black people (people in the Third World) were primarily engaged in this kind of liberation struggle. News of feminist struggles in Western countries that filtered through sounded alien—burning one's bra to declare one's liberation as a woman did not connect psychically as did the act of a Buddhist monk who made a human pyre of himself to protest the American occupation of Vietnam. And perhaps this was the point—we were a people under siege. As women we identified with this—the national liberation struggle was our struggle. In this context we accepted Black Consciousness—"Black man" we interpreted as inclusive of Black women, Black youth, everyone who comprised the Black community.
>
> In short, the circumstances of the time imposed a need for solidarity within the ranks of Black people—firstly to inspire, build, and consolidate resistance. A few years later, when cadres and organizations were systematically detained and banned, the priority was to regroup and rebuild—this was an ongoing process as the government systematically sought to destroy the movement. It was not a scenario which encouraged the confronting of gender issues, nor did they appear anyway as the major issues of the time within the country.
>
> How was this sort of confrontation going to take place anyway, with people in prison or banned and removed to remote corners of the country—or even dead? Survival dictated that we viewed gender contradictions as nonantagonistic ones, which meant that their existence was acknowledged but for the time being would not be taken to issue.

However, having taken on co-responsibility for waging the political struggle, for sustaining and conserving it when it was really embattled, there was no way women would continue their silence ... their suspension of the gender struggle. When they said then that the liberation of women was "inextricably linked" with the national liberation of the country, they did not mean that political liberation meant overall freedom for women. It was to imply a warning that at some time in the future, when they deemed it fit to do so, there would be also be a direct confrontation with patriarchy. Within organizations, within whatever new political dispensation came into being, within society as a whole.

The 1980s saw renewed attempts to establish women's organizations that would resist the state at the grassroots level by addressing local concerns and engaging in local struggles. The groups, many of which affiliated to the United Democratic Front (UDF),[16] included the Federation of Transvaal Women, which consisted mainly of urban women in the Transvaal province; the United Women's Congress (UWC) in the Western Cape; organized women workers in the trade union movement; Rape Crisis; and the Natal Organization of Women (NOW). Nozizwe Madlala was involved in NOW from its inception in the early 1980s:

The character of our organization was largely Black working class, and our approach was to mobilize and organize a strong united front in the struggle against apartheid. The women in our organization determined what issues we took up. The fact that we had our own source of funds and resources allowed us this kind of flexibility.

The issues we took up were largely around state repression, high rents, lack of housing, poor education and health facilities, and the high cost of living. We organized marches and demonstrations against local authorities, and we sent petitions to the central government. Participation in these struggles served to raise political awareness among our members. It also showed our male comrades that women had the capacity to organize and to lead.

As the level of political awareness grew, we began to demand that issues of the specific oppression of women be integrated into the national agenda. We debated the question of which issues our organization should prioritize. As we did so, however, we were conscious of the specific context in which women experienced oppression in South Africa, where gender, race, and class are intertwined. It was this specific context which influenced our decision to adopt an approach that sought to integrate gender issues into those of national oppression and class exploitation.

To popularize this approach within the national liberation movement, we used various methods. At our meetings and in our publications we popularized slogans like "Women's issues are people's issues" and "The nation is not free if women are not free." At the practical level we demanded that meeting times and venues be changed to suit women and that child care be provided at meetings so that women could participate. We demanded that meetings be run in a participatory way in order to allow greater participation by women.

We began to mobilize the support of women in other organizations, such as the trade unions and the churches. Through joint action our position as women was strengthened and our demands gained wider support. This laid the foundation for the broader alliance of women, known as the Women's National Coalition, which came into being during the period of constitutional negotiations.

Often women's organizations had to address wider political issues, such as the implications of state policy for Black women, as well as the issues of sexism in interpersonal relations with lovers and political comrades. As Elaine Salo remembers, in a branch of the UWC

> there was constant tension between spending time on gender consciousness raising, such as talking about our experiences in relationships with men [or about] sexual assaults against women, and meeting the needs of national struggles, such as the occupation of white beaches or the protest against detentions.
>
> At the same time we were expected to participate in broader campaigns. These campaigns included marches during the Defiance Campaign in 1989, providing safehouses for men and women who were on the run from the police, or putting up posters in the dead of night to protest against the detentions. At one time the National Association for Democratic Lawyers requested us to provide the tea and snacks at a national conference on media and the state. We discussed the obvious sexism contained in this request. Some women felt that we should accede to the request in the interest of solidarity. A few of us refused to participate in this activity because we regarded it as a reinforcement of the stereotypes of women as providers. There were times when struggles against sexism and racism coincided.
>
> During the Defiance Campaign in 1989, seventy of us were arrested in central Cape Town during a women's march against capital punishment. The march was stopped by white policewomen and men. However, we were unceremoniously hauled into the back of police vans by burly white policemen. I remember thinking, "Don't go quietly—scream, shout, challenge!!" At the Caledon Street prison where we were held, the men taunted us while they took fingerprints and photographs, telling us to "Call upon our savior Mandela to free us." They attempted to intimidate the old Black women who appeared fearful. Some bolder women crowded around the older women and challenged the policemen in turn. I think that these men were a bit flummoxed by women who danced and sang in prison and who dared to challenge the very authority of the South African police. We had to cast aside our fears of the dreaded police in order to cope with our situation, even though individually we were very scared indeed.

The 1980s also saw the transformation of some predominantly white feminist groups that had previously remained outside of the national liberation struggles. The group Rape Crisis, initiated in 1979 by survivors of rape, at first confined its energies to addressing the needs of rape victims. Its perspective was broadened, however, when members began to understand the political violence against Black women that often resulted in the rape or sexual assault of female detainees by state police. This predominantly white, self-identified feminist group had to learn that the white state, not the Black male or the family unit, was for many Black women the primary patriarchal enemy. Understanding this formed the basis for the decision to join the UDF, even though that decision caused some of Rape Crisis's members to resign. That Rape Crisis has survived and expanded its base among Black women is testimony to the fact that it transformed its feminism.

The weakening of the apartheid state and, to some extent, the powerful white patriarchy during the late 1980s and early 1990s has redefined the terrain of struggles against oppression in South Africa. It has also allowed tensions in the Black community that had to remain obscure for fear of exploitation by the white government to become visible. It is in this context that the Rural Women's Movement has begun to challenge the authority of traditional leaders and to debate on national television with the Council of Traditional Leaders of South Africa, the organization of tribal authorities, and that urban-based skilled Black women can now be seen publicly demanding their right to equality alongside white women without feeling that they are betraying the national liberation struggle. Black women all over are beginning to articulate their own distinct goals and interests so as to introduce issues of gender and racial equity into both public discourse and the political bodies that will affect their lives.

South African Feminisms

Until recently self-identified feminist writings and debates in South Africa drew mostly on Western-centered feminist thought to analyze the situation of a largely Third World female population in this country. The theoretical position that women's primary struggle is against patriarchy, or against a capitalist patriarchy, has been advanced mainly by well-educated white women and a few Black women. Though Western feminist analysis seeks to conceptualize women's oppression in a South African context and to make gender visible in South African social theory, such analysis has served to silence many Black women and alienate them from mainstream feminist discourse. According to Lewis and Hendricks, this view's "prescriptive, Western-centric, middle-class, and white orientation drove many South African women activists ... to nationalist discourses and uneasiness with the 'feminist' label."[17] Throughout the 1970s and 1980s, therefore, many Black women dismissed the Western-based feminism they heard and read about. For example, in 1987 Nora Chase, a Black Namibian activist, rejected feminism because "the minute you hear about feminism one immediately puts it in the connotation of the European and North American women's struggles. These are women from societies which have long been independent—people who ... support the governments that ... support our oppression. I could never feel solidarity with that. ... I think there will be a different kind of feminism coming out of Africa."[18]

Patriarchy, in South Africa and everywhere else, is differentiated; power is not equally shared among men. The related notions of public and private spheres cannot, however, be simply transplanted to South Africa from European and North

Young people react with joy on hearing the outcome of the March 18, 1992, referendum that started the unraveling of apartheid.

American discourses. In fact, Black South African women have often felt compelled to confine their disputes with Black men to a sphere knowable only to their specific communities. This has been a strategic choice made in the face of opposition from a seemingly invincible white nationalist party-state that was quick to exploit any sign of division in order to subjugate Black people even further.

Theorizing a single patriarchy without regard to the multiplicity of experiences created by race, class privilege, and oppression has effectively caused feminist discourse to marginalize Black women's resistance. It is not useful to characterize women who organize a bus boycott, mount rent strikes, or march against pass laws as lacking a feminist consciousness while at the same time considering the women who establish a group such as Rape Crisis, for example, to be sufficiently feminist. We argue that Black women fighting for national liberation, living wages, or clean, accessible water engage multiple systems of domination simultaneously. As the experience of the women who resisted the pass laws in 1912 and 1913 shows, African and coloured women had to assert themselves not only against the British colonial government but also against patriarchal assumptions and structures within their own communities. The key challenge for South African women throughout this century has been to negotiate successfully how and when these contradictions are confronted.

Black women have long been aware of gender inequities and have not lacked a feminist consciousness in the past. On the other hand, strategic decisions had to be made about how and when they could afford to make gender issues public given the real threat of a genocidal state to their very lives.[19] This is not to say that no struggles have been waged between Black men and women. In the Qwa Qwa Bantustan in the 1980s, for example, when unemployed male migrants who had returned from urban areas protested against the employment of women at a small local factory, the women resisted this effort to deny them their livelihood and won their battle for employment. Though they were fully aware of the role of the apartheid state in limiting the options for Black men, the Qwa Qwa women chose to fight for their own interests.[20]

South African Black women understand that they need to make strategic alliances, recognizing that these alliances may be temporary and limited to particular common interests rather than built on assumed, ongoing sisterhood. Further, these interests are fluid, and struggle over their validity across class or race lines will help deepen our solidarity and strengthen our position. As bell hooks writes, "Radical commitment to political struggle carries with it the willingness to accept responsibility for using conflict constructively, as a way to enhance and enrich our understanding of one another, as a guide directing and shaping the parameters of our political solidarity."[21] To cite one example, this became clear during the Women's National Coalition negotiations over the rights that should be included in the Women's Charter for Effective Equality. One participant took issue with the inclusion of the right to accessible clean water, maintaining this was not a "women's issue." Rural women, however, argued that this was a critical women's issue because water for cooking and cleaning was the responsibility of women in rural households. In effect, the rural women did not allow their class and gender to be separated. The demand for clean, accessible water remained in the charter.

The notion that national liberation means only the abolishment of institutions that oppress people simply on the basis of race effectively marginalizes those for whom race exclusion intersects with class, gender, and regional background, among other factors. As Kimberle Crenshaw argues, "Adoption of a single-issue framework for discrimination not only marginalizes Black women within the very movements that claim them as part of their constituency but it also makes the illusive goal of ending racism and patriarchy even more difficult to attain."[22] Positing the goal and activities toward the liberation of an entire people as feminist allows the experiences of Black women who are part of whole groups of oppressed people to be central to the discourse of struggle. If the African to be liberated is presumed to be male, then reconstruction will probably not benefit African women equally. The work of women within the battle for national liberation, who emphasized the struggle against the state even while they negotiated the struggle with patriarchy within their own organizations, has laid the basis for the intensified battle over, and education about, gender oppression that is being waged by the new South African feminists today.

The RWM and the WNC

When we asked participants in three regional focus groups what they considered to be the most important struggle from which to draw lessons and discuss the achievement of South Africa's women's movements, the Women's National Coalition emerged by consensus. However, many participants also highlighted the achievements of the Rural Women's Movement. In this section, our discussion of the RWM demonstrates how this organization centers on the interests of poor African women in its battles with both the state and traditional tribal structures. We then describe the WNC and its efforts to bring race and gender interests together in a coalition composed of many conflicting groupings.

The history of the Rural Women's Movement is rooted in the resistance of Black communities to policies of forced removals and loss of their South African citizenship through incorporation into the Bantustans. These policies were the hallmarks of successive apartheid regimes and had major effects on the lives of rural women: Men were often away for eleven consecutive months providing labor for South African industry, and women were dependent on transfer payments from their husbands as the primary source of income. As government repression increased and detentions became more and more commonplace, this source of income was interrupted; eventually nearly every rural family was affected.

Rural women's already difficult lives were exacerbated in the early 1980s by the brutality and repressive tactics, including harsh interrogation and beating, of the police and vigilante groups hunting their husbands or activist children. Young people often belonged to student organizations; these youths served as an important source of information for women living in isolated areas, and they became particular targets of the homeland authorities. In desperation, rural communities sought the assistance of the Transvaal Rural Action Committee (TRAC), an NGO that had evolved from the women's organization Black Sash. The Rural Women's Movement grew out of the work initiated by TRAC.

Noting the exclusion of rural women from the traditional community decision-making processes (*pitsos*) and forums (*kgotlas*), TRAC appointed Lydia Kompe, who had spent a good deal of her life in the rural Transvaal, to work with rural women, encouraging them to speak of and recognize the common experiences they shared. It did not take long for the women to agree, for example, that if in the absence of their husbands they passively accepted eviction notices from government officials, then they were accomplices to their own removal.

TRAC's work with local communities made increasingly clear the extent to which women's concerns were intertwined with community issues such as poor water supply and inadequate health services, education, and child care. Addressing these concerns challenged women's resolve, forcing them to face squarely the traditional and cultural sanctions that continued to restrict their full participation in decisions affecting their lives. For example, denied land for gardening, women in the northern Transvaal observed the following about the power of the chiefs:

> Women shouldn't have to go through members of the royal family to get access to the chief because these people do not understand women's problems. Women want to be able to send their own representatives to speak directly to the *kgotla*. ... Recognised women's committees should be part of the land distribution mechanism. Currently, men are in charge of land distribution and women are discriminated against. Women must therefore be part of the *kgotla*.[23]

While women remained largely dependent in their relationships with men, they seemed to gain a new measure of confidence. The unbanning, combined with outreach by political parties through their women's desks, NGOs, and service organizations, provided the space for women in rural areas to voice concern over their inability to influence events and contribute to the financial well-being of their families. The RWM helped cast issues in a new light and was eventually able to broker direct representation on the *kgotlas*, a major breakthrough for rural women. Women also began to engage in local income-generating activities, which helped fill the void left by the reduction in transfer payments.

Stronger links were forged between rural women and the more organized urban women's groups. Both groups discovered, for example, that they suffered from the limited response on the part of the authorities to violence against women, particularly domestic violence. While gaining political independence and establishing a legitimate government remained their first priority, women began to ask a new series of questions that lay within the domain of the relationship between African men and women: Why should I be treated as a minor in marriage? Why does equity built over the years with my husband flow to my son rather than to me? What is the meaning and intent of *lobola* (bride-price) prior to marriage—am I my husband's property? Should a man have more than one wife?

These questions are sensitive and complex, and women themselves have not yet reached consensus on them. The struggle to challenge traditional male authority is ongoing and must, of course, affect the domestic lives of rural women. New technologies and improved communications are likely to reduce the isolation of rural areas and provide a greater variety of role models and life choices for women there, some of whom have begun openly on television and in the other mass media to challenge polygamy and the patriarchal structure of the chiefs. At the same time, however, other women articulate the need to maintain a delicate balance within relationships as men and women adapt to new expectations and circumstances. These women feel the need to have a better understanding of the issues and the impact of change upon their lives. While sensitive to these concerns, the RWM believes that the best way to achieve change is through building the leadership skills of women and securing women's full participation both in the *kgotlas* and as informed voters and candidates in provincial and parliamentary elections.

Certainly the achievements of the RWM to date confound the stereotype of rural women as unable to speak for themselves, as has been demonstrated clearly by their actions within the Women's National Coalition.

Key leadership within the African National Congress's Women's Section, which became the Women's League in 1990, had begun to set the stage for a national women's consortium in the late 1980s by calling for a reinstatement of the Federation of South African Women and by reestablishing the Women's Alliance. Neither of these groups actually enjoyed national participation, however. While FEDSAW had an explicitly political agenda, its support was primarily among charterist women. The membership of the Women's Alliance was broader, but the group limited itself to activities such as cultural celebrations that did not directly confront the apartheid regime.

In 1990 ANC women began calling for the formation of a national women's organization that would exercise power not only by challenging the apartheid regime's treatment of women but also by placing gender issues on the agenda of all political parties. In summing up the ANC Women's Section and the Dutch antiapartheid movement's Malibongwe Conference in January 1990, Mala Singh identifies three major tasks key to advancing women's liberation, one of which was "the formation of a strong national women's organization which could play a key role in the struggle towards a democratic non-sexist society."[24]

This view and the subsequent formation of the Women's National Coalition marked a major shift in many Black women's conceptualization of gender and national oppression. As we have already noted, many, perhaps the vast majority, of Black women in the liberation movements had rejected the feminism they had been exposed to, dismissing it as the "indulgence of bored rich white Americans."[25] They were also concerned that raising issues of gender oppression would dilute and distract the urgent discourse of national liberation. As activist Nora Chase remembers, "If we become feminists we are going to divorce ourselves from the liberation struggle."[26]

Frene Ginwala, the first convener of the WNC, argued the limitations of the ANCWL in a roundtable discussion on the May 1990 ANC Statement on the Emancipation of Women in South Africa. Ginwala pointed out that, while the league was an autonomous organization under the umbrella of the ANC,

> the ANC's overall priority is national liberation. ... But we have progressed by moving to integrate into it an understanding of gender oppression and a commitment to the emancipation of women. But being realistic we have got to accept that when it comes to the choice either/or, the decision is more than likely to fall towards national liberation. ... Therefore while the League has a particular role to play, we still need a national women's organization. ... Unless we empower women organizationally, we can't liberate ourselves.[27]

*More than ten thousand people met in Durban in August 1990 to relaunch the African Na-
tional Congress (ANC) Women's League.*

Another ANC discussant at the roundtable, Lulu Gwagwa, argued that a women's
organization "can agitate and push gender issues" and demand accountability
from decisionmakers, male or female. "This means the women's organization
must not only mobilize women for the national struggle but must also be concerned with gender oppression and gender struggle."[28]

While the need for women to struggle around gender both inside and outside
the ANC inheres in both women's views, Ginwala called for an organization distinct from the league, whereas Gwagwa argued, "But if you have a strong women's
organization, like the ANC Women's League for example, you can agitate and
push gender issues and demand accountability from decision makers." Ginwala
saw a need for women to build a power base both inside the ANC and outside the
organization in order to "force the decisions in our favor when it comes to the ei-
ther/or situation, in a budget debate or anything else." Her vision of a national
women's organization is broad enough to include "all women, and women's organizations which do not necessarily subscribe to particular ANC positions."[29]

Ginwala's call for a national independent women's organization whose views
could conceivably be different than those of the ANC was indeed breaking new
ground. As a member of the ANCWL Internal Leadership group in 1990, she was
deeply committed to building the league's strength. Ultimately, however, she saw

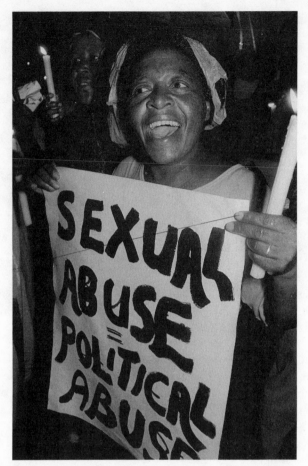

*Women in Johannesburg mark International Women's Day,
March 8, 1991, with a march to protest crime and violence
against women. This poster reflects the women's movements'
commitment to linking women's concerns with broader political issues.*

the empowerment of women both inside and outside the league as necessitating a
separate organization: "I mean politics is about power and women's liberation is
about power. Unless we empower women organizationally, we can't liberate ourselves."[30] Ginwala is clearly a new South African feminist.

Not all Black women activists in the liberation movements agree with Ginwala's
view. For example, Patricia De Lille, chief representative for the PAC at the Convention for a Democratic South Africa (CODESA) and current member of Parlia-

As apartheid crumbles and the transition to majority rule be-
comes inevitable, women of all races and classes from a wide
range of organizations meet at the University of Witwaters-
rand in 1992 to develop a women's agenda. Despite inherent
tensions and differences, women articulate common interests
put forward by the Women's National Coalition.

ment (MP), argues that "I am an African before I am a woman. ... This is the way that all African women should see themselves. Liberal feminists say women face a triple oppression, on the basis of race, gender, and class. This is a move away from the main problem."[31] Michele Miller of the South African Women's Political Party, a Western Cape regional party, claims that "women have to define who and what they are. They must first unite as women and then unite with men."[32] Clearly for Miller the main problem is gender, and the first basis of unity is woman-ness, whereas De Lille's bottom line is race. Nonetheless, the notion of a single core oppression to which all others add inheres in both views. And, interestingly, both groups have affiliated to the WNC, recognizing as all its affiliates do the clear need for women to come together to present their concerns or risk invisibility in the new constitution.

Launched as a loose coalition in April 1992 with the original aim of being an instrument to organize a national participatory campaign that would compile

Women join together in a Johannesburg march for women's equality in September 1993.

women's opinions and concerns into a women's charter, the WNC soon had to institutionalize itself by acquiring staff, securing funding, creating leadership bodies, and identifying decisionmaking processes. The coalition currently has eighty-one organizational affiliates and thirteen regional alliances of women's organizations. Representing a cross-section of South Africa's women's movements unique in the country's history, the WNC now includes the women's caucuses or gender desks of all the major political parties. This is extraordinary because during the liberation struggle antagonisms among these parties had reached the point of sustained armed conflict between the ANC and the Inkatha Freedom Party, while sporadic skirmishes erupted between the PAC's armed wing and the National Party's Security Forces. Other major political parties represented include the Azanian People's Organization, which neither participated in other important alliances (such as CODESA and the Transitional Executive Council [TEC]) nor contested the April 1994 elections, and the Democratic Party, which was the opposition party in the Afrikaner-dominated Parliament. In addition to these political parties, groups as diverse as the Rural Women's Movement and the Executive Women's Club, the Methodist Women's Manyanos and the Union of Jewish Women, the South African Domestic Workers Union and the South African Association of University Women, are affiliated to the WNC.

This extraordinary convergence of women across geographical, racial, class, religious, and political lines probably could have occurred only during the period of negotiation (1990–1994) when the unbanning of liberation organizations, the subsequent establishment of forums such as the Convention for a Democratic South Africa (CODESA I and II), and the emergence of issue-specific bodies such as the economic forum, the housing forum, and the education forum all occurred. The negotiation of constitutional guidelines, the cessation of armed struggle, and the emergence of principles of representation among groups previously identified as absolute enemies or betrayers of the liberation struggle supplied a model and a justification for the formation of a forum through which women who harbored deep animosities could also identify common concerns. In creating the WNC, all of the major women's organizations allowed something larger and more representative to command an authority that none of them could achieve alone, making the WNC something that they could not avoid affiliating to as well as something that could not be controlled by any one organization.

The new South African feminists charted new territory in the WNC as they attempted to exercise power as a distinct constituency without relinquishing their active loyalty to the national liberation struggle through their political parties. After noting that none of the parties had female representation at the early stages of the talks, for example, women in the ANC had put forth a proposal that at least one delegate to CODESA be a woman. The proposal became a rallying cry and subject of public debate and protest when the WNC endorsed the proposal and sought to use its position to "put forward the women's point of view." That the women won their point and that a public discourse concerning a nonsexist as well as a nonracist South Africa was generated illustrate the WNC's potential to exercise a power greater than the sum of its individual affiliates.

The public image of the WNC as the voice of women and its continued actions reinforced its prime position and unique authority. For example, the WNC and its affiliates lobbied successfully for the establishment of a subcouncil on the status of women, which, along with the other subcouncils on foreign affairs, finance, and defense, constituted the Transitional Executive Authority. The subcouncil's task was to provide strategies on leveling the field for women in the electoral process, both as voters and candidates. No other constituency had achieved such recognition during the negotiation process, and no single women's organization had been able to achieve this kind of legitimacy for women's issues on its own. Ironically, it is this strength of the WNC that has been a major factor in fueling the constant tensions and threatened resignations that continue to beset the coalition.

The process of institutionalization has been contentious as the WNC has moved from being a coalition formed for research purposes to a proactive political organization. Anxious not to be left out of critical CODESA decisions simply because it had not yet finished its lengthy research process, the WNC became both a political player and powerful institution. The issue of power and voice within the coalition has remained a question that affiliates and WNC officeholders must continually reassess. Are their individual and organizational interests served by this particular coalition? The WNC's legitimacy and power are derived from eighty-one member organizations; if many of these organizations resigned, the coalition's claim to broad representation would be sharply undermined. However, if one organization resigned and the coalition continued, that single organization might lose the benefits of being involved in what is arguably the most important platform for constructing and advocating women's interests in the country and might also risk becoming marginalized.

These issues of control and power within the organization have challenged the WNC's administration as well as its mechanisms for decisionmaking with its affiliates. Problems appeared early on and continue to challenge the WNC's relations with its affiliates. For example, the Congress of South African Trade Unions (COSATU) pulled out of the coalition because a provisional constitution was adopted without consultation and because as a federation itself, COSATU could not affiliate with another federation. The problem was solved by adding a special constitutional clause that allowed for COSATU's participation without affiliation. Only days before the conference to adopt the Women's Charter in February 1994, the National Party pulled out of the coalition, charging that it was dominated by the ANC. Interestingly, interviews at regional levels indicated that ANC-leaning women felt the coalition was dominated by the National Party in particular and white middle-class women in general.

There has been no formal voting within the coalition because the basis upon which affiliates would vote could not be agreed upon. Of the eighty-one member organizations, some clearly have larger memberships than others. Some have demonstrated a large mass base through demonstrations and protests. Still others have access to resources and long histories in South Africa. COSATU's female membership exceeds a quarter of a million, mainly Black women, clearly larger constituencies than the Union of Jewish Women or the Women's Legal Status Committee. In the same fashion the ANC's female membership dramatically outnumbers the Democratic Party's female membership. More important still, although African women outnumber every other single racial classification, this is not reflected within the coalition because of the large number of white women's affiliates. One vote per organization could magnify the voice of white women. The solution thus far has been operation on the basis of broad consensus, which in practice means a clear majority perspective emerges in a given discussion.[33]

With all the problems membership in the WNC entails, the clear commitment to nonracialism it inherited from the ANC and its emphasis on reconciliation and inclusivity have been important forces in sustaining the coalition. Thus far, the unlikeliest of allies have remained affiliated. The RWM, whose inclusion is key to the WNC's claim of broad representation, has successfully used the coalition to fight a key CODESA battle. As late as October 1993 traditional leaders, including chiefs and other tribal authorities, sought to subordinate the Bill of Rights to customary law, aspects of which explicitly discriminate against African women. The RWM sharply criticized this action and, supported by the WNC, successfully countered the traditional leaders' position. By mobilizing resources and maintaining a high media profile, the WNC publicized the issue in mainstream and alternative media. In a briefing paper the WNC argued that the effect of the traditional leaders' recommendations was that two states would be established in the new South Africa: the democratic South African state and an "invisible" traditional state. "The former will be subject to the Constitution and the Bill of Rights, and its citizens will have resort to the Bill of Rights to challenge discrimination. In the latter, rural communities (and particularly rural women) will be isolated in a traditional state with no resort to the full rights of citizenship. Like the apartheid state, we will be creating two classes of citizens."[34]

Further, the RWM had its agenda included in the draft Women's Charter for Effective Equality that the WNC produced in February 1994. For example, Article 2, Law and the Administration of Justice, calls for women to be represented and participate in the selection of all judicial candidates, including those in traditional courts, and states that "women shall have equal legal status and capacity in civil and customary law." Article 5, Development, Infrastructure, and the Environment, identifies as basic needs women's participation in development programs for adequate, accessible, and safe water and sanitation; electricity; access to land and security of tenure; and safe transport and effective communication services. While the issues under Article 2 might fit the conventional notion of women's rights, the claims made in Article 5 are relatively new to the discourse of women's liberation; they are a direct result of the new South African feminism, which has given a voice to the concerns of many formerly unheard women, including the members of the RWM.

The draft Women's Charter for Effective Equality was ultimately adopted in principle in February 1994, demonstrating both the WNC's ability to withstand walkouts and vocal disagreements and its clear recognition that the opportunity to present such a document would not be likely to come again. Fissures continue to appear within the coalition, however, raising questions as to what the basis of unity is and whether the WNC serves to marginalize an affiliate's goals or means of exercising power. After the charter was adopted, the constant balancing of forces and interests led much of the WNC's key leaders, especially those within the major political parties, to advocate the coalition's dissolution as called for by the original constitution, which limited its life to the completion of a charter. However, many of the WNC's smaller nonparty political affiliates argued for the coalition's continued existence because its efforts placed their local issues squarely in a national context and because its resources empowered women in terms of both information and access to powerful institutions and individuals. As former WNC project manager Preggs Govendar concludes:

The most important thing about the [Women's Charter] campaign is that local women owned the campaign. Experience from the campaign will only grow and grow into other experiences. We'll continue to see the fruits of this. We wanted to release the power people actually have. This is a process not easily measurable. At the level of structures, those more experienced, those more skilled at using committee structures could manipulate these to gain power. But in the long term, it's the [former] that's real power. Because once it's there, it cannot be destroyed. It's a stepping stone, a foundation.[35]

The June 1994 meeting of the WNC confirmed the desire of the affiliates as a whole to keep the coalition alive. In addition to carrying on research initiatives, the coalition will continue its mandate to "empower women and strengthen their public voice by mobilizing and reinforcing women's organisations to secure the objectives of the Charter."[36] However, the WNC now bars individuals who hold public office from taking official positions within the coalition; its new convener, Jean Ngubane, hails from the South African Council of Churches. This makes it difficult to project the WNC's future, as many of its key players, including Ginwala, who is now speaker of Parliament, have moved into government posts. Thus far in many ways the new South African feminists have successfully placed the intersection of race and gender, and to some extent class, at the center of the coalition's demands. However, many issues continue to challenge the WNC since the groups that make up the coalition continue to represent widely different economic, social, and political interests.

Claiming Our Place in the New South Africa

The new South Africa and its Government of National Unity were formally inaugurated on May 10, 1994. Looking at its composition, the *Sunday Times* observed:

> From being one of the world's most sexist governments our new Parliament, with its 106-strong contingent of women, has emerged as one of the world's most progressive. South Africa has moved from 141st place on the list of countries with women in Parliament, to seventh. ... With a jump from 2.7 percent to 26.5 percent, South African women are now better represented than their British and American counterparts.[37]

The presence of these women parliamentarians and ministers is surely due to the significant struggle waged by progressive women's movements within the national liberation struggle and, since 1990, as distinct voices articulating a separate agenda. If numbers signify progress, then the current number of women in Parliament is certainly an improvement on the past. Overall, however, the top layers of the new government remain bulwarks of male power, and women remain numerically weak at all levels of government. Only sixteen of the ninety senators are women, and in the thirty-member cabinet only two ministerial positions and

South Africa's first multiracial election in April 1994 heralded the end of apartheid and the beginning of a new era in the struggle for women's equality.

three deputy ministerial positions are held by women. While some ministries, for example, the health, agriculture, and welfare and population portfolios, are generally viewed as being conducive to the pursuit of strategic gender interests, the same optimism is not felt about others.

This unequal representation of women also extends to the provincial parliaments, where all nine provincial premiers are men. Women are still absent from effective seats of power such as the regional executive committees. Activist women have expressed their unhappiness at the number of women in all levels of government and have raised fundamental questions about representation. They are also skeptical about the ability or willingness of some of the women ministers to apply a gendered analysis and approach to the general responsibilities underlined by their positions.

It is too early to comment on delivery. Women members of Parliment have formed party caucuses to strategize ways of coping with their relatively small numbers. For example, the 84-strong women's caucus of the ANC (out of a party total of 252 seats) says it will lobby to integrate women's issues with state affairs and to ensure that "women's issues maintain visibility."[38] It is also a positive factor that a number of the women MPs are prominent women's activists who have worked together in the WNC and in the drawing up of the draft Women's Charter for Effective Equality. Their energy, experience, and vision, coupled with the con-

South Africa's new majority government includes a number of women in leadership roles. Other women activists continue to work independently on gender-related issues. Here, a counselor works with a rape victim in Johannesburg.

tributions of women who participated at CODESA and the TEC, could be effectively marshaled into a powerful lobby for meaningful gains on behalf of women at a government level. Conjecture that these groups will form their own internal network to strategize and lobby on women's issues is rife, but it is too early to judge the truth of such conjecture.

One of the options considered by women prior to the installation of the Government of National Unity was the establishment of a women's ministry, although this was sharply contested. While some women argued that such a ministry would marginalize gender analysis and absolve other ministries from their responsibility to work toward gender equity, others called for a "total package" that would include a women's ministry supported by gender desks in other ministries. This second concept was generally supported at the December 1993 conference on women's ministries sponsored by the Institute for a Democratic South Africa.[39] It is quite possible that all these options will now be considered at a government level, as many of their advocates are currently sitting in Parliament.

There are also many possibilities for change in the constitutional and legal arenas, where the foundations have been laid through the Bill of Rights to prevent discrimination against women, promote women's equality, and ensure the protection of women's rights under a new government. Brigitte Mabandla, senior legal researcher and gender project coordinator at the Community Law Centre, University of the Western Cape, surmises that "the lobby and advocacy for women's human rights has been successful. The interim constitution substantially promotes equality between women and men."[40] Cathy Albertyn of the Gender Research Project at the Centre for Applied Legal Studies concurs with Mabandla but warns that women will still have to "engage in political and legal struggle to give meaning to the constitution in ways that will further their interests and rights."[41]

Albertyn's statement points to the crossroads where South African women currently find themselves. A vast dichotomy still exists between the possibilities for women's achievements and the reality of the majority of women's lives. Representation by women at the parliamentary level and considerable constitutional and legal advances have been attained at a certain cost. They represent in very large measure a top-down approach, and the gains in these areas have been made mainly by middle-class women, both Black and white, with better access to education and other resources. While women's organizations have played an important role in putting women's issues on the national agenda, the majority of women in South Africa, both Black and white, remain unorganized. They still suffer from the secondary status imposed on women in the community and at home through a patriarchal ideology expressed through religion, culture, customary law, and tradition.

If the gains women have made at the constitutional, legal, and parliamentary levels are to be meaningful, the legacy of gender, race, and class exploitation and oppression handed down mainly to Black women, particularly Black working-class and rural women, will have to be aggressively addressed by both the government and society as a whole. Major change must be made in the material conditions of the oppressed majority; those who have been denied access to education, decent homes, health facilities, and jobs must have their needs addressed immediately.

The setting up of information, education, and support networks that will ensure communication and a sense of solidarity among women is critical. This will be even more important as African women's conflicts with male-dominated structures become more apparent.[42] The fundamental challenge today is to ensure that the structures now in place avoid further entrenching a race and class hierarchy among women even while they challenge the domination of men.[43]

A recent report identified a "startling consensus for skills building as the most immediate priority" among national women's organizations. Ellen Kornegay, executive director of the Women's Development Foundation, cited "the need to transfer knowledge and information and nurturing of the ability to analyze one's position so that Black women can speak, write and think for themselves." Literacy for women was identified as a "pressing concern" by COSATU, while "the development of leadership skills among women" was expressed as a key objective by the Young Women's Christian Association (world affiliated) and the South African Council of Churches. Even more encouraging was the vision of the Zamani Soweto Sisters (a self-help community-based organization), who wish to include bricklaying and car maintenance as part of a training program for women geared to make women look beyond the traditional realms of women's work.[44]

In an article entitled "The Need for Gender Bias," Jennifer Shreiner emphasizes the necessity for women to have access to resources and skills building. She states that "the real and substantial emancipation of women is dependent on a reconstruction and development program which is based on empowerment, social emancipation and fundamental national democratic transformation."[45] The reconstructing of gender relations is integral to the process of obtaining full emancipation for women. The provision of child care facilities, the sharing of housework, a commitment to dealing with rape and domestic violence, and access to financial, health, and educational facilities are only examples of some of the necessary practical solutions that will free women to participate more fully in the policies of the new state.

The new government's Reconstruction and Development Programme holds out the promise to achieve all this. However, any change will be significant only to the extent that it has a positive impact on, for example, the situation of a woman who walks several kilometers a day to collect fuel and water or the situation of a woman who faces violence from her partner and her community. To be able to deliver on its promises, the new government must heed the voices of women's movements. And in order to lead effectively, those movements must in turn listen to the most oppressed women.

As this chapter's discussion on the WNC demonstrates, forging unity that takes into account differential access to power and various kinds of power will remain an ongoing and challenging process as women continually redefine their interests. As Mmatshilo Motsei from the Alexandra Women Abuse program points out, "You don't give someone power. They must claim it for themselves." Motsei locates power sharing and transformation in a dialogue between those with "expertise or resources" and those whose knowledge is marginalized. "It's a two-way process. We're reminding each other of our power. I come back from a workshop of rural women on domestic abuse empowered by them."[46]

South African women's movements have scored some important victories over the four years between the unbanning and the installation of the first democratically elected government in the nation's history. This chapter has argued that these gains were made possible by of the fluidity and dynamism of the period and the emergence of a new South African feminism that consistently intersected race and class with gender. The space afforded by national liberation negotiations enabled Black women to build constituencies and organizations that centered their interests, such as the Rural Women's Movement; it also afforded women the opportunity to found the Women's National Coalition, thus creating a higher profile than ever before for women's interests. Whereas previously most Black women, particularly those active in national liberation movements, had spurned the ideas of the feminisms to which they were exposed and distrusted alliances built on gender interests, some now accepted the potential power they could exercise as Black women by making gender-based alliances.

At their best, the dialogues women hold with each other disrupt authority and redefine all the issues. This means that access to running water and the electrification of rural areas become women's issues and that appropriate responses to domestic violence and rape become integral parts of the campaign to reconstruct the nation. The current convergence of progressive women's movements, orchestrated by the new South African feminists and with the interests of Black women at its center, clearly holds the possibility of refashioning the priorities of the struggles for national liberation and reconstruction in South Africa.

NOTES

1. Under apartheid all of the Black opposition parties in South Africa and most of their leadership were banned. Beginning in 1960, banned organizations were prevented from operating and in effect became illegal. A banned person could not attend public meetings or be mentioned or quoted in publications. Further, he or she could not be in the company of more than one person or of any other banned individuals. Anyone who was thought to be furthering the aims of a banned organization could be prosecuted and, if found guilty, imprisoned.

2. The word *Black* was introduced by the Black Consciousness Movement in 1968 as a term that included all Africans, coloureds, and Asians. However, the South African government lowercased the word and perverted its meaning to include only Africans. Today the borders of the term are shifting, but in this chapter we capitalize it and use it once again as an all-inclusive term.

3. Although the apartheid state was male dominated, white women on the whole supported it—the notable exception being the organization Black Sash.

4. Chandra Mohanty, ed., *Third World Women and Feminism* (Bloomington: Indiana University Press, 1991), p. 12.

5. *Bantustans* were desolate, impoverished regions where the majority of Africans were confined by a constellation of acts, passed between 1920 and 1980, that prevented Africans from owning land in an area demarcated as White South Africa. *Influx control* comprised

policies that rigidly controlled Africans' access to white urban areas; violation was met with harsh fines or imprisonment. *Pass laws* required all Africans and coloureds to carry passes, or identification cards, outlining their legal status and permission to be in particular areas.

6. Caroline White et al., eds., *Status of South African Women: A Source Book in Tables and Graphs, the Reason for Change* (Marshall Town: ANC Women's League, 1993).

7. This family form also exists among poor urban coloured communities, although for different social reasons.

8. Francis Wilson and Mamphela Ramphele, *Uprooting Poverty: The South African Challenge* (Cape Town: David Philip, 1989), p. 50.

9. Klugman, 1990.

10. The appointment of a pro-choice female minister of health, Dr. Nkosazana Zuma, offers some hope in this area. Dr. Zuma has already enacted policies that allow for free medical care for all children under the age of six and pregnant mothers.

11. Shireen Badat, "'Guilty' Secret in South Africa," *Democracy in Action* 8, no. 1 (1994):24–25, writes that one of every two South African women has been or will be a rape victim and that one of every four South African girls will have been sexually abused by the age of sixteen—in most cases by a family member.

12. Frene Ginwala, "Women and the African National Congress, 1912–1943," *Agenda* no. 8 (1990):77–93.

13. The SANNC later became the African National Congress.

14. For more on the 1912–1913 antipass campaign, see Ginwala, "Women and the African National Congress."

15. The march took place on August 9, 1956; August 9 is now celebrated as South African Women's Day.

16. With the National Forum (a large nationwide meeting of antiapartheid groups), the United Democratic Front was launched in 1983 to revive united opposition to the state. The National Forum focused on cultural boycotts and opposed the 1984 Indian and coloured elections. The UDF was an umbrella organization for all the opposition groups claiming allegiance to the Freedom Charter promoted by the ANC in the 1950s and calling for a nonracial, democratic South Africa. The UDF organized collective action against the state and, unlike the Black Consciousness Movement, emphasized nonracialism to unify Black and white South Africans and accommodated all organizations that fought localized struggles. Despite this philosophy of nonracialism, UDF organizations tended to be racially segregated, reflecting the impact of the state's racial policies. Emphasizing unity, the UDF did not address the issue of differences in material wealth and power within its ranks. According to erstwhile Black Consciousness supporter Aubrey Makoena, "We cannot have a struggle within a struggle. Everybody is invited to come under the big umbrella of the UDF." A. Marx, *Lessons of Struggle: South African Internal Opposition, 1960–1990* (Cape Town: Oxford University Press, 1992), p. 133.

17. Cheryl Hendricks and Desiree Lewis, "Voices from the Margins," *Agenda*, no. 20 (1994):64.

18. *Crisis News* 17, no. 1 (July-August 1987).

19. In the current climate of reconciliation it is important to remember the extreme repression and brutality of the Nationalist Party government. For example, the three South

African authors of this chapter were all jailed for legitimate opposition and nonviolent protest.

20. L. Bank, "Angry Men and Working Women: Gender Violence and Economic Change in Qwa Qwa in the 1980s," *African Studies* 1 (1994). The Unemployed Workers Union in Qwa Qwa still continues to campaign against women's employment in this former homeland.

21. bell hooks, "Sisterhood: Political Solidarity Between Women," *Feminist Review,* no. 23 (Summer 1986) (Special issue).

22. Kimberle Crenshaw, *Demarginalizing the Intersection of Race and Sex: A Black Feminist Critique of Anti-discrimination Doctrine, Feminist Theory, and Antiracist Politics* (Chicago: University of Chicago Legal Forum, 1989), p. 387.

23. Transvaal Rural Action Committee, "Rural Women's Movement: Holding the Knife on the Sharp Edge" (January 1994), p. 8.

24. Mala Singh, "Malibongwe Conference," *Agenda,* no. 6 (1990):25.

25. Mamphela Ramphele, "The Dynamics of Gender Within Black Consciousness Organizations: A Personal View," in Braney Pityana et al., eds., *Bounds of Possibility: The Legacy of Steve Biko and Black Consciousness* (Cape Town: David Philip, 1992), p. 221.

26. *Crisis News* 17, no. 1 (July-August 1987).

27. Jo Beale, "Picking Up the Gauntlet: Women Discuss the ANC Statement," *Agenda,* no. 8 (1990):13–14.

28. Ibid., p. 11.

29. Ibid., pp. 13–14, 11.

30. Ginwala, "Women and the African National Congress."

31. Rosalee Telela, "Patricia de Lille: I Am African Before I Am a Woman," *Speak,* no. 54 (October 1993):5–7.

32. Cape Town focus group meeting, March 4, 1994.

33. The coalition borrowed the method from CODESA negotiations, where voting had also presented problems.

34. Women's National Coalition, "Briefing on Women, Culture, Customary Law, and Equality" (unpublished ms.), p. 3.

35. Preggs Govendar, interview with Amanda Kemp, Johannesburg, March 16, 1994.

36. Women's National Coalition, "Briefing on Women."

37. J. Wilhelm and D. Streak, "SA Parliament a World Leader in the Fight for Sexual Equality," *Sunday Times,* May 29, 1994.

38. Ibid.

39. Formerly called the Institute for a Democratic Alternative for South Africa, this organization's name was changed in February 1994.

40. Cathy Albertyn, "Two Steps Forward," *Work in Progress,* no. 94 (February 1994):24.

41. Ibid., p. 22.

42. Consider, for instance, the experience of the Rural Women's Movement. Initially, when the RWM organized over broad community issues, its "struggle" was approved by men in the community. However, when members moved their focus to the control of resources within the community, rural men were threatened and sought to entrench their "traditional" powers.

43. It is probably in this area, where there is a need for a conduit between women in government and women on the ground, that the WNC could formulate a new role for itself. Alternatively, the individual members of the WNC or other independent women's NGOs could form strategic coalitions to put pressure on the government around specific interests.

44. Amanda Kemp, "A New Day: South African Contemporary Women's Movements" (January 1994), unpublished paper.

45. Jennifer Shreiner, "The Need for Gender Bias," *Reconstruct,* no. 16, supplement to *Work in Progress,* no. 95 (March 1994):2.

46. Mmatshilo Motsei, focus group meeting, Johannesburg, March 3, 1994.

6

The Many Faces of Feminism in Namibia

DIANNE HUBBARD & COLETTE SOLOMON

As A STARTING POINT, it is difficult to determine whether there is something that can validly be called a women's movement in Namibia at present. On the one hand, it is possible to speak of a Namibian women's movement in two senses. First, although there is no single organization that speaks for all Namibian women, various nongovernmental organizations (NGOs) and governmental bodies concerned about women have on occasion been able to put aside their differences to work together to achieve common aims. Second, there is a growing perception among Namibian women that many of their social and economic problems are related to their position as women, and they are showing an increasing interest in organizing to address such problems jointly. On the other hand, it may be misleading to speak of "a" women's movement in a nation divided by race, ethnicity, class, political affiliation, geography, and historical experience. Most formal women's groups are dominated by black, urban, educated women, who cannot be viewed as representing the needs of the majority of Namibia's women.

Namibian women have not yet discovered how to utilize their combined political strength effectively to advance the position of women. Past attempts at achieving organizational unity have been unsuccessful, and there is now a trend toward looser alliances around specific issues. Despite the existence of a government body to coordinate the efforts of women's groups, the most dynamic forces for the advancement of women are independent nongovernmental and community organizations with their own issues and agendas.

We take the view that there is a sufficient degree of networking and mutual support among these groups to warrant the use of the term *women's movement*. In

NAMIBIA

GENERAL

type of government: Republic
major ethnic groups: Ovambo (50%); Kavango (10%); Herero (7%); Damara (7%)
language(s): English (official); Afrikaans common to most; indigenous languages
religions: Predominantly Christian (90%)
date of independence: 1990
former colonial power: Germany, South Africa

DEMOGRAPHICS

population size: 1.57 million
birth rate (*per 1,000 population*): 45
total fertility (*average number of births per woman*): 5.4
contraceptive prevalence (*married women*): 23%
maternal mortality rate (*per 100,000 live births*): 479

WOMEN'S STATUS

date of women's suffrage: 1989
economically active population: M 83%   F 24%
female employment (*% of total workforce*): 24
life expectancy   M 58   F 63
school enrollment ratio (*F/100 M*)
   primary   108
   secondary   127
   tertiary   *not available*
literacy   M 45%   F 31%

this chapter we provide an analytical description of the evolution of the Namibian women's movement. While clear strengths and weaknesses can be identified, the major developments that have taken place do not yet seem to fit into a single pattern.

Historically, discrimination against women was compounded by the racial discrimination and underdevelopment of the colonial era. Gender was first used as a framework for analysis by the women's wings of the liberation movements, which were fighting first and foremost for national self-determination. Grassroots organization of women around bread-and-butter issues intensified within the country in the latter years of the liberation struggle.

In 1990 Namibia became an independent, democratic state with a constitutional commitment to eradicate all sex discrimination. The early years of independence have given impetus to action around issues of special concern to women, as patterns of life under colonial rule are slowly being reshaped. It is a time of opportunity for women.

The decision to abandon the vision of an all-embracing unity in favor of the idea of strategic "unity-in-diversity" seems to be a wise one. The women's movement has been fairly successful in ensuring that women's concerns are articulated at a national level and in increasing gender sensitivity in public policy. However, action on matters of concern to women is moving slowly, and the groups that promote women's issues are not yet adequately representative of the broad spectrum of women in Namibian society. In short, the women's movement has not yet managed to mobilize the full power of Namibia's women.

The Context: Points of Diversity and Unity

In order to understand the challenges faced by the women's movement in Namibia, it is necessary to examine the complex divisions and diversity that characterize this small nation. The population of approximately 1.5 million is spread over a landmass more than six times the size of England and includes at least twelve major ethnic and language groups.[1] These in turn are divided into overlapping subgroups, which sometimes speak distinct dialects.

During the colonial period, the Namibian population was stratified into three racial groups—blacks, whites, and "coloureds," a colonially created category for mixed-race persons. As a divide-and-rule tactic, eleven "population groups" identified by the colonial authorities were assigned second-tier governing bodies, with the black groups relegated to different geographical homelands. Namibia's rich cultural variety became the basis for profound political and economic discrimination, the effects of which are proving difficult to eradicate in the postindependence era.

As a result, the experience of sexual oppression was and still is heavily intertwined with race and class distinctions. Independence has given rise to a new black elite that shares more common interests with middle-class whites than with black members of the working class, thus blurring racial differences among the privileged classes. Meanwhile, both race and class distinctions continue to operate as divisive forces in the women's movement.

These intricate planes are overlaid with much political fragmentation. Namibia became a sovereign nation on March 21, 1990, following a twenty-three-year struggle to achieve freedom from South African rule. Although the South West African People's Organization (SWAPO) was the clear leader in the liberation struggle[2] and is now a strong majority party, more than forty political parties participated in Namibia's first free and fair elections in 1989. Political activity has since been rationalized, leaving only a handful of active parties, with SWAPO remaining predominant.[3] However, party-political loyalties remain a divisive factor.

Since independence, political diversity has been supplemented by an increasing number of nongovernmental organizations active in different spheres. The NGOs often acquire party-political associations, voluntarily or involuntarily,[4] which have been subtle and complex and often problematic. Another point of diversity is the differing experiences of the forty to fifty thousand people who engaged in the liberation struggle from exile compared to the experiences of the majority, who remained in Namibia. While both men and women in exile benefited from contact with other feminisms, they inevitably lost touch with practical conditions inside Namibia. Returning Namibians who benefited from educational opportunities abroad now form the backbone of a new black elite, from which grassroots women often feel alienated.[5]

Namibia is characterized by complex geographical and ethnic distinctions that complicate the nation's urban-rural divide. For example, there are crucial distinctions in organizational style and characteristics between Windhoek, the nation's capital and center of political activity, and the smaller towns that also function as "urban" centers in some respects.[6] There are also fundamental differences in community dynamics in both rural and "urban" settings between the broad geographical areas of north and south. Different problems and priorities also exist for women in Namibia's thirteen political regions, which are in some cases isolated by long distances and difficult traveling conditions.[7]

Namibia's ethnic groups, which still have different geographical centers as a legacy of both history and apartheid, follow distinct customs and traditions. To cite only one example, some groups in Namibia are matrilineal, while others are patrilineal. Thus, a Namibian woman's individual experience may be shaped not only by her race and class but also by political affiliations, by whether she lives in Windhoek or a smaller town or rural area, by the characteristics unique to her region, and the ethnic identity of her community. This wide range of experience creates an enormous challenge for national organization by women's groups.

Amidst all this diversity, there are some significant unifying factors. Approximately 90 percent of Namibia's population is Christian;[8] although the church played a role in the colonial occupation and subjugation of the indigenous people, most denominations ultimately became ardent and consistent challengers of the apartheid state.[9] The church is an important force at the community level, and Christianity provides a common moral ground on certain issues. However, Christian beliefs in Namibia are often manifested in conservative Christian doctrine that works against the interests of women. For example, biblical teachings are often cited in both personal and political settings to justify the subordination of women, particularly in the family. Therefore, the potential of the church as a vehicle for organizing women is limited.

Another point of convergence is a slowly growing sense of nationhood. There is a political commitment to encouraging a concept of Namibian nationality that will unite the diverse population and to deemphasizing political assertions of ethnic identity.[10] Nevertheless, ethnic, political, racial, regional, and class-based conflicts remain strong and are influential in determining divisions and alliances around women's issues.

Organization of Women Prior to Independence

While it is difficult to generalize about precolonial gender relations in Namibia's many ethnic groups, many communities had a sex-based division of labor in which women played an important, if unequal, role in both production and reproduction. For example, in the mixed-farming Owambo communities, the harvest from the wife's plot was consumed by the household, while that from the husband's plot was disposed of by him as surplus profit. Thus, even though women were involved in production, their economic role was marginalized.

Positions of influence in precolonial communities were generally held by men, although there were some exceptions, and men usually had larger economic decisionmaking power within extended family units. *Lobola* (bride-price) also contributed to the relatively inferior position of women; men often believed that they could exercise total control and power over their wives since they had "paid" for them. Polygamy, while ensuring household labor and arguably reducing the workload of individual women, intensified sexual inequality by linking a woman's status to her rank as wife. While women's precolonial position was later interpreted as conferring inferior status, it has been asserted that notions of gender equality or inequality were simply nonexistent during this period and that men and women were perceived as inhabiting and controlling different and complementary spheres.[11]

During this period, the missionary influence was undermining traditional ideology and religion and holding up submission and subordination as model behavior for women. Paradoxically, it also provided useful educational opportunities for women in some parts of the country. In the white settler communities, women generally remained in the home, while the realm of public activity was completely male dominated.

Colonial rule brought new legal, social, and economic bases for women's subordination. Gender dynamics were profoundly affected by the system of migrant labor that was imposed in 1925, primarily to ensure a supply of cheap labor in the country's mines. A range of influx control laws ensured that workers' families remained in rural "native reserves." This resulted in an increased workload for women, as they assumed tasks traditionally performed by men in addition to their own productive and reproductive duties. This rarely, however, gave them more decisionmaking power, as men often continued to control the household's major economic resources during their infrequent visits home. Furthermore, men engaged in wage employment did not always send regular remittances home, thus increasing the burden on women to find alternate sources of income for the household's cash expenses.[12]

As the years passed, environmental degradation, increasing poverty, a greater reliance on a cash economy, and the dangers of the liberation war all encouraged increasing numbers of people, including women, to flee the rural areas in search of wage employment in cities and towns. Unfortunately, women were concentrated in domestic work, where they had no legal protection and were vulnerable to exploitation by employers. The majority of black women, particularly those who remained in rural areas, were forced to rely on subsistence agriculture, informal economic activities, and, in some cases, prostitution. Women's economic marginalization contributed to their overall disempowerment in the preindependence era.[13]

Although it is difficult to pinpoint a particular time or event as the beginning of Namibia's women's movement, it clearly has important roots in the liberation struggle. Women had always been active in resistance to colonial domination. For example, during a war of resistance to German rule in 1904–1905, Herero women vowed not to bear children until German rule ended. In later years, black urban women defied the pass laws imposed on them by the colonial administration. (Pass laws required blacks and coloureds to carry identity cards at all times, which were then used to strictly segregate and control the movement and settlement of these groups.) Women also played a leading role in a seminal struggle against the forced removal of blacks to ethnically segregated townships in 1959—an event that was an important catalyst for crystallizing the nascent liberation movements. When political attempts to achieve independence were supplemented by armed struggle in 1966, women overcame initial male opposition to participate as combatants in the People's Liberation Army of Namibia (PLAN), the guerrilla force that was the military wing of SWAPO. An equally important role was played by women who remained inside the country and provided crucial material and psychological support to the freedom fighters. Women also suffered from the direct and indirect consequences of the liberation war—rape, torture and imprisonment, and health, social, and economic hardships stemming from unemployment and underdevelopment.[14]

Against this background, a SWAPO women's council was formed in 1969 and formally inaugurated as a wing of SWAPO in 1976, soon establishing an active

Women members of the People's Liberation Army of Namibia joined in the struggle to establish the independent nation of Namibia, which was administered as part of South Africa's Cape Province from 1919 until independence in 1990.

presence both inside and outside Namibia. The South West African National Union (SWANU), a smaller liberation movement, also established a women's wing during this period. While these groups discussed steps to end the oppression of women, this goal was subordinated to the achievement of national independence, considered a prerequisite for improving the condition of women. While black women experienced a combination of race, class, and gender oppression, it was the experience of living under apartheid colonialism that most affected them. Thus, the struggle for national liberation was accorded more prominence than the struggle for women's liberation. Although this approach has been criticized by some Western feminists, it has been the reality in a number of other African countries, including Zimbabwe and Mozambique.

Namibian women were mobilized to support the liberation struggle, while the hierarchy of the liberation movements remained male dominated. Nevertheless, the women's wings were an important conscientizing force, as they provided the first significant framework for discussion and analysis of gender issues. In the years immediately preceding independence, women became increasingly active in local organizations formed to address community issues that affected their daily lives and in local church groups that focused on basic needs. There was some coordination among local church groups through the women's desk of the Council of Churches of Namibia (CCN), an ecumenical institution that spoke out strongly against the injustices stemming from apartheid.[15] A chapter of the Young Women's Christian Association (YWCA) became active in Namibia in 1985, focusing on small income-generating projects and educational programs for women.

The most significant women's group in Namibia in the preindependence era was another ecumenical organization, the Namibia Women's Voice (NWV). Initiated in 1985 by women from church groups, the NWV rapidly acquired a broader identity as an alliance of women across party-political and denominational lines to address a spectrum of "women's issues."[16] The NWV established thirteen regional branches in its first two years. It had a strong grassroots appeal in both urban and rural areas, and its membership also included educated women in professions such as teaching, nursing, and social work. Although there were a few progressive white women among the members, the NWV was predominantly a black organization; since the apartheid regime succeeded in keeping black and white Namibians apart on all fronts, it was difficult for women of different races to identify their common interests as women.

The NWV's mechanism for organization was small income-generating and development projects. It brought women together for workshops on topics such as literacy, health education, and leadership, providing a forum to facilitate discussion and action on community problems. The NWV also took action on national issues; for example, it organized campaigns against the use of Depo-Provera and against the "hearts-and-minds" tactics employed by the colonial government.[17]

Although there are conflicting accounts of the reasons for the dissolution of the NWV in 1989, one frequently cited factor is the opposition engendered by its challenge to male authority in church and political party hierarchies. The autonomy and success of the group were apparently threatening. Some SWAPO leaders were concerned that the NWV was competing with the SWAPO Women's Council, even though all of the NWV leaders also belonged to SWAPO. There were tensions between the NWV and some of the churches, which pressed the NWV to formalize its relationship with them. Other groups envied the NWV's ability to mobilize grassroots women and its success in attracting funding. Some women have also cited personal conflicts within the leadership as contributing to the NWV's ultimate demise.

The NWV was unique in its emphasis on the practical problems faced by grassroots women. It played a seminal role in alerting women to the political dimension of the gender-related problems they faced daily and in mobilizing women around the integration of gender issues into the liberation struggle. It was also significant because, as the first major women's group to operate independently of party-political, church, or other superimposed structures, it provided a forum where gender issues were not subordinated to other priorities.[18]

The Impact of Independence

Since Namibia became independent on March 21, 1990, there has been a widespread sense of building anew. This has included a receptivity to changes relating to gender issues. Women's issues were discussed in campaigns leading up to the country's U.N.-supervised elections in November 1989 but did not prove influential, as the election was dominated by party loyalties.[19]

The framework created by the new constitution and the ratification of the Convention on the Elimination of All Forms of Discrimination Against Women (CEDAW) in 1992 gave the women's movement important tools. The constitution employs a gender-inclusive formulation of "he and she" throughout. It explicitly forbids discrimination on the grounds of sex and authorizes affirmative action "with regard to the fact that women in Namibia have traditionally suffered special discrimination and that they need to be encouraged and enabled to play a full, equal and effective role in the political, social, economic and cultural life of the nation."[20] The constitution also guarantees that men and women of full age "shall be entitled to equal rights as to marriage, during marriage and at its dissolution."[21] Customary law is still recognized, but only to the extent that it does not violate the constitution.[22]

However, the constitution also provides that all laws in force at independence remain in place until altered by Parliament or declared unconstitutional by a court.[23] Women have not yet challenged in court any existing laws that are in conflict with the constitution or developed political skills sufficient to become a powerful lobby for change through the political process. Thus, while the legal tools for change are available, discriminatory laws on many gender-related issues remain.

The first postindependence legal reforms specific to women have been primarily aimed at the small proportion of women in formal employment. Gender inequalities in the civil and customary laws on marriage and inheritance, which have a profound impact on the status of all women, have yet to be addressed. It is likely to be much more difficult for the state to take effective action to improve the status of women in private family settings than in the public sphere.

Shortly after independence, the Department of Women's Affairs (DWA) was established in the President's Office to facilitate liaison between women and the government and to help identify priorities for action. While some women feared that channeling gender issues through a single department might have a marginalizing effect, the establishment of the DWA was viewed as a symbol of the government's commitment to gender issues.

Since independence, recognition of gender issues has increased at policy levels. Nevertheless, there is still a tendency to compartmentalize women's issues instead of integrating gender concerns into overall policymaking. Many government initiatives designed to benefit women have been donor driven and have not garnered

Women wait to cast their ballots at the polling station at Ariamsvlei in November 1989. More than 90 percent of eligible voters participated in electing seventy-two delegates to draw up Namibia's constitution.

sustainable momentum. The DWA and the government's National Planning Commission recently established an interministerial gender network to monitor gender issues in government policy. As of 1993, there were plans to expand the role of this network as well as to incorporate more input from the NGOs.

Independence has also brought a new level of participation by women in government structures. Women constituted almost one-third of all local government representatives in 1993, due partly to a statutory affirmative action provision requiring political parties to include a specified number of women on their lists of candidates.[24] Women still constitute only a tiny minority of the representatives at national and regional levels.[25] However, at the national level the presence of even a small number of women has been significant, as they have used their influence to draw attention to gender issues.[26] Still, the political arena and the major political parties remain male dominated.

Since independence, Namibia has moved from an era of relative isolation into a period of intense international contact. This has given stimulus to the treatment of gender issues by both state and nongovernmental organizations, although international networking is not yet carried out as strategically as it might be. In general, independence has brought high and often unrealistic expectations for rapid change that have inspired both energy and frustration. People have looked to the new government to bring change to every aspect of their lives, while the govern-

Namibians celebrate their independence on March 21, 1990.

ment faces the task of rebuilding the nation while being hampered by severe economic constraints. Gender issues must compete for attention on a crowded national agenda. It is in this climate that the women's movement has taken new forms and directions.

The Dynamics of the Postindependence Women's Movement

In recognition of the strategic importance of unity for effective lobbying and political action, efforts were made around the time of independence to create an umbrella body to speak on behalf of all Namibian women. Shortly after indepen-

This mural in Windhoek illustrates women's willingness to work together in the transition period to promote their rights and interests.

dence, a steering committee composed of two delegates from each of thirteen interested women's groups began lengthy deliberations aimed at forming this body.[27] While it was not difficult to reach agreement on aims and objectives—demonstrating a certain unity of purpose among the groups—there was strong disagreement over the form the group should take. The women's wings of political parties tended to favor an organization that women would join as individuals to avoid the constraints of their party structures. The NGOs preferred a federation of groups on the grounds that this would be the most powerful form of alliance.

Before this debate was resolved, the effort fell apart, primarily because of splits along party-political lines exacerbated by personal competitiveness.[28] The result was the emergence of two different umbrella bodies operating on a national level: one federation of women's organizations and one national organization open to individual women. Partly because of their origins in the failed efforts at a more comprehensive umbrella, each group acquired political connotations, with one being characterized as a SWAPO grouping, while the other had its base among the opposition parties. In fact, both umbrella bodies drew their members from more than one political affiliation, but the party-political identities endured. The more apolitical NGOs withdrew from the efforts at unification altogether and have remained independent. There have been several subsequent initiatives to draw women together across party lines, primarily in Windhoek, but these have remained informal and ad hoc in nature.

Since the failure of this effort to establish a single women's group, there seems to be more acceptance of the notion of unity-in-diversity. The process of attempting to achieve unity, acrimonious though it was, seems to have been a maturing process that helped key individuals and groups work together strategically to achieve common aims.

As of 1993, there were several different types of women's groups active in the country. First, women's wings of political parties are still active. Although several facilitate ongoing projects, their primary focus is mobilizing women for elections and the advancement of women within the parties. It is difficult to gauge the degree of committed involvement in these groups. For example, every woman who becomes a member of SWAPO is automatically made a member of the SWAPO Women's Council.

Second, after the attempt at unification, there were for a time two national organizations that attempted to speak for "women" on a broad range of issues. The federation associated with Namibia's opposition parties is now dormant, but the Namibia National Women's Organization is active and growing. This group is still perceived by many as being aligned with the ruling party. While it tries to reach out to a broad cross section of women, at present it remains dominated by an educated elite.

Third, there are special interest groups that focus on particular issues. Examples include a group that provides education and counseling around the issue of violence against women and a group that publishes a feminist magazine in accessible language. Both of these groups have a small membership, which includes black and white women, but they are primarily composed of educated, middle-class women who attempt to provide services that will benefit women on a broader scale. A small organization of business and professional women has been one of the few initiatives to attract a significant proportion of white women.

Fourth, there are grassroots-based groups. The strongest among these are church based, operate locally, and focus on practical community needs rather than women's issues as such. For example, many members are active in local choirs, Bible study groups, or small income-generating projects. The only grassroots-based women's group known to operate in towns both north and south of Windhoek is Concerned Women Against Violence Against Women, which has relatively autonomous local groups in eight locations. Their focus is not only sexual violence but also all violent crimes that impact women. More recently, they have included other areas such as education on legal rights, income-generating projects, and the development of improved organizational skills. While there are a few men and educated black and white women who play a supportive and active role, control of the groups remains decisively in the hands of grassroots women. Concerned Women has been fairly successful in reaching across ethnic and political-

Women in Windhoek demonstrate against violence in June 1992.

party boundaries; however, the profile of the group varies from place to place.[29] There have been some tensions between Concerned Women groups and some other women's organizations, partly because of competition for grassroots loyalty.

A number of other NGOs, while not specifically women's groups, mobilize women around specific concerns. The trade unions are also potential organizing structures. Although most of the existing trade unions, like most of the sectors of formal employment, are male dominated, a domestic workers' union and a teachers' union—both of which have a majority of female members—have taken a lead in addressing gender issues.[30]

The Namibian National Students' Organization (NANSO) has been particularly successful at integrating gender concerns into its overall platform and structures. There are women's subcommittees with their own budgets in every branch; they hold an annual national conference on their own, in addition to NANSO's full national conference, to ensure the fullest possible participation by women. NANSO ensures that women are represented on its highest decisionmaking bodies. Roughly half the members of NANSO are women, and careful attention to gender issues has produced a high level of gender sensitivity in both male and female NANSO leaders. In recent years NANSO has actively taken up several gender-related issues, such as teenage pregnancy and the promotion of family life education in the school curriculum.

Organization of women in rural areas, where approximately 70 percent of the Namibian population resides,[31] centers around income-generating and church-related activities. The precarious economic position of rural households, often headed by women, makes the appeal of income-generating activities understandable.[32] Before independence, churches were the main sponsors of such projects; since then various other organizations have become involved in this arena. Many activists have realized that these projects can serve as an entry point for further mobilization. Donor funding and assistance have also contributed greatly to the proliferation of such projects.

The empowering effect of most such initiatives has been minimal. Many income-generating projects for women focus on traditional skills—such as sewing, baking, gardening, and poultry rearing—thereby perpetuating gender stereotypes.[33] These projects are generally modest in scope and lack sustainability due to inadequate feasibility studies or lack of appropriate managerial skills. A number of Windhoek-based groups that assist small business enterprises now offer management skills training and evaluations. Lack of adequate access to productive resources such as land and credit also remains a limiting factor for women's economic activity.[34]

Church activities such as prayer groups and choirs are the other major focal point for rural women. In addition to providing moral and sometimes financial support, such groups are for many women the only source of social diversion from the routine of their daily lives. Although these church structures are not normally "woman centered," they indisputably reach the largest numbers of rural women. As a result, many mainstream women's organizations have cooperated with church structures but without substantially altering the issues taken up by the church groups.

Mobilization of rural women is hampered by a range of constraints, including a heavy workload and resistance by male family members who fear that organizational involvement by women might threaten men's position of power and authority. In addition, some community activists have identified a "dependency syndrome" whereby rural residents expect that improvements in their situation will come from the government or from donor agencies. This syndrome causes apathy and affects women's attitudes and their level of participation in women's organizations.

The DWA endeavors to coordinate the wide variety of groups operating in rural areas. However, it has faced serious difficulties in balancing the enormous expectations from the government and the public against the reality of a small staff and a limited budget—while being advised by numerous donor agencies, each with its own ideas about the ideal approach. After inviting a range of organizations to discuss strategy, the DWA has wisely chosen to focus on networking and facilitating, rather than implementing, projects.

The DWA thus tries to coordinate the activities and projects of existing women's groups and NGOs, to put these groups in touch with appropriate government ministries and donors, and to undertake needs assessments as a basis for project initiation.[35] It has also made the CEDAW a focal point for a communications strategy designed to encompass conscientization and action on a range of gender issues.[36] Because the DWA is located within a SWAPO government, it is perceived as being SWAPO oriented by some, in spite of its work with a broad range of women's organizations. The DWA has also been criticized for favoring some groups while intentionally shunning others.[37] Another widespread criticism is that the DWA has failed to establish adequate mechanisms for accountability.

Such criticisms can be viewed as a sign of a healthy dialogue between a state structure and an active and vital NGO community; the government will clearly not be allowed to shape the women's movement unilaterally. The DWA itself seems to have become increasingly sensitive to such criticism and is attempting to give a greater appearance of openness and inclusiveness to its efforts to prepare for the 1995 United Nations Fourth World Conference on Women. At the same time, the DWA has had to struggle for meaningful recognition within the government. It is still not consistently consulted on legislation and policies that include critical gender components, and there is no DWA representative at the cabinet level.

While there is a general recognition that the DWA has been performing admirably under difficult circumstances, there is still a widespread view that it has not sufficiently articulated and acted upon rural concerns and priorities. Rural women are alienated from the processes that take place in the urban centers, feeling excluded from policy debates and uninformed about their outcomes. It has been suggested that the DWA adopt a more aggressive approach in rural areas in order to keep women informed about relevant matters and relay their concerns back to the government and to the rest of the women's movement.

The same criticisms of rural neglect that are leveled at the DWA can be applied to most other Windhoek-based women's groups. The majority of Namibian women are still isolated from the mainstream women's movement. For example, preliminary results of a survey of women in Windhoek indicate that most grass-roots women, even in the capital, are unaware of the activities of the DWA or any of the Windhoek-based women's groups, with community activity centering around local church groups. Women who have heard of any of the women's organizations perceive them as being for educated women. Those few women who have attended meetings felt isolated and intimidated by the level of the discourse or the use of English. At the same time, an abiding racism complicated by class distinctions continues to divide women in these communities; for example, middle-class coloured women, who seem to be one of the groups most thoroughly neglected by the women's movement, were found to expect long hours of work for low wages from their black domestic workers.

With the exception of a few progressive thinkers, white women are largely absent from the women's movement. This is partly the result of the apartheid era in the sense that white women are perceived as being relatively privileged. They are reticent to assert their interests in the context of the larger women's movement, and some black women are suspicious of their involvement. Furthermore, most of Namibia's white population was traditionally intent on preserving the status quo, producing a general conservatism incompatible with fundamental changes in gender relations.

Since less than five years have passed since independence, it is perhaps understandable that the vestiges of the preindependence racial divide still remain. There is more interracial meeting and mixing than before, which is largely confined to a small group of educated, middle-class Namibians. For the majority, racial barriers still exist, even if they are no longer legally enforced. This makes it difficult for most women to meet and organize across racial lines. Thus, the driving engine of the women's movement at this stage is a small urban elite dominated by educated black women who have achieved some impressive and well-intentioned results but who have not yet managed to transcend the barriers of race and class to extend the women's movement to the majority of the population.

Emerging Priority Issues

At a 1991 conference organized by the DWA, women from all parts of Namibia identified a range of women's needs that stemmed from the position of women

As a result of women's efforts, Namibia's new constitution provides for gender equality in many areas. However, in other areas traditional law still prevails, precluding women from exercising their rights. Here a legal aid organization conducts a seminar to inform women of their rights.

relative to men and from the persisting social and economic impact of apartheid and underdevelopment. Conference participants found women to be primarily concerned about the general conditions that affect them and their families. The persistence of discriminatory and inadequate laws is a frequent focus of discussion.[38] One of the most frequently cited problems is the law on maintenance (child support), an economic issue as much as a legal one. This problem reflects the frequent failure of fathers to take financial or emotional responsibility for their children. Another often-cited priority is the set of family laws that address marriage, divorce, inheritance, and domestic violence.[39] In general, violence against women—widespread rape and domestic violence as well as more generalized crime and violence—is a common problem that cuts across race and class lines and has been identified as a priority in both urban and rural areas. As one of the few issues that inspires consistent grassroots action, it functions as a key mobilizing issue and has inspired several public protests in Windhoek and other locations.

An issue of growing and widespread concern is the need for more access to family planning services. Before independence, family planning was complicated by a general political debate around population control, which was seen as a government strategy to control the number of blacks. Since independence, the issue has become depoliticized. Birth rates in black communities are still high, and many men and women continue to define women as mothers. But women are now increasingly questioning the close linking of womanhood with fertility and are challenging male resistance to birth control.

As already noted, improving the economic position of women is a fundamental rural priority. Although this goal is shared by many urban women, it is even more pressing in the tenuous economy of rural households. There is also an urgent need for improved agricultural extension services for rural women who remain the primary producers in subsistence agriculture. Access to clean water and adequate sanitation is another major concern of rural women. The time and distance involved in collecting water are borne by women, and lack of water and sanitation is also a key contributing factor to the health problems of women and children.[40]

The effect of customary laws and practices is also of major concern to rural women, particularly in the north. Widows, who often lose all their land and property to the family of the deceased, are particularly vulnerable. Access to land and exclusion from traditional decisionmaking structures such as headmen's courts are other areas of concern. In the southern regions, rural women often cite a nexus of interrelated family and social problems that include unemployment, alcohol abuse, and family violence. An additional problem is an intensified feeling of exclusion from rural development projects, which have been concentrated in the north.[41]

These priority issues specific to rural women have tended to be addressed, if at all, by government ministries and donor agencies rather than by women's groups. While the mainstream women's movement has acknowledged in principle the importance of including the concerns of rural women, there has been little concrete action to back up this assertion. As a result, it is not surprising that rural and urban poor women do not generally view the women's movement as a primary vehicle for the assertion of their needs. In order to attract a broader following, the women's movement must prove that it can produce tangible results on issues that concern a wider range of the nation's women.

Characteristics, Strengths, and Weaknesses

The Namibian women's movement is a nascent one about which only a few generalizations can be made. For example, "feminism" is an unpopular word in

Namibia, although many women apply feminist analysis without labeling it as such. Similarly, "gender" is still an unfamiliar concept to many. Gender issues have understandably had to compete with a wide range of other issues for attention in a nation that is busy building itself anew. Namibia has been inundated with well-meaning and generous donors, many of which have given special priority to matters relating to gender. While the aims of donor agencies have for the most part been consistent with those of women's organizations, donors often set differing priorities and a different pace.

The Windhoek-based women's movement is characterized by the high visibility of a few prominent women involved in multiple endeavors. There has not yet been a unifying issue strong enough to mobilize women more broadly. It is unlikely that preparation for Beijing will serve this function; in fact, Beijing could prove to be an interruption of the more pressing business of internal organization and action on the ground. A few individuals have had contact with international women's organizations, but this has not yet filtered through to Namibian women's groups in any meaningful way.

Some of the difficulties faced by the women's movement have been noted. The challenge of articulating a feminism that will encompass the needs and aspirations of women ranging from subsistence farmers to urban professionals is immense. The women's movement is still searching for a way to bridge the gap between grassroots women and the educated elite as well as the gap between Windhoek and the rest of the nation. The continuing divisiveness of race, class, ethnicity, and political persuasion constitutes a serious obstacle to united action. An additional constraint is personal competitiveness and a similar sort of organizational competitiveness that encompasses competition for members, influence, and donor funds. Even the most active women are still strengthening their networking, lobbying, and strategizing skills.

Despite these limitations, the women's movement also has significant strengths, such as individual women with untiring personal commitment to the advancement of women, a slowly increasing consciousness among Namibian women of the impact of gender discrimination on their daily lives, and a receptive national climate with a growing level of gender sensitivity among policymakers. Younger Namibian women and men seem to be less divided by the experiences of the past than their parents, with less deeply entrenched gender stereotypes, as evidenced in NANSO.

The women's movement has clearly matured and evolved in the few short years since independence. There is still a need for more organization around specific initiatives instead of attempts to organize women to address the entire spectrum of women's issues at once. There is an even more critical need to create spaces in which *all* Namibian women can assert their own priorities in their own ways. Even though the women's movement is reaching only a small minority of women at present, it has already had a significant impact on national politics and has the potential to become a vibrant and powerful force in Namibia.

NOTES

1. Population figures are from a 1991 government census.

2. Other groups that were active in the liberation struggle included the Herero Chiefs' Council and SWANU.

3. For instance, SWAPO made a strong showing in the 1992 regional and local government elections, and a number of leaders from other political parties have chosen to join SWAPO in the last few years.

4. For example, the nation's largest trade union federation is formally affiliated to SWAPO, while the major students' organization suffered a split over its decision to disaffiliate from SWAPO. There are two different umbrella bodies for NGOs, each with a different political profile, even though neither has any formal ties to any party.

5. This point should not obscure the fact that only a small proportion of exiled Namibians (perhaps 15 percent) underwent comprehensive post–secondary school training. Many returning Namibians have faced severe difficulties in finding employment and in reintegrating themselves into Namibian society.

6. Bruce Frayne, *Urbanization in Post-Independence Windhoek* (Namibian Institute for Social and Economic Research, University of Namibia, February 1992); UNICEF/NISER, *A Situation Analysis of Children and Women in Namibia* (UNICEF, March 1991), p. 20. In 1991, the population of Windhoek was estimated at 150,000, although this figure could have grown to 200,000 by 1992 due to migration caused by drought. Windhoek is approximately eight times larger than its nearest urban rival, Rehoboth, and accounts for about one-third of the nation's entire urban population.

7. For political purposes, the nation is divided into thirteen different regions, each with its own elected regional council. Local authorities, classified as municipalities, towns, or villages, depending on their size and level of development, exist within each region.

8. It has also been estimated that some 70 percent of the population attend church regularly.

9. In rural Namibia, especially in the parts of northern Namibia that fell within the operational area during the liberation war, the church provided a safe meeting place as well as various forms of practical and symbolic support.

10. See Republic of Namibia, *Report by Commission of Inquiry into Matters Relating to Chiefs, Headmen, and Other Traditional or Tribal Leaders* (Republic of Namibia, 1991), pp. 8–9, where it is affirmed that the "concept of a Nation must prevail over that of a tribe or ethnic group."

11. Heike Becker, "From Anti-Colonial Resistance to Reconstruction: Namibia Women's Movement, 1980 to 1992" (Ph.D. diss. University of Bremen, 1993), pp. 41–60. (This thesis provides an extremely useful and detailed synthesis of information about the women's movement.)

Information about the changing gender dynamics in particular communities is available in a number of sources, some of the more recent of which include Megan Biesele, *Women Like Meat: The Folklore and Foraging Ideology of the Kalahari Ju/'hoan* (Witwatersrand University Press/Indiana University Press, 1993); Gordon D. Gibson, Thomas J. Larson, and

Cecilia R. McGurk, *The Kavango Peoples* (Franz Steiner Verlag, 1981); Robert J. Gordon, *The Bushman Myth; The Making of a Namibian Underclass* (Westview Press, 1992); Margaret Jacobsohn, *Himba—Nomads of Namibia* (Struik, 1980); Karla O. Poewe, *The Namibian Herero: A History of Their Psychological Disintegration and Survival* (Edward Mellon Press, 1985); Frieda-Nela Williams, *Precolonial Communities of Southwestern Africa: A History of Owambo Kingdoms, 1600–1920* (National Archives of Namibia, 1991).

12. For more information on the gender impact of migrant labor, see Ndeutala Hishongwa, *The Contract Labour System and Its Effects on Family and Social Life in Namibia: A Historical Perspective* (Gamsberg Macmillan, 1992).

13. Although the laws supporting migrant labor were repealed in 1978, this employment pattern persists as a result of wage employment being concentrated in Windhoek.

14. See, for example, Tessa Cleaver and Marion Wallace, *Namibia—Women in War* (Zed Books, 1990); Denis Herbstein and John Evenson, *The Devils Are Among Us: The War for Namibia* (Zed Books, 1989); Manfred Hinz and Nadia Gevers, *Koevoet Versus the People of Namibia* (Working Group Kairos, 1989).

15. The CCN was established in 1978, with eight different denominations among its original members. The CCN women's desk, established in 1987, has focused on income-generating projects and educational programs as well as providing opportunities for women from churches from different regions to come together to discuss issues of common interest.

16. The NWV grew out of the first national women's conference in Namibia, convened in June 1985 by a number of church women who were establishing an ecumenical group. This conference drew together almost three hundred women from all parts of the country to discuss a broad range of issues. (See Becker, "From Anti-Colonial Resistance," p. 156, for more details.)

17. Under colonial population control policies, Depo-Provera (a long-acting hormonal contraceptive often accompanied by side effects) injections were often forced on Namibian women without their consent. The colonial regime also established a number of groups that organized cultural, religious, and sports activities at a local level to provide platforms for the spread of propaganda. The NWV helped raise community awareness of the true aims of these activities.

18. More details about the NWV are available in Becker, "From Anti-Colonial Resistance," pp. 155ff; and Cleaver and Wallace, *Namibia,* pp. 89ff.

19. See, for example, Bience Gawanas, "Namibian Independence," in Susan Bazilli, ed., *Putting Women on the Agenda* (Raven Press, 1991), p. 249.

20. Namibian constitution, Article 23(3). Article 10(2) prohibits discrimination on the grounds of sex, race, color, ethnic origin, religion, creed, or social or economic status.

21. Namibian constitution, Article 14(1).

22. Namibian constitution, Article 66(1). The same is true of common law in force at the date of independence.

23. Namibian constitution, Article 140(1).

24. For a detailed study of the operation of this affirmative action provision, see Dianne Hubbard and Kaveri Kavari, *Affirmative Action for Women in Local Government in Namibia* (Legal Assistance Center, 1993). The statutory provision applied only to the first local gov-

ernment elections that were held at the end of 1992; in subsequent local elections voters will select individual candidates rather than political parties.

25. For example, there were only seven women in ninety-eight seats in Namibia's two houses of Parliament at the end of 1993. Only three out of ninety-five seats on Namibia's thirteen regional councils were filled by women in 1992.

26. For example, the affirmative action provision in the Local Government Act was sponsored by one of Namibia's woman ministers. Women parliamentarians have used their positions to encourage parliamentary debate on issues of particular interest to women.

27. The regular meetings of this steering committee took place in Windhoek. While many of the groups involved operated outside of Windhoek as well, no regional representatives were involved in the deliberations. There was a plan to invite women from all parts of the country to a launching meeting that would make final decisions on the aims and structure of the umbrella body, but the initiative fell apart before this meeting took place.

28. The catalyst for the breakdown was disagreement on how many representatives would be allocated to the various women's groups at the launch of the umbrella body.

29. The Windhoek branch was the first to be established, in 1992. It has since stimulated the formation of similar groups in other locations and provided follow-up support.

30. Although gender issues in general have not been high on the overall trade union agenda, it is noteworthy that some male-dominated unions have entered into collective agreements that include provisions for maternity leave and that the nation's major trade union federation took a strong stand on the issue of maternity leave during negotiations around the new labor act that came into force in November 1992. See International Labor Organization, *Namibian Women and Employment: Strategies and Policies for the Promotion of Equal Opportunity and Treatment for Women and Men in Employment in Namibia* (ILO, 1992).

31. UNICEF/NISER, *A Situation Analysis,* p. 20.

32. The large number of female-headed households is another consequence of the extensive migration of male members of the family in search of wage employment. For example, a recent UNICEF survey of three rural areas in northern Namibia found that the percentage of female-headed households ranged from 40 to 49. UNICEF, *Household Health and Nutrition in Namibia* (UNICEF, 1990).

33. This is a function both of the interests of the women concerned and the availability of funds, as many donors are inclined to support such "traditional" programs rather than "risk" backing an unconventional project that might fail because it is "culturally unacceptable."

34. A national land conference organized by the government in June 1991 highlighted the need for affirmative action for women in the areas of landownership, inheritance, training, and credit and resolved that women should be fairly represented on all future bodies that administer communal land. However, these principles have yet to be translated into action. Similarly, while the government has repeatedly expressed its commitment to changing aspects of the laws on marriage that hamper women's economic capacity, such changes have not yet occurred.

35. More detailed information about the DWA's activities is available in Maria Kapere (undersecretary, DWA), "Report on the Department of Women's Affairs to the Inaugural

Annual Sharing Forum of Agencies Engaged in the Promotion of the Status of Women (Mariental, November 14–19, 1993)" (DWA, 1993), mimeo.

36. See DWA, *National Communication Strategy in Support of the U.N. Convention on the Elimination of All Forms of Discrimination Against Women, 1993–1995* (DWA, July 1993).

37. The DWA has a list of twenty-two different women's groups with which it regularly networks. However, other groups that attempt to play a networking role make use of a wider pool of contacts.

38. In fact, women in Namibia may be placing overly high expectations on what can be accomplished through law reform. While legal changes will certainly be important for women, they are unlikely in themselves to bring about the desired transformations in social and family life.

39. The issue of inheritance is particularly acute for women in some communities, where a widow may be deprived of her home, her land, and virtually all of her property upon the death of her husband. In advance of comprehensive law reform in this area, Parliament passed a resolution appealing to traditional leaders to show more compassion for the plight of widows, particularly during the current drought.

40. In 1990, it was estimated that 53 percent of the population had no access to clean water and 77 percent had inadequate sanitation facilities. This situation was clearly linked to a high incidence of gastrointestinal disease, which produced high levels of infant mortality. UNICEF/NISER, *A Situation Analysis*, p. 88.

41. The majority of Namibia's population is resident in the north of the country. However, it is also possible that the northern regions receive more attention from donor agencies because they suffered the most direct forms of war damage. As noted earlier, some people also believe that the SWAPO government gives priority to Oshiwambo-speaking areas in the north because so much of SWAPO's membership is drawn from this population.

7

The Mother of Warriors and Her Daughters: The Women's Movement in Kenya

WILHELMINA ODUOL

& WANJIKU MUKABI KABIRA

WHEN WE WERE FIRST approached about writing on the women's movement in Kenya, one question emerged in both of our minds: Is there a women's movement in Kenya? When we considered this, we simultaneously answered, "No." After more reflection, we began to ask, "If there is no women's movement, what is this intense activity going on around us of women's group meetings, workshops, seminars, and even individual women agitating for women's rights in the courts, in the media, and on the streets?" We were thus faced with the dilemma of deciding whether a women's movement does exist in Kenya and, if so, what it implies in the Kenyan context.

Our conceptualization of a conventional definition of a movement, emphasizing a common objective, continuity, unity, and coordination, led to our initially negative reaction on the question of a women's movement in Kenya. It is true that the Kenyan context has always been characterized by women's active participation in activities aimed at improving the status of women in all spheres of development. These activities are manifested in individual efforts, self-help groups, occupational associations, nongovernmental organizations, business enterprises, and social welfare activities, among others. In fact, women's group efforts are so vibrant that researcher and writer Patricia Stamp once described them "as the source of the most radical consciousness to be found in the countryside providing

KENYA

GENERAL

type of government: Republic
major ethnic groups: Kikuyu (21%); Luhya (14%); Luo (13%); Kalenjin (11%); Asian
language(s): Swahili (official); English and multiple tribal languages
religions: Protestant (38%); Catholic (28%); Muslim (6%); indigenous
date of independence: 1963
former colonial power: Britain

DEMOGRAPHICS

population size: 26.5 million
birth rate (*per 1,000 population*): 44
total fertility (*average number of births per woman*): 5.4
contraceptive prevalence (*married women*): 33%
maternal mortality rate (*per 100,000 live births*): 170

WOMEN'S STATUS

date of women's suffrage: 1963
economically active population: M 90%   F 58%
female employment (*% of total workforce*): 39
life expectancy   M 60   F 64
school enrollment ratio (*F/100 M*)
    primary   95
    secondary   78
    tertiary   36
literacy   M 80%   F 58%

---

women with a basis for resistance to exploitation."[1] This vibrant activity is equally
evident in urban settings, where women from all walks of life transcend individual, cultural, class, tribal, religious, and other barriers to identify issues of common concern and design strategies to address them.

    However, these efforts are often uncoordinated and fragmented, with individ-
ual women or women's groups developing specific structures and agendas in response to local situations. This approach to the movement often beguiles both
women themselves and the rest of the public into believing that the women's

movement either does not exist or is insignificant. In a few instances the movement has manifested itself as being coordinated and cohesive. This occurred during the social and political upheavals of the 1950s, when the whole country was agitating for political independence from colonial domination. The same cohesiveness was apparent during the democratization process of the 1990s, when women organized two national conventions to map strategies for the future development of Kenyan women. However, these moments of cohesiveness have been so limited that few people recognize their significance for the movement as a whole.

Perhaps the diversity that characterizes the women's movement is a strength rather than a weakness. In a social context where tribal, class, educational, and geographical differences make the identification and pursuit of common issues of concern difficult, it seems realistic to highlight this heterogeneity and strategize accordingly rather than operate under an illusion of homogeneity, which in reality *does not* and *cannot* exist in the Kenyan context. Janet Burja underscores this point by asserting that "we cannot belabor the fact that women cannot be thought of as a single category, even though there are important and occasionally unifying struggles in which they engage."[2] For Diane Margolis, the major strength of the 1985 United Nations Third World Conference on Women held in Nairobi was "recognizing and accepting that women have different perspectives, issues and priorities and strategizing to meet these needs."[3] The diversity that characterizes the women's movement in Kenya does not in any way detract from the strength of the movement. On the contrary, it helps stimulate the movement's activism and creativity.

The women's movement is not a recent phenomenon in Kenya. Its origins lie in the precolonial period, when women formed self-help groups and work parties to assist one another during periods of economic and social stress. This tradition of forming women's groups to consolidate efforts for addressing problems has carried forward into the contemporary period. As a result of socioeconomic and political changes occurring in Kenyan society, the women's movement now faces a number of major challenges. Kenyan society is still characterized by overarching patriarchal dominance and repressive sociocultural practices. Women are divided based on educational, economic, and geographic differences. Finally, the state and donor organizations have tended to be a co-optive and divisive influence.

In examining the evolution of the women's movement in Kenya from precolonial times to the present, we consider the women's movement to be synonymous with the emergence of women's groups. After providing a brief overview of Kenyan political and economic history and its impact on women, we examine these group activities at three levels: the women's group movement, largely rural and grassroots in nature; formal women's organizations; and the actions of individual women. We discuss the role played by the dominant patriarchal structures and existing sociocultural practices in shaping the women's movement. We analyze the extent to which the state has undermined these efforts by manipulating those in

In 1985, Kenya hosted the conference marking the end of the United Nations Decade for Women and the parallel Non-Governmental Organization Forum, drawing more than twenty thousand women to Nairobi.

leadership positions and interfering with the autonomy of existing organizations. We examine the role of donor agencies and Western development approaches in shaping the movement. Finally, we assess women's efforts to empower themselves at the personal level.

Background: The Social and Political Context

The country now known as Kenya encompasses diverse ethnic groups and geographical features. Along the coast its ports have supported an extensive and sophisticated trade economy for centuries. Its fertile highlands encouraged colonization and continue to support extensive cash crop production. However, it is estimated that only about 20 percent of Kenya's land is suitable for intensive agriculture. Much of the rest is semiarid and can support only periodic grazing. Distinct societies developed in these diverse conditions; this diversity has at times led to bitter tribal competition and conflict, which remain a dominant feature of Kenyan political and social life.

As European influence in the region increased, these distinct and often conflicting groups were brought together as a British protectorate in 1895 and annexed as a colony in 1920. The temperate climate and fertile soil of the highlands drew large numbers of European settlers, who appropriated land for large plantations, which primarily produced coffee and tea. The colonial administration instituted a series of laws and policies to ensure adequate cheap African labor to support large-scale plantation production. Both men and women initiated organized protests against these polices and the appropriation of their land and independence. A number of smaller protests culminated in the guerrilla independence war of the 1950s that came to be known as the Mau Mau war.

After an experimental period of shared rule, Kenya gained independence in 1963. Jomo Kenyatta, a Kikuyu leader and head of the Kenya African National Union (KANU), became president. Sometimes bitter struggles for leadership occurred in the new nation, and loyalty to rival political parties closely followed tribal lines. Although there was official provision for multipartyism, Kenyatta effectively silenced any opposition. His ability to quell the opposition and concentrate power within his own Kikuyu ethnic community led Kenyatta to become one of the most powerful leaders in Africa. In spite of his often repressive tactics and their lingering legacy for the country's political development, his reign, which lasted until his death in 1978, was marked by relative peace, political stability, and economic prosperity.

KANU continues to dominate Kenyan politics under Kenyatta's successor, Daniel arap Moi. Moi moved swiftly to consolidate his position by amending the constitution to legitimize a one-party state, silenced all dissident activity, and strengthened KANU's power. He effectively controls all three branches of government, his words and directives are law, and he brooks no opposition. The recent movement for democracy and the official emergence of multipartyism in 1992 have done little to alter this situation.

For women, this increasingly repressive political climate has clearly not been conducive to challenging state policy or organizing protest. However, the women's movement has built on many of its strengths to overcome the legacy of patriarchy. Women have continued to build on their traditional modes of organizing to galvanize into an increasingly powerful economic and political force.

Collaborative Effort: A Strategy Against Cultural and Patriarchal Dominance

In traditional times women cooperated and mobilized themselves to assist one another through self-help groups; membership was based on friendship, kinship networks, and common need. Work parties were formed to perform crucial labor activities within the household and on the farms, especially during peak agricul-

Kenyan women have a long tradition of working cooperatively in farm production. In the community of Kanyaa, women farmers work together cultivating maize and millet.

tural seasons and during illness and childbearing,[4] thus providing a form of maternity and sick leave. This tradition of community self-help was practiced by ethnic groups throughout much of Kenya,[5] providing a firm foundation for women's
self-help activities and a strong women's movement.[6]

The formation of women's self-help groups evolved as a coping mechanism in
male-dominated societies whose patriarchal structure ensured that most women
did not have adequate access to and control of resources, including land, cattle,
and other basic commodities. In an economy revolving around agriculture,
women had only user rights to land passed through the husband's patrilineage;
these traditional land tenure systems made few provisions for unmarried, divorced, or widowed women. In most societies all property was inherited through
the male line. When women today ask for control of title deeds or access to credit,
they are challenging these deep traditions.

These structures also denied women access to decisionmaking processes. Almost all societies now part of Kenya had political systems in which clan elders
made decisions concerning the political and legal affairs of the community; these
councils of elders were male dominated, and women rarely participated in them.[7]
In some strongly male-dominated societies, such as pastoral communities,
women were not even accorded adult status. This gender-based ideology of oppression was institutionalized through a number of mechanisms, including the legal system, educational and religious institutions, and customary beliefs and
practice.[8]

The gender-based division of labor also revealed the culturally determined and
socially constructed power relationships evident in traditional societies. Despite
this stereotyping of gender roles, in reality women performed all productive and
reproductive functions in addition to off-farm community activities. They
fetched water, cooked, collected firewood, and cared for both animals and family
members; they also did most of the manual agricultural work, tilling the land,
planting, weeding, harvesting, and processing food. In addition to ensuring that
women and girls did most of the work, these norms accorded higher status to the
male roles, a situation that continues in the present.

Women's realization that their marginalized position in society resulted in
common problems not experienced by men motivated them to initiate ways of
sharing and addressing these problems. Forming cooperative work parties was a
positive strategy for coping with the work burden. Women also expressed their
dissatisfaction through various cultural forms, such as song, poetry, and dance. In
a Maasai prayer described by writer and researcher Wanjiku Kabira, a young
woman describes her grief at the prospect of an arranged, polygamous marriage:[9]

> *My father*
> *Why do you send me to*
> *Ole Kasero*

> *Why do you send me*
> *to such an old man*
> *Ole Kasero has eleven wives*
> *You say he can look after me*
> *but he is too old*
> > *Father why do you send me to*
> > *Ole Kasero*

Such songs are not unusual in traditional Kenyan societies. Women challenged gender-based oppression in institutions such as marriage, polygamy, and political governance, which perpetuated their marginalized position, and found nonconfrontational artistic methods of expressing their challenge.

The Growth of the Women's Movement

During the colonial period the form and substance of women's resistance changed considerably. These changes were catalyzed by colonial policies and labor laws designed to meet the demand of a market-oriented economy, which disrupted traditional social structures and shifted responsibilities. The colonial period saw the strengthening of the women's movement. This was typified by two parallel movements that were formed almost simultaneously, and both drew their roots from the traditional support networks and self-help groups.

The first movement was composed of militant but informal associations of women who mobilized existing women's groups to rebel against those colonial policies that were destroying the local culture and economy and institutionalizing colonial structures and ideology. The colonial government imposed a series of laws and legislation that drew Kenya into the exploitative colonial global market economy. In 1902 an ordinance was enacted that "empowered" traditional village headmen to enforce forced labor policies. Between 1912 and 1922 the Native Authority Ordinance reinforced this policy by legalizing forced labor on European farms with minimal pay. The 1926 Native Ordinance and the hut and poll tax further ensured the availability of labor in European farms by necessitating cash income to meet tax obligations.[10] This resulted in massive male out-migration in search of wage employment.[11] Traditional family and social networks were profoundly disrupted.

As a direct consequence of these policies, many women became heads of households,[12] and their labor time greatly expanded as they continued to shoulder all their traditional responsibilities while taking on those of men. Women relied on their traditional work groups to help meet these responsibilities. Furthermore, in areas where cash crops were predominant, women performed all the manual tasks, such as picking coffee and tea, while men dominated the mechanized agricultural work. The Swynnerton Plan of 1955 led to the privatization of land and the issuing of title deeds to men by the colonial government. The plan sanctioned large tracts of land for cash crop production while sharply reducing land available for subsistence production, a sector dominated by women. This resulted in the erosion of women's customary rights and further limited their access to land.

The situation was exacerbated by the exploitation of natural resources for cash crop production, which resulted in extensive overcultivation, overgrazing, and soil erosion. To rectify this situation, the colonialists forced women to undertake soil conservation measures such as terracing, planting trees, intercropping, and engaging in mixed farming. This compounded women's workloads and left them with limited time to attend to their numerous other responsibilities.

All of this led to intense debate among women, which culminated in open rebellion in the 1930s and 1950s. A few women mobilized existing women's groups in a series of riots. According to the colonial commissioner at that time, "If left unchecked, [they] might have precipitated a landslide in government authority."[13] Women in Muranga district mobilized their groups to resist soil conservation measures in 1948: "2,500 women from Muranga danced and sang and informed everyone that they would not take part in soil conservation mainly because they felt they had enough to do at home. [When the District Commissioner ordered their arrest,] they were quickly released by a large crowd of their own sex brandishing sticks and shouting Amazon war cries."[14] Igembe women looted an Indian shop whose owner was not giving them a fair price for their produce.[15] In 1947 Kiambu women refused to pick coffee because they felt they were being underpaid.[16]

Numerous examples of women's mobilization also occurred during the Mau Mau war of 1952, which was fought to liberate Kenya from colonial domination and reclaim lost lands. Up to 5 percent of the forest fighters were women, and women also supported the war by organizing their work groups to prepare and carry food into the forest, hide firearms, and convey messages. As is discussed later, some women also rose to prominent leadership positions in the liberation struggle. In addition, women in central Kenya broke away from the most influential African political group of the time, the Agikuyu Central Association. Women characterized the group as chauvinistic in its approach toward issues and dominated by men, who assumed all the leadership positions and marginalized women. The women left to form their own group, the Mumbi Central Association, named for the mythical mother of the Agikuyu.

These examples of women's militant activities during the colonial era demonstrate that women were fighting oppression at two levels. They were fighting colonial domination, which denied them control of their lives in all spheres and totally disrupted the mechanisms that organized society. They were also fighting a patriarchal structure that provided all the opportunities to men while marginalizing women. Men engaged in cash crop production and reaped its benefits; they also reduced their workloads by using modern technologies, leaving the more menial tasks to women. As a result of disruptions in the traditional division of labor, women shouldered all responsibilities, while men worked away from home. The women resented this and fought against it.

Parallel to this more militant movement was the establishment in 1952 of a nationally based women's organization called Maendeleo Ya Wanawake (MYWO), which means "Progress for Women" in Swahili. It was formed by a group of white settlers and administrators' wives who sought to advance the status of women according to Western values. They mobilized traditional women's work groups and trained them in child care, hygiene, cooking, home sanitation, handicrafts, and other traditional activities.

The colonial government hoped that the interactions between white and black women within this organization would diffuse the tensions that were culminating in the liberation war. This is clearly evidenced in MYWO's close alliance with the colonial government during the Mau Mau uprising of the 1950s. In return for this support, the government awarded MYWO an annual grant for capital development and equipment, and its members were exempted from forced labor by the colonialists.[17] In fact, for many in Central Province in the 1950s and early 1960s, MYWO was synonymous with the colonial government and its homeguards. This created clear tensions between Mau Mau activists and those women's groups that supported them, on the one hand, and members of MYWO on the other. Ironically, after independence the new government sought to maintain this close association with MYWO. MYWO's close relationship with the ruling party, KANU, has created similar tensions with other women's organizations and activists in the contemporary period.

Scholarly opinion is divided on MYWO's success in promoting the cause of women. Some see MYWO as one of the few organizations that has successfully mobilized women's groups from all over Kenya and coordinated their activities in an effort to improve the status of women. Authors such as Ruth Nasimiyu and Shanyisa Khasiani, for example, quote escalating membership figures to support this assertion.[18] They argue that, while there were only 508 women's groups with a membership of 36,970 in 1954, today there are more than 3,000 registered groups coordinated by MYWO. They further assert that MYWO is the only women's organization that has provided a sense of continuity for the women's movement over the last three decades. It has weathered all sorts of obstacles since the colonial era, yet still retains its vitality.

Opposing views hold that MYWO has been vulnerable to political manipulation by the existing regime. Nzomo, for example, notes that in 1989 the organization was co-opted by the ruling party government.[19] Its elections were grossly interfered with by male KANU politicians who had picked their own candidates for the leading posts. Audrey Wipper also asserts that MYWO's acceptance of the status quo has limited its effectiveness as a membership organization since the leaders spend their time promoting the interests of the ruling party while ignoring the members' needs.[20] As already noted, KANU and the regime have used increasingly repressive measures to consolidate power. One tactic has been to try co-opting and controlling popular organizations, including MYWO. Because of MYWO's popularity and influence among women's groups all over the country, the government has a strong interest in co-opting it to win its members' support.

The Women's Movement in a Postcolonial Context

In addition to the efforts of Maendeleo Ya Wanawake, a number of other women's organizing and advocacy initiatives have emerged in the postcolonial era. These efforts can be classified into three broad categories: the women's group movement, which is concentrated in rural areas; formalized women's organizations largely based in urban centers; and the efforts of individual women. The following sections highlight the objectives and activities of these categories of women's initiatives and assess the extent to which they have succeeded in improving the overall status of Kenyan women.

The Women's Group Movement

The women's group movement refers to the informal voluntary women's groups that have proliferated all over the countryside and, to a lesser extent, in the urban centers. These groups are typically formed to engage in business enterprises, community projects, and revolving loan programs. The popularity of these groups is so marked that the 1988 *Women's Bureau Annual Report* put the total number of groups at twenty-seven thousand, with more than 1 million members.[21] Just as traditional self-help groups based their efforts on welfare-oriented and economic activities and utilized social, friendship, and kinship networks to draw their members, the women's group movement in the postcolonial era uses similar mechanisms as the basis for group formation. Membership is usually small (between five and twenty), with the majority coming from the same community and having little or no education. This reflects Kenya's low female literacy rates; of the 80 percent of women who live in rural areas, 62 percent are illiterate.[22] Leadership within the groups generally depends on popularity, although in some groups women with more education and higher socioeconomic status tend to dominate leadership positions. They bring skills and exposure that facilitate managing their group's programs. For this reason, a few groups also have male members. Many of the groups are linked with national or international women's organizations, which act as channels for technical and financial assistance to the groups from donors or the government.

Women's self-help groups increasingly work to provide members with skills and income, some-times in nontraditional areas. Under contract with the African Housing Fund, members of the Kayole Women's Self-Help group in Nairobi produce building materials, such as cinder block, and work in construction.

The groups' activities are wide ranging and often defy generalization. Mazingira Institute describes the myriad activities in the following way: "A group whose main goal is to own a business may also create an emergency welfare fund (through regular contributions) to help needy members, destitute children or homeless mothers in the community. Groups also incorporate educational activities in their meetings, welcome visits from health workers and agricultural advisors."[23]

Nevertheless, broad categorization is possible. Welfare groups generally concentrate on providing moral and material support to members during times of need, such as weddings, births, and funerals. Self-help groups organize to actively address community needs, such as constructing water cisterns, schools, bridges, dispensaries, and roads. Income-generating groups seem to have made the greatest strides toward the self-empowerment of women, particularly in the rural areas. Since traditionally women did not own resources or handle income, income earned and projects owned by women either individually or collectively to some extent help reduce their dependence. Illustrative examples of this include initiatives taken by women in Central Province to provide permanent roofing for their houses;[24] these efforts were so successful and prominent that the groups came to be known as *mabati* (iron roofing) women groups. Mazingira Institute also provides examples of women's groups that have transformed mutual welfare activities into revolving loan societies, investor groups, highly structured labor collectives, and so on.[25] Even more revolutionary, women's groups have bought land, business premises, and other properties. This signifies that women are moving away from merely coping with their traditional status to challenging and redressing it. The sense of empowerment derived from ownership of property is described by Rahab Wabici, a woman from Central Province, in referring to the land her group bought: "I am a free woman. I bought this piece of land through my group. I can lie on it, work on it, keep goats or cows. What more do I want? My husband cannot sell it. It is mine."[26]

However, while the women's group movement continues to make major strides in addressing issues of concern to women, it also faces major obstacles. The patriarchal administrative machinery blocks many of the women's attempts to challenge existing structures—land is not subdivided, title deeds are not released, and legal cases sometimes remain in court for decades. A formidable obstacle also emanates from the state and KANU, which realize that as a majority of voters are women, they have the potential to greatly influence the political direction of the country. Furthermore, if united, the women's group movement poses a major threat to male superiority and dominance in Kenyan society. To dilute this threat, the state has often manipulated and shaped the direction of the movement to suit its purposes. It does this by using divisive politics based on class, rural-urban, ethnic, and educational differences among women. Politicians often coopt women's

groups by appointing their own wives, relatives, or other partisan women as leaders, thereby ensuring votes during election periods.

Another threat to the women's group effort is the influence of donor agencies in
shaping its structures, objectives, and activities. Donors work with women's
groups through national coordinating organizations such as MYWO, the National
Council of Women of Kenya (NCWK), and the Young Women's Christian Association (YWCA). Because many of the donor agencies still adhere to a women-in-
development (WID) approach, they focus largely on welfare-oriented projects.
WID posits that women, as a disadvantaged category, need to be integrated into
development projects. Carefully designed strategies and projects have been implemented in attempts to improve women's status, but without challenging fundamental gender relations. Typically, women engage in small projects in areas such
as beehive keeping, poultry, goats, and kitchen gardens; often the benefits are
minimal compared to the input. Other projects are based on outside ideas and
technologies such as water pumps or grinding mills. When these break down,
members tend to disassociate themselves from the project since the program idea
was not internally generated. However, not all projects undertaken by women's
groups are donor sponsored, nor do all those that are sponsored by donors fail.
Nevertheless, groups that are affected negatively by donor influence find it difficult to achieve a sense of independence or empowerment.

Formalized Women's Organizations
and Associations

Apart from the women's group movement at the grassroots level, there are many
formalized women's organizations and associations that have raised strong voices
in the women's movement. These organizations are nongovernmental, and most
are formally registered under the statutes governing organizations in Kenya. Most
of them are affiliated with international women's organizations whose objectives
they largely adhere to. A few of them, such as the Kenya Finance Trust (KFT), the
YWCA, and the NCWK, are umbrella organizations for grassroots women's
groups.

The efforts of these organizations complement those of the small rural groups
just discussed. They see women as agents of social change who should have their
voices heard, and the activities and programs of these organizations are oriented
toward empowering women at different levels. For many, empowerment implies
the capacity of women to increase their self-reliance and internal strength through
group effort and mobilization. Some also vocally challenge existing social structures and institutions and advocate for the elimination of discriminatory practices against women at all levels.

These organizations use a variety of approaches. For example, while the YWCA
primarily conducts welfare programs, it also worked aggressively for women's po-

The National Council of Women of Kenya (NCWK) was founded in 1964 and is widely known for its successful Greenbelt Movement to combat desertification. Women carrying seedlings march in Nairobi in 1981.

litical empowerment during the democratization period of 1992, when it organized voter education for women throughout the country. The KFT focuses on economic empowerment of women by providing loans and business skills. This does not, however, prevent it from engaging in welfare activities such as child care, family nutrition, and hygiene.

Perhaps the organization that best exemplifies these diverse activities is the NCWK. The NCWK was initiated as an affiliate of the International Council of Women in 1964 to coordinate women's organizations and groups in Kenya. While many of its programs, such as dressmaking, crafts, and home economics, reinforce women's traditional roles, it also works actively for women's empowerment. For example, during the multiparty era in the early 1990s, the NCWK launched the National Committee on the Status of Women to educate women on democracy and their political rights as Kenyan citizens. The organization also sponsors scholarships and training institutions for girls and women and initiated the well-known Greenbelt Movement to combat desertification in Kenya. It was instrumental in the First and Second Women's Conventions that took place in 1992 and 1993 and brought women together to strategize and demonstrate their solidarity in the struggle against gender-based oppression.

Women's organizations increasingly form partnerships to address pressing issues. Girl Guide leaders participate in a training session on gender violence conducted by the Kenya Anti-Rape Organization.

Several other organizations have been at the forefront of the women's movement and bear mention. The Kenya chapter of the International Federation of Women Lawyers has advocated for legal protection for children and women, especially widows; conducted outreach programs to educate grassroots women on their legal rights; provided legal counsel; and challenged laws that discriminate against women. The League of Women Voters undertook a voter education program during the democratization process of 1992, published a booklet on women and democracy, and advocates for women's rights in all spheres. The Antirape Organization conducts educational and policy programs against violence against women and provides support to women who have been physically assaulted by men.

Of special interest is the contribution of research organizations and writers to the liberation of Kenyan women. A major example of this is the Kenya chapter of the Association of African Women in Research and Development (AAWORD). AAWORD engages in action-oriented research on women's issues for policy implementation. Its publications, which include *Democratic Change in Africa, The Women's Movement in Kenya,* and *Women in Politics,* provide information to influence policy on a range of issues affecting women. AAWORD also conducts seminars in areas such as research methods, women and democratization, and vi-

NCWK takes an active role in the political education of women. Here women campaign during a parliamentary election.

olence against women. Its impact is largely felt in educated and professional circles.

Writers of fiction and poetry have continued the tradition of using cultural expression to articulate women's perspectives, concerns, and aspirations. In *Our Secret Lives*, by Wanjiku Kabira and Akinyi Nzioki,[27] women express their individual suffering. They reveal how the sanctioned status of women and girls continues to destroy the body, mind, and soul of women. In *They Have Destroyed the Temple*, women condemn their own alienation and the destruction of the temple within them and express the desire for full autonomy and a full life.[28] While these writers target both the public and academia, a major emphasis is on providing material to schools to reverse the socialization process in educational texts that portrays women as subordinate. While these writers have taken important and often courageous steps, given Kenya's strong patriarchal orientation, major changes in the perception of women require sweeping policy changes.

While formalized organizations work for women's rights, they face a number of problems. Just as the state developed mechanisms to weaken women's groups at the grassroots level, it also manipulates these formal organizations and employs divisive strategies that hamper unity. While the ruling party rewards and financially supports organizations such as MYWO that promote its interests, it harasses and heavily censures those organizations that challenge its oppressive patriarchal structure. For example, under the strong leadership of Professor Wangari Maathai, the NCWK was censored by KANU and the government for publicly challenging government policies that undermined women's progress and the promotion of human rights.

A major omission by the formalized organizations is that, while they concentrate on power relations in the public sphere, their members compromise their rights at the personal level. For many women, practicing at the personal level and within the home what they advocate in public is impossible. Many women stay in unhappy marriages because divorce is culturally unacceptable. Many cannot make personal decisions on whether to stay single or whether to have children because they are going against societal expectations. Many activist women also continue to perform multiple roles at home and at work without expecting assistance from men because they risk being ostracized.

Without empowering themselves, women who advocate for female liberation cannot act as effective role models. It is therefore quite unfortunate that this vital element of women's liberation efforts has been largely ignored by existing organizations. Few groups have programs that deal with strengthening the personal lives of individual women through hotlines, counseling services, or centers for women who are victims of domestic and other forms of violence. Until these issues are effectively addressed, the impact of the women's movement will be limited in the real lives of Kenyan women.

Efforts of Individual Women

The importance of individual women's efforts toward individual and group liberation cannot be underestimated. While there is a paucity of literature on women's heroic actions during the precolonial era, colonial history abounds with examples of women who sacrificed their lives to fight for the cause of liberation and attain personal empowerment.

Scores of women joined men in the forests to fight colonial domination during the Mau Mau war of 1952. Of these women, a few rose to very senior ranks within the military. Likimani describes the case of Field Marshall Muthoni, a woman who attained this high military rank in a male-dominated army because of her courage and individual discipline.[29] She later defied all traditional constraints when she divorced her husband after the war by returning the dowry paid for her; he had told her that she needed to remember that she was just a woman.[30] At a time when divorce was a rare phenomenon and cultural inhibitions were at their height, this action was considered an extreme act of courage by female activists and total rebellion by the rest of society.

Wanjiru Nyamarata acted as a judge in the Mau Mau courts in Nakuru town in the center of Mau Mau activities. She passed sentences and was intensively involved in administering oaths and recruiting new guerrillas. As a result of these activities, she earned the name *Nyina-wa-Anake* (Mother of Senior Warriors).[31] This is particularly significant because during this period it was unheard of for women in any of the Kenyan ethnic communities to participate in judicial matters, let alone act as judges. The courageous feats of these individual women reversed societal perceptions of women from dependent and submissive to politically active, at least as long as the Mau Mau war lasted. Academic Tabitha Kanogo supports this assertion in noting that during this period "leadership ceased to be a male preserve and there was no difference between male and female leaders."[32]

In the postindependence period heroic women have persisted. Two cases that have had wide repercussions in Kenyan society are the famous 1987 Wambui Otieno case, where a woman fought to reverse patriarchal laws that prohibited her from burying her husband, and the case of Professor Wangari Maathai previously mentioned.

S. M. Otieno, a legal practitioner from the western Luo tribe based in Nairobi, died in 1986. His wife, Wambui Otieno, a Kikuyu, and his relatives and clan members could not agree on a place of burial. She filed a suit in the high court claiming the right to bury her husband on their farm near Nairobi. Otieno's relatives claimed that no respected member of the Luo tribe could be buried away from his rural ancestral lands. This case generated heated debate and forced examination of a range of policies relevant to women. What are the rights of Kenyan women in relation to burial of their nearest kin and inheritance of property both in constitutional law and traditional customs? What is the relevance of constitutional law in a society in transition from a traditional to a modern economy? What are the tensions and conflicts resulting from ethnic intermarriages?

After four months of what the *Washington Post* described as "the most sensational legal struggle in Kenya's history," Wambui Otieno lost her case.[33] The judge declared that according to Luo custom, which is considered customary law, the deceased would be handed over to his brother, who would bury him in his rural home village. This case was illustrative of a society torn between adherence to familiar traditional norms and values and the need to adopt and respond to new values. More important, the case epitomized patriarchal gender-based oppression. The details revealed that in Luo customary law women were not only denied the right to bury their husbands and other close kin but were also not considered their husbands' closest kin. After a man's death, his brother would be considered the next of kin and would look after the estate until the eldest son married; the wife would then be inherited by the husband's relatives. These customs also applied in many other Kenyan tribal communities.

The case also clearly revealed the openly discriminatory nature of Kenyan constitutional law. The court of appeal admitted that the constitution permits discriminatory laws on matters of personal law. The court did not even refer to the section of the constitution that specifically deals with the protection of fundamental rights and freedoms of the individual. In his concluding statement, the judge categorically stated that "the plaintiff had no right to bury her husband under Luo customary law. She does not become the head of the family upon the death of her husband."[34] Such blatant statements have led to a number of changes, such as the formation of a high-level commission dominated by women, to look into and change discriminatory laws and regulations.

Wangari Maathai has committed her life to the struggle against gender-based oppression and violation of human rights. A Ph.D., scientist, and internationally renowned environmentalist, Maathai headed the NCWK in the 1980s and initiated the Greenbelt Movement to mobilize women for environmental conservation efforts. During her participation in public life, she has spearheaded the women's movement by taking a position on national issues adversely affecting women's rights. In 1986 the NCWK challenged the validity of the queuing method, where votes are counted by persons publicly standing in line, rather than secret balloting. When Wambui Otieno was fighting for the right to bury her husband, only the NCWK under Maathai actively lobbied for the introduction of burial laws that protect the rights of women. She broadened the agenda of the women's movement by challenging the government on the environment and human rights. The most celebrated incident was her battle to stop the government from erecting a skyscraper in the middle of the largest recreational park in Nairobi.[35] She was threatened, harassed, and thrown out of the offices she had occupied for over a decade. In March 1992 mothers of political prisoners being detained without trial went on strike; Maathai was the only elite woman who actively joined and fasted with the mothers. When these women were attacked and brutally beaten by the police, she was among the victims, beaten unconscious and admitted to the intensive care unit in Nairobi Hospital.[36] When she was endorsed as the presidential candidate by women delegates in June 1992, she turned the offer down, maintaining that she could best serve women in her capacity as an environmental conservationist and not as a politician.

Conclusion

In the introduction to this chapter, we emphasized that, while conventional notions of social movements do not fully explain the women's movement in Kenya, the movement does exist and is vibrant with activity. However, these efforts are often uncoordinated and fragmented, with individual women's groups developing specific strategies to suit local situations. We also noted that the movement has its roots in traditional forms of resistance to gender-based oppression. We argued that this resistance was expressed by developing strategies for coping with the burdens imposed by unequal gender division of labor and expressing silent resistance in artistic forms.

These less confrontational forms of resistance evolved in the colonial era to a more militant stand against colonialism and gender-based oppression, as embodied in protests and women joining in the guerrilla independence struggle. In the postcolonial context the movement has become more diversified. Women fight against male dominance as individuals and as members of groups. They strategize and formulate coping mechanisms ranging from welfare-oriented approaches to initiatives that aim at transforming the status of women in all areas of society. They are not satisfied with perpetuating the stereotyped roles of wife and mother that have been mapped out for them by society. They want equal pay for equal work, their own title deeds and other property, a share in reproductive work, and the freedom to shape not only their destiny but also the whole nation.

However, to attain their objectives, they must continue to fight the negative challenges posed by state, tribal, class, ideological, and cultural mechanisms that perpetuate their marginalized position. This requires more effective strategizing, the more vigorous pursuit of existent goals, and the ability to withstand opposition and harassment from a male-dominated society.

NOTES

1. P. Stamp, "Kikuyu Women's Self-Help Groups: Towards an Understanding of the Relation Between Sex-Gender System and Mode of Production in Africa," in C. Robertson and I. Berger, eds., *Women and Class in Africa* (New York: Holmes and Meier, 1986).

2. J. Burja, "Urging Women to Redouble Their Efforts: Class, Gender, and Capitalist Transformation in Africa," in C. Robertson and I. Berger, eds., *Women and Class in Africa* (New York: Holmes and Meier, 1986).

3. D. Margolis, "Women's Movements Around the World: Cross-Cultural Comparisons," *Gender and Society* 7, no. 3 (1993):380.

4. R. Nasimiyu, "The History of Maendeleo ya Wanawake Movement in Kenya," in S. Khasiani and E. Njiro, eds., *The Women's Movement in Kenya* (Nairobi: Association of African Women for Research and Development, 1993).

5. B. Thomas, *Politics, Participation, and Poverty: Development Through Self-Help in Kenya* (Boulder: Westview Press, 1985), pp. 7–8.

6. Mazingira Institute, *Women and Development: A Kenya Guide* (Nairobi: Mazingira Institute, 1992).

7. W. M. Kabira and A. Nzioki, *Celebrating Women's Resistance* (Nairobi: Women Perspective Publications, 1993).

8. J. B. Ojwang and J. Mugambi, eds., *The S. M. Otieno Case: Death and Burial in Modern Kenya* (Nairobi: Nairobi University Press, 1989).

9. Kabira and Nzioki, *Celebrating Women's Resistance*, p. 27.

10. A. Pala, "Daughters of the Lakes and Rivers: Colonization and the Land Rights of Luo Women" in M. Eteinne and E. Leacock, eds., *Women and Colonization: Anthropological Perspectives* (New York: Praeger, 1980).

11. T. Kanogo, "Kikuyu Women and Politics of Protest: Mau Mau," in P. Halden MacDonald and A. Ardener, eds., *Images of Women in Peace and War: Cross-Cultural Perspec-*

tives (London: Macmillan, 1987). Kanogo notes that in Central Province up to 50 percent of the men were short-term migrant laborers.

12. Republic of Kenya, *Agricultural Survey* (Nairobi: Government Printer, 1986). In Kitui district, male out-migration resulted in up to 36 percent of households being female headed.

13. Kenya National Archives, DC/FHI/27. 1948, p. 1.

14. Kanogo, "Kikuyu Women."

15. H. E. Lambert, *A Guide to Women's Organizations and Agencies Serving Women in Kenya* (Nairobi: Mazingira Institute, 1985), p. 100.

16. Kanogo, "Kikuyu Women."

17. J. Nzomo, "The Kenya Women's Movement in a Changing Political Context," in S. Khasiani and E. Njiro, eds., *The Women's Movement in Kenya* (Nairobi: Association of African Women for Research and Development, 1993).

18. Nasimiyu, "The History of Maendeleo ya Wanawake."

19. Nzomo, "The Kenya Women's Movement."

20. A. Wipper, "Equal Rights for Women in Kenya," *Journal of Modern Studies* 9, no. 3 (1971):427–442.

21. Republic of Kenya, *The Women's Bureau Annual Report* (Nairobi: Ministry of Culture and Social Services, Women's Bureau, 1988).

22. Republic of Kenya, *Kenya Literacy Survey* (Nairobi: Government Printer, 1988).

23. Mazingira Institute, *Women and Development*, p. 14.

24. M. Monsted, *Women's Groups in Rural Kenya and Their Role in Development* (Copenhagen: Center for Development Research, 1978).

25. Mazingira Institute, *Women and Development*, p. 8.

26. Kabira and Nzioki, *Celebrating Women's Resistance*, p. 75.

27. W. M. Kabira and A. Nzioki, *Our Secret Lives* (Nairobi: Phoenix 1992).

28. A. Nzioki and W. M. Kabira, eds., *They Have Destroyed the Temple* (Nairobi: Longman, 1993).

29. M. Likimani, *Women of Kenya: Twenty Years of Independence* (Nairobi: Giant Printers, 1983), p. 7.

30. Kabira and Nzioki, 1993.

31. W. A. Oduol, "Kenyan Women in Politics: An Analysis of Past and Present Trends," in G. S. Were, ed., *TransAfrican Journal of History* Vol. 22; 166–180. Nairobi: Gideon S. Were Press, 1993).

32. Kanogo, "Kikuyu Women."

33. *Washington Post*, May 25, 1987.

34. Okechi-Owiti, "Some Socio-legal Issues," in J.B.O. Ojwang and J.N.K. Mugambi, eds., *The S. M. Otieno Case: Death and Burial in Modern Kenya* (Nairobi: Nairobi University Press, 1989), p. 12.

35. Nzomo, "The Kenya Women's Movement."

36. *Standard*, March 4, 1992.

8

Wifeism and Activism: The Nigerian Women's Movement

HUSSAINA ABDULLAH

THE POPULATION OF NIGERIA, the largest in sub-Saharan Africa, is composed of more than three hundred distinct ethnic groups, which were brought together under British colonial rule in 1914. Long-standing ethnic and religious rivalries, reinforced by the British, remain a dominant feature of Nigerian political and social life. In general, the north is dominated by the Muslim Hausa and Fulani; the southeast, by the predominantly Christian Igbo; and the southwest, by the Yoruba, who include both Christians and Muslims. Since independence in 1960, competition for control of the nation's economic and political resources has led to brief efforts at democracy interrupted by prolonged periods of military rule. Most recently, the military government spent years proclaiming its commitment to a return to civil rule. After numerous delays, presidential elections were finally held in June 1993. When the government's candidate appeared to lose, the results were promptly canceled.

The government influences every sector of Nigerian life through layers of administrative structures that reach far into rural areas. Despite increasing urbanization, approximately 70 percent of the population still live in rural areas, where they engage largely in agriculture and small-scale economic activities. Agriculture was traditionally the core of the Nigerian economy, a situation that dramatically changed with the discovery of oil in the 1970s. This vast oil wealth has brought some infrastructure and industry to Nigeria. However, the country's enormous economic potential has remained largely unrealized. Much of the country's oil revenue has been concentrated among a small elite or lost to poor economic planning and corruption. Few, if any, of the benefits have reached the majority of Ni-

NIGERIA

GENERAL

type of government: Federal Republic; in transition
major ethnic groups: 250 groups, 10 of which account for 80% of population; Hausa
    (21%); Yoruba (20%); Ibo (17%); Fulani (9%)
language(s): English (official); Hausa, Yoruba, Ibo
religions: Islam (50%); Christianity (35%); animist
date of independence: 1960
former colonial power: Britain

DEMOGRAPHICS

population size: 88.5 million
birth rate (*per 1,000 population*): 48.5
total fertility (*average number of births per woman*): 6.6
contraceptive prevalence (*married women*): 6%
maternal mortality rate (*per 100,000 live births*): 800

WOMEN'S STATUS

date of women's suffrage: 1957
economically active population: M 88%   F 46%
female employment (*% of total workforce*): 35
life expectancy   M 48.8   F 52.2
school enrollment ratio (*F/100 M*)
    primary   76
    secondary   74
    tertiary   39
literacy   M 62%   F 40%

---

gerians. These problems, combined with the severe global recession of the 1980s, led the government to adopt a mandated structural adjustment program (SAP) to increase foreign exchange earnings to service the country's foreign debt. This has dramatically curtailed funding for social programs and has had severe effects on the standard of living of Nigerians at all levels.

In many areas, the brunt of these economic problems have been felt most acutely by women as few women are steadily employed in the formal economy. In urban areas, women's work is concentrated in the informal sector, especially in food production and sale and in trading. In rural areas, women generally work in food crop agriculture, food processing, petty trading, and a host of time-consuming, unremunerated household tasks. Most households, especially those in rural areas, are large and multigenerational; approximately 40 percent of Nigerian marriages are polygynous, and the total fertility rate, while declining, still averages more than six births per woman.[1] This rate reflects prevailing attitudes, which value large families and base women's status primarily on their roles as wives and mothers, especially of male children.

These familial roles were traditionally the basis on which Nigerian women organized within their villages and communities around activities such as circumcision, childbirth, and marriage rites. The groups organized around these activities as well as savings societies and work groups formed the basis of women's rich associational history in precolonial times. Women were also active in organizations established to protect their communities. These associations unquestionably provided women with necessary support and camaraderie. However, in keeping with the values that underlay "tradition" and religion, these activities also tended to reinforce and reproduce the structures of patriarchy through which women were subordinated.

During the British colonial period, women continued to address their traditional socioeconomic and political concerns, while also protesting against the economic and political policies of the colonial government. Two well-known examples of women's activism are the Aba women's riot of 1929 and the Egba women's protest of 1947. In both cases, women organized and took to the streets to protest the colonial administration's most egregious taxation policies and those prohibiting assembly. Out of these anticolonial struggles emerged the first women's association that crossed ethnic, religious, and class barriers. The National Women's Union was started in 1947 by Funmilayo Ransome-Kuti, a dynamic leader who organized the Egba women's protest.[2]

The Women's Movement in Nigeria Today

In contemporary Nigeria there is at least some general level of national awareness of the importance of women's roles in development. A host of women's organizations operate at the national and/or at the grassroots community level. Of necessity, these groups are primarily concerned with conventional issues of livelihood and welfare. However, questions of women's emancipation and empowerment are also debated, and women's organizations are posing significant challenges to patriarchal structures.

Concomitant with the onset of the ongoing Nigerian economic crisis, since the 1980s rural and urban Nigerian women—sometimes joined by men—have increasingly organized to empower women and help them devise strategies to combat the effect of the economic crisis. These organizations have tackled not just the difficulties posed by the relics of traditional cultural practices but also newer problems caused by the dynamics of "modernization." Generally, rural women's groups identified with traditional activities such as initiation rites have declined in number and significance as cultural values and practices have changed. Presently, the majority of women's organizations that have emerged to champion the rights of women and to advance gender consciousness in society are located in the principal urban centers.

In Nigeria there is general agreement that there is a women's movement comparable to other social movements with a visible presence around the country. However, sociologist Mere Kisekka is substantially right in stating that "it cannot, however, be accurately inferred that there is a women's movement in the country which is vociferously engaged in the exposure and challenge of gender inequality in most of its ramifications. Rather, most women's associations have striven to operate cautiously within traditional gender boundaries articulating the theory of complementary rather than competitive roles in gender relations."[3]

Only a few activists take the view that the objectives of the women's movement are similar to those of labor, human rights, and student groups, which clamor for restructuring society. Many see the objectives of women's groups as different: "The Nigerian women's movement is an unarmed movement. It is non-confrontational. It is a movement for the progressive upliftment of women for motherhood, nationhood and development."[4] Very few women leaders accept that the movement is feminist in orientation. Those objecting to the feminist label view it as Western terminology that should not be employed in Africa, as captured in the words of a woman lawyer: "When African women demand equality, we are only asking for our rights not to be tampered with, and the removal of laws that oppress and dehumanize women. We are not asking for equality with our husbands. We accept them as the bosses and heads of the family."[5]

The concept of feminism should thus be contextualized within each society where it applies. Yet in a certain sense, the Nigerian women's movement can be considered feminist in orientation because it is attempting to transform gender relations in society. To buttress this point, a leader of the group Women in Nigeria asks, "What is Western feminism anyway? African men see nothing wrong in their relationship with Western governments and institutions, but object to African women having relationships with these same institutions. Why? Because they feel threatened by the prospects of feminism."[6] The women's movement is evolving as women build coalitions. Examples of this are the establishment of the Community Development Association by grassroots women's groups, the formation of the National Task Force on Vesico-Vaginal Fistulae (VVF),[7] and the formation of the Nigeria National Safe Motherhood Movement by women's health groups.

The notion that women are bound together by a common history of oppression and a common struggle to achieve liberation does not hold true in Nigeria. There are secondary divisions in any social movement that create obstacles for the realization of group objectives, even within a single-sex movement like the women's movement.[8] In Nigeria these cleavages are based on age, religion, marital status, ethnic origin, educational level, and social class. Tensions and conflicts within the women's movement have been based in part on differences over strategy and policy and in part on leadership struggles. The Nigerian movement cannot be faulted for not being a homogeneous organized body. Rather, it consists of several groups, all of which are arguing in different, and at times conflicting, ways about matters affecting women based on differing perceptions of women's interests.

Throughout Nigerian history, numerous individual women have gained national prominence in their own right. It is also the case that wives of men in certain occupations have had ceremonial responsibilities. The roles of politicians' wives have recently been institutionalized in a manner that has far-reaching implications for an autonomous, genuine women's agenda oriented toward full emancipation. The role of the Nigerian state in relation to the women's movement can be examined in the expression of this peculiar phenomenon of "wifeism" in women's affairs. In this chapter I examine the emergence of wifeism and the bureaucratization of women's concerns in Nigeria through state involvement, especially since the early 1980s. I pay particular attention to the relations between state-sponsored women's programs and autonomous groups in the women's movement. Finally, I explore the implications all these issues have for developing and moving forward a truly emancipatory feminist agenda in Nigeria.

Government-Sponsored Women's Bureaucracies: Wifeism in Nigeria

As part of the United Nations Decade for Women (1975–1985), all member governments were encouraged to establish appropriate national machinery to aid women's integration into development. Nigeria's response led to the increasing bureaucratization of women's issues. The National Committee on Women and Development (NCWD) was established within the federal Ministry of Social Development, Youth, and Sports in 1982. The NCWD was set up to liaise between women's nongovernmental organizations (NGOs) and the government to coordinate all activities relating to women, to advise the government on women's issues, and to design programs to facilitate women's integration into the development process.[9] The NCWD's activities were fairly traditional, such as training in home economics, arts and crafts, health and personal hygiene, literacy, and income-generating activities. The committee's composition reflected an urban, upper-class bias; although 90 percent of Nigeria's female population work in the agricultural or informal sectors of the economy, there was no one to represent their interests on the NCWD's twelve-member board.

After reverting to military rule in the 1980s, Nigeria began for the first time since independence to pay specific policy attention to women's issues at the highest level of state power, the presidency. This interest in women can be understood in the context of the overall objectives of the SAP. One of the SAP's provisions was to facilitate opening up the rural areas by providing incentives to male farmers to increase productivity and generate higher monetary income. This was central to the government's export promotion drive aimed at boosting foreign exchange earnings for debt servicing and repayment.

To involve women more fully in development, and to counter the negative effects of these export promotion policies on rural families, the government initiated the Better Life for Rural Women Programme (BLP) in 1987, launched as an arm of the Directorate of Food, Roads, and Rural Infrastructure. This program ushered in a new era in the development of the women's agenda in Nigeria. It heralded the twin processes of direct intervention by the state in the formation and funding of women's organizations and the systematic appointment of wives of high-ranking government officials as leaders of these organizations. I refer to these phenomena as state pseudofeminism. By introducing the BLP, the Nigerian government brought rural women, long excluded from the capitalist nexus, directly into the capitalist arena.[10] While the BLP first targeted only rural women, eventually all rural inhabitants were included in order to encourage men to support the program.

Mrs. Maryam Babangida, wife of the then-military president, Ibrahim Babangida, was the founder and national coordinator of the BLP, which she came to personify. In this capacity, she was assisted by a team made up of the wives of ranking service chiefs and a select group of professional academic women. This pattern was replicated at other government levels, with wives of state governors who were appointed military officers and local government chairmen heading BLP branches in their husbands' areas of jurisdiction. Only in the few cases where a woman herself was a local government chairperson were other women appointed as leaders within the BLP organization.

The BLP's stated aim was to create a "new rural woman"—economically strong, politically active, socially aware, psychologically fulfilled, and thus equipped to play her role in society to the fullest.[11] To achieve these objectives, the BLP began literacy and vocational training courses, social welfare and health programs, enlightenment campaigns, and income-generating projects for women. By 1991, the BLP was claiming 9,422 cooperatives, 1,435 cottage industries, 1,094 multipurpose centers, and 495 shops and markets scattered throughout the country. There were BLP branches in all thirty states and the federal district of Abuja, from the ward level to the national level. Their activities were covered extensively in the print and electronic media. By 1992, the BLP had built the ultramodern Center for Women's

Mrs. Maryam Babangida, wife of military president Ibrahim Babangida, was the founder and national coordinator of the controversial government-sponsored Better Life Programme.

Development in Abuja, named for Maryam Babangida, appointed the BLP's national patron and the only life member of the board.

Ideologically, the BLP reinforced gender subordination in the guise of women's activism. As a state-sponsored women's group, it mirrored the state's conservative image of women as wives, mothers, and secondary income earners. The BLP leadership structure was both hierarchical and completely unrepresentative of its professed constituency of poor, uneducated, rural women. The automatic appointment of women to positions based on their husbands' rank in the state political and military hierarchy and regardless of suitability or merit was undemocratic and reinforced the prevailing societal image of women as appendages to male power.

The BLP's cooptation of the women's agenda and use of government funds were challenged in several ways. Most notable was a legal complaint filed in 1989 by Lagos lawyer and human rights activist Gani Fawehinmi seeking a court injunction to restrain the federal military government from authorizing additional public funds to Mrs. Babangida. Fawehinmi maintained that Babangida had "no legal and constitutional function of duty assigned to her and consequently ... no legal and constitutional right or backing to use or expend public funds for any purpose."[12]

While the government did not respond to Fawehinmi's suit, it decreed the institutionalization of the BLP's activities. Shortly afterward, the government created a new body, the National Commission for Women. It was mandated to take over the activities of both the NCWD and BLP, among other functions.

Both the commission and BLP enjoyed patronage from the government in the form of yearly grants. Between 1987 and 1992, the BLP received 400 million naira ($18 million); the commission was allocated 77 million naira ($4 million) for its three-year plan. These funds have provided office buildings in nearly every state, staff salaries, media coverage, overseas travel, vehicle purchases, and the presence of the top government functionaries at the organizations' events. The impact on actual programs and the lives of rural women is somewhat less clear.

While at first relations between the new commission and the BLP were cordial, discernible cracks soon appeared in their facade of solidarity. In keeping with the mandate to take over the BLP's activities, the commission's board wanted to streamline the BLP and subject it to examination and monitoring. However, the BLP coordinators and advisers refused to submit to this scrutiny. This initially resulted in a standoff between the two organizations and eventually in a 1992 military decree that repealed the previous decree establishing the commission. This essentially left the BLP and its leaders unaccountable to any constituency or monitoring body.

The new decree dissolved the board of the commission and named a new national advisory council (NAC) in its place. First Lady Maryam Babangida, already the chair of the BLP, was also designated the chair of this new council. Fourteen additional members were to reflect a cross section of national interests but did not include representation of the rural women whose interests the BLP was supposed to advance. On the role of the NAC, the decree states, "The National Advisory Council shall be charged with the responsibility of advising, guiding, and monitoring the activities of the National Commission [for Women] on national policies and programs pertaining to the objectives and functions of the National Commission and the Better Life for Rural Women Programme." [13]

The government gave no explanation for these actions. Apparently, the board of the commission had tried to fulfill its mandate of monitoring the BLP by subjecting the wives of the ruling military junta to rules of accountability and the laws of civil society, and in response the board was dissolved. The BLP coordinators, like their husbands, seemed to be above the laws of society and legal procedures. The dissolution of the board of the commission further entrenched the tactics of wifeism. In the eyes of many, this dissolution embodied a thinly disguised attempt by the military state to completely take over organizing within the female sphere.

After General Babangida was forced out of office in August 1993, the BLP's and NAC's fate appeared to be in doubt. The uncertainty surrounding the NAC's future was reinforced by the clamor in some sectors of civil society to dismantle everything the Babangidas represented. Moreover, Mariam Abacha, wife of the present military head of state, General Sani Abacha, had not been part of the BLP but had concentrated on her own activities as president of the Nigerian Army Officers' Wives Association. The BLP anniversary parade and fairs for 1993 were canceled, and Mrs. Abacha indicated that she would launch her own initiative, the Family Support Program. Without the first lady as patron, the future of the BLP remains uncertain.

Relations Between the State and the Women's Movement: Conflicting Viewpoints

Perceptions of the state's involvement in the women's sphere and its relationship to the women's movement differ appreciably among Nigerian women leaders. The BLP and the National Commission for Women see the state's role in their formation as an indicator of state recognition of women's centrality to development and the national interest. They expect that this will lead to women's increased participation in government and the economy. They are joined in this view by leaders of the nongovernmental National Council of Women's Societies (NCWS).

The NCWS was formally established in 1959, but its history can be traced back to the early National Women's Union, which in 1953 became the Federation of Nigerian Women's Societies (FNWS). The FNWS's primary aims were to bring Nigerian women together to protect their rights under colonial rule and to raise the general status of women to win equal opportunities with men.[14] The FNWS allied with the International Federation of Women, which had links with the East European socialist bloc. It concerned itself with several international issues, such as condemning French atomic tests in the Sahara, and with local issues, such as fighting for the enfranchisement of women in the northern region of Nigeria. As a result of harassment of the FNWS leadership by the colonial state and damaging internal rivalry, it was unable to maintain a national presence, although it continued to function until the 1978 death of its radical and dynamic leader, Funmilayo Ransome-Kuti.

A breakaway faction of the FNWS formed the NCWS in 1959 with a very different ideological orientation. The NCWS was far less critical of government since it was dominated by the wives of nationalist politicians and bureaucrats. It was also much more distant from the mass base of the FNWS. It redirected women's pro-test strategies from mass demonstrations for action to petition writing and dia-logue with government.[15] The NCWS is now recognized by the federal govern-ment as the only umbrella NGO representing women's interests. All women's groups in Nigeria are required to affiliate with the NCWS if they are to be recog-nized by the state.

More recently, elections at the NCWS's biennial conventions have been marred by controversy. On the surface, the reasons center on south-north, Christian-Muslim bids for control, which are common divisions in Nigeria. In reality, these divisions only partially explain the elections' contentious nature. The underlying cause centered on the state patronage the NCWS enjoys at the federal, state, and local government levels in the form of ministerial and parastatal appointments, overseas travel, grant support, and other favors. In essence, elite women within the NCWS were wrangling on the platform of the state-recognized women's organiza-tion over the state's largesse and over access to political power and available re-sources.

The NCWS's policy calls for having the wife of the head of state as its patron. The NCWS has thereby maintained good relations with the state, generally giving its unconditional support to the state and its policies. Consequently, the organiza-tion has been labeled a supporter of the "AGIP" party—any government in power—by its critics.[16] Confirming this stance, the immediate past president of the NCWS describes the organization's relationship with government as follows: "It is cordial; we owe absolute loyalty to the government irrespective of the gov-ernment in power. That is the reason why we have never fallen out of grace. We criticize when necessary, but when we do, we do not publicize it. All in all, we pre-fer dialogue to confrontation."[17]

In recent times, the NCWS's few open criticisms of the state have been based on too few women in federal or state cabinets and the national Armed Forces Ruling Council and on objections to a provision in the national population policy rec-ommending a limit of four children per woman without stipulating any limit for men. This close relationship between the state and the "nongovernmental" NCWS is interpreted by many more explicitly feminist activists as direct govern-ment interference.

In contrast to the close and generally uncritical relationship the NCWS has with the state, other women's activists view the government's recent involvement in women's issues as unnecessary interference aimed at neutralizing women's au-tonomous actions and promoting patriarchy and male domination within the fe-male sphere. Proponents of this viewpoint generally take a more explicitly femi-nist perspective, as typified by the group Women in Nigeria (WIN). Its identification with radical antigovernment groups and condemnation of the SAP, the military junta's unfulfilled transition to civil rule, and the proscription of the

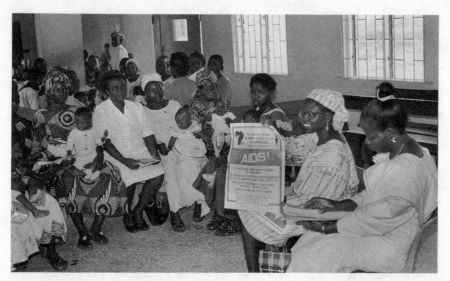

Despite the government's growing control over women's activities, independent women's organizations continue to emerge, especially to tackle difficult and politically sensitive issues. Here a leader of the Society for Women and AIDS in Africa (Nigeria) informs women about the risks of HIV/AIDS.

democratic formations and labor unions are a far more critical stance than that espoused by the NCWS. In general, WIN's relationship with the state is strained.

The emergence of WIN in 1983 as a national women's organization qualitatively transformed the debate on the "woman question" in Nigeria both in form and in content. WIN's emphasis, activities, and approach with regard to gender and national issues are aimed at the entire transformation of society. WIN's socialist feminist ideology holds that women's subordination stems from both class and gender oppression. WIN is urban based and made up of lower-middle-class women and men from the universities and other professions. Although it seeks to represent the interests of poor women and men, the organization has not successfully recruited or maintained members from this class. This can be attributed in part to a lack of financial resources for programs or staff, conflicts within the organization over strategy, and the fact that most of its members combine career and family responsibilities. It may also be due to analyses and perspectives that differ from those of the poor. WIN's activities have been mainly in the areas of research and documentation, dissemination of information and policy recommendations, political conscientization (training and discussion to raise women's political awareness and/or awareness of gender discrimination), and project work.

The emergence of WIN transformed the debate on the nature of gender subordination in Nigeria, as WIN embraced a multidimensional approach to the subject of gender inequality. It moved beyond articulating the importance of income-generating projects to improve women's economic status and independence. WIN also included issues of women's reproductive rights and choice, sexual harassment and violence, and consciousness-raising programs in the broader discourse on women. With its research and documentation programs, WIN has been able to generate data for policymakers and researchers on the conditions of Nigerian women. These achievements notwithstanding, WIN's impact has been limited by its inability to broaden its membership base.

WIN's relationship with the state has been uneasy and at times confrontational. The state has attempted at one level to coopt WIN by suggesting that it affiliate with the NCWS and seek to effect change from within. WIN has steadfastly and publicly refused to join the NCWS. WIN is ideologically opposed both to the NCWS's progovernment stance and the government's insistence that all women's organizations affiliate with the NCWS. In response, the government has refused to register WIN as a legal entity and has also threatened incarceration and detention of some of its leaders.

WIN, recognizing that its ideals of democratically transforming gender and class cannot be achieved by working on its own, has cooperated and identified with other social movements and progressive organizations interested in democratic change. The only time WIN did work with the state, in a political bureau set up by the Babangida government to discuss the political future of Nigeria, it linked up with other popular democratic organizations in the country.

Other women's groups with an entirely rural base, such as the Country Women Association of Nigeria (COWAN), have also cooperated with the movement for democracy in the shared objective of popular participation. The achievements of such voluntary development organizations lie not only in providing services to grassroots women but also in articulating the principles that guide such work. Grassroots organizations are generally managed by rural women for themselves and therefore base their programs on the actual needs of their members. In fact, their success among rural women was precisely what prompted the government to establish the Directorate of Food, Roads, and Rural Infrastructure, the BLP, and people's and community banks all over the country. However, the state to date has not been able to replicate the effectiveness of grassroots organizations. COWAN's leader was in fact imprisoned for "insubordination" as a result of a clash with the BLP, which tried to appropriate and take credit for COWAN's long-standing work with rural women. COWAN's participation in the prodemocracy campaign became even more pronounced after the cancellation of the presidential election results in June 1993.[18]

For one prominent activist-scholar, the mutual relationship of these organizations to the state can be regarded in class/political terms. Groups such as the NCWS, the BLP, and the commission have never threatened the dominant classes that control the state apparatus and have generally been supported by and sup-

The majority of Nigerian women live in rural areas where there are few opportunities to earn income. Rural women who belong to the Country Women Association of Nigeria (COWAN), an outspoken independent women's organization, earn income in a variety of programs such as weaving and cloth production.

portive of the state.[19] As creations of the state, the BLP and the commission have had the closest relationship with the state. This relationship has been likened to that which traditionally exists between a husband and wife, based on the love and obedience of the wife to the husband. In a recent interview, the current director of the BLP aired a desire for Nigerian women "to be grateful to the president before his wife because without his support the BLP would have been an unrealized dream of the first lady."[20]

A question that emerges is whether the activities of these more conservative women's groups are emancipatory or subordinating. In the period since independence in 1960, there has been continuity in the organizational forms in which women intervene in society. There have also been changes both in the content and mode of organization of women's associations, indicating important progress. The combination of continuity and change in women's organizations suggests, however, that the question of whether Nigerian women are moving toward achieving emancipation or remain subordinated is not a simple one. While the women's movement is fluid and historical shifts in its class and urban-rural composition are evident, it is clear that winning over the rural women who form the backbone of the nation is key to its continued progress. Thus, the government's selection of rural women as its target, singling them out as state beneficiaries, has the potential to split alliances within the movement.

Few women's programs effectively reach the majority of women in rural areas. This coopera-
tive mill, started by COWAN, processes cassava into garri, a staple food, thus dramatically
saving labor for women who would otherwise pound the cassava by hand.

An Agenda for the 1990s and Beyond

What is the vision of the Nigerian women's agenda for the 1990s and beyond?
Does it reflect our situation, which is characterized by economic adjustment policies, repression, and democratic struggles? The National Commission for Women
has formulated a national women's policy, which has yet to be signed into law by
the government. The policy reflects the agenda of women active in development,
which is based on a vision of economic independence, self-reliance, and sustainable development for women. The policy largely neglects other issues of importance to Nigerian women, including those related to reproductive rights such as
contraception and abortion and health issues such as incest. In general, however,
the women's movement in Nigeria, despite internal differences and inherent
weaknesses, has been successful in putting the woman question, however defined,
on the national political agenda. In all this militancy and activism, however, no viable women's agenda has been put forward to lead women into the twenty-first
century.

On the surface, it appears as if the state's vision for its development projects in
the mid-1980s, characterized by interest in mobilizing women for development,
self-improvement, and democracy, has been fulfilled. However, while the state can
point to its support for and close involvement with the NCWS, the BLP, the commission, and other groups essentially conservative in nature, the reality of any dis-

cernible impact on most Nigerian women's lives is quite different. The bureaucratization and cooptation of women's mobilization efforts have meant that in many cases propaganda and fanfare have tended to substitute for substance and results. The very structure of the state's efforts, top-down and top-heavy, has meant that the projects have been subject to the whims of their initiators, who presented themselves as benefactors to the rural women. Not surprisingly, such benevolent posturing has often degenerated into a patronizing attitude. In the end, we may see that a major factor in the eventual downfall of the state's efforts at mobilizing women was the selection of a group of urban, privileged women to lead, unqualified except by accident of marriage, whose modus operandi was starkly out of tune with the realities of the poor rural women the programs were supposed to benefit.

Ironically, for all the government's efforts and publicity at mobilizing Nigerian women in general and rural women in particular, women's involvement in the government's other programs, especially those for transition to civil rule, has been minimal. This certainly does not suggest any major departure from the practice of previous regimes. Women have not emerged as a credible political force able to stamp their influence on the local and national political landscape. This can be traced, at least in part, to the bureaucratization of women's issues and the rise of Nigerian state pseudofeminism, the hallmark of which was the policy of wifeism. Wifeism's effect on the majority of women has been far from emancipatory. To the contrary, it has tended to reinforce the structures and ideologies that have long characterized the domination of women. Rather than emphasizing autonomy, state pseudofeminism has emphasized incorporation and patronage. The net effect has been apathy at the grass roots.

In order to be sustainable in the long term and achieve results, any programs to mobilize women should have several characteristics. First, the program should have the ultimate objective of empowering women in order to free them from the yoke of patriarchal domination and gender discrimination. Second, it should be aimed at involving economically active women in productive activities that could assist them in increasing their independent income. Third, it should encourage women to become leaders in articulating their own interests and in tackling wider societal issues. Given these criteria, the potential for a lasting impact of the Nigerian government's initiatives on behalf of women is questionable.

The Nigerian women's movement is at a crossroads. The movement faces at least two alternatives: It can move forward independently to challenge patriarchy and seek to liberate women, or it can risk being completely coopted by the state and by other interests. Which of these will prevail depends on how the women's movement defines its agenda and how well it succeeds in popularizing its struggle. The movement can embrace its full role in society and become more integrated into the trade union, human rights, and democratic movements. It can develop a women's platform as a basis for negotiating and forming coalitions with other

mass movements and as a catalyst for supporting women to take part in party politics. A true feminist agenda challenges the state. If the Nigerian movement believes in emancipation, it must divorce itself from the grip of the state.

NOTES

1. Government of Nigeria, Federal Office of Statistics and IRD/Macro International, *Nigeria Demographic and Health Survey, 1990* (Lagos: N.p., 1992).

2. Nina Mba, *Nigerian Women Mobilized: Women's Political Activity in Southern Nigeria,
1900–1965* (Berkeley and Los Angeles: University of California Press, 1982), p. 166.

3. Mere Kisekka, "Women's Organized Health Struggles: The Challenge to Women's Associations," in Mere Kisekka, ed., *Women's Health Issues in Nigeria* (Zaria: Tamaza, 1992),
pp. 105–121.

4. Interview with Mrs. Theresa Chukwana, Mrs. Hannatu Fika, and Mrs. Theresa
Oguibe at the National Commission for Women, Abuja, February 2, 1993.

5. Interview with Obiageli Nwankwo, project coordinator, the International Federation
of Women Lawyers, Enugu, February 12, 1993.

6. Interview with Dr. Bene Madunagu, national coordinator (1991–1993), Women in Nigeria, Calabar, February 11, 1993.

7. Vesico-vaginal fistulae are tears in the wall between the vagina and urinary tract that
result from prolonged, obstructed labor. They are particularly common among very young
women whose bodies have not sufficiently matured to accommodate passage through the
birth canal. VVF result in constantly leaking urine; woman suffering from VVF are commonly ostracized by family and community and often become homeless and destitute.
While VVF can usually be corrected with surgery, the cost is prohibitive for most women.
The National Task Force on Vesico-Vaginal Fistulae is an unusual coalition among women's
groups, lawmakers, and medical experts. It has sought to bring public attention to VVF,
prevent them by advocating raising the legal age of marriage to eighteen and improving access to maternity care, and raise funds for medical and vocational rehabilitation of women
suffering from VVF.

8. Amrita Cchachhi and Renee Pittin, "Multiple Strategies: Confronting State, Capital,
and Patriarchy" (Paper presented at the International Workshop on Women Organizing in
the Process of Industrialization, the Hague, Netherlands, April 15–26, 1991).

9. Interview at the National Commission for Women, Abuja, February 2, 1993.

10. Hussiana Abdullah, "Transition Politics and the Challenge of Gender in Nigeria," *Review of African Political Economy* 56 (March 1993):27–37.

11. Maryam Babangida, text of a speech at the 1991 Africa Prize for Leadership for the
Sustainable End of Hunger, reproduced in *New Nigerian,* October 13, 1991.

12. *Tell,* April 20, 1992, quoted in Renee Pittin, "Women's Work: Parameters of Representation and Action" (Paper presented to an international workshop on Women and Work:
Historical Trends, Center for Basic Research, Kampala, Uganda, September 1992), p. 16.

13. Government of Nigeria, Decree no. 42, 1992.

14. Mba, "Kaba and Khaki."

15. Ifi Amadiume, "Contemporary Women's Organizations, Contradictions, and Irrele-
vance in the Struggle for Grassroots Participatory Democracy in Nigeria" (Paper presented

at the CODESRIA Workshop on Social Movements, Social Transformations, and the Struggle for Democracy, Algiers, Algeria, July 1990).

16. Ayesha Imam, "The Dynamics of Winning: An Analysis of Women in Nigeria (WIN)," in Chandra Mohanty and Jacqui Alexander, eds., *Third World Feminism* (London: Basil Blackwell, 1993); Ahmed K. Shettima, "Engendering Nigeria's Third Republic" (Paper presented at the CODESRIA conference on the Politics of Structural Adjustment in Africa, Dakar, Senegal, September 1991).

17. Interview with Emily Aig-Imokhuede, president (1988–1993), the National Council of Women's Societies, Abuja, March 22, 1993.

18. Interview with Chief Bisi Ogunleye, national coordinator, the Country Women Association of Nigeria, Akure, December 18, 1993.

19. Ayesha Imam, "The Women's Movement, State, and Democracy in Nigeria" (Paper presented at the Akut workshop on Social Movements and Democracy in the Third World, Delhi, India, October 1992).

20. Interview at the National Commission for Women, Abuja, February 2, 1993.

9

Claiming Feminism, Claiming Nationalism: Women's Activism in the Occupied Territories

ISLAH JAD

IN FEBRUARY 1968, ABOUT three hundred Palestinian women gathered in the courtyard of the Church of the Holy Sepulchre in Jerusalem and marched through the narrow, stone-paved streets of the Old City, holding banners denouncing Israel's deportation of Palestinians and confiscation of Palestinian land. The demonstration echoed older protests: A similar number of women attending the first Arab Women's Congress in Palestine in 1929 had taken to the streets chanting slogans against Britain, then the colonial power in Palestine. Some removed their veils as a form of protest.

From that time on, as the tortured history of Palestine unfolded, Palestinian women banded together as women and undertook a number of forms of nationalist activity. A significant portion of this history remains to be recovered, particularly that of rural women, who have historically constituted the majority of Palestinian women. The formal Palestinian women's organizations that emerged before 1967 were characterized and limited by their urban, upper-class leadership and their ancillary status to the male-dominated nationalist movement. These groups shared the national priority of ending both British and Zionist colonialism and a focus on charitable and humanitarian activity.

While linked to and formed by the protests of the past, the women walking on the rainy streets of Jerusalem in 1968 were marching into a new era, both in Palestinian history and for the Palestinian women's movement. Israel's conquest and

OCCUPIED TERRITORIES

(Figures given separately for Gaza and West Bank)

GENERAL

type of government: Transition; limited self-rule
major ethnic groups: Palestinian Arab (99.8%/88%); Jewish (0.2%/12%)
language(s): Arabic; Hebrew (Israeli settlers); English
religions: Muslim (99%/80%); Jewish (0.2%/12%); Christian

DEMOGRAPHICS

population size: Worldwide Palestinians: 4.5 million
            (Gaza: 731,000; West Bank: 1.4 million)
birth rate (*per 1,000 population*): Gaza: 45; West Bank: 32.5
total fertility (*average number of births per woman*): Gaza 7.4; West Bank 4.2
contraceptive prevalence (*married women*): *not available*
maternal mortality rate (*per 100,000 live births*): *not available*

WOMEN'S STATUS

date of women's suffrage: not applicable
economically active population: M 36%   F 4%
female employment (*% of total workforce*): 17
life expectancy   M Gaza: 66.4; West Bank: 68.8
            F Gaza: 69.1; West Bank: 72
school enrollment ratio (*F/100 M*)

primary	*not available*
secondary	*not available*
tertiary	*not available*

literacy: *not available*

---

occupation of the West Bank and Gaza in the June war of 1967, expanding Israeli rule to all of historic Palestine, opened a new chapter in Palestinian resistance and ushered in new political, social, and economic realities that profoundly affected women. The new Palestinian women's movement that has developed since 1967 has been shaped by these forces. In turn, the women's movement has contributed both to Palestinian national resistance and the creation of a new consciousness of and about Palestinian women. This distinct new consciousness, new forms of organization and mobilization, and a concomitant expansion of activities, program, and constituency constitute the features of a new Palestinian women's movement.

During this period, the Palestinian women's movement has been linked inextricably to the nationalist movement and has shared its fortunes, its burdens, and its vision of Palestinian independence. For both, the ideology has been shaped by the imperative of national self-determination and an end to the harsh rule of Israeli military occupation. As they have developed inside the Occupied Territories, these movements have been tied to, and in the case of the nationalist movement guided by, exiled Palestinian leaders and organizations outside Palestine.

Both movements developed in the particular and rather unique situation of prolonged occupation and the absence of a state. This absence, however deleterious to social and economic development, afforded space for mobilization and public activity that gave a special empowering character to Palestinian grassroots movements, including a new formation of the women's movement that emerged in the late 1970s. This movement, embodied in the women's committees, decisively widened the circle of activist women and played an important role in mobilizing women for the intifada, the nationalist Palestinian uprising launched in December 1987. With the more recent waning of the intifada and the emergence of new political forces, the link between the nationalist and women's movements has been subject to serious stress and strain. Paradoxically, the heightened nationalist activism and responsibilities undertaken by women during the intifada led to a new gendered consciousness among Palestinian women activists. The women's movement today is deeply involved in a serious debate over its future agenda, just at the time when the emergence of a limited Palestinian authority signals a new era for Palestinian society.

Women's Role in the Crucible of Occupation

Although the history of Palestinians under Israeli occupation since 1967 is complex, there are several general observations that can be made about the role of Palestinian women during this turbulent period, both in terms of change and continuity. From its inception in 1967, the Israeli occupation destructured Palestinian society by subjugating it to the Israeli economic system and by transforming communities through massive land confiscation and Israeli settlement. The profound challenge posed to Palestinian society to survive and resist was also a challenge to its basic institutions, among them the family. The family is a central institution in Palestinian society in particular and Arab society in general. While remaining hierarchical and patriarchal in character, the ideology of the family, and to some extent its practice, is based on each member's "complete and unconditional commitment" to family members.[1] But this commitment's assumption of mutual sacrifice often conceals the greater burden laid on the less powerful members of the family, particularly women.

In both family and society as a whole, a central role for Palestinian women has been to preserve tradition, national heritage, and culture and its symbols, instilling in children respect for national values and knowledge of their history.[2] While this role can be conservative, in conditions where cultural survival is at stake, it is critical. This role was a necessary cultural and social precondition for the Palestinian intifada, for example, and a sustaining element in Palestinians' commitment to that prolonged uprising. Some of the traditional roles that women have customarily played in the family and in society have been critical to Palestinian society's ability to withstand extremely repressive conditions.

Of equal importance is how this traditional role has been extended and thus partially transformed. As a consequence of the harsh conditions of military occupation, many women have been separated from their husbands and other male family members when the men have been arrested or deported. In these instances, women have effectively assumed the role of head of household. Israeli measures, from land confiscation to house demolitions to school closures, have greatly affected the presumed stability and security of family and home, spurring women into action to protect their families. A visitor to an Israeli prison, military court, or defense attorney's office will inevitably witness Palestinian women assuming the role of negotiator, or intermediary, between their children or husband and the authority. As is demonstrated in this chapter, this extended role took on new dimensions during the Palestinian intifada.

The period of occupation also witnessed greater participation of women in the formal economy, although labor force participation remains relatively low at less than 17 percent of the total labor force in the Occupied Territories.[3] As the highest participation is still among educated women and among women from upper- and middle-class households, the direct effect of formal employment on women's position in society is strongest among elites. However, the increase in women professionals clearly has a wider social effect. In general, the Palestinian working class is employed inside Israel as unskilled, construction, or agricultural labor. While this kind of employment is not common among poor working women, many do work inside their homes for Israeli or Palestinian subcontractors. Because of the underdevelopment of the Palestinian economy, and the severe restrictions imposed on it by Israel, substantive change in the role of women through labor force participation is so far insignificant, although it remains a future possibility.

Women and Resistance

The 1967 war transformed the Palestine Liberation Organization (PLO), founded in 1964, into a mass representative organization. The defeat of the Arab armies

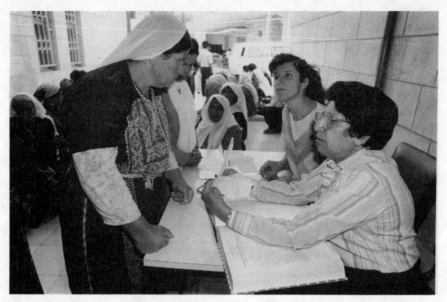

When male family members are imprisoned or detained, women handle negotiations and business matters, including collecting relief checks from the In'ash Al-Usra organization.

confirmed the message of the Palestinian resistance that became the leadership of the PLO after 1967: Palestinians had to liberate Palestine through their own struggle. The PLO charter focused on popular mobilization and a self-reliance that stressed the necessity of engaging the whole population, including women.

Outside the Occupied Territories, in Jordan first and then in Lebanon, the Palestinian resistance organizations in the PLO recruited women to a limited extent for armed actions and even airplane hijackings. The PLO's mass organizations included the General Union of Palestinian Women (GUPW), founded in 1965 but activated only in the wake of the 1967 war. The history of women's activities in the diaspora, while not examined here, is rich and varied, particularly during the PLO's years in Lebanon prior to 1982. Women's concerns were subordinated to Palestinian liberation, as demonstrated in slogans such as "Women will be liberated when society is" or "Men and women side by side in the battle."[4] This subordination reflects women's lack of representation in the PLO's decisionmaking bodies. A woman has never served on the PLO Executive Committee, and the Palestine National Council, the parliament of the Palestinian people, had only 8 women out of 426 members in 1987. All 8 represented the GUPW.[5]

Inside the Occupied Territories, women first confronted the occupation through channels provided by charitable organizations and the GUPW, both linked to the Palestinian leadership. Although women's role in the initial armed resistance was considerably less than men's, by 1968 about one hundred Palestinian women were in Israeli prisons accused of such offenses as contact with guerrillas, concealment of weapons, incitement, or membership in armed organizations. Like male Palestinian prisoners, women were subjected to torture and maltreatment. Their courage in the face of this treatment began to change the concept of women as weak and to undermine the traditional notion of "women's honor."[6] By 1979, about three thousand women had been imprisoned, reflecting an increase in the number enrolled in political and military organizations.[7]

In the wake of the Palestinian armed resistance defeat in Jordan in 1970–1971, the Palestine National Front was established. Started in the West Bank by a group of community leaders, including one woman, its vision was one of mass mobilization and civil resistance rather than armed struggle. It encouraged young people to engage in community projects and voluntary work to aid beleaguered villagers struggling with the economic problems of occupation. For the first time, young men and women met in a communal setting and discussed their and society's problems. The front's agenda of community activity and struggle offered an important entry point for women's political participation.

In the mid-1970s, as local colleges expanded and universities were founded, new student organizations with active female participation launched grassroots mobilization efforts. At the same time, women's charitable organizations began to see protest, in addition to service, as part of their mandate, and women's sit-ins and protests occurred sporadically. In general, these were responses to national, rather than women's, issues. This new era of organizing still did not include the voices of rural women and women in refugee camps. Charitable organizations offered some medical assistance and traditional vocational training in knitting, sewing, and food processing, with the goal of helping women face harsh economic conditions in the event of the death, deportation, or imprisonment of male kin. While these efforts were important in the absence of a national authority, the charitable societies participated in women's struggle only on a national level and in a limited fashion.

Several other factors contributed to the mounting involvement of women in political resistance. Granted the right to vote for the first time in the 1976 municipality elections, women, contrary to Israeli predictions, voted overwhelmingly for the pro-PLO candidates rather than the conservative politicians favored by Israel. At the same time, a boom in higher education saw nine colleges and community colleges open. These were heavily attended by young women, who made up from 35 to 55 percent of various student bodies. In addition, dynamic cultural movements arose with a progressive vision and an interest in women's issues that were reflected in theatrical performances and literary productions. These interrelated developments throughout the 1970s resulted in the birth of a new women's vanguard within the Palestinian national movement.

The Women's Committees:
Women's Vanguard

On International Women's Day, March 8, 1978, a new generation of women activists, formed in the student and voluntary work movements as well as inside Israeli prisons, held an important meeting that resulted in the creation of the Women's Work Committee. The committee was born to reach the majority of Palestinian women living in villages and in the refugee camps of the West Bank and Gaza. The activists were also seeking an alternative to the charitable societies, whose leaders excluded them in order to preserve their own position and power.

Although the Women's Work Committee was initially made up of active cadres regardless of political affiliation, a partisan power struggle soon emerged. The only solution found was one that had already occurred in other mass organizations, such as trade unions: Each Palestinian faction was to found its own mass women's organization.[8] Although all the women's committees started from the initiative of women political cadres, their organization later diverged. The membership of some committees came only from within the political faction itself, while others were open to members from outside the organization. This determined the degree of independence of each women's committee from the political faction that was its "sponsor." Each committee was, to a greater or lesser extent, an extension of a particular Palestinian political faction.

This division of the women's movement, which continues to the present, did not reflect a difference in agenda and goals. The first goal of all these organizations was political: to involve the greatest possible number of women in the national movement. To achieve this, the committees developed flexible conditions for participation and membership. This flexibility contrasted with the membership conditions of the charitable organizations, which restricted their membership to middle-class women. This flexibility was therefore critical in enabling women from different social classes to participate.[9]

The first committees took their internal structures from the other grassroots organizations at that time, primarily trade unions. Almost all of the committees had the same internal structure when they began. Led by an executive committee and divided into regions, the committees implemented programs in local branches, often a particular town, village, or camp. Each branch elected an administrative committee; in the absence of elections, this committee was composed of members of the political faction.[10] Even in an election, the results were often controlled indirectly by the political organization to promote trusted members, or pressure was exerted on the winners to join the organization.[11] In addition, general assemblies of each organization met annually. In the early and mid-1980s, these general assembly meetings, usually held in Jerusalem, encompassed hundreds of participants gathered in a lively, festive atmosphere, where electioneering, nationalist statements, and cultural performances mingled. However, as Israeli policy toward Palestinian mass organizations became more harsh, especially after the "iron fist" policy in 1985 (which used a wide range of illegal practices, including administrative detention, town arrests, and collective punishments, against political activists), security concerns often caused meeting postponements. The women's committees with the strongest political overtones tended to hold elections less frequently due to fears about security.

Most of the women's committees were formed first in the West Bank and only later in Gaza. Women in the West Bank and Gaza experienced several obstacles in working together. The committees worked primarily with housewives and poor women, who for the most part lacked mobility. There was also resistance from the male party members who did not want their wives involved in political work. Another major factor was the geographic isolation of Gaza from the West Bank, which intensified during the intifada when the Israeli authorities prohibited Palestinians from leaving Gaza without permission. The links between women's committees in the West Bank and Gaza were always among the leadership rather than the grass roots, preventing development on an equal basis. As restrictions on freedom of movement for residents became even more severe during the numerous military-ordered closures of Gaza, even the "elites" were often banned from leaving. This necessitated women in Gaza taking decisions independently of their colleagues in the West Bank. For example, the committee Women's Action formed a regional council in Gaza that was independent of the executive committee in Jerusalem.

"Emancipating Palestinian women" was an item on the agendas of all the committees, especially those with a leftist orientation. Demands were raised concerning equal pay for equal work and various types of social protection for working women. However, the public agenda for women, while it embraced a notion of equality, was often reduced to workplace issues, which had little relevance for the majority of Palestinian women. Women's publications before 1987 contained little mention of the more broadly discriminatory laws that governed women's status in society or of issues such as male violence against women, the sexual division of labor, or traditional cultural notions that devalued women. Avoiding many gender issues was justified by asserting that they were not a priority in the period of national struggle and that opening an internal debate was dangerous when unity was needed to end the occupation. At the same time, women activists often used informal means to intervene in individual cases of domestic violence or restrictions on women's activity.

On the surface, the programs used by the women's committees to achieve their goals did not differ greatly from the charitable organizations' programs. The former included nurseries; traditional training programs in sewing, knitting, and embroidery; literacy centers; workshops; and small-scale cooperatives. The major difference was that these programs were designed to mobilize and empower women politically rather than simply meet immediate needs. The political consciousness of the women who supervised the programs evoked a similar consciousness in participants. The structure of the programs gave participants self-confidence and experience in democratic decisionmaking, the holding of elections, and the articulation of common agendas. All projects undertaken by the women's organizations recruited a wider circle of women for national or women's activities in the village, refugee camp, or city. The projects were not in themselves the goal but rather a means of mobilization. In spite of these overlapping efforts, the number of organized women members (rather than participants in an individual project) was low, not exceeding 3 percent of the population.[12]

In this initial period of less than a decade (1978–1987), the women's committees achieved a number of important things. They fostered and supported a large number women activists, broke down divisions between women, reached out to women in all social settings, and contributed to giving women greater visibility, self-esteem, and self-respect.

The Intifada and the Women's Movement, 1987–1990

Many observers were surprised at the strikingly visible role played by Palestinian women in the initial popular stage of the Palestinian intifada, which erupted on December 9, 1987. It was not new, of course, for Palestinian women to take on a political role in society, especially in times of emergency. What was new were the scope and multiple manifestations of this role. In the streets of villages, towns, and refugee camps, women from all ages and social classes took part in demonstrations, threw stones, burned tires, built roadblocks, raised Palestinian flags, and prevented soldiers from arresting people. From a woman in traditional peasant dress carrying a bucket of rocks on her head to a middle-class woman in Beit Sahur, her high heels in one hand and a rock in the other, images of women permeated the first months of the uprising. These activities were most intense in poor urban neighborhoods, in villages, and in refugee camps.

Although women's actions were sometimes violent, and women engaged in serious confrontations with the army, women's activities were particularly characterized by acts of peaceful civil disobedience and resistance. In the uprising's first months, every Friday became an occasion for women's marches from mosques and every Sunday, for marches from churches. International Women's Day 1988 witnessed the largest celebrations of this occasion ever. In the town of Ramallah, over five hundred women, from teenagers to grandmothers, marched through the streets, calling to the youth, "No stones!" Soldiers attacked the marchers with teargas and rubber bullets several times before the women dispersed. The Women's Day marches were the last large public organizing effort of women activists as

Palestinians rise against Israeli occupation of their country in December 1987. Women, embracing the cause of nationalism, participate with men and children in demonstrations. From George Baramki Azar, Palestine: A Photographic Journey *(Berkeley: University of California Press, 1991).*

army repression and arrests led to protests and community survival became an urgent task.

As the toll of dead and wounded rose and Israel mounted an offensive to crush the intifada, new critical needs for the people appeared. The grassroots organizations responded with new programs and activities. When the Israeli authorities closed all primary and secondary schools in the West Bank in February 1988 "until further notice," affecting three hundred thousand school-age children, women organized neighborhood and home classes throughout the West Bank. The isolation of cities and towns from the countryside through curfews and restrictions on mobility revealed the importance of each community being self-reliant. This resulted in an emphasis on conservation, local production, and boycotting of Israeli goods. With increasing numbers of prisoners and martyrs, health insurance programs were instituted for prisoners' wives,[13] adoption of children of prisoners and martyrs was broadened, and solidarity visits with families became a daily activity. In all these activities, the women's committees and individual women played a leading role, often undertaking much of the practical work, whether teaching in their homes, growing and canning food, or extending emotional and practical support to stricken families.

Rural women wave the Palestinian flag, banned by the Israelis, during the intifada. From George Baramki Azar, Palestine: A Photographic Journey *(Berkeley: University of California Press, 1991).*

Women protest Israeli treatment of prisoners in June 1991 at an International Red Cross office in Gaza City.

Beneath all the impressive mobilization and courageous activity of women activists and ordinary women, the structure of the women's committees had been transformed. The goals of the women's movement were subsumed not only to national priorities but also to the male-dominated political organizations that set these priorities. The impact of the intifada on the Palestinian women's movement has been contradictory. It demonstrated simultaneously both the strength and limitations of the existing women's organizations and their programs as well as the power and influence of the movement and its activists. It also revealed the existence of traditional social and political forces that had been relatively unacknowledged before the uprising, in particular political fundamentalist Islam.

Political Organizations and the Women's Committees

During the uprising, the difference between the programs of the clandestine political organizations and those of the grassroots women's committees converged. The masses were in the streets, and everyone experienced oppression. The women's committees had been founded primarily to mobilize for nationalist activity, and the moment of opportunity had now arrived. Integration of the women's committees' structure and the political parties' structure occurred quickly. A ma-

In 1988 boys and girls attend an "illegal school" set up to replace those closed by Israelis on the West Bank. Women played a crucial role during the intifada by establishing and running these schools. This activity built on women's traditional roles as conveyors of culture as well as giving them an important new political role.

jor reason for this integration was that both shared the same main aim: mobilization. In addition, it was dangerous and often impossible, due to curfews and restrictions on movement, to gather people together for general assemblies or other mass meetings. The massive scale of arrests led the political organizations to put women activists to work because women were less visible.[14] As the Israeli army's search for what it considered the "leadership" of the uprising intensified, women expended endless energy in seeking new hiding places for wanted men and women.

The formation of neighborhood committees in early 1988 provided a new focus for community survival and empowerment, which brought many women temporarily into political activity at a local level. At the same time, the women's committees strove to adapt to these new forms of organization: "We dissolved the organizational units as they had been before and replaced them with specialized activity units like social solidarity, production units, health committees, etc."[15] In the end, however, the relationship between the political factions and the women's committees became one way, with women's independent activities subsumed. One leading woman activist, also a political cadre, noted, "It was no longer possible to have the existence of a women's bureau within the organization as before. ... Women's branches became subsumed within the organization's regional offices, which were mixed and mostly headed by men. We used to receive enormous amounts of complaints about the inability of comrades in the regions to understand and to follow the previous women's work. Their focus was only on how many women could be organized for the organization."[16] All of the women's committees had essentially the same experience—that the political organization, through orders coming from above, was dictating to a great extent the women's committees' programs and the details of their work.

Institutionalization

At the same time as the women's committees were losing their autonomy, they were, ironically, expanding their activities, due to the increase in relief and urgent services programs. Combined with new funding sources, this led to hiring full-time workers instead of relying on volunteers. Most of these workers were loyal organization members with little or no professional experience, especially in production projects, cooperatives, and small factories. Increased institutionalization led some committees to substitute internal relations of a voluntary, democratic type for ones that were centralized and businesslike; to substitute volunteers with employees; to become increasingly dependent on running offices with expensive equipment; and to rely on big budgets instead of on human resources as the basis of the work.[17] Dependency on outside financial resources coming from the PLO or from international donors to the proliferating nongovernmental organizations in the Occupied Territories became a major dynamic.

This phenomenon had negative repercussions for popular mobilization. Women started to deal with the committees as a source of income, and when the flow of money started to slow down, women employees simply looked for other jobs. Leadership now required both managerial capacity and mobility, creating a wider gap between the leaders and the grassroots base of the committees.[18] In general, popular participation by grassroots women in decisionmaking dwindled almost to nothing.[19] As one member stated, "The women's union's executive bureau became a head without legs."[20] This led to increased intervention from the political organizations in the women's programs. Financial matters came under the purview of the political parties, which often made even personnel decisions.[21] With increased bureaucratization, the committees' programs lost the flexibility to continue responding to members' changing needs. In some cases, the committees were ordered to continue programs that at one time had addressed needs stemming from the uprising but that had failed to adapt to the changing reality.[22]

Crisis in the Women's Movements, 1991–Present

With the decline in intensity of the uprising in 1991 and the waning of national resistance in general, women's action, which was mainly nationalist, also dimin-

University professor Hanan Ashrawi, shown here with Palestine Liberation Organization chairman Yasir Arafat in 1993, became Palestine's official spokesperson during the Middle East peace talks.

ished. In the wake of the Gulf War in particular, the Palestinian national movement experienced a profound crisis in confidence and direction. Women's committee leaders began to reexamine their own activities, their relation to the political organizations, and women's status in society. The heroism of women in the intifada was not matched by concrete improvements in the status of women. As a result of a real deepening in the committees' feminist consciousness, they began to realize the necessity of both returning to women's programs and creating new women's agendas.

This intensification of feminist consciousness occurred for many reasons. The enormous family, community, and political responsibilities that women took on during the uprising was not acknowledged by the political leadership or matched by any lasting political power. As male leaders were imprisoned during the uprising, many women activists took on leadership positions. One such leader described what happened when the men returned:

> After the release of political cadre, they came to me demanding that I choose between the political party and the women's committee. I refused the choice. I replied to them that they didn't put me in my place to remove me from it; my effort and my people were the reasons I was in this position. I was running the whole political party for six

months, alone in very difficult circumstances. All my energies and time were completely dedicated to the point that my young son started to call me "aunt."[23]

The uprising also brought together independent academic women and the organized political women leading the women's committees. Thus began a process of mutual enrichment, with the academic women's experience in research, theory, and international networking meeting the deep practical experience and political consciousness of the activists. During the uprising, the Palestinian women's movement was exposed to the different feminist perspectives brought by scores of foreign delegations. Participants in the international women's movement raised questions on feminist issues that Palestinian activists realized needed to be tackled.

The Fundamentalist Challenge

Among the important developments of the uprising, and one that deeply affected women, was the increased influence of the Islamic movements in the Occupied Territories. In 1988, Hamas, the Islamic Resistance Movement, was founded by activists of the Muslim Brotherhood (a pan-Islamic political movement founded in Egypt in 1937). The Palestinian nationalist movement found itself faced with an organized Islamicist challenge whose young activists in the streets were fully as willing to struggle against the occupation as the secular nationalists. The issue of women became, with its overlapping meanings of national purity, honor, and tradition, an important tool of the Islamicists. Women's role in the ideology of Hamas was defined for the first time in the movement's covenant (*mithaq*) in Article 17: "In the resistance, the role of the Muslim Woman is equal to the man's. She is a factory to produce men, and she has a great role in raising and educating the generations."[24]

In 1990, Islamicist activists launched a highly organized campaign to attack women wearing jeans and Western dress while participating with men in the demonstrations. Women were urged to show respect and modesty in their behavior by covering their heads. According to anthropologist Rima Hammami, "The hijab (wearing a head scarf) was promoted (and to some extent became understood) as a sign of women's political commitment, as women to the intifada." The most prominent, and quelling, redefinition made the scarf a sign of respect for martyrs, depicting bareheaded women as vain, frivolous, and antinationalist.[25] These campaigns resulted in the imposition of head scarves on all women in Gaza, including Christians, through such means as writing slogans, throwing stones at bareheaded women, and calling from the mosques. Leftist and nonreligious men started to urge women to wear head scarves to avoid problems in the streets. Some other nationalist groups, particularly Fateh, participated in the campaigns as an intifada activity.[26]

Hamas, founded in 1988 by Muslim fundamentalists, urges women to wear head scarves as a mark of respect for the dead. To be without a head scarf is considered vain and antinationalist. These women are seated under a Hamas banner at a 1992 rally.

The first organized reaction came from independent women in a seminal December 1990 conference entitled "The Intifada and Some Women's Social Issues."[27] The women's committees also began to mobilize and in particular pressured the male leadership of their political organizations to take a principled stand. The underground leadership of the uprising finally issued a belated condemnation, and Islamicists were unable to succeed in similar campaigns launched in Nablus and Hebron. The struggle over the *hijab* underlined several trends, from new forms of feminist consciousness and activism, to the silence of the male-dominated nationalist movement, to the growing strength of fundamentalism. Most recently, in the wake of the signing of the Israeli-Palestinian Declaration of Principles in September 1993, women activists are grappling with a new alliance of Hamas and secular leftist groups opposed to the agreement.

New Forms of Organization, New Agendas

The profound crisis of the women's committees has led them to take several important steps. A number of activists have also begun to set up independent interest groups specifically concerned with women's issues. Within the women's committees, efforts have been made to expand democratic participation, simplify cumbersome bureaucracy, and remove the factions' control. Paradoxically, one result has been the women's committees taking on the form of their old opponents by registering as charitable societies. Some women activists see transforming the committees into legal entities such as charitable societies as a deliberate strategy to make it more difficult for a future state to dissolve them based on political affiliation. These same concerns are behind the campaign to change the GUPW, the only official women's organization in the PLO.[28]

The problem of internal bureaucracy has diminished as women's committees are forced to close many of their projects due to lack of money and, often, the failure of the projects themselves. For many, the organizations' emerging feminist orientation has pushed them to deemphasize service programs. First, the committees are seeking to redefine themselves as advocates for women's rights. Second, the women's committees now anticipate that the future Palestinian authority, whether a state or quasi state, will take charge of offering basic services for women, such as kindergartens, nurseries, income-generating projects, health services, and education. With the elimination of service programs, the committees have begun to divest themselves of full-time employees,[29] particularly the politicized ones. The committees' task has then become a different one: formulating a women's agenda for social change.

It is too early to assess whether these organizational changes will be successful in involving more women and advancing women's issues. What is clear is that women activists are studying their own experience and that of earlier women's movements. Their aim is not to offer services in the traditional concept of the charitable society: "We put forward the idea of associations with a feminist concept, not with a charity concept."[30] Membership will be open to all women. Programs will be designed according to the interests of the members themselves and not according to a political decision coming from a political organization or from a strong-minded leader of a women's charity. The view of women's issues and of the different sectors of Palestinian women is much more inclusive. Whether these new structures will diminish factionalism remains to be seen. With the establishment of a Palestinian authority, their success will depend mainly on the evolution of the democratic Palestinian experience in general and on the democratic evolution within the women's committees in particular.

New Structures: Women's Studies

In developing a more inclusive view of women's issues and of Palestinian women in society, the women's movement has been spurred by the development of new initiatives, in particular women's research centers and institutes. These centers emerged as the crisis in the women's movement crystallized a new feminist consciousness. Previously avoided issues such as domestic violence and personal status laws could now be researched, discussed, and debated, at least in limited forums. While programs differ, these centers share the common goals of researching and documenting the situation of Palestinian women as well as providing women, and the women's movement in particular, with the skills, knowledge, and resources to transform society. Thus, training and information have been a theme in all their programs. These centers also offer important forums where activists and academics can meet to discuss issues that have hitherto been taboo, such as violence against women and discriminatory personal status laws.

The key relationship between the research centers and the women's committees has not always been an easy one. The independent women active in the research centers fear political control, while the women's committees sometimes resent the academic women's more easy access to international funding and contacts. However, unlike the experience of contemporary women's movements in Egypt or Algeria, the link is a living and dynamic one. Activists and researchers emerged from the same context and share many experiences and concerns. The research centers' training programs focus on women's movement activists. The relationship offers both present and future possibilities for important interaction between intellectuals and grassroots activists as well as for these categories not to be too fixed and rigid.

The new era ushered in by the Middle East peace process has also brought another new form of women's organization. A women's technical committee is one of a range of quasi-governmental committees established to prepare for the Palestinian authority. There is one striking difference between this and the other committees: It was established on the initiative of women and maintains a skeptical attitude toward the emerging authority. It has been active in developing a women's agenda, lobbying for women's participation in governance, and working with other groups on a women's bill of rights.

New Directions?

The struggle of women activists to draft a women's bill of rights offers a clear example of the potential and the pitfalls facing the Palestinian women's movement today. While the new era has necessarily led the women's movement to develop new directions, it has also imposed obstacles, among them the divisions within the women's movement itself over the direction of Palestinian politics and the future authority. For the first time, however, the Palestinian women's movement is engaged in setting strategic feminist priorities to advance the interests of women rather than a purely nationalist agenda. The women's bill of rights is one important example.

Beginning in December 1993, at the same time a constitution was being drafted by a PLO committee, Palestinian women activists in the Occupied Territories began serious and sustained discussion on the women's bill of rights. This charter of women's basic demands and rights would be offered to Palestinian women, supported through a mass signature campaign, and presented to the new authority and other relevant bodies for inclusion in a new Palestinian constitution.

After lengthy consultations and debates, women overcame many obstacles, including the reluctance of women opposed to legitimizing the Palestinian national authority by presenting it with women's demands. The draft Declaration of Women's Rights that finally emerged from this lengthy and democratic process is a strong document reflecting a growing women's consensus. After a preamble noting the basic principles of equality enshrined in the Palestinian Declaration of Independence and U.N. declarations, the Declaration of Women's Rights affirms:

> We, the women of Palestine, from all social categories and various faiths, including workers, farmers, housewives, students, professionals, and politicians, promulgate our determination to proceed with our struggle to abolish all forms of discrimination and inequality against women, which were propagated by the different forms of colonialism on our land, ending with the Israeli Occupation, and which were reinforced by the conglomeration of customs and traditions prejudiced against women, embodied in a number of existing laws and legislation.[31]

The reference to law is extremely important. The draft declaration opens a debate against discriminatory legislation, implicitly including personal status laws as codified in *shari'a*, the religious Islamic laws that govern Muslim women's personal status. The declaration also states that the law should protect women from family violence and affirms women's right to independent citizenship, political participation, freedom of movement, and other basic rights. The declaration represents a major step forward for the Palestinian women's movement.

On August 3, 1994, the declaration was ready for public presentation, and a historic press conference and meeting were called in Jerusalem. Women's committee activists, representatives of the General Union of Palestinian Women, leaders of the charitable societies, and women from all parts of the Occupied Territories gathered to hear the declaration read and explained by leading activists. As an overflow audience listened to the speakers, a controversy erupted over the unexpected presence at the speaker's table of a woman with a high post in the Palestinian national authority. For half an hour, national political passions and the deep political divide in Palestinian society over the present course of the Palestinian leadership overshadowed the unity among women's organizations that had been so patiently forged over the course of nine months of discussion on the declaration.

Yet that unity of purpose over the rights of Palestinian women, reflected in the declaration, is a living reality, but one that inevitably collides with and is influenced by the profound transformations in the Palestinian national movement today. These transformations and the institution of a limited form of Palestinian self-rule make the struggle for women's rights even more urgent. The Palestinian women's movement, armed with its own organizations, a constituency in the grass roots, supporters from the political parties and democratic elements, and hard work, is determined not to let this opportunity for women pass.

NOTES

I wish to thank Penny Johnson, my colleague in women's studies at Birzeit University, for her contributions to this chapter, including but not limited to her invaluable editorial assistance.

1. Halim Barakat, *Arab Society* (Beirut: Center for Arab Studies, 1984), p. 167, in Arabic.

2. See Rosemary Sayigh, *From Peasants to Revolutionaries* (London: Zed Press, 1978).

3. Mariane Heiberg et al., *Palestinians in Gaza, the West Bank, and Arab Jerusalem: A Survey of Living Conditions* (Oslo: FAFO, 1993), p. 200.

4. Ghazi al-Khalili, *The Palestinian Women and the Revolution* (Dar al Aswar: Akka, 1981), p. 113.

5. Nahla Asali, "The Palestinian National Movement and Its View of Women," in Women's Studies Committee, *The Intifada and Some Women's Social Issues* (Ramallah: Bisan Center, 1991), pp. 41–42, in Arabic.

6. Raymonda Tawil, *My Home, My Prison* (London: Zed Press, 1983), p. 131. The notion of women's honor comprises a strict control by male family members of female sexuality and a highly defined pattern of respectable behavior.

7. Soraya Antonious, "Femmes prisonieres pour la Palestine," *Revue d'etudes palestiniennes* (1981):76. The majority of female prisoners were from left-wing organizations, while the majority of male prisoners were from Fateh.

8. The original Women's Work Committee (later the Palestinian Federation of Women's Action Committees) became affiliated with the Democratic Front; the Union of Palestinian Working Women's Committees, founded in March 1980, was linked to the Communist Party; the Palestinian Women's Committee (later the Union of Palestinian Women's Committees), founded in March 1981, gave its loyalty to the Popular Front; and the Women's Committee for Social Work, established in June 1982, was affiliated with Fateh.

9. See Lisa Taraki, "Mass Organizations in the West Bank," in Naseer Aruri, ed., *Occupation: Israel over Palestine*, 2nd ed. (Belmont, Mass.: AAUG, 1989).

10. Many of the administrative committees belonging to the Palestinian Union for Social Work are appointed or are composed of women who, because of their having initiated the work, merely took the positions on the committee without being formally elected or appointed.

11. In one of the women's committees, a crisis occurred because a woman offered her candidacy even though her name was not on the preordained list drawn up in advance by the party.

12. Union of Women's Work Committees, *The Development of the Palestinian Women's Movement* (Jerusalem: Union of Women's Work Committees, n.d.), in Arabic.

13. This program was applied mainly in Gaza by the Women's Committee for Social Work.

14. In one party, a leader from the women's committee took over the leadership of the party for the West Bank and Gaza. In another party, women were leaders of huge geographic areas such as Gaza, Nablus, Hebron, and Jerusalem.

15. Interview with Dahani abu Dakka, member of the executive committee of the Gaza Women's Action Committee, Gaza City, September 1993.

16. Interview with Siham Barghouti, a founder of the Women's Action Committee, Ramallah, September 1993.

17. Samir Helilah, "The Dynamics of Alternative Development Schemes: The Emergence of Palestinian Grass-root Organizations in the Occupied Territories," *Afaq Filastiniyyah*, no. 6 (1991):68.

18. Women's Action, "Renovation and Renaissance: Report of the Meeting of the Executive Committee, July 7, 1993," (Jerusalem: Palestine Federation of Women's Action Committees, n.d.), p. 36.

19. Interview with Barghouti.

20. Ibid.

21. Ibid.

22. This happened to the Palestinian Women's Committee, which was obliged to reactivate the neighborhood committees after their collapse. Interview with Randa Nassar, member of the executive committee of Palestinian Women's Committee, Ramallah, August 1993.

23. Interview with Rabiha Diab, head of the Women's Union of Social Work, Ramallah, September 1993.

24. *The Covenant of Harakat al-Muqawama al-Islamiyya* (Hamas, August 18, 1988).

25. Rima Hammami, "Women, the Hijab, and the Intifada," *Middle East Report* (May-August):26.

26. Interview with Naima al-Shiekh, head of the Women's Union for Social Work, Gaza, September 1993.

27. Hammami, "Women, the Hijab, and the Intifada."

28. Women's Action, "Renovation and Renaissance," p. 21.

29. Ibid.

30. Interview with Barghouti.

31. General Union of Palestinian Women, Jerusalem-Palestine, "Draft Document of Principles of Women's Rights" (Jerusalem: GUPW, August 3, 1994), p. 1.

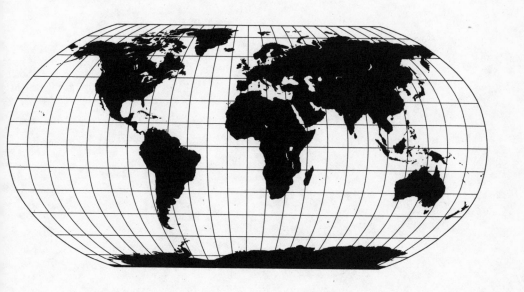

10

Out of the Kitchens and onto the Streets: Women's Activism in Peru

CECILIA BLONDET

IN PERU TODAY, THE presence of women and women's movements in the public sphere is widely recognized. No one is surprised to see a woman conducting the national symphony orchestra or to see women working as journalists, business owners, mayors, members of Congress, and cabinet ministers. The presence of women poets, painters, and art critics expressing feminist positions is widely accepted. Women lead two traditional political parties and actively participate in the most radical leftist parties, playing an important role in the Sendero Luminoso (Shining Path) terrorist group's top leadership and death squads.

Just a few decades ago, all this would have been unthinkable. Women had little opportunity to participate in public life. With rare exceptions, their world was limited to family and the four walls of home. Today women participate socially and politically, and to the public their presence seems natural. Nevertheless, the situation is far from ideal. Not all women in leadership positions defend women's rights. Educational and labor statistics show that a great gender gap persists. School desertion, job discrimination, and segregation are common. Sexual violence and domestic violence are still considered private, protected by the shroud of family dignity and intimacy.

How did these changes occur in Peru? Do the new images correspond to real improvements in the lives of the majority of women? In this chapter I trace this process of change: the development of, and the limits encountered by, the women's movement in Peru from the late 1970s to the mid-1990s. I discuss the impor-

PERU

GENERAL

type of government: Democratic Republic
major ethnic groups: Indigenous (47%); Mestizo (37%); Caucasian (15%); Black;
   Asian
language: Spanish (official); Quecha; Aymara
religions: Roman Catholic (90%)
date of independence: 1824
former colonial power: Spain

DEMOGRAPHICS

population size: 22.8 million
birth rate (*per 1,000 population*): 28
total fertility (*average number of births per woman*): 3.7
contraceptive prevalence (*married women*): 55%
maternal mortality rate (*per 100,000 live births*): 165

WOMEN'S STATUS

date of women's suffrage: 1955
economically active population: M 79%   F 25%
female employment (*% of total workforce*): 24
life expectancy   M 63   F 67
school enrollment ratio (*F/100 M*)

primary	93
secondary	83*
tertiary	53*

literacy   M 92%   F 82%

*Data from 1980–1984

---

tant attempts to unite interests and describe the difficulties that women encountered in their efforts to forge and consolidate a social movement in a fragmented
and impoverished society at a time when political polarization and disorder
reached historic proportions. In this sense, it is more accurate to speak of the experiences of various movements rather than one unified experience. Thus, while

the focus is on the emergence and development of the women's movement in Peru, I argue that women organized in various ways to address the specific social and economic conditions confronted by different sectors of Peruvian society. Moreover, precisely because of these varied experiences, the women's movement(s) mirrors the complex conditions in Peru during the past two decades and can be understood as representing a microcosm of the country.

The historical changes have taken place in a geographically diverse nation with marked social and cultural differences. Most of Peru's population of 22 million speak Spanish, although its indigenous populations continue to speak Quechua and Aymara. They live in isolated communities and villages nine to twelve thousand feet above sea level. Peru is also an Amazon nation, with diverse native groups, each with a distinct language and customs. In this variegated territory, different cultures, races, and languages coexist without completely blending or understanding each other.

While the heavy weight of colonial domination still pervades Peru, after World War II new social demands forced the state to intervene in an active effort to integrate this diverse and complex nation.[1] One of the developments that most affected women's position was the growth of the educational system. In the 1950s, great numbers of boys and girls began to attend school. When these girls became women, this education helped lessen their isolation inside the home, broadened their realms of interaction, and gave them access to information and to Spanish. Education expanded the voting population when literate women won suffrage and later fostered a growing number of scholars and professionals who acted as a powerful mechanism for democratization.[2]

As their educational levels rose, women slowly began to join the labor market, a phenomenon that became massive in the 1970s.[3] Clear demographic changes resulted from this process: The average age at marriage rose, family size declined, and women began to demand birth control methods. Paradoxically, these changes increased distances within society and especially between women. Unequal access to education, to Spanish, and to university and the professions widened the cultural and social gap between poor and middle-class women and between rural and urban women. The spheres open to women expanded, but in a stratified way that reinforced Peru's cultural heterogeneity.

Even as social mobility and economic participation increased, the country's political life remained oligarchical. The 1968 coup d'état by General Juan Velasco Alvarado and his "Revolutionary Government of the Armed Forces" helped shake up the country's traditional social and political structures.[4] The government introduced social and economic reforms accompanied by a radical ideological discourse that promoted grassroots participation and gave the state a central role in the life of the nation and its citizens.

This led to mobilization and formation of a variety of grassroots organizations around Peru, which the poor used to pressure the state for services such as light and water, jobs and social security, and better wages. The intensity of grassroots participation arose from the military government's reformist agitation and from the leftist political parties that influenced these organizations. However, this reform process could not be consolidated. In the mid-1970s, Peru's economy, dependent on foreign credit, went into crisis. A military countercoup interrupted the reform process and created further social disorder. Strikes and demonstrations against the new government's economic stabilization program followed. Into this turbulent environment of social and political participation and protest the women's movement was born.[5]

Toward the end of the 1970s, different groups of women led a process of integration unique in the country's recent history. Accompanied by economic crisis, and by the emergence of the political Left and feminist discourse, an enormous number of women's organizations were formed. Politics, poverty, and feminism flowed together to produce a complex women's movement in Peru. Women political party activists, women from barrios, and middle-class feminists, working separately or together, identified their interests and took to the streets. Their demands included changes in living conditions, subsidies and food supplies for their organizations, and an end to domestic violence. As the movement progressed, women's view of themselves and their place in society changed radically.[6]

Despite the social and cultural heterogeneity of these groups of women, their leaders began to articulate, with great difficulty, a common discourse and a shared platform that linked the right to their families' basic survival and the fight against sexism in a single political agenda. But these movements, which were moving toward political integration, ran into obstacles: the worsening economic crisis, terrorist violence, and the loss of legitimacy of the state and of the political and social organizations in the country. In addition, since 1990 the current government has applied a severe structural adjustment program that has helped destabilize and break apart this movement.

In the first two sections of this chapter, which describe this process, I focus on the principal social actors and how they came together. Shared interest and needs arising from poverty, politics, and feminism led the different groups to build alliances through which each would be strengthened. In time, women became interlocutors recognized by both the state and political parties. In the third section I examine the emergence of conflicts between women's organizations and social and political institutions as the state and the political parties went into severe crisis. The impact of terrorist violence and the structural adjustment measures on the already weakened women's movement once again reduced their expectations as citizens to those of survival. As an epilogue, I briefly analyze the chief accomplishments of this movement and look at the questions surrounding the future of the women's movement(s) in Peru.

The Actors

The women's movement in Peru drew on different roots, among them the feminist discourse discussed at the 1975 World Conference for International Women's Year in Mexico; the message of liberation theology from the Puebla bishops' conference (1979); and, on a political level, the Cuban and Chinese Revolutions, whose principles found expression in Peru in the formation of the parties of the New Left.

Peru was ripe for these new ideas and influences. More middle-class women were entering university in the late 1960s, and they took a strong interest in both their country and themselves. The universities were a focal point for political activity as well as for women's search for new forms of expression. Many young women embraced political or feminist activism, promoting women's participation and equality. At the same time, grassroots women, mostly migrants from the countryside, were already playing an active role in building their neighborhoods. Defending against and fighting off police, building homes, and organizing daily life instilled confidence and won women recognition in the new shantytowns.

When the economic crisis began to emerge, women were alert and ready to intervene. At home, traditional family models were already breaking down. With the job market shrinking, men could no longer fully support their families. This meant a revolution in female roles, which the men reluctantly had to accept. In public, a new channel of expression emerged in the women's food assistance organizations and the nongovernmental organizations (NGOs). The expansion of women's roles as a result of modernization, social participation, and the collapse of existing economic and social structures provided fertile ground in which the women's movement could develop.

Poverty and Survival: The Grassroots Organizations

Since the beginning of the 1980s, Peru's grassroots women's organizations have been one of the most significant symbols of the growing visibility of women in Latin American political and social life. These organizations first appeared as an emergency response to the economic crisis at the end of the 1970s. As the economic situation deteriorated and poor families tightened their budgets, the organizations consolidated into permanence. Foreign aid organizations, governments, feminists, and women from the leftist political parties all participated in their creation and development.

Though different, these organizations are associations of women, usually mothers. Often reliant on foreign aid or some external support, these organizations meet concrete needs by providing food, health care, legal aid, education, and training to poor women.[7] Each organization becomes an effective arena of per-

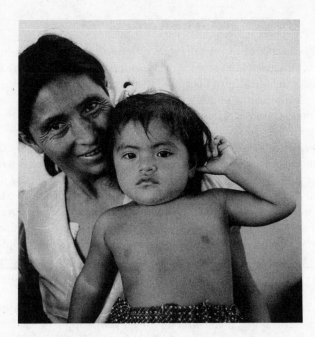

This woman helped manage one of the "people's kitchens" in Lima's shantytowns in the 1980s. Encouraged by the government as a condition of poor people's receiving grain and food supplements, the kitchens provided women with a forum for developing and asserting community leadership skills.

sonal recognition, social integration, and political awareness. Given the cultural heterogeneity and unequal opportunities for women in the shantytowns, these social functions make the organizations especially valuable to their members.

In broad terms, we can identify four kinds of grassroots women's organizations. The "mothers' clubs," the classic women's organizations, are dependent on the state's welfare program. "People's kitchens," supported by the Catholic church and NGOs, are organizations in which members collectively share the tasks of food purchase, preparation, and distribution. The "Glass of Milk" committees, promoted by the United Left municipal government of Lima (1983–1986), are neighborhood groups of women who meet daily to prepare and distribute among local children the milk they receive free from the municipal government. The networks of grassroots health and legal aid promoters, formed and advised by feminist NGOs, are organizations of women specially trained to provide these services in poor neighborhoods.

As indigenous women migrated to the cities to escape the war between the army and the Sendero Luminoso, many became involved in women's groups. These groups later became integral to the development of popular feminism in Peru. This indigenous woman is attending a national meeting of peasant women in 1988.

The organizations' numbers and importance have varied over time in direct proportion to the worsening economic crisis and the state's progressive withdrawal from providing social services. Grassroots women's organizations now serve approximately 17 percent of all families in metropolitan Lima and 25 percent of the poor families.[8] These organizations are fundamentally an urban phenomenon concentrated in the capital city. Though organizations exist in many provincial cities, and mothers' clubs receive food in rural areas, outside Lima these organizations are not as influential or large. Kinship networks take precedence in the survival strategies of the poor in Peru's provinces.

Internal and External Changes: The Feminists

While the women of Lima's poor neighborhoods and shantytowns were beginning the daily labor of the first people's kitchens, middle-class feminist women were also building their first organizations. Between 1968 and 1975, while the reformist military government was in power, events of profound importance in Peru and around the world were challenging the established course of social and political life. As in other parts of the world, the universities of Lima and the provinces were subject to intense student pressure for a voice in curricula, administration, and other aspects of university life. Students from private and public universities marched together in the streets demanding attention and expressing solidarity with other sectors: striking miners, teachers, the Vietnamese fighting to drive out the United States, or the Nicaraguans fighting Somoza. Tension, camaraderie, mutual recognition, a sense of a shared identity as part of an important segment of the national and global population, and a shared belief in social and political change united young Peruvians during the 1970s. Within this context of mobilization, a new feminist vision started to take shape. Strengthened by the increasingly ubiquitous ideas of international feminism, a small group of urban, mostly middle-class women formed Action for the Liberation of the Peruvian Woman (ALIMUPER) in 1973. ALIMUPER led the first protests against beauty contests, and its members began to speak out for all women's right to control their own bodies.[9]

Women or Feminists? During the late 1970s, the first four middle-class feminist organizations were formed: the Flora Tristán Center for the Peruvian Woman, the Manuela Ramos Movement, Women in Struggle, and the Women's Socialist Front. Linking national, social, and political issues with a challenge to patriarchal oppression, a varying number of women, ranging from fifty to three hundred, mobilized against the criminalization of abortion, the commercialization of Mother's Day, and in support of Nicaragua's Sandinista front. They soon formed the Women's Organizations' Coordinating Committee to develop joint political action that demonstrated their commitment to social change.

At this early stage, their beliefs fit within the outlines of feminist socialism. Linking the problems of class and gender, they recognized social inequality and added the specifics of women's subordination to their discourse. Before long, most had renounced the platforms of the leftist parties and moved toward an openly feminist position. As the movement headed toward feminist autonomy, the women of the political parties who had founded or accompanied this process began to distance themselves from it. They instead insisted on the importance of creating a broad front that would press for reforms to improve the lives of poor women.[10]

The Feminists and the Feminist Political Party Militants. The different groups defined themselves during the early 1980s. To safeguard their identity, feminist groups tended to isolate themselves from other institutions and from national political activity. By the time of the Second Feminist Meeting of Latin America and the Caribbean, held in Lima in 1983, two styles had become explicit: the feminist political party militants, whom the others denounced as "not feminist," and the feminist activists, labeled "bourgeois" by the politicians. Without dramatic ruptures, the two groups defined separate spheres of action.

The party feminists concentrated on preparing platforms and government programs to combat the marginalization of the poor, particularly poor women. These proposals were as numerous and varied as the leftist parties. Feminist organizations emphasized building an autonomous movement, with both organic and ideological independence, that would raise women's consciousness about the oppressiveness of patriarchal power. There is a continuing debate on whether this was a key moment in the development of Peruvian feminism or whether it merely bogged the movement down. Still, while emphasizing gender oppression, the movement's isolation kept it from recognizing the different ways this oppression affected the different women of Peru. The discourse thus reached only one segment of the population.[11]

Between 1978 and 1983, new feminist groups formed and existing ones divided to form new organizations in Lima and in many provincial cities. NGOs working with grassroots women also proliferated. During the same period, the Women's Bookstore and the Center for Women's Documents opened in Lima, two magazines were in print, and an increasing number of pamphlets on topics such as health, sex education, and women's rights were being published. At the same time, Peru's first two homosexual organizations were founded—the Lima Homosexual Movement and the Group of Lesbian Feminists.[12] Although numerically small, their presence at this time was another example of the extent to which women were determined to establish their presence in the public sphere.

The milestone that demonstrated the limits of feminist self-isolation was the participation of two feminists as candidates in the 1985 general elections. While they lost the election, feminists in general won publicity and broad dissemination of their demands.[13] Perhaps the most positive aspect of this experience was that it forced feminist NGOs to reexamine their own programs. They found that in order to broaden their social base, they needed to build stronger ties with women in different sectors, using a discourse and a practice that incorporated the demands of these other sectors.

Building Grassroots Feminism. The years that followed were filled with new initiatives relating to women. Many were projects that trained women in areas such as health and family planning, literacy, and nutrition and also served as a mechanism for raising consciousness and promoting women's rights. Feminist training on legal affairs, women's identity, and sexuality was adapted to the conditions of poor women. These activities also played a crucial role in developing leaders among poor women.

While many of these programs enjoyed great success, they also had limitations. First, their exclusive orientation toward women was limiting. Introducing gender issues was difficult, above all because of men's resistance to these types of projects.[14] A second problem was the NGOs' frequent lack of specialized training in the program areas they worked in. Finally, the priority placed by funding sources on concrete projects with short-term results also contributed to dispersion in programs for women's advancement. Activism and a short-term outlook often led to improvisation, as institutions dependent on external financing carried out projects with more attention to the interests of funders than the real needs of women.

Nevertheless, in later years many of these problems began to be addressed. In the late 1980s, development NGOs working with women and feminist organizations formed networks by areas of interest and activity; at present more than ten networks coordinate their activities. Many of these groups have had important results. Most but not all of these networks function in Lima,[15] attesting both to the centralized nature of Peru's institutions and to the varying degrees of development—and fragmentation—of the women's movement around the country.

Class Before Gender: The Party Activists

A third group of women activists comprised the women militants of the political New Left. Mostly university graduates in the social sciences, between 1970 and 1980 these young sociologists, anthropologists, social workers, and teachers went to the shantytowns, built ties with labor and neighborhood organizations, and formed political action circles as part of their party activism. Likewise, as workers from the NGOs or as employees in state programs for health and literacy, they strengthened the grassroots movements while trying to consolidate a base for their parties.

At first, many of these young women did not make a special effort to relate with poor women. In the debate between class and gender, their priority was class, and most identified exclusively with a party. However, over time their own feelings of marginality began to sensitize them to women's issues. Discontent with the unequal value placed on women's work in the political parties led many to prioritize working with women. They also saw the emergence of a new dynamic in Lima's shantytowns as the grassroots women's organizations went to work. These developments led many young women militants into relationships with women's organizations.

Later in the 1980s, many of these women activists went to work in development NGOs and feminist centers, mixing their partisan classism with a commitment to women rather than to feminism per se. Within this wordplay lay a host of contradictions. Yet this combination of interests was felt in the development NGOs, which broadened their perspective to include projects working with women, and in the parties themselves, as they recruited new militants from among the leaders of the grassroots organizations. For their part, the feminist "politicians" reinforced this process. They remained in the parties when the feminist organizations and movement became isolated, and despite resistance from both men and women, won space and legitimacy for their ideas.

History of a Meeting of Interests and Needs

The offer of foreign food donations to address hunger and the desire of different institutions to broaden their base of social support activated the latent demand for food assistance among poor women. The formation of women's organizations to distribute food was encouraged by the government, churches, and political parties as they sought to broaden their bases of support. The convergence of interests between donors and recipients helps explain the speed with which these groups multiplied. Food aid was later supplemented with services and technical assistance from development and feminist NGOs as they sought their own bases of support and legitimacy.

This process strengthened both the grassroots organizations and their external counterparts but did little to promote integration among different grassroots organizations. Instead, the presence of outside entities reinforced separate and fragmented social identities among the leaders, emphasizing difference and competition for resources. This tendency was also indirectly influenced by the need of these external institutions to preserve and differentiate their bases of support. The grassroots organizations thus developed in an environment characterized by conflict and sectarianism.

The Potential of Charity

In 1979, the Peruvian and U.S. governments signed an agreement under which the United States, through the Agency for International Development, would donate to Peru surplus agricultural products. The accord reflected the U.S. policy of basing food donations on its foreign policy goals.

Churches, along with the state, played a key role in food distribution. Through their philanthropic agencies, these vast programs conditioned the distribution of foodstuffs on the existence of organized groups of women who cooked collectively.[16] This favored the formation of Christian-based communities and broadened the pastoral constituency of the "church of the poor." The first people's kitchens developed in this context, and between 1980 and 1986 hundreds emerged. President Fernando Belaunde (1980–1985) used the food supply to strengthen his own patronage networks. The office of "Popular Cooperation," led by the president's wife, Violeta Correa, inaugurated what would come to be known as "Violeta's kitchens."

In April 1984, the Glass of Milk Program was inaugurated in Lima. The leftist municipal government gave the women in the government's allied parties a chance to do as the church and the central government had already done and directly organize women in the barrios. Militants, NGO workers, and municipal officials joined the mobilization, and by 1986, 100,000 women were organized in these groups, with 1 million beneficiaries in metropolitan Lima alone. Glass of Milk committees in the provinces started functioning regularly a year later.

In this fertile field of women's organizations, the Popular Revolutionary Alliance of America (APRA) party (in government from 1985 to 1990) launched the Program of Direct Support (PAD), led by President Alan García's wife, Pilar Nores. Building on existing networks of women's organizations, PAD clubs, as they were known, received both foodstuffs and cash.[17] The government also promoted a jobs program in which the majority of the participants were women. Membership in many poor women's organizations declined as the members chose to work for income instead of continuing in their organizations. This forced external advisers to rethink the choices and preferences of grassroots women, and NGOs also began promoting income-generating projects. When the jobs program ended in a year, the members returned to their organizations.

Poor women entered into these relationships with the collaborating agencies for a variety of reasons—as different as the women themselves. Those with previous ties to the parishes or the government's assistance programs and a certain degree of family stability emerged as leaders in their communities through the collective food preparation programs. In contrast, the youngest and best educated women brought with them a more political outlook, a feminist perspective, or both. The neediest women, battered by the economic crisis, showed little interest in becoming leaders. They took part in the training programs because they had to, often to avoid paying the fines the organizations charged for nonattendance. Thus, the movement advanced in the context of the mingled and often conflicting interests and needs of these distinct actors.

As they organized, these women initiated important social innovations. They learned how to establish rules and procedures, manage shifts, keep purchase and distribution records, participate in assemblies, elect delegates and authorities, and establish control and oversight mechanisms that built a foundation of trust. These lessons complemented the exercise of representative democracy that the women leaders embodied as they met with donor agencies to conduct business.

Collective cooking also had its inconveniences. Women leaving the home changed family life, creating problems with their spouses and children. Earning the right to go out often led to confrontation with close relatives, especially fathers, husbands, and eldest sons.[18] Envy, gossip, doubts, and ill-humor often occurred in the organization, the neighborhood, and the family. Without any models these women developed organizations, and in doing so they had to overcome deep-rooted traditions. Collective cooking thus helped integrate culturally distinct immigrant families of the shantytowns. Despite fear, shame, and family problems, women ventured from their homes to hear about, and discuss in open assemblies, the problems that affected them.[19]

In January 1985, after a massive demonstration demanding official recognition, the Glass of Milk Program won passage of a law that for the first time recognized the women's organizations and assigned them a financial allotment in the national budget. Around this time, the local Glass of Milk committees formed a centralized metropolitan coordinating committee. The collective kitchens began a similar process in 1986 with the First National Meeting of People's Kitchens, attended by nearly three hundred delegates.[20]

The Moment of Integration

In 1986, conditions existed for grassroots leaders, feminists, and party militants, many of them working in NGOs, to act together. After their electoral loss, the feminist organizations adopted different strategies in relation to the grassroots women's organizations. While some strengthened their own positions, clearly differentiating their interests and demands from those of the grassroots movement, others came to accept the need to work with the poor sectors and introduced them to specific concerns affecting women as women. The feminist NGOs and those working with women in development expanded their efforts in poor neighborhoods and the provinces. A significant amount of money was invested in the development of grassroots women, generating important experiences in educating and training leaders to provide legal, educational, and health services to women in their own communities. Perhaps the most significant aspect of the work of the NGOs at this time was their dedication to training new women leaders.[21] The NGOs provided transportation, funding and materials for assemblies and board meetings, technical assistance, and consulting. This both strengthened the grassroots organizations and facilitated these women's participation in public life. The convergence of feminists, development NGOs, and grassroots leaders strength-

Peruvian women celebrate International Women's Day 1988 with a march through Lima.

ened the women's movement as a whole as well as the individual institutions involved.

The feminists increased their projects and broadened their social base. Women from NGOs, many of them former party militants, received funding from foreign foundations to work with women in development, bringing secure jobs and increased legitimacy. The community leaders also benefited from attending training courses, examining their own traditions, and growing themselves. The personal style of leadership that had at first predominated began to blend with more democratic practice and teamwork among the different groups. They learned, and informed their neighborhoods, about women's rights and their ability to exercise those rights. They began to speak to judges and police, cabinet ministers, and members of Congress as they sat down at the negotiating table with labor unions and business. They attended social functions, and such public recognition reinforced their self-esteem.

Relations with external advisers, also women, became indispensable for the leaders to efficiently fulfill their responsibilities, which took on an increasingly political tone. Their ability to mobilize important sectors of Lima's poor barrios increased their bargaining power. At the same time, midlevel leaders also participated in public affairs. The arena open to women's participation expanded so much that the older leaders willingly brought along younger colleagues, allowing the younger leaders to learn and exercise leadership.[22]

`Men and women join in on a neighborhood improvement project. Such projects have been critical in bringing poor women into contact with the wider world and developing their leadership skills.*

The members of these organizations also benefited. Though at first most joined organizations to receive rations, the obligation to attend training courses in exchange for food helped raise the members' awareness and enriched their own personal growth. They allowed women to meet and relate to other women in the same condition.

Despite intense activity, these organizations never managed to articulate a clear agenda that tied together the principal interests of all the women's groups and gave them the strength to negotiate in the political realm. Later, as the economic crisis became widespread, the lack of a cohesive political vision surfaced in a lack of coordination among the groups. Advisers, without necessarily meaning to, often exacerbated this fragmentation. The NGOs and political parties "privatized" the grassroots organizations to guarantee control over their bases. In order to be more efficient in their institutional programming, the NGOs worked with different leaders without assuring a minimum level of coordination. The political parties sought to co-opt the leaders in order to build up their own influence. Each grassroots organization reinforced its own circle of advisers and never laid the foundation for even minimal agreement among themselves. Later, that task would prove difficult, if not impossible.

Conflict and Fragmentation

The trends just outlined seemed to foreshadow a process of integration among the different women's groups. While the process would be characterized by conflict and time would be needed to integrate these vastly different groups of women, the movement seemed to have the strength to resolve these contradictions. Instead, the economic and political situation began to exhibit the terrible signs of decomposition that would soon bring the collapse of the state. Generalized crisis, economic adjustment, and violence marked this period. In response, programs for the advancement of women also changed radically from legal and health training to projects aimed solely at keeping poor families from starving. This sudden change eliminated the potential for integration.

Beginning the Adjustment

In September 1988, the García government decreed a set of measures that sought to stabilize the shaky economy. The price of gasoline rose 300 percent, the currency was devalued by 650 percent, and real wages fell 30 percent as a result. The state instituted programs that sought to lessen the impact of the crisis among the poor. These programs, however, merely reoriented food distribution toward the government's supporters and away from existing organizations. Established procedures for food donations changed, and the donations themselves were restricted. Meanwhile, the demand for food and for new organizations to distribute it increased.

These drastic changes left the grassroots organizations deeply shaken. Internally, the distance between their leaders and members widened as the need for efficiency and pragmatism clashed with the principles of democratic practice. Channels of communication and internal functioning frequently broke down in disputes over a handful of food. Loyalties and trust dissolved, laying bare the conflicting extremes of institutional life. At the same time, the political crisis facing the parties and the government also affected the grassroots women's organizations as organizational action clashed with the political leaders' interests. The organizations began to split into fragments as a result.

As the crisis continued, the parties ceased to act as effective mediators between the interests of the state and those of neighborhood, labor, and women's organizations. Yet the parties' struggle to maintain control over the organizations hampered the unification of the women's movement. Partisan disputes repeatedly cost leaders their legitimacy when they were seen to participate, directly or indirectly, in political manipulation to keep their party or themselves in power. These actions caused many intermediate leaders and women members to distrust their leaders because of their party links.

While political-partisan and organizational interests clashed, a growing mass of women turned to welfare dependency in order to receive food. This combination of economic and political factors debilitated the still weak institutional structure of the grassroots organizations. The NGOs' work now centered on backing and advising the grassroots leaders on strategies to pressure the state into guaranteeing a minimum level of aid for the popular kitchens.

Meanwhile, the number of grassroots organizations was growing every day. They maintained a precarious level of activity cooking and distributing food rations acquired through donations and a small fee from each family. More and more restricted to a purely local level, they broke away from the higher leadership, which was acting on a political level. In this denouement, a strategy based on using the organizations as a lever to demand state attention and depending on donations and advisers became less relevant. With day-to-day problems commanding attention, women had no time to articulate the common problems of women. All women, middle class and poor, feminist activists and party militants alike, had to focus on the centrality of poverty. There was no more talk of the right to an adequate social policy, education, jobs, or health, no more discussion of the defense of women's dignity, the outlawing of sexual assault and domestic violence, or the legalization of abortion. These demands began shrinking to fit into the framework imposed by the economic and political crisis and the government's meager social compensation programs.

The government of Alberto Fujimori continued this trend and worsened the population's misery. When Fujimori took office in July 1990, the country's annual rate of inflation was roughly 2,000 percent. The state apparatus was inefficient, the political system widely scorned, and the economy increasingly recessive. Terrorist violence was breaking down, polarizing, and tearing apart Peruvian society. The new president, contrary to his campaign promises and with the goals of fighting hyperinflation and reinserting Peru into the international financial community, applied a drastic adjustment "shock" that quickly slashed hyperinflation but dramatically increased poverty.

This so-called Fuji-shock on August 8, 1990, quintupled prices from one day to the next. The greatest price increases hit kerosene, the basic cooking fuel in poor households, which rose nearly 7,000 percent; bread, up 1,567 percent; and vegetable oil, up 639 percent. Meanwhile, private-sector salaries fell an average of 42 percent, and public-sector salaries were cut by 50 percent.[23]

Women leaders were called to meetings to design a compensation program, but the government had neither the interest, the ability, nor the resources to implement it. With no social emergency plan, survival, for the vast majority of Peruvians, became each family's individual responsibility. The total number of people's kitchens and their variants more than doubled; in many poor barrios the number of kitchens rose four or five times. The change marked the end of all activities not directly related to feeding programs.

The leaders of the women's organizations were increasingly finding themselves in a "no-(wo)man's-land." Their members thought them ineffective because they could not secure even a minimum level of support. The government ignored their demands. Trapped between an all-powerful executive branch, a few weak parties with no real political presence, and an anxious and demanding membership, they felt the pressure of disregard and the loss of legitimacy.

The situation had changed dramatically. The effects of the new economic policies upset an already precarious social situation. The lack of a social welfare program left organized and unorganized women alike to their fate. And a fearsome force, Sendero Luminoso (the Communist Party of Peru), began at this time to penetrate the women's organizations in Lima's shantytowns with increasing ease. For Sendero, the organizations existed only to serve the party and the revolution. The women leaders lost ground, and their conflicts with their members grew.

Sendero Luminoso's Violence Against Women

Sendero Luminoso launched its armed struggle in the community of Chuschi, in the southern Andean department of Ayacucho, in May 1980. In the decade that followed, the struggle spread to other areas around the nation. The years of war took a terrible toll: twenty-seven thousand dead in political violence, over twenty-three thousand attacks, and material damages exceeding $21 billion, an amount similar to the country's foreign debt. The war also forced more than half a million people from their homes for a life of displacement and wandering. Widows, mothers, orphaned children, devastated and charred communities, groups of armed civil defense squads waiting for the next ambush, distrust, fear, and generalized misery—these were the results of Peru's political violence.[24]

Though at first the war took place in the country's interior, in Lima those in poor neighborhoods heard the dramatic tales from the highland families that began seeking refuge in the capital. But Sendero Luminoso did not remain in the countryside, and by the mid-1980s its presence in Lima was already known. The real shift came after 1989, when Sendero Luminoso placed strategic value on the poor neighborhoods surrounding Lima and started to assassinate authorities and grassroots and labor leaders. By 1991, Sendero had begun to realize the strategic importance of the women's organizations and launched a strategy that sought to co-opt or destroy them. As they were, the organizations were an obstacle to Sendero because they mobilized the population and fed the poor, moderating their misery and, presumably, their eagerness for revolution. Ironically, they also ended up feeding the Senderistas. Above all, Sendero sought to break down the women's organizations because they united poor women around concrete issues and strengthened the social fabric Sendero sought to destroy.

Rather than attack the organizations per se, Sendero sought to undermine and intimidate their leaders by fanning old jealousies and accusations of entrenchment in power between intermediate- and higher-level leaders. Sendero encouraged this conflict in order to co-opt these middle ranks. To do so, it sought to isolate individual leaders from their group by "choosing" a leader for an individual relationship. Sendero militants would then visit the woman's home in a relentlessly helpful campaign, showing what felt like friendship but proved to be a trap. Little by little, some women became involved, and somewhere between the terror and the attention, they found themselves prisoners of the party. Of course, not all the middle-ranking leaders followed this pattern. Many resisted and found themselves targets of threats, blackmail, blows, and even murder. One way or another, using persuasion or fear, Sendero pursued its objective of winning them over or neutralizing them.

With the problems and distrust dividing the leaders, and with some of them co-opted or trapped, Sendero fomented confusion to "capture" the grassroots women. If an organization set a date for a march or demonstration, Sendero put up posters announcing a similar date. If an accord was reached, Sendero later denied it. If the group decided to attend an event, Sendero spread rumors that there might be attacks by Sendero or the police. The strategy proved highly efficient for dealing with the frightened people of Lima's shantytowns. Before long, a wall of silence had been built. The rules were clear: No one should take responsibility or speak out. Everything that went on, the comings and goings, the rumors and gossip, seemed to happen behind a curtain, with no one clearly responsible. There were just voices, whispers, or screams feeding uncertainty, exhaustion, fear, insecurity, distrust.

Sendero also created new support groups among the displaced women recently arrived from the highland emergency zones. As these women did not yet understand the workings of urban institutions, or know the language and customs of the city, they organized their own collective kitchens. Sendero used them as a way to isolate these women from the other women's organizations. The Senderistas told them in their language, Quechua, "The others see you and me as Indian, dirty, useless. I'm like you. No one wants us in this country, yet we're the majority." "You ran away from there like a dog, but you can't run from here. You just shut your mouth, and don't say you saw me."[25] These women were thus condemned to silence and isolation.

While hounding and threatening the grassroots leaders and their organizations, Sendero also went after intellectuals, NGO promoters working in the provinces and the capital city's shantytowns, and, increasingly, the population in general. Between 1990 and 1992, many NGOs and foreign aid programs were forced to leave the provincial emergency zones and in the end even withdrew from the poor areas of Lima, closing down many development programs. As fear grew, a feeling of vulnerability seized every Peruvian.

All that remained in this context of war were to survive, to lower expectations to a minimum, to keep silent in order to avoid arousing the suspicions of the police or Sendero, to work twice as hard just to cover the barest necessities. Though the organizations were more important than ever, many were too frightened to open their doors. Members stopped coming because their leaders had been threatened and their husbands had forbidden them to continue. Distrust devoured every-thing—anyone could be a Senderista or a police informant. After the threats against the leaders of the people's kitchens and the murder of María Elena Moyano in February 1992, the central committees essentially stopped functioning because of security problems. The organizations diminished, turned inward, and cut off relations with other organizations as a way of demonstrating their rejection of political activity. Those who continued worked only at a very local level and strictly limited themselves to cooking and distributing rations. A highly prag-matic attitude motivated them, along with a clear vision of the need for isolation in order to survive.

Starting in September 1992, the capture of Abimael Guzmán and the top leaders of Sendero and another group, the MRTA, radically changed the panorama in Peru. Though terrorist attacks continue, Peruvians have begun to recover trust and a sense of life in the medium and long term. The question on the minds of Pe-ruvians today is, What will come now that the end of the war seems to be ap-proaching?

The Challenges of the Future

In contemporary Peru, the power to regulate society has been given to the market, and the state has withdrawn to its older social functions. This is a dangerous deci-sion, leaving the majority of Peruvians, already affected by structural adjustment and battered by Senderista violence, to compete under very unequal terms. The women's movement, whose germination and move toward unification I have de-scribed, has fallen apart. Today's grassroots women's movement has serious prob-lems impacting on politics but is able to fill the need for a minimum welfare net-work among the poor.

The government's lack of interest in the fate of grassroots women is clear. The 1994 national budget did not include funds for the legally mandated subsidy for the women's food support organizations. Despite grassroots leaders' work lobby-ing Congress, and a motion put forth by the Democratic Movement of the Left to pay the subsidies with international aid, the effort failed. In this new setting, the fate of the grassroots women's organizations is increasingly uncertain. In the past, international aid agencies and NGOs occupied the space left by the state. But to-day new conditions exist. Multilateral financial agencies posit new ways to fight poverty, which differ from the traditional practices of the NGOs and the grass-roots organizations.

Prospects for the future are uncertain. The grassroots organizations, which played such an important role providing a minimal safety net for the majority, are in crisis and face the risk of complete isolation from the new forces dominating the country. The tradition of receiving donations led to the notion that donations were a right; the idea of rights was based on a dependency relationship in which the state was expected to protect the poor, who won attention through collective action.

Today, the generally accepted discourse echoes the market and emphasizes personal initiative and individual growth and accumulation. If organizations fail to reorient their objectives to the market, they run the risk of collapse. This means replacing the idea of donations and subsidies with a new entrepreneurial identity and implies that women leaders must become small-scale entrepreneurs, while the mass of beneficiaries become the workforce for these new productive organizations.

Some NGOs have opted for a new approach emphasizing the personal development of women willing to become "entrepreneurs." While these programs seem to have a greater chance for success than the former, they face other problems. Due to shortcomings in the women's training, their products do not meet even minimum quality control standards. They continue to be goods for which no market, local or international, exists.

This process of change needs time to mature. But time is what seems most lacking in Peru. As these organizations undergo this slow and difficult process of change, what are they and their members to do in the meantime? The risk is that in an effort to become something new, the food aid organizations will simply be destroyed without achieving in the short term a reorientation toward productive activities.

Expansion of the job market in the short term, and a resulting rise in employment, would free these organizations from the need to be mechanisms either for aid distribution or income generation. In this scenario, the organizations would have a greater chance to become part of civil society. This outcome would put the history of these organizations to work in a new exercise of democracy and citizenship. They could redefine their relationship with the public sector and pressure the state to fulfill its role as a regulator of services while ensuring that the majority has access to them.

The feminist and development NGOs have gone through a period of reflection and evaluation. While not abandoning their ties with the grassroots organizations, they now seek to broaden their impact on the general public through programs in the mass media and contracts with universities and government agencies that disseminate and protect women's rights. For example, the Feminist Radio Collective was formed in 1991 by four organizations that conduct radio programs for women to inaugurate the first feminist radio station in Peru. At the initiative of the Flora Tristán Center for the Peruvian Woman and other feminist institutions, an accord was signed with the national police for feminists to consult in forming "women's police stations" around the country. Another valuable initiative is a series of agreements with universities to encourage graduating law students' "civil service" toward legal aid. Feminist organizations have also promoted political and legal changes that favor women, including changes in the civil and penal codes and in the constitution. Despite these efforts, the major victories that have been achieved for the legal recognition of women recognize the role of women in the fight against poverty rather than equal rights.

In some senses the new constitution is a step backward for women's rights since it annuls affirmative action based on women's real inequality with men, included in the 1979 constitution. It also grants "personhood" from the moment of conception, effectively eliminating the possibility for decriminalization of abortion. In contrast, a law is currently being debated that would guarantee women a quota of 30 percent participation in political parties.

There has been an impressive accumulation of intellectual works on women's issues. Most of these publications have been related to the work of the NGOs and the universities. Three specialized magazines are currently in circulation: *Viva, La Tortuga* (The Turtle), and *Musa.*[26] Since the mid-1980s, articles on women's issues have been published in various specialized social science and psychoanalytical journals as well as other magazines. These publications cover a range of topics, including women in shantytowns and grassroots organizations, reproductive health, women in the job market, political participation, and legislation.

In general terms, there has been an emphasis in literature and in political action on the problems of urban poor women, women's leadership and grassroots feminine identity, and citizen participation. Less attention has been given to the problems of campesinas and even less to middle-class women. The national drama of poverty and economic crisis was reflected in the feminist intellectual production of the past decade. Production related to the theoretical and conceptual development of gender problems and the construction of women's identity is still very limited.

Some Closing Thoughts

The women's movement in Peru did not emerge as a unified whole because the conditions of women in the country varied according to their social and economic status. In the postwar period, university women, professional women, and poor women burst onto the public scene to fight for their social rights. From inception the movement was heterogeneous in its composition, interests, and goals.

The structural factors that sparked the growth of the women's movement in Peru were the modernization process and the economic crisis. The breakdown of the traditional order and the collapse of the "statist" development model prompted greater flexibility in the division of labor and changed women's place in society. The church, the political parties, the NGOs, the international aid agencies, and the grassroots organizations were the movement's institutional channels. Among these groups, relations arose that were marked by a tension between cooperation and conflict.

In these forums, women began to acquire a basic knowledge about the social order, gender inequality, rights, and power. They also began to develop their own new leaders, feminists or grassroots leaders, who worked for their own, different interests. Nevertheless, the co-optation of the leadership positions through what inadvertently became a divisive approach by these institutions set one of the most important limits to the movement. There was never a shared leadership recognized by the different groups or a common agenda that integrated women's varied interests. Instead, there were many agendas, as many as the diverse interests that existed among the women of the movement. The political parties and the NGOs also contributed to the process of fragmentation. Their patronage was in many ways a destabilizing factor among the women's organizations.

Under these conditions and in a context of poverty, violence, and neoliberalism, the women's movement(s) faces an enormous challenge. A new scenario has emerged in which the state explicitly withdraws from its social functions and leaves the market to order society. This change has meant a rupture in the trajectory of the women's movement and demands new structures and new leaders who can adapt to the new conditions. Peru has not completed its transition to modernity, and today the situation is an uncertain one. Women, today more "citizens" than ever before despite their inequality, have learned that their new place in society will depend on them and only on them. A long path has led them here.

NOTES

This chapter is dedicated to María Elena Moyano. I wish to thank Julio Cotler, Jürgen Golte, Carmen Montero, and Patricia Oliart, who read and made valuable comments about the manuscript. My thanks also to Carmen Yon for her thoughtful and efficient assistance and to Rafael Leon and Corinne Schmidt for their patience and excellence in translating this in Spanish and English. Others have accompanied me with their love and support during the months of writing: my three sons, who are an endless source of trust and pride for me, and my sister Marta, who in the past year has become the person I turn to every day to talk about life.

1. Julio Cotler, *Clases, estado, y nación en el Perú* (Lima: IEP, 1978).

2. Jill Ker Conway and Susan Bourque, *The Politics of Women's Education: Perspectives from Asia, Africa, and Latin America* (Ann Arbor: University of Michigan Press, 1993).

3. Maruja Barrig, *Investigaciones sobre empleo y trabajo femenino,* Documento de Trabajo (Lima: ADEC-ATC, 1988); Peri Paredes and Griselda Tello, *Los trabajos de las mujeres* (Lima: ADEC-ATC, 1989); Lidia Elias and Cecília Garavito, *La mujer en el mercado de trabajo* (Lima: ADEC-ATC, 1994).

4. On this point see Barrig, 1988; Cotler, 1978; and Cynthia McClintock and Abraham Lowenthal, *El gobierno militar: Una experiencia peruana, 1968–1980* (Lima: IEP, 1985).

5. Maruja Barrig, "The Difficult Equilibrium Between Bread and Roses: Women's Organizations and the Transition from Dictatorship to Democracy in Peru," in Jane S. Jaquette, ed., *The Women's Movement in Latin America: Feminism and the Transition to Democracy* (Boston: Unwin Hyman, 1989); Cecilia Blondet, *Las mujeres y el poder: Una historia de Villa El Salvador* (Lima: IEP, 1991).

6. Virginia Vargas, *El aporte de la rebeldía de las mujeres* (Lima: Flora Tristán, 1986).

7. Blondet, 1991; Ana Boggio, et al., "Estrategias de promoción y comedores," in Nora Qaler and Pilár Nuñez, eds., *Mujer y comedores populares* (Lima: SEPADE, 1989); Patricia Cordova and Carmen Luz Gorbiti, *Apuntes para una interpretación del movimiento de mujeres: Los comedores comunales y los comités del vaso de leche en Lima* (Lima: SUMBI, 1989).

8. Cecilia Blondet and Carmen Montero, *Los comedores populares: Balance y lecciones de una experiencia* (Lima: UNICEF, 1994); José Reyes, "No sólo comen los pobres: El impacto del programa de ajuste social," *Cuadernos laborales,* no. 93 (October 1993). These statistics are based on information from the 1992 Household Poll of Metropolitan Lima.

9. Virginia Vargas, *El aporte de la rebeldía de las mujeres* (Lima: Flora Tristan and CONCYTEL, 1989), p. 33.

10. Barrig, 1989.

11. Maruja Barrig, "Democracia emergent y movimiento de mujeres," in *Movimiento sociales y democracia: La fundación de un nuevo orden* (Lima: DESCO, 1986).

12. Vargas, 1989, p. 47.

13. Vargas, 1986; Virginia Vargas, *Como cambiar el mundo sin perdernos: El movimiento de mujeres en el Perú y América Latina* (Lima: Flora Tristán, 1992); Barrig, 1986.

14. Patricia Ruiz Bravo, "Promoción de la mujer: Cambios y permanencias, 1975–1985," in Patricia Portocarrero, ed., *Mujer en el desarrollo: Balances y propuestas* (Lima: Flora Tristán, 1990).

15. Amelia Fort, *Mujeres peruanas: La mitad de la población del Perú a comienzos de los 90* (Lima: CENTRO, 1993).

16. CARITAS (Catholic), OFASA (Adventist), SEPAS (evangelical), and CARE (lay) are the most important food distribution agencies through which AID channels donations.

17. CARE, *I censo metropolitanao de comedores comunales, 1990* (Lima: CARE, 1990). Official recognition by the new government prompted a multiplication of the people's kitchens, which grew by some 60 percent, from 884 in 1985 to 1,383 in 1987.

18. Carmen Lora et al., *Mujer: Víctima de opresión, portadora de liberación* (Lima: Instituto Bartolomé de las Casas, 1985).

19. Blondet, 1991.

20. See María Mercedes Barnachea, *Con tu puedo y con mi quiero* (Lima: Tacif, 1991), for more on the centralization of the kitchens in Lima's eastern cone.

21. Blondet, 1991; Narda Henriquez, "¿Cerrando brechas?" (Lima: 1993), manuscript.

22. Blondet, 1991.

23. Cecilia Blondet, *Mujeres latinoamericanas en cifras-tomo Perú* (Santiago de Chile: Instituto de la Mujer, Ministerio de Asuntos Sociales de España y FLACSO, 1993). Employment, health, and educational indicators bear eloquent witness to the effect of the adjustment measures on an already impoverished nation. From mid-1990 to October 1991, employment levels fell drastically: In commerce, jobs fell 36 percent; in manufacturing, 30.6

percent; and in the service sector, 9 percent (Gárate 1991). Between June and November 1990, the number of lower-class persons falling ill rose 20.6 percent, and those in the middle class rose 19.3 percent. Over the same period, spending on medicines fell sharply, by 90 percent in the lower strata and 62 percent in the middle.

24. See Carlos Iván Degregori, *Qué difícil es ser Dios: Ideología y violencia política en Sendero Luminoso* (Lima: El Zorro de Abajo Ediciones, 1989); Carlos Iván Degregori, *Ayacucho 1969–1979: El surgimiento de Sendero Luminoso* (Lima: IEP, 1990); and Ponciano del Pino, "Los campesinos en la guerra: Una aproximación a explicar los Comités de Defensa Civil a partir de la expansión rural," in *SEPIA IV* (Iquitos, 1991), for more on Sendero Luminoso.

25. Coral, 1991.

26. Between the early 1980s and the early 1990s *Micaela, Mujer y Derecho* (Women and Research), *Manuela* (now changed to *Fotonovela*), and *Mujer y Sociedad* (Women and Society) were circulating. The latter was distributed as a supplement to one of the most important newspapers in Lima.

11

Democracy in the Country and in the Home: The Women's Movement in Chile

ALICIA FROHMANN & TERESA VALDÉS

SINCE ITS HISTORIC BEGINNINGS in the early twentieth century in the nitrate mining towns of the north, the Chilean women's movement has passed through a number of stages, all of them closely related to the political developments of the time. A high point in women's organizing was the struggle for female suffrage in the 1930s and 1940s; another one came in the 1980s with the combined struggle against the military regime and for women's rights during the dictatorship and the transition to democracy. We describe these developments in the first three sections of this chapter. Since the return to democratic rule in 1990, the women's movement has faced the challenge of retaining its identity and a certain degree of autonomy. Putting gender issues on the political agenda and struggling for empowerment and equal opportunity within the political establishment have made the movement more prone to being absorbed by the dynamics of the political process. In the fourth section of the chapter we evaluate the women's movement in this democratic context, drawing on a number of indicators (institutionalization, variety of issues, policy proposals, regionalization, and articulation) in order to compare this with previous stages. However, while the political context significantly influenced the women's movement, there was also a process of evolution, development, and maturation of the movement that followed a logic of its own.

The cultural, social, and political forces determining the discrimination against women in Chilean society have been pervasive ever since the Hispanic colonial period. The heritage of the *Marianismo* cultural ethos both enshrined and ex-

CHILE

GENERAL

type of government: Republic
major ethnic groups: Mestizo (66%); Spanish (25%); Indian (5%)
language(s): Spanish
religions: Roman Catholic (89%); Protestant; Jewish
date of independence: 1810–1818
former colonial power: Spain

DEMOGRAPHICS

population size: 13.5 million
birth rate (*per 1,000 population*): 21
total fertility (*average number of births per woman*): 2.7
contraceptive prevalence (*married women*): 56%
maternal mortality rate (*per 100,000 live births*): 40

WOMEN'S STATUS

date of women's suffrage: 1934 (municipal); 1949 (national)
economically active population: M 75%   F 29%
female employment (*% of total workforce*): 29
life expectancy   M 71   F 77
school enrollment ratio (*F/100 M*)
    primary   95
    secondary   106
    tertiary   75
literacy   M 94%   F 93%

---

cluded women.[1] In addition, the peculiar development of democratic institutions in the nineteenth and twentieth centuries created a system based on a politics of negotiation and compromise (*acuerdos de caballeros,* or gentlemen's agreements) among tightly knit political elites, which only marginally considered other social sectors and definitely excluded women.

The process of urbanization and early industrialization that occurred during the late nineteenth and early twentieth centuries affected the lives of women, many of whom shifted from subsistence economies in the countryside to informal labor in the urban areas. Very soon, however, working-class women were pushed into low-paying service and manufacturing jobs. Urbanization and workforce participation did not automatically help change the condition of women. While upper- and middle-class women enjoyed a higher standard of living, they were also discriminated against socially and politically.

Female suffrage, which was obtained in 1949 after decades of struggle, did not alter this situation significantly. It has taken much longer to modify the traditional and patriarchal aspects of Chilean society that have molded the status of women. When higher levels of participation and democratization were achieved during the 1960s and early 1970s, the specific needs and demands of women were subsumed within those of Chilean society as a whole. It was taken for granted that whatever was the driving force of the political system at that moment—modernization, economic growth, or the transition to socialism—would also redefine and improve the status of women.

The military coup of 1973 and the seventeen-year dictatorship that followed brought an abrupt end to those expectations. Women's struggle for survival and against human rights abuses emerged alongside a new consciousness regarding the patriarchal and authoritarian traits of both the military regime and Chilean society and family life. These factors served as strong catalysts to the women's movement.

The women's movement grew and flourished in the context of a struggle against the dictatorship.[2] This explains some of the specific characteristics of the Chilean movement, such as its very political nature and considerable level of political mobilization, the participation in the movement of women from both the popular sectors and middle class, and the close, although often troubled, links with the political parties of the Left and Center-Left.

The significant role played by the women's movement in the transition to democracy in the late 1980s encouraged considerable expectation regarding the empowerment of women within a democratic regime. However, though some gender-just public policies and legislative inroads have been made, women and the women's movement have remained largely absent from politics and government.

What has happened? The women's movement has not disappeared, but it has had difficulty adjusting to the rules of the new political context, where political parties and organic structures prevail. While a political women's movement still exists in a state of latency and may organize cohesively in a moment of crisis, women's issues and politics today have a stronger presence in the cultural sphere than in the political arena.

Today, women's groups are thriving everywhere—in the workplace, neighborhoods, universities, unions, and nongovernmental organizations (NGOs). There are a women's radio station and a women's newspaper. Gender issues are discussed in the media, and there is an increased public awareness of gender discrimination and its implications. The women's movement has become very diverse, loose, and dispersed, and even if its impact on the political system is more indirect, its mid- and long-term impact on prevailing social and cultural mores and patterns seems to have greater potential than ever before.

The Early Stages of the
Women's Movement

In Chile, as in many other Latin American countries, the origins of the women's movement can be traced to efforts by the working class to organize, unionize, and struggle for better wages and working conditions in the early twentieth century. In the nitrate mining towns in the north of Chile, women workers began organizing around both class and gender issues around 1910.[3] This resulted in a number of women's associations, lecture groups, and newspapers and first put women's issues on the agenda of the emerging progressive parties and labor unions. Other catalysts to the movement were women's increased access to education, the development of a lay and freethinking movement in the early twentieth century, and the influence of European writers such as John Stuart Mill, Karl Marx, and Friedrich Engels. At the time, the predominant belief was that discrimination against women was just part of a more general system of injustice and that overall social change would also bring about equality for women.

With the crisis of the nitrate economy and the increased political and ideological polarization of the period following the Russian Revolution, the relative importance of women and women's issues within the social struggle declined. By then, a number of women were engaged in the new forms of political participation and organization—labor unions and political parties. The most visible women's groups were middle- and upper-class charities or cultural associations. However, there were also a number of groups demanding civil and political rights for women: The first bill advocating female suffrage was introduced in 1917 by the Conservative Party, and the first two women's political parties were created in the 1920s.[4]

Nevertheless, by the early 1930s women were still lacking the most elemental political rights, and they only began to vote in municipal elections in 1934. The political system did not favor women's suffrage: The conservative parties were content to limit women to their traditional roles in the home and in the family, and the progressive parties feared that the women's vote would be very conservative and only benefit their adversaries.

The second big catalyst to the women's movement in Chile came in the late 1930s and in the 1940s with the struggle for women's suffrage. The creation of the Movimiento por Emancipación de Mujeres de Chile (Movement for the Emancipation of the Women of Chile, or MEMCh) in 1935, the Federación Chilena de Instituciones Femeninas (Chilean Federation of Feminist Institutions) in 1944, and the Partido Femenino de Chile (Feminist Party of Chile) in 1947 highlighted a long period of mobilization around women's issues. Their efforts were focused on suffrage but also addressed other issues related to the status of women. This period of activism culminated in 1949 when Chilean women were finally granted the right to vote and to stand as candidates in legislative and presidential elections.

At the time, the lack of political rights had seemed the major impediment to the emancipation and increased participation of women in the political sphere. Women assumed that, with their participation growing in education and in the labor force and with birth control beginning to be more widely available, their status in Chilean society would definitely change once political rights were achieved. It appeared that incremental, rather than radical, change was needed to complete the emancipation of women, and many of the women who had mobilized in the suffrage movement in the 1940s joined political and trade unions during the 1950s and 1960s, participating in the broader political struggle.

Gender issues were seldom raised during the period of social and political turmoil of the 1960s and early 1970s. Although during this period Chilean society experienced greater social democratization and political participation than ever before or since, the status of women remained basically the same. *Centros de madres* (CEMAs, or mothers' centers), which had been created in the 1940s to organize and educate low-income women in urban and rural areas, became institutionalized in the 1960s, especially under the Christian Democratic government, which advocated communal organization of both urban and rural poor women. These centers promoted a slightly modernized version of the traditional female role. While they were very effective in engaging women in community affairs, they also acted as a mechanism of social control.[5] Approximately 1 million women were enrolled in the CEMAs in 1973, and many of them participated actively in existing social and political organizations. Although they rarely articulated gender-specific concerns, this organizational experience helped mold the grassroots women's movement of later years.

The only women to mobilize as political actors by themselves during the early 1970s were right-wing women, who, within the group El Poder Femenino (Women's Power), organized against the Allende regime from 1971 to 1973, prior to the military coup. While these women organized as women, they did so not for themselves, but against socialism and for their families and the *patria* (fatherland).

The Women's Movement and the Struggle Against the Dictatorship

The Pinochet dictatorship (1973–1990) was a period of hardship, repression, and misery for most Chileans. This was especially true for Chilean women, who were active in the struggle for survival. They defended human rights and organized for their own and their families' subsistence.[6] During the first decade of the military regime, unemployment and poverty deeply affected the Chilean people, and women suffered additionally through the feminization of poverty. It was only after the mid-1980s that a process of economic restructuring and modernization began to bring about economic growth and increasing employment and wage levels.

The Pinochet government developed special organizations and a discourse to discipline and depoliticize women, building on the "motherhood and fatherland" ideals and activism of the right-wing women who had mobilized against Salvador Allende. Thus, a network of female support for the military regime was structured through the CEMAs, headed by Augusto Pinochet's wife, Lucía Hiriart; the Secretaría Nacional de la Mujer (National Women's Agency); and voluntary charity organizations.[7]

The roots of the present women's movement can be found in the first years of the military dictatorship in the mid- and late 1970s. The Chilean movement presents a near-textbook case of the three groups that have contributed to the formation of the modern women's movement in Latin America: women from human rights organizations, urban poor women, and feminists.[8] However, in contrast to many other Latin American countries, the movement's links with political parties, although troubled, were also strong, at least until the end of the military regime.

Shortly after the coup of 1973, women began to organize for survival and in defense of human rights. Initially they sought the protection of churches; this parish work multiplied and diversified into soup kitchens, handicrafts workshops, child care centers, and health groups. Women whose families had suffered directly from human rights abuses joined organizations in order to engage in solidarity work with the victims of political repression. A feminist scholar has stressed that "it was precisely women's traditional public invisibility which allowed them to become political actors at a time when it was extremely dangerous for anyone to do so."[9] These groups were not concerned specifically with gender issues, but they initiated a strong presence of women in the struggle against the dictatorship, which would be a central aspect of the transition to democracy of the mid- and late 1980s.

Another important component of the women's movement at this time was urban poor women, the *pobladoras*.[10] They were driven to organize by the economic crisis and the need to provide for themselves and their families. However, once these women left the isolation of their home or workplace to join with other women, many of them learned to recognize and articulate their own oppression as a point of departure for political action.

A third component of the Chilean women's movement was feminist women, many of them middle-class professionals who joined the movement because of specific gender issues and linked a critique of patriarchal oppression to that of the military dictatorship.[11] Some of these women had been active in the parties of the Left and had experienced gender discrimination there; others had been in exile in

Europe and North America and had been exposed there to women's movements and feminist thinking. A few of these women joined the Círculo de Estudios de la Mujer (Women's Studies Circle), founded in 1977, to discuss their condition as women in consciousness-raising groups. The Círculo was the first specifically feminist organization created in contemporary Chile.

Even though in Chile the women's movement has never been synonymous with the feminist movement, from the early 1980s on the qualitative impact of feminist thinking was strong. "Democracy in the country and in the home" became the rallying cry first of feminist women and then of the entire women's movement, combining gender issues and the struggle against the dictatorship.

With these objectives in mind, numerous women's groups and organizations were created in the wake of the social and political protest movement of 1983–1984. Some of them, such as the Centro de Estudios de la Mujer (Center for the Study of Women), created in 1983 as a successor of the Círculo, were oriented toward women's studies and feminist research. Others, such as the Casa de la Mujer La Morada (La Morada Women's House), engaged in feminist activism and offered counseling and workshops for women; the Casa became the umbrella for the incipient Movimiento Feminista (Feminist Movement).

Two other important organizations created during this period were MEMCh'83, named to honor the organization that had worked for women's suffrage in the 1930s, and Mujeres por la Vida (Women for Life). MEMCh'83 was established to coordinate all of the women's organizations that opposed the dictatorship; Mujeres por la Vida began as a group of sixteen well-known political leaders who joined together to demonstrate unity for the anti-Pinochet establishment. Both groups included feminist and nonfeminist organizations and individuals, and their histories provide interesting examples of how the various components of the Chilean women's movement developed an increasingly feminist perspective. The Movimiento de Mujeres Pobladoras (Movement of Urban Poor Women) is another organization that, begun by *pobladoras* to discuss and act upon their condition, gradually developed into a "popular feminist" organization.[12]

The dialectics of class and gender was debated in groups such as the feminist socialist collective Furia (Fury) and the Movimiento de Mujeres por el Socialismo (Movement of Women for Socialism), which combined "an analysis of capitalism and the need for women's autonomy and self-determination in the political process."[13] Two other women's organizations that grew out of parties of the Left but without a feminist analysis, at least initially, were Mujeres de Chile (Women of Chile) and the Comité de Defensa de los Derechos de la Mujer (Committee for the Defense of Women's Rights). The latter developed into a feminist socialist organization.

Chile has traditionally been a country very open to ideas and influence from abroad, and the women's movement was no exception. Exile and the predomi-

Women protesters walk through downtown Santiago in 1987, their hair wet from police water cannons that disrupted an opposition rally. The poster reads, "We demand justice. No more impunity! Punish the assassins!"—a remembrance of three opposition activists kidnapped and killed in 1985.

nance of women of the Left, which also had a strong internationalist tradition, accentuated this tendency. The local debates were, at least in part, similar to those of other countries. The Chilean movement, as did many others, developed in the wake of the U.N. Decade for Women (1975–1985). The women's movement of the 1970s and 1980s was an international movement, and whatever happened concerning women, both in the industrialized and the developing countries, influenced debates and initiatives elsewhere. The Encuentros Feministas (Feminist Encounters, 1981, 1983, 1985, 1987, 1990, and 1993) served as regular meeting places where Latin American and Caribbean feminists came to know each other and exchange ideas and points of view.[14] For Chilean feminists they also provided an opportunity to discover their own relative homogeneity vis-à-vis the great diversity of Latin American feminisms as well as to confirm the specifically political and antiauthoritarian nature and strong leftist legacy of the Chilean movement.

The mid-1980s are seen in retrospect as the most "heroic" period of the women's movement. Women participated massively in all the social and political protest against the military dictatorship. In fact March 8, International Women's Day, became the annual celebration that inaugurated the political year.

In 1986, the women's movement was for the first time represented within a cross-party body, the Asamblea de la Civilidad (Civilian Assembly), which represented different sectors of Chilean society. Women's demands were included in the organization's public statement, the *Pliego de Chile* (Charter of the Chilean People). This was possibly the highest point in the struggle of the women's movement for political legitimacy. It signified momentum in the effort to link gender issues to the struggle against the dictatorship and also demonstrated women's very active involvement in the forces engaged in bringing about a change of regime in Chile.

The organization and mobilization of women were undoubtedly aided by the creation and the development of a network of nongovernmental organizations oriented toward women, most of which were initiated by active participants in the women's movement.[15] These NGOs were instrumental in giving the women's movement a sense of its own worth and potential. This network also served as a very effective channel of communication and mutual support.

Another important component of the women's movement was composed of many of the female members of political parties, including Socialists, Communists, Christian Democrats, and others. Some organized specific women's organizations within their parties, often with great difficulty, while others were plain party members but saw themselves as part of a wider women's movement.

Especially during the early 1980s, the word *feminist* had a negative connotation for many people, both men and women. Within the more traditional and ideological Left, feminists were considered "bourgeois" and elitist and not sufficiently committed to class struggle and the interests of the working class. As elsewhere in the world, long debates were waged among socialist feminists about whether class or gender was the primary contradiction within society. Within conservative sectors, especially those close to the Catholic church, feminists were viewed as immoral because of their defense of birth control, divorce, and abortion. However, together with the growth and consolidation of the women's movement during the final and more liberal stage of the military dictatorship, feminism also experienced a process of relative legitimation. By the time of the democratic transition in 1990, the women's movement was advancing feminist objectives as a condition for the democratization and modernization of Chilean society.

The objectives of the women's movement during the years of antiauthoritarian struggle were very broad. They included putting an end to the military dictatorship, changing the status of women in Chilean society, achieving justice and equal opportunities for all, and changing the nature of the political and the practice of politics. This last objective definitely challenged the modus operandi of the political parties and accounted for much of their unease and distrust regarding the women's movement in general and feminists in particular.

The attempt at redefining what is political was a success: There was a process of politicization of everyday life and of the private sphere. The home, the family, and the neighborhood also became a locus of political activity in addition to the state, the party, the union, and the workplace.[16] These shifts in the locus of political activity deeply affected the characteristics of the women's movement in the period after the transition to democracy. In this process, women also became political actors in their own right and stopped acting exclusively for others: children, family, party, or fatherland.

The goal of advancing democracy in the home by changing the pattern of relationships within the family and the organization of housework also came closer during this period. Some of the elements that influenced this process were directly related to urbanization, modernization, and women's workforce participation. However, women's organizational experience and increasing gender awareness affected their statutes in the home and the relationships and roles within the family. Issues related to sexual differences were raised by a few lesbian collectives, but at the time their influence was marginal because of the strong drive within the women's movement to seek political legitimation.

The women's movement was not successful, however, in effectively changing the practice of politics. A more democratic style better suited to an egalitarian social movement was sought within women's groups but never really achieved. In fact, the strongly egalitarian traits of the women's movement conspired against raising women to leadership positions where they could negotiate with their peers in the political parties. Without legitimate and representative women leaders, it became increasingly difficult for the women's movement to participate in and affect larger political groupings.

Women leaders who were active both in the women's movement and in a political party found it very difficult to maintain and expand their political legitimacy. Many women opted to make their party allegiance primary in order to maintain and improve their political visibility. This proved to be a catch-22: Without the support of the women's movement, their leadership positions were almost impossible to maintain; however, when they sought the movement's support, their party loyalty was seriously questioned. Thus, when "politics as usual" returned with the transition to democracy, the women's movement found itself in a no-(wo)man's-land: The days of public protest and mobilization were apparently over, but there seemed to be no place for the women's movement in an institutional setting.

The Women's Movement and the Transition to Democracy

The women's movement played a significant role during the period of transition to democracy, from 1988, the year of the plebiscite that defeated Pinochet, to 1990, when Patricio Aylwin was inaugurated as president after almost seventeen years of military rule. Before the October 5, 1988, plebiscite, the women's movement played primarily a mobilizing role, organizing at the grassroots level and through public demonstrations to bring about the defeat of the apparently invincible and omnipotent dictator. *"Somos más"* (We are more) became the rallying cry during this period, expressing the quantitative superiority of both the opposition to the dictatorship and women. The network of women's NGOs helped register voters to get people to the polls to vote against Pinochet. For feminist women, publicizing the no vote became an excellent opportunity to say no also to sexism, gender discrimination, patriarchy, and the authoritarianism of Chilean society.

However, it also became necessary to move beyond merely articulating and denouncing gender discrimination and to place women's issues on the agenda for democracy.[17] Feminist women organized in mid-1988 and issued the *Demandas de las Mujeres a la Democracia* (Women's Demands to Democracy), which presented demands in three different areas: women as persons and citizens, addressing their civil rights; women as mothers, addressing reproductive, parental, and family issues; and women as workers, addressing labor issues.[18] The *Demandas* also proposed a special executive agency at the ministerial level to introduce gender issues in public policies, ratifying the U.N. Convention on the Elimination of All Forms of Discrimination Against Women, eliminating the reproduction of sexism and inequality through the educational system, and adopting an equal rights amendment to the constitution. This was the first time that feminist organizations presented themselves as legitimate interlocutors of the political parties.

The political establishment that opposed the military disliked this initiative, considering it excessively ambitious, sectorial, and divisive, and little attention was paid to it at the time. However, many of the specific issues presented in the *Demandas* were taken up by the women's movement and later included in the government program, becoming public policy after March 1990. The one demand that did not receive much response during the transition to democracy was that calling for women's empowerment within the state apparatus, specifically that 30 percent of all government decisionmaking positions be reserved for women.

Another interesting mobilizing and consciousness-raising effort was the campaign *Soy mujer, tengo derechos* (I am a women, I have rights) developed by a network of urban grassroots women's organizations in 1988.[19] This initiative showed the potential for collaboration between grassroots women's organizations and NGOs.

The Concertación Nacional de Mujeres por la Democracia (National Coalition of Women for Democracy, or CNMD) was created in early 1989 as an autonomous women's coalition in support of the overall Concertación de Partidos por la Democracia (Coalition of Parties for Democracy), the Center-Left political coalition that campaigned throughout 1989 in order to win the presidential and legislative elections of that year. The CNMD was a unique coalition effort by political party members, feminists, and women from NGOs, many of them with mixed allegiances. It had the explicit aims of preparing a government program, supporting

These women, family members of men who have been disappeared, attend a human rights rally in Santiago in December 1988. Women from many walks of life joined the opposition to the military dictatorship and its brutal policies.

women candidates, including gender issues in the political agenda during the transition, and publicizing women's discrimination in all sectors of Chilean society.

The first objective, preparing a government program, was definitely the CNMD's greatest success. Women with great professional expertise from different political spheres organized in eleven commissions to make gender-specific policy recommendations in the areas of education, health, family, communications, arts and culture, labor, political participation, rural and urban working-class women, legislation, and the National Office for Women (the executive agency responsible for public policies vis-à-vis women).

The effectiveness of the CNMD's programmatic efforts can be observed at several different levels. The government program of the Concertación de Partidos por la Democracia included a special chapter on women and the need to implement gender-specific public policies.[20] This also forced the parties of the concertación to include gender issues in their own programs. In response, even the right-wing presidential candidate supported by Pinochet, Hernán Büchi, had to include equal rights for women in his political discourse. In addition, the CNMD used the recommendations of its eleven commissions to prepare an elaborate program.[21] This was the first time that the women's movement offered Chilean society a concrete proposal for change, and it has served as the basis of public policies on women and for the development of further proposals. Finally, most of the gender-specific policies implemented by the democratic government between 1990 and 1994 were initially proposed by the CNMD. This included the creation of the ministerial-level Servicio Nacional de la Mujer (National Women's Service, or SERNAM). Many of these issues had already been outlined in the *Demandas* presented by feminists in 1988. Thus, even though the change in regime did not seem to facilitate the immediate empowerment of women in the political sphere as demonstrated in a substantial increase in the number of women elected or appointed to government office, many of the gender issues raised by the women's movement and the CNMD were in fact included in the public agenda for the transition to democracy.

Another aim of the CNMD, making women and gender issues visible in the political arena during the presidential campaign, was only partially achieved. Possibly the greatest achievement in this area was that concertación presidential candidate Aylwin, a traditional and Catholic Christian Democrat, made the women's demand for "democracy in the country and in the home" his own.[22] Not only were "women added to the constituency of social actors to whom Aylwin's campaign was addressed," but also the parallel between oppression in the public sphere and oppression in the private sphere, drawn by feminist thinkers, was implicitly accepted.[23] Although this may have only been political campaign discourse, it had never been used in this way in any other presidential campaign in Chile or, to our knowledge, in Latin America. Thus, it signified an important ideological breakthrough for the women's movement.

What had happened? Did the Chilean political leadership have a sudden revelation regarding women's discrimination and oppression? Not really. What occurred in 1989, a moment when the political establishment was particularly open to new ideas, was a combination of different factors that the women of the CNMD took advantage of successfully. First, there was a recognition of the important political and mobilizing role the women's movement had played during the struggle against the military dictatorship. Second, gender discrimination in its most blatant forms began to be seen as an anachronism, incompatible with a modern, democratic society. Third, women were perceived as particularly prone to vote conservatively; thus a proposal for change necessarily had to include some elements that especially appealed to women. Finally, a few women from the CNMD enjoyed easy access to the presidential candidate and were thus able to influence him directly.

In spite of their success in influencing the discourse of the campaign, the members of the CNMD failed to find effective channels to negotiate the empowerment of women within the political parties and the concertación. It paid the price for the women's movement's inability to develop strong, legitimate, and representative leaders. When the time came to negotiate and defend the presence of women on the lists of legislative candidates and government posts, this difficulty proved fatal, and the traditional interests of the political parties prevailed.

By 1989, most of the parties of the Center and Left had included gender concerns and propositions for change in their political platforms and were at least paying lip-service to the need to promote women in leadership positions. The Socialist Party and the Party for Democracy also included affirmative action programs in which 20 percent of all decisionmaking posts would go to women. The Humanist Party even had a woman president, Laura Rodríguez, who was also the first female presidential candidate; several other parties had women as vice presidents after the 1990 elections. However, even though women seemed to reach more and more formal leadership positions, the locus of decisionmaking and political power always shifted to where women were absent. Whenever tough decisions had to be made within the parties regarding politically powerful positions, women were absent or relegated to the background.

Nevertheless, the important difference of the 1989 campaign was that political parties appealed to women for the first time as "citizens, as workers and as participants in the creation of the new democracy" and not only in their "traditional roles of wife, mother and guardian of hearth and home," thereby formally and publicly recognizing "the existence of inequality and discrimination of women."[24] The efforts of the women's movement and of the CNMD had borne fruit. Many of the issues that had previously been only on the agenda of a few feminist groups were about to become state policy. However, some crucial issues, such as divorce and abortion, remained off the mainstream agenda, mainly due to pressure by the Catholic church; others, such as the empowerment of women, were taken up only rhetorically.

The Women's Movement in a Democratic Context

The achievement of the women's movement after the return to democracy in 1990 can be viewed from different perspectives. On one hand, at the government level many women's issues were included in the agenda of the new democratic government. SERNAM was created to introduce and implement gender-specific public policies. María Antonieta Saa, a feminist socialist leader of the women's movement, was designated mayor of Conchalí, the largest working-class municipality in the Santiago area. Two out of seven women legislators in the House of Representatives, Adriana Muñoz and Laura Rodríguez, were feminists and longtime members of the women's movement.[25] A number of professional women who had been active in the movement were appointed to government posts. Several bills regarding women's rights were introduced into the legislative process in areas such as domestic violence, labor rights, divorce, abortion, marriage law, adultery, and the status of children. Many of them, however, have not been passed by Congress because they do not have sufficient support among the legislators and women have not been able to organize effectively to lobby for passage of these bills.[26]

However, on balance there has been relatively little progress in empowering women in the formal political sphere. In 1993, there were only three women senators and six representatives in Congress, or 6 percent of the total. Ironically, this represented a smaller proportion than in 1973 prior to the military coup. Women accounted for only 10 percent of those elected to local councils in the municipal elections in 1992 and 11 percent of the congressional candidates in 1993. In the Congress inaugurated in March 1994, there were nine women representatives (7.5 percent), two of them leaders of the women's movement, and three women senators. This was only partly due to the undemocratic nature of the electoral laws; the virtual invisibility of women in the political sphere was once again gender related.[27] In the executive, there was only one woman cabinet minister, the minister of SERNAM, until President Eduardo Frei appointed three women cabinet ministers in March 1994.

The political parties, which after 1990 reasserted their traditional role as mediators between the state and civil society, still discriminate strongly against women candidates. The parties not only reproduce the gender discrimination found in Chilean society at large but also aggravate and reinforce it.[28] Even though women have gained some leadership positions within the parties, they are still viewed with unease and distrust by their male peers, who are bothered by the women's "otherness" and try to avoid or push them aside. Women are subject not only to discrimination but also to the political control of their male peers in government and within political parties. Often this political control is practiced, implicitly or explicitly, by a family member or spouse. Thus, quite a few women who have been nominated to decisionmaking posts are directly related to a male political leader. Even though these women certainly have credentials of their own to make them eligible, their family links seem to make them more trustworthy in the eyes of the political establishment.

The political dynamics of the democratic transition have encouraged the resurgence of an elitist, all-male, tightly knit political establishment, where politics has become once again an *acuerdo de caballeros*. By 1990, a great deal of pressure had accumulated within this elite to regain access to positions of political representation after seventeen years of military rule and suspension of political rights.

However, it is also true that the women's movement, which developed outside the party system, has lacked the internal political cohesion to confront these challenges and effectively raise women to leadership positions. The process of acquiring political expertise has not been easy. The few women leaders who have managed to break through all these barriers have encountered additional difficulties because they lack experience in the dominant style of political negotiation and

have given insufficient attention to the financial aspects of political campaigning.[29]

SERNAM itself has been a target for criticism within the women's movement.
Some consider it too cautious and conservative. Others perceive that it is the instrument through which the government has co-opted feminist discourse and that
it has displaced the movement as the main interlocutor of the state. Finally, many
women complain that no fluid and organic links exist between women's organizations and SERNAM.

It is true that SERNAM has had a difficult time legitimizing itself, that it enjoys
only limited autonomy within the state apparatus, and that it has endured strong
direct and indirect mechanisms of political control that have limited its scope of
action.[30] However, it has also shown great initiative, even if it lacks the political influence to implement some of its plans, and it is the only institution that attempts
to deal with and articulate most of the great variety of gender-specific issues that
concern women. Some examples of SERNAM's work during the Aylwin administration include campaigning against violence in the home; developing a national
policy for female heads of households; revising educational policies, including
those on sexuality issues; initiating a program to prevent cancer of the uterus and
cervix; starting a program to support pregnant teenagers; conducting training
programs on gender-specific issues for public officials; and creating a national
network of women's rights information centers. Finally, the Plan for Gender
Equality that SERNAM presented to the Frei administration in 1994 is the most
comprehensive agenda for women's rights ever developed in Chile.

The role of SERNAM should not be distorted: It is only a government agency,
not the locus of women's empowerment. It neither represents nor replaces the
women's movement within the government. It should ideally be a close interlocutor of women's organizations in order not to lose touch with their demands and
aspirations and to enhance and reinforce its political clout. The women's movement should not expect SERNAM to advance further than it has itself or envision
a government agency that represents the movement. A combination of pressure,
criticism, support, and active lobbying is likely to be the most effective relationship the movement can develop with SERNAM in the future.

The role of the women's movement in the new democratic context has been
quite different from what it had been before. Some analysts and former activists
even go so far as to say that there is no longer a women's movement in Chile and
that democracy co-opted the feminist discourse and demobilized the movement.
We strongly disagree with this interpretation. We believe that, together with the
change in the political context from an authoritarian, repressive dictatorship to a
more open, democratic regime that respects civil rights, the nature of the women's
movement and of other social movements has also changed. The heroic days of
barricades and demonstrations seem to be over, at least for the time being. Authoritarianism and patriarchy are not so easily identified and fought against as in

the past. Pinochet has not left the political scene completely, and many authoritarian enclaves remain, but most people perceive that democracy is in the process of consolidation. The 1993 democratic election went smoothly, and Frei's inauguration as president in March 1994 marked a continuity of the democratic process.

The way in which women, and society in general, perceive social change has also suffered dramatic transformations. The crisis of marxism and socialism has affected feminist thinking worldwide, and it has had a definite impact on the Chilean women's movement, which has traditionally had strong links with the Left. There is, of course, an agenda of gender-specific issues that grows with the changes achieved in the condition of women. However, the more general ideological context within which these issues are placed is in a state of flux. Thus, many of the women's movement's earlier concerns that were not gender specific have either disappeared or become uncertainties, urging a redefinition of the movement.

There are some elements of continuity. Poverty remains an important concern because of both the movement's roots among urban poor women and the more general problem of the feminization of poverty. Strategies for poverty alleviation have evolved from the subsistence organizations of the Pinochet years into more structured initiatives, such as cooperatives and microbusinesses, with the support of women's organizations and NGOs. Organized women continue to be the main constituency demanding truth and justice in the many pending cases of victims of military repression and abuse. Finally, the demand for political and social participation remains a central issue for women's organizations.

In the past, the antiauthoritarian struggle and the overall concern for social change provided links with the political establishment. Today, the absence of a common set of concerns has been worsened by the movement's lack of legitimate and representative leadership, which might have provided adequate channels of communication and negotiation with the state and the political parties. In the present context it has become more complex to place a feminist agenda within the conceptual and practical framework of antiauthoritarian struggle and social change. This is one of the great challenges that the women's movement faces in the 1990s and that it has not yet resolved.

In addition to these changes in the political and ideological context, we have identified five dimensions where there have been significant variations in the nature of the women's movement if the developments in the 1980s are compared with those of the 1990s; the transition period (1988–1989) is a category by itself (see Table 11.1). These dimensions are institutionalization, variety of issues, policy proposals, regionalization, and articulation, by which we mean linkages, cohesiveness, and a sense of common purpose. These characteristics are present at varying levels of development, which we categorize as low or high. Of course, this comparison is schematic, and none of the periods or dimensions is as clearly defined in reality as on paper. However, it does serve as an instrument to evaluate re-

TABLE 11.1   Dimensions of Development of the Women's Movement in the 1980s and
1990s

Dimension	Dictatorship (1978–1987)	Transition (1988–1989)	Democracy (1990–1994)
Institutionalization	Low	High	High
Variety of issues	Low	High	High
Policy proposals	Low	High	High
Regionization	Low	Low	High
Articulation	High	High	Low

cent developments in the women's movement and to reveal the nature and role of
the women's movement after the return to democracy.

Institutionalization

Perhaps the most salient aspect of the development of the women's movement
during the past decade is the number of women's NGOs, institutions, networks,
social organizations, and grassroots groups that emerged in response to the need
to change the status of women and the quality of women's lives.[31] These organizations began to appear during the struggle against the dictatorship, and they
flourished especially during the transition and after the return to democracy.
Many of them established women's centers and offered workshops for consciousness-raising, leadership training, and other subjects of interest to middle- and
low-income women. While these organizations developed for very different reasons, including solidarity, participation, health, handicrafts, work, education, human rights, food, and violence against women, all shared a common gender-specific concern. In the popular sector, many soup kitchens were redeveloped into
cooperatives or microbusinesses with the support of NGOs.

This trend toward institutionalization helped strengthen and diversify women's
organizations. The effect on the movement was not directly symmetrical. In many
cases, once the organizations had an internal structure, a budget, and institutional
goals, their need for survival and legitimation vis-à-vis the rest of society also
made them more cautious in their involvement with the rest of the movement. In
addition, the more organizations existed, the more difficult it became to relate to
one another and to achieve close, trusting, and meaningful relationships. However, in many cases the organizations developed very effective networks, which en-
hanced the public visibility of the women's movement. We believe it likely that in
the medium and long term, if the organizations maintain and expand their gender-specific purposes, the trend toward institutionalization will in fact result in a
stronger and more powerful movement.

Institutionalization does not only mean creating new institutions; it also means that demands that were formerly voiced in simpler forms in meetings or on the streets have become more formal political platforms of organizations and are included in the public debate and in the media. Feminist women have even created their own radio station and a feminist newspaper. Gender studies, which were formerly limited to small, rather marginal research centers, have been introduced in the public universities. The small research centers have now become solid and very productive institutions, and their professional services are often sought by SERNAM and other government agencies.

Simultaneously, there has been a tremendous increase in women's creative expression and cultural production, which is manifested in academia, in literature, and in the arts. Women and gender-specific cultural manifestations have a greater presence than ever before. Part of this is due to the renewed freedom of expression within a democratic context, but it also indicates women's new sense of identity and often shows the support of the women's institutional network.

A complementary trend, toward professionalism, has also taken place. In the late 1980s, feminist activism was no longer enough to run organizations, and a large group of professional women and women specially trained to work in these organizations developed. Today there is a more institutionalized and professional movement in lieu of the formerly more spontaneous and activist movement. However, even though some of the more romantic and idealistic aspects of the struggle for women's rights might get less attention, if bureaucratic practices are avoided, and the gender-specific goals are not only maintained but also enlarged, these trends might help further the movement in the long run.

Variety of Issues

The Chilean women's movement originally focused on a limited number of issues, which can be considered classic women's issues: legal and political discrimination, divorce, abortion, day care, and birth control. While the movement also addressed issues related to the antidictatorship struggle, such as human rights, freedom of speech, hunger, and deprivation, on the whole its perspective was similar to that of other social and political actors.

Increasingly, with the transition and the return to democratic rule, the movement engaged in a two-way process. On the one hand, the traditional "women's issues" were presented as, and increasingly became, issues that concerned society as a whole. On the other hand, women began to bring a gender-specific orientation to their involvement in more general issues, such as the environment, housing, health, education, poverty, labor rights, communications, democratic governance, and civil-military relations. This process of diversification went hand in hand with that of institutionalization and professionalization of the women's movement. New work environments and skills had to be developed to deal in a meaningful way with this new array of issues. This process is clearly reflected in the production of knowledge by and for the women's movement of this period: In 1982 women's studies focused on six different areas; by 1989 this number had increased to eighteen.[32] Clearly, there is no "single-issue" women's movement in Chile today. While this diversification has catapulted women to arenas where they were formerly absent, it has also dispersed some of the leverage a more focused movement might have had.

Issues formerly considered women's issues receive a great deal of public attention. They are covered extensively in the media, where they are treated as human interest issues. Even though this treatment of the issues often takes away some of the gender-specific edge of feminist analysis, it effectively meets the goal of advocating public debate of these topics. The issue of sexual difference is also being raised more forcefully, often in coordination with male homosexual activists. Women have also been busy trying to "engender" different realms of public discourse and policies.[33] These efforts have been more successful, for the time being, in influencing political programs and discourse than in affecting policies. Possibly it will only be through the direct empowerment of women that legislative results and policy implementation will effectively change.

Policy Proposals

During the decade 1983–1993, the political platforms and policy proposals developed by the women's movement became less and less denunciatory, schematic, and general and more and more proactive, comprehensive, and specific. The increasing growth and maturity of the movement can be traced through an analysis of these political platforms. The *Manifiesto Feminista* (Feminist Manifesto) of 1983 was possibly the first of these documents.[34] It was rather sketchy but contained most of the themes the movement would develop later: links between authoritarianism and patriarchy, violence against women, and recommendations on overcoming the discrimination against women in politics, employment, jurisprudence, and education. The *Plataforma de la Mujer Chilena* (Platform of Chilean Women), developed by MEMCh'83 in 1984, had a more complex structure and closely followed the contents of the U.N. Convention on the Elimination of All Forms of Discrimination Against Women.[35] The *Pliego de las Mujeres* (Women's Charter), presented in 1986 within the context of the *Asamblea de la Civilidad*, was another step forward. We have already described the significant role of the *Demandas de las Mujeres a la Democracia*, presented by feminist women in 1988, in setting the women's agenda for the transition to democracy.

A significant conceptual leap was made in 1989 when the CNMD prepared its *Propuestas* (Propositions), which covered a large number of areas and presented most of the gender-specific public policies later implemented by the Aylwin administration.[36] From a political point of view, the CNMD's programmatic achievements were a landmark in completing the transition from denouncing gender discrimination to proposing specific measures and policies to transform the condition of women in Chilean society.

Since the return to democracy, policy proposals have become more numerous but also increasingly specific and technical. Organizations and individuals have worked on and tried to influence legislative proposals concerning women. Few of these efforts have been coordinated and have thus not had the necessary impact to push through legislation. One of the challenges the movement faces is to create an effective women's lobbying group to coordinate technical and political efforts, influence policy proposals, and mobilize women to press for the passage of bills concerning women's rights.

The women's movement did not engage as actively in trying to influence the political platforms of the 1993 elections as it had in 1989. However, gender-specific issues had a prominent status within the "antisystem" presidential campaign of Manfred Max-Neef, who was backed by many feminists. Even if gender issues were not as prominent, they were dealt with in a more comprehensive way in Frei's political platform, which at least partly serves as the basis of his government's policies.[37]

The most comprehensive policy proposal concerning changes in the condition of women is the Plan for Gender Equality that SERNAM presented to the Frei administration in 1994. Although it is a document prepared by a government agency and not by the women's movement, it incorporates many of the proposals regarding gender equality developed by the Chilean movement as well as many ideas that originated in women's movements elsewhere in the world.

Regionalization

Geographically, Chile is a very long and narrow country; its political system, however, is extremely centralized. The capital, Santiago, is a real metropolis, where almost 40 percent of the population is concentrated and the political and economic power elites are centered. It is also the locus of contacts with the rest of the world, which in a geographically isolated country such as Chile is of great importance.

In spite of its historic stand in the nitrate mining towns of the north, the women's movement has had its traditional stronghold in Santiago. Thus, the history of the women's movement in the 1980s is almost exclusively that of the Santiago movement. During the late 1980s, however, a few women's groups and organizations began to appear in larger towns: Arica, Antofagasta, Valparaíso, Concepción, Temuco, and Puerto Montt.

This pattern changed dramatically during the transition to democracy. Together with the mobilization against Pinochet and in support of the democratic presidential candidate, ideas about women's rights began to travel quickly, and very soon there were active women's NGOs and social and political organizations in most regions of Chile. Many organizations activated after 1989 in urban and rural areas involved indigenous women, campesinas, housewives, and industrial workers. In the Santiago area itself, many new organizations developed at the district and municipal levels, thereby also decentralizing the women's movement in the capital. In many cases the NGOs served as the link between the grassroots women's groups and the more political organizations within the movement. Some of these initiatives were activated by SERNAM's regional and municipal delegations; others by the Fundación para la Promoción y Desarollo de la Mujer (Foundation for Women's Promotion and Development), a government agency oriented toward poor women and headed by the president's spouse. In addition, the process of institutionalization described previously also occurred in the provinces where NGOs had not developed as much during the previous period as they had in Santiago.

Articulation

There is no articulated, cohesive, and highly visible women's movement in Chile today. This may be the main reason some analysts and activists argue that at present there is no women's movement at all. During the struggle against the dictatorship and in the transition period, the level of articulation, or internal cohesion and linkage of the movement, was certainly higher. Articulating the women's movement in the 1980s was simpler than it is in the 1990s. In the 1980s, the struggles against authoritarianism and patriarchy merged and became a driving force for organizing International Women's Day celebrations, political demonstrations in the streets, and a few large public meetings. Agreement was only necessary on a few basic issues. At that time, the movement was much smaller and less complex. There were fewer organizations and individuals, and they focused on a limited number of issues; most of the women activists knew one another and were concentrated in Santiago. In contrast, in the 1990s increased levels of institutionalization and professionalization, the larger variety of issues and more comprehensive policy proposals, and the growing process of regionalization and decentralization have changed the movement. It is much larger, more heterogeneous, very fluid, and rather dispersed; as such, it has become very difficult to articulate.

Another important factor contributing to cohesiveness, the antidictatorial struggle, has disappeared. This was in itself a unifying force for the women's movement, reinforced by the opposition political establishment's interest in supporting and highlighting the importance of the social movements in the struggle against Pinochet. It was this interest that helped introduce the women's movement's actions to the media. This interest disappeared after the return to democracy, when politics as usual displaced the social movements as a frontline political actor.

Much of the articulation and cohesion that does exist is organized around regional and/or issues-oriented women's networks. Achieving greater articulation in Santiago and at the national level is the biggest challenge the women's movement faces. Articulation and public visibility are not necessary conditions for the existence of the women's movement. The movement may persist in a state of latency and even grow, develop, and mature without a high level of articulation.[38] However, if the movement is seeking a real breakthrough in the condition of women within Chilean society and in their relationship with the state, and is advocating comprehensive cultural changes and very ambitious policy proposals, these can be achieved only by a movement that has gained leverage through significant levels of internal articulation and public mobilization.

Conclusion

The main challenges to the women's movement in the late 1980s, "building a mass movement, developing cross-class alliances, coordinating the mobilization of the women's opposition, and, importantly, maintaining autonomy to ensure that social movements would not be marginalized by political parties in the transition," have not been achieved during the early years of the return to democracy.[39] However, the women's movement is flourishing in Chile today, and it is more extensive and diverse than ever before. It is a movement that consists of thousands of women's groups, NGOs, and social and political organizations, with a variety of orientations and purposes, focusing on many different issues, and spread throughout Chile. In spite of their great variety and considerable dispersion, all these groups and organizations share gender-specific concerns and have in common a desire to change the status of women.

In comparison to the women's movement of the 1980s, the current movement shows an increased level of institutionalization and professionalization. It focuses on a greater variety of issues and has been able to develop much more comprehensive policy proposals. And it has spread from Santiago to most regions of Chile. Its impact in the cultural sphere is considerable. There are two dimensions, however, where the development of the movement has lagged behind: (1) the internal articulation and consequent public visibility necessary to enhance and give leverage to women's proposals for social change and (2) the placement of the feminist agenda within a more general framework of social change without any loss of autonomy and specificity and with a modification of the presently gender-specific characteristics of power relationships. These are the great challenges for the women's movement of the mid- and late 1990s.

NOTES

1. S. Montecino, *Madres y huachos: Alegorías del mestizaje chileno* (Santiago: Editorial Cuarto Propio—CEDEM, 1991); E. Stevens, "Marianismo: The other face of machismo," in

A. Pescatello, ed., *Female and Male in Latin America* (Pittsburgh: University of Pittsburgh Press, 1977).

2. We define the women's movement as a comprehensive and heterogeneous social process that includes individual as well as collective actors and that defines itself through a shared identity, an awareness of conflict, and a will to transform the social condition of women.

3. J. Kirkwood, *Ser political en Chile: Las feministas y los partidos* (Santiago: FLACSO, 1986); E. Hutchinson, "El feminismo en el movimiento obrero Chileno: La emancipación de la mujer en la prensa obrera feminista," *Contribuciones* no. 80 (Santiago: FLACSO, 1992).

4. E. Gaviola et al., *Queremos votar en las próximas elecciones: Historia del movimiento feminino chileno, 1913–1952* (Santiago: La Morada, Fempress, Isis, Librería Lila, PEMCI/Centro de Estudios de la Mujer, 1986).

5. E. Gaviola et al., "Chile centros de madres. ¿La mujer popular en movimiento?" in Isis Internacional, *Nuestra memoria, nuestro futuro: Mujeres e Historia.* Ediciones de las Mujeres no. 10 (Santiago: Grupo Condición Femenina—FLACSO, 1988).

6. M. E. Valenzuela, "The Evolving Role of Women Under Military Rule," in P. Drake and I. Jaksic, eds., *The Struggle for Democracy in Chile, 1982–1990* (Lincoln: University of Nebraska Press, 1991).

7. P. Chuchryk, "Protest, Politics, and Personal Life: The Emergence of Feminism in a Military Dictatorship, Chile, 1973–1983" (Ph.D. diss., York University, Canada, 1984); N. Lechner and S. Levy, "Notas sobre la vida cotidiana III: El disciplinamiento de la mujer," *Material de Discusión* no. 57 (Santiago: FLACSO, 1984); G. Munizaga and L. Letelier, in Centro de Estudios de la Mujer, *Mundo de mujer: Continuidad y cambio* (Santiago: Centro de Estudios de la Mujer, 1988); M. E. Valenzuela, "La mujer en el Chile militar: Todas ibamos a ser reinas," *Ediciones Chile y América* (Santiago: CESOC-ACHIP, 1987); T. Valdés et al., "Centros de madres, 1973–1989. ¿Sólo disciplinamiento?" *Documento de Trabajo* no. 416 (Santiago: FLACSO, 1989).

8. J. Jaquette, ed., *The Women's Movement in Latin America: Feminism and the Transition to Democracy* (Boulder: Westview Press, 1994).

9. P. Chuchryk, "Feminist Anti-Authoritarian Politics: The Role of Women's Organizations in the Chilean Transition to Democracy," in J. Jaquette, ed., *The Women's Movement in Latin America: Feminism and the Transition to Democracy* (Boulder: Westview Press, 1994), pp. 70–71.

10. T. Valdés and M. Weinstein, *Mujeres que sueñan: Las organizaciones de pobladores en Chile, 1973–1989* (Santiago: FLACSO, 1993).

11. Kirkwood, 1986.

12. Chuchryk, 1994; Valdés and Weinstein, 1993.

13. Chuchryk, 1994, p. 77.

14. N. Saporta et al., "Feminisms in Latin America: From Bogotá to San Bernardo," *Signs: Journal of Women in Culture and Society* 17, no. 21 (1992).

15. A. M. Arteaga and E. Largo, "Los ONG en el área de la mujer y la cooperación al desarrollo," in Taller de Cooperación al Desarrollo, *Una puerta que se abre: Los organismos no gubernamentales en la cooperación al desarrollo* (Santiago: Taller de Cooperación al Desarrollo, 1989); A. M. Arteaga and R. Delsing, *Directorio nacional de servicios y recursos para la mujer* (Santiago: CEDEM, 1992).

16. Chuchryk, 1994.

17. N. Molina, "Propuestas políticas y orientaciones de cambio en la situación de la mujer," in M. A. Garretón, ed., *Propuestas políticas y demandas sociales* (Santiago: FLACSO, 1989).

18. This document was issued by twenty-one collectives belonging to the Movimiento Feminista and a group of well-known women. It was published in its full length in the newspaper *La Epoca* (Santiago), July 1, 1988.

19. Valdés and Weinstein, 1993.

20. Concertación de Partidos por la Democracia, *Programa de gobierno* (Santiago: Concertación de Partidos por la Democracia, 1989).

21. S. Montecino and J. Rossetti, eds., *Tramas para un nuevo destino: Propuestas de la Concertación de Mujeres por la Democracia* (Santiago: Concertación de Mujeres por la Democracia, 1990).

22. "Discurso de Don Patricio Aylwin," Teatro Caupolicán, August 20, 1989.

23. Chuchryk, 1994, p. 86.

24. Ibid., p. 87.

25. Laura Rodríguez died in 1992 and was therefore not able to finish her legislative term; Adriana Muñoz stood for reelection in 1993 and lost, due at least in part to lack of support within her own party.

26. Instituto de la Mujer, *¿Cómo les ha ido a las mujeres chilenas en la democracia? Balance y propuestas: Mirando al 2000* (Santiago: Instituto de la Mujer, 1993).

27. The peculiar binomial electoral system devised by the Pinochet regime was aimed at securing the representation of the Right, a numeric minority, in Congress well beyond its share of the ballot.

28. E. Hola and G. Pischedda, *Mujeres, poder, y politica: Nuevas tensiones para viejas estructuras* (Santiago: Centro de Estudios de la Mujer, 1993).

29. Institutions within the women's movement have been quick to react in order to overcome these shortcomings, and they have developed numerous leadership training courses for women at different levels of social and political participation, many of them from grassroots women's organizations.

30. The organizational task SERNAM had to carry out in a short time span was very large: Regional offices were created in thirteen regions, and most of the personnel had to be specially trained and prepared for their new work.

31. T. Valdés and E. Gomáriz, coord., *Mujeres Latinoamericanas en Cifras: Chile* (Santiago: Ministerio de Asuntos Sociales, Instituto de la Mujer, España/FLACSO, 1992).

32. T. Valdés, "Movimiento de mujeres y producción de conocimientos de género en Chile," in G. Briones et al., *Usos de la investigación social en Chile,* 43 (Santiago: FLACSO, Foro 90, 1993).

33. V. Guzmán and R. Salazar, "Los problemas de género en el debate de las políticas públicas," in E. Lahera, ed., *Cómo mejorar la gestión pública* (Santiago: CIEPLAN, FLACSO, Foro 90, 1993).

34. M. A. Meza, *La otra mitad de Chile* (Santiago: CESOC-INCH, n.d.).

35. Within the political parties or political movements, women also developed platforms of their own, such as the *Proposiciones de Políticas para la Mujer* (Policy Proposals for Women) of the Christian Democratic Party and *Mujeres por Socialismo* (Women for Socialism) of the Socialist Women's Movement (Meza, n.d.)

36. Montecino and Rossetti, 1990.

37. Eduardo Frei was the candidate of the Center-Left government coalition (Concertación de Partidos por la Democracia, *Un gobierno para los nuevos tiempos,* Bases programáticas del Segundo Gobierno de la Concertación [Santiago: Concertación de Partidos por la Democracia, 1993]).

38. A. Melucci, "Social Movements and the Democratization of Everyday Life," in J. Keane, ed., *Civil Society and the State* (London: Verso, 1988).

39. Chuchryk, 1994, p. 94.

12

Brazilian Feminism and Women's Movements: A Two-Way Street

VERA SOARES, ANA ALICE ALCANTARA COSTA,

CRISTINA MARIA BUARQUE,

DENISE DOURADO DORA,

& WANIA SANT'ANNA

WOMEN HAVE BECOME an increasingly visible and important presence in Brazilian cultural, economic, and political life since the early 1970s.[1] They have played an active role in bringing about Brazil's dramatic political changes and have influenced the way democracy has been defined. For women in Brazil, and in particular for those in the feminist movement, this period has been characterized by both rich potential and serious challenges.

Our concept of feminism is based on the principle that feminism is the political action of women. Feminism includes both theory and practice and centers on women as agents effecting change in their own condition. Feminism supports the proposition that women should transform themselves and the world. Although feminism is expressed in collective, individual, and existential action in the arts and in culture as well as in politics, this chapter focuses on women's political action.

We view the feminist movement as one segment of a large and increasingly heterogeneous women's movement that is creating opportunities for women's politi-

BRAZIL

GENERAL

type of government: Federal Democratic Republic
major ethnic groups: Portuguese (55%); Mulatto (38%); African (6%); Indigenous
language(s): Portuguese (official); also Spanish, English, French
religions: Roman Catholic (89%)
date of independence: 1822
former colonial power: Portugal

DEMOGRAPHICS

population size: 158 million
birth rate (*per 1,000 population*): 26
total fertility (*average number of births per woman*): 2.8
contraceptive prevalence (*married women*): 66%
maternal mortality rate (*per 100,000 live births*): 140

WOMEN'S STATUS

date of women's suffrage: 1932
economically active population: M 81%   F 30%
female employment (*% of total workforce*): 28
life expectancy   M 62   F 68
school enrollment ratio (*F/100 M*)

primary	95
secondary	*not available*
tertiary	100

literacy   M 82%   F 81%

---

cal participation. In general, these efforts focus on demanding better conditions in women's daily lives and addressing issues stemming from women's socially defined reproductive roles. Currently in Brazil, the feminist and women's movements are movements against human misery and for the exercise of citizenship. They generate new rights for women by demanding new public policies, participating in the administration of social services, and struggling for new laws. The women's movement also includes women workers, who are increasingly visible in the labor market and within trade unions.

In this chapter we describe the trajectory of the feminist movement in Brazil since the 1970s in order to examine both the ruptures and continuity in women's activism. This analysis of feminism is necessarily embedded in a discussion of the Brazilian political and economic situation, which we briefly outline. We construct a history of feminist struggles and organizing. Then we explore the relation between the feminist movement and the larger women's movement. We examine some of the gains and compromises in the evolution of feminist dealings with the state. Finally, we review several challenges that the movement continues to face.

Politics and Economics in Brazil: An Overview

Brazil, the largest country in Latin America, is marked by stark regional contrasts. The south-central region, where almost half the population is concentrated, is largely industrialized and developed, accounting for 80 percent of industrial output and more than 75 percent of farm goods production. In contrast, the north and northeast remain mostly underdeveloped, essentially agricultural regions where large landed estates and informal wage labor still prevail. Negative social indicators such as poverty, illiteracy, and hunger are far higher in the north and northeast. This dichotomy is also reflected in the country's income distribution, one of the most unequal in the world.

The Portuguese colonized Brazil beginning in the early 1500s and brought with them large numbers of African slaves. Two significant legacies of this colonial period are the complexities of race relations and the strong and influential role of the Catholic church. Brazil has the largest population of African origin outside of Africa; the 1991 census indicates that 44 percent of the Brazilian population is nonwhite.[2] Brazilians have been led to believe that the absence of overtly segregationist legislation like that of the United States and South Africa made Brazil a racial paradise where there were no distinctions based on race. In reality, the abolition of slavery did little to modify the society's profound racial prejudice or create conditions where Black women and men could effectively exercise their civil rights. Social disparities based on racial discrimination continue to be dramatic. The Catholic church, which claims more than 89 percent of Brazilians as adherents, has had a mixed legacy for the country. Many of its most conservative stances on issues such as contraception and abortion have strongly influenced government policies and thwarted the efforts of women activists in these areas. However, its more liberal parishes have provided a place within which community organizing and activism have developed and matured, especially among the poor.

Brazil became an independent monarchy in 1822 and a republic in 1889; since then governance of the country has alternated between democracy and military rule. The military coup of 1964 was essentially a conservative reaction to the growing popular mobilization around grassroots reforms favored by the populist government of João Goulart. From 1964 until 1985, Brazil was ruled by a sometimes brutal military dictatorship characterized by periods of greater and lesser political openness, with a gradual process of political opening beginning in the mid-1970s. Following an indirect election for a civilian president in 1985, Fernando Collor de Mello was elected president in 1989 in the first direct presidential elections in twenty-five years; three years later he resigned, facing impeachment for corruption.

Shifting political systems have helped make Brazil's potentially strong economy volatile and unstable. During the 1970s, Brazil had the leading economy in Latin America, with strong output and growing exports in both the industrial and agricultural sectors. However, corruption, soaring inflation, income maldistribution, and enormous foreign debt have precipitated a cycle of economic crisis that has had particularly devastating effects on the poor. The resulting climate of political repression, economic crisis, and concomitant organizing by the poor has had significant influence on the evolution of the Brazilian feminist and women's movements.

A History of Brazilian Feminist Struggles

In its political actions, the Brazilian feminist movement seeks to denounce the mechanisms that thwart women's liberation. This feminism in essence denies the existence of the public and private spheres as two separate, mutually exclusive arenas and challenges the failure to recognize women's reproductive role as a productive one. Feminism seeks to redress women's subordination and dependence in the civic, political, economic, sexual, and psychological spheres and seeks to overcome the isolation and atomization of women's problems.[3] Brazilian feminists have struggled in Congress, in the streets, and in the home to guarantee women's access to formal education, the vote, equal salaries, and suitable working conditions; recognition of the value of domestic work; women's control over their bodies and sexual pleasure; and construction of a more just and egalitarian society where women can be fulfilled as women and citizens.

Feminist thought first appeared in Brazil in the nineteenth century through the action and work of Nisia Floresta Brasileira Augusta. An early advocate of women's right to formal education, Augusta published several works addressing the formation of a critical consciousness about women's condition.[4] Since then, the feminist movement in Brazil, as elsewhere, has embraced various forms of struggle and diverse issues. These struggles have paralleled the country's historical evolution as the women's movement has become politically engaged and incorporated into Brazilian society. As Zuleika Alambert states, "The struggle that we now join to make clear the subjective character of oppression, the emotional aspects of consciousness, etc. … is an extension of our grandmothers' and great-grand-mothers' struggle for women's access to the labor market and to education, at a time when neutrality was attributed to individual space and only the public, objective sphere was defined as political."[5]

Brazil's feminism was expressed in the suffragist campaigns of the early twentieth century, and women's right to vote was finally granted in 1932.[6] Parallel to this liberal movement for civil rights, another movement developed with support from organizations of the Left, particularly the Brazilian Communist Party. This movement mobilized low-income women to strive for better living conditions and participate in the broader struggles of society. Many women's organizations were started through such mobilizations, especially after the 1940s, and a number of them remained active until the military coup of 1964.[7] Independent of its ideological ties, the women's movement legitimated and consolidated the traditional family by trying to protect it during the period of authoritarian rule. In many ways, the women's movement itself reinforced the ideology of women's oppression by underscoring woman's subordinate status as mother, wife, or daughter.

After the 1964 military coup, the women's movement, along with other social movements in the country, was largely silenced. Many middle-class women played important roles in supporting the coup and the military regime, organizing and leading movements that came to be known as Marchas com Deus pela Pátria e pela Família (Marches with God for Fatherland and for the Family).[8] These movements advocated maintaining order, preserving the traditional family, protecting property, and obeying the church, family, and military hierarchy. These activities projected and reinforced an image of women's political participation as defending conservative and traditional values. These conservative women largely disappeared from the political arena after the coup, and the women's movement then reorganized, breaking away from these traditional ideas about women.

Until the mid-1970s, Brazilians were subjected to strong repression by the military regime, and there was little public protest. At that time, the first demonstrations and political activity resurfaced within the popular sectors (i.e., civil society), including the feminist movement. This movement built on the history of women's political participation but broke the barriers of women's traditional roles. While it developed its own identity, it was influenced by the ideas that arose in Europe and in the United States in the 1960s, especially in the feminist, Black, and antiwar movements. The movement questioned the role of women in the family, at work, and in society and struggled to transform human relationships by eliminating those based on social and gender discrimination.[9]

This "new" feminism insisted that power relations permeated all spheres and levels of society, not just the public and state arenas. This view broadened the conventional conception of politics and called on those subordinated to the existing power structure to transform it. Because this movement emerged during a period of political repression, it played a key role in the struggle for democracy and was vocal in denouncing political repression as well as introducing new themes, such as sexual violence against women. During the military regime, when torture was used against political prisoners—men, women, and children—the women's movement articulated the connections between such violence and violence against women in the domestic sphere.[10]

. During the early phase of the military government, all opposition movements had been strongly repressed. This left little or no room for the development of a radical liberation movement, such as those that were mobilizing women in other countries.[11] Instead, feminism reemerged among activists of leftist parties, and women engaged in the struggle for democracy. In this sense, from its inception, feminism in Brazil sought to join the struggle for women's full citizenship to the struggle for democracy. The Brazilian feminist movement's key role in broader social struggles is similar to that of feminist movements in several other Latin American countries that also endured military regimes in the 1970s and early 1980s.

In 1975, in commemoration of the United Nations International Women's Year, a conference was held in Rio de Janeiro that brought together women interested in discussing women's condition in Brazilian society in light of the "new" feminist movement then developing in Europe and in the United States.[12] Following this and similar meetings held in other cities, a number of women's groups emerged throughout the country. Many were organized on the model of the consciousness-raising groups in other countries and emphasized study and reflection.[13] Others engaged in action as well as reflection and established links with other organized groups of women. These feminist groups were composed primarily of middle-class women, intellectuals, and others from the liberal professions.[14]

The feminist movement was ideologically aligned with the Left in its vision of changing society, particularly on the issue of democracy. However, there was a profound divergence concerning the manner in which women's struggles should be waged. The majority of feminists had prior political experience in student movements, clandestine organizations of the Left, and political parties that had been outlawed. After amnesty for political prisoners was decreed in 1979, many women returning from exile and from prison became active in the feminist movement.[15]

Feminists increasingly rejected the tutelage of leftist organizations. The principle of autonomy was one of the polemic points in the ensuing confrontation with political parties. This was particularly true with parties of the Left, which were accustomed to controlling progressive people's movements and organizations. Feminists wanted independence in defining their forms of organization and action, independent of the state, parties, labor unions, churches, or other structures.

Adhering to the principle of autonomy, feminist groups and individuals sought alliances with other women's groups in the country, hoping to promote a discussion of their own in order to deepen the discourse on questions of specific interest to women, such as abortion, sexuality, and women's condition. They experi-

mented with diverse ways to define the movement's actions and to conduct national campaigns. Autonomy was critical in enabling feminists to engage in these
discussions without compromising their principles of decentralization and
nonhierarchical organization.

Two fundamental forces that defined the second half of the 1970s and all of the
1980s also impacted social movements in contemporary Brazil, including the feminist movement. Repeated economic crises and the process of political opening
both affected and mobilized the middle and working classes. The Brazilian party
system, which for fourteen years had been forcibly restricted to two parties, became increasingly complex beginning in 1980, when other parties emerged. The
opposition to the military regime, which had been exclusively represented by the
Brazilian Democratic Movement (MDB), was fragmented into three parties: the
Party of the Brazilian Democratic Movement (PMDB), the Democratic Workers
Party (PDT), and the Workers Party (PT).[16]

Within this context, the feminist movement also became more organizationally
complex and more ideologically diverse, and the areas of feminist action were increasingly formalized. The party reorganization of the 1980s surfaced the old divergence between autonomous women's groups organized around their own demands and political party organizations seeking to extend control over popular
organizations. The first direct elections for state governments, held in 1982, also
polarized the movement on whether to participate in government initiatives to
define public policies for women. During this time, the first centers for women
and gender studies were created in the universities, and a number of feminist
groups adopted more formal structures, becoming specialized in dealing with issues such as health, sexuality, and violence. Feminist nongovernmental organizations (NGOs) were created, providing feminism with physical and organizational
structures where members developed skills in administration as well as political
action. Gradually many "activist" members of these groups became "professionals."[17]

Questions initially raised by feminists, such as women's rights, female sexuality,
sexual violence, and even abortion, that had previously provoked sharp controversy, if not outright scandal, started to be discussed quite openly in public.
Through television these issues entered the living rooms of the "best" families and
the classrooms of the most traditional schools, were incorporated into the programs and platforms of political parties, and appeared in the campaign speeches
and television programs of candidates for public office. Finally, with the promul-
gation of a new constitution in 1988, many feminist demands were transformed
into constitutional rights,[18] and even the state incorporated some feminist proposals and actions.

In the 1980s, the Brazilian feminist movement incorporated other segments of
the women's movement, including women from the periphery of large cities, rural
and urban workers, Black women, and lesbians. The feminist movement had

coexisted for some time with lesbians without bringing lesbianism into its agenda. Initially, lesbians organized themselves within the homosexual movements that emerged in Brazil during the 1970s. National feminist meetings provided additional opportunities for lesbians to organize, and they subsequently created their own forums. Similarly, the Black women's movement incorporated feminist ideas as it became increasingly autonomous from both the Black and feminist movements. This was due in large part to the insensitivity of the Black movement to the specific demands of Black women and the feminist movement's inability to incorporate a thorough analysis of Brazil's racial problems. Black women became increasingly organized and developed their own agenda and a perspective on feminism that prioritized their ethnicity.

Feminism was also expanded and transformed by women from the popular sectors and low-income women who took on increasingly important leadership roles. For example, in a 1987 national feminist conference, approximately 79 percent of the participants were active in labor unions, in the Black movement, in neighborhood associations, in mothers' clubs, in the church, and in political parties. Feminists from autonomous groups, known as "historic" feminists or "fossils," came to be in the minority at these meetings.[19] The growing interest in feminist conferences from women's groups organized around broader social issues as well as from women workers reflected a complex relationship of collaboration and conflict that had developed since the mid-1970s.

The increasing participation of diverse women from the popular sectors in the contemporary feminist movement grew out of their own organization and the "invisible work" carried out by autonomous feminists among these sectors over many years. This took the form of a struggle for day care centers, a fight against violence against women, a struggle for women's health programs, and work within the Black movement, where Black women began to articulate their own oppression.[20]

In the 1990s, the movement "left the streets" and developed new forms of activism; this did not, however, signify demobilization. According to some studies,[21] among women from the popular sectors, consciousness of gender progressively developed, bringing in issues of class and race. This, along with the rise of lesbian feminist and Black feminist groups, led to the recognition of various "feminisms," each arising with its own distinctive mark.

Relations Between the Feminist and Women's Movements

In Brazil, as elsewhere in Latin America, women made and make themselves visible through a variety of demands, organizational expressions, and forms of struggle. The heterogeneity of the women's movement reflects the many dimensions of

women's subordination as well as the social, cultural, ethnic, and generational diversity of its participants. These characteristics determine how women organize
themselves and construct their identity. In addition to being heterogeneous, the
movement is also spontaneous. This leads to a varied presence in the national
arena and sometimes to ambiguous and contradictory demands. The movement
combines immediate objectives related to improving family and community well-
being and longer-range objectives of transforming gender relations in society. The
common ground where the streams within the women's movement meet in all
their diversity can perhaps be seen along two dimensions: the discovery of a common identity as women and the emphasis on daily life.[22]

The women's movement is commonly characterized as composed of several
segments, with the feminist movement being but one expression of a broader
women's movement. Women from the periphery of urban centers, those from
small rural communities, and those active within labor unions make up the other
major segments. Each part of the women's movement could be analyzed as a social
movement in itself, with its own dynamics and modes of expression. These parts
intersect, interrelate, and, at times, conflict. Therefore, our use of the term *wom-
en's movement* acknowledges a plurality of processes and a multitude of collective
actions.[23]

Women's movements, like other "new" social movements, occur in nontraditional spheres of organizational and political action. They have made visible large
sectors of society usually marginalized in social analysis, illuminating previously
obscure aspects of life and society and questioning old paradigms of political action. One of the women's movement's main contributions has been to demonstrate the complexity of social dynamics and actions, the multidimensional and
hierarchical nature of social relations, and the existence of great heterogeneity in
the arenas of conflict.

In Brazil, the popular segment of the contemporary women's movement
emerged from neighborhood groups on the periphery of large urban centers. This
part of the movement organized around family subsistence, grounded in domestic
life. It was composed of poor women, mostly housewives, and some salaried
workers. Such movements organized mainly around women's concerns, though
not necessarily questions of identity and specific demands concerning their subordination or exclusion as women.

The negotiated transition of the authoritarian regime in the second half of the
1970s was accompanied by a proliferation of popular movements, consolidation of
the opposition, remobilization of the Left, reemergence of opposition political activities, and expanded pastoral action of the Catholic church. During the time of
strong repression, women had had more latitude than men in political activities
due to the popular view of women as intrinsically apolitical or depoliticized. Consequently, the first public demonstrations sprang from movements composed primarily of women. While labor unions and political parties had been closed and

the students' movement silenced, women's organizations from poor districts had continued to operate; their activities had been perceived as nonpolitical and, as such, deemed relatively harmless by the military regime.[24]

Beginning in the 1970s, these women from the poor districts created their own political dynamic. In their socially designated roles as wives and mothers, they organized the first protests against the military regime. They fought against increases in the cost of living and demanded adequate schools, health centers, running water, transportation, electricity, housing, and other necessities of urban infrastructure. They demanded conditions adequate to care for their families and educate their children.[25] Political scientist Sonia Alvarez uses the term *militant motherhood* to characterize these movements.[26]

At the end of the 1970s, two large social movements led by women emerged: the movement against the high cost of living and the struggle for day care.[27] Organized around survival issues, women in these movements transcended domestic confinement, identified interlocutors, and increased their self-esteem. While they were not able to change the profound gender segregation within society or alter the course of social programs, they became, and remain, the primary interlocutors of feminism.

Examining the strong presence of the Catholic church in women's lives is critical to any analysis of the women's movement in Brazil. From 1964 to 1974, the church-sponsored Christian base communities (CEBs) responded to the repressive military government by providing space to organize unarmed resistance. The progressive church served as an organizational umbrella for the opposition, covering its activities with a cloak of moral legitimacy. As part of these efforts, the church also encouraged and gave shelter to many women's organizations.[28] Many women were changed by participating in the CEBs, redefining themselves as legitimate public actors and modifying the traditional norms that had limited women's participation in the public arena.

The church hierarchy, including some progressive priests, was doctrinally opposed or even hostile to some feminist demands, especially concerning abortion and contraception. However, the women in church-based movements often objected to the church's practices and teachings and undertook many joint activities with feminist groups.[29] These women developed a degree of autonomy from the church and expanded the range of their demands. A sometimes conflicting but solid relationship developed between women from CEBs and feminists, leading to the emergence of an extensive women's movement.

Urban and rural workers form another critical part of the women's movement. As women's presence in the labor force grew, more women joined trade unions. Along with the emergence of women's movements, women's growing participation in the labor force and trade unions influenced women's perceptions about their roles as workers, and the relationship between women and trade unions.[30] Women's participation in union leadership had been minimal (and remains so).

Unions had traditionally refused to acknowledge women as political subjects and disregarded their specific needs in labor relations. Women's public denunciation of sex discrimination at work, the double work shift for women workers, and men's absence from domestic tasks and child care were decisive in strengthening the relationships between women trade unionists and feminists and in charting a new course for union action and debate on women workers. The implementation of policies on gender within several union organizations was a result of this dialogue and alliance.[31]

Rural workers, "be they small rural producers, landless or slum dwellers, day laborers or employees in the large plantations, have been transforming the political and social scene in Brazilian agriculture, demonstrating their combativeness and determination in the struggle to conquer a new social identity, that of women rural workers."[32] They form part of an extremely complex dynamic generated by the commercialization of agriculture in Brazil. The struggle for agrarian reform and land, for better conditions and better prices, for higher salaries and more rights, unites women and men in rural areas. All are linked to the specific struggle of women peasants for citizenship and recognition as workers.

Feminists maintained often tense relationships with these various currents of the women's movement; some of these were mutually enriching, and others were problematic. These different currents have become intertwined, so that today the boundaries between them are less clear, and it is more difficult to separate these currents, even analytically. Many popular organizations and labor unions now refer to themselves as feminist, and other actors, such as Black women, have appeared within the movement.

Along with the emergence of popular women's organizations and early feminist consciousness, the second half of the 1970s was also marked by the flourishing of Black movement organizations, which vehemently contested the myths of "racial democracy" and harmony in Brazil. In this context of denouncing existing inequalities from a racial perspective, Black women organized. While they initially organized as part of the broader Black movement, by the late 1980s Black women had developed their own autonomous movement at the national level. This movement highlighted several issues pertinent to Black women: their position in the labor market, where they were concentrated in the service and informal sectors; their high rates of illiteracy and exclusion from political participation; and the stereotyped and incomplete images of slavery presented in formal education.[33] The Black women's movement thus identified sharp inequalities among women and denounced the fact that racial disparity was being obscured in the analysis and actions of other women's movements. Today, many Black women declare themselves feminists but not in the same sense as white feminists.

One of the women's movement's striking characteristics is that it ebbs and flows. The process of constructing a new political action is diffuse and subject to shifting influences, pressures, and the weight of tradition. It is a deeply subjective process that also brings about disorder and insecurity as part of the actions and consciousness of its actors.[34] The feminist movement's ability to establish and maintain close and direct relationships with organized women in different spheres has been central to creating what is often referred to as the largest, most varied, most radical, most diverse, and most politically influential women's movement in Latin America.[35]

The Adventure of Power: Feminism and the State

As women actively participated in the struggles for democracy and presented their own demands, they made themselves visible interlocutors in the reorganization of the state. As previously argued, the reformulation and creation of new political parties were part of the slow and gradual transition to democracy. Many feminist activists began to participate in political parties, and as a result of this activism and the gradual transformation sparked by the women's movement, government plans and electoral campaigns began to incorporate feminist issues.

One of the demands women presented was the creation of a "place" in the government to deal with sexual inequality. The proposal to create councils on women's rights was formulated by feminists from the PMDB, the opposition party that won the 1982 elections in several states. This proposal generated controversy regarding the feminist movement's autonomy from the state and the forms that dialogue and interaction should take.

In 1983 in Minas Gerais and São Paulo, the first State Councils for Women's Rights and the Feminine Condition were created; they were composed of representatives from the women's movement, an advisory council, and a technical executive body. During the 1980s, numerous such councils were created at the state and municipal levels. Absorbing the growing political importance of feminist issues, parties often manipulated and depoliticized these councils.

In 1985, the first civilian president of the republic, José Sarney, took office after twenty-one years of military rule. Creation of a women's council or department at the national level was already being discussed, and after much controversy, participants in the Seventh National Feminist Encounter endorsed the creation of a national council for women's rights. "Some of the feminists present at the Encounter sought the support of the movement as a whole for this proposal. Others, at that moment criticizing the action of the existing councils, saw it as a great threat to the movement's autonomy. The webs of power appeared as an intricate net full of obscure and evil intentions. The 'State' and the 'System' appeared as large entities remote from our existence."[36] The movement was divided into those who supported a place for women's issues within the executive branch and those wary that

Members of the National Council for the Rights of Women gather in Brasilia during the constitutional convention meetings in 1988. At that time the CNDM included members of the women's movement who worked hard to incorporate many of the movement's proposals into the new constitution.

this would constitute a form of co-optation and jeopardize the movement's political autonomy.

The resulting National Council for the Rights of Women (CNDM), established in 1985, was linked to the Ministry of Justice and by law had the power to formulate policies to eliminate discrimination against women. It was composed of representatives of the women's and feminist movements as well as a technical staff to coordinate implementation. The CNDM was active until July 1989, when conservative hegemony was consolidated within the Sarney administration: By an act of the minister, the CNDM's councilors were replaced by women with no links to women's movements. The CNDM's president and technical advisers promptly re-

Women from many sectors of the women's and feminist movements celebrate International Women's Day, March 8, 1990, in Rio de Janiero.

signed. No government body has since replicated the first CNDM's representativeness or legitimacy with the feminist movement.

There is consensus among feminists from progressive parties and the movement on the need to reevaluate collaboration with the state to more effectively combat women's inequality. The presence of feminists in the councils signaled a commitment to the women's movement's demands and demonstrated that bureaucratic difficulties could be overcome through the force of militant identity. This presence, however, did not ensure that feminist demands would be addressed throughout the state apparatus and did not produce efficient responses to the problems faced by the country's women. Responsibility for implementing gender-fair policies depended on the women's councils; it did not permeate government structures and programs. One lesson from this experience has been that in order to be effective, women need their own institutional place within the state structure and need to develop political party ties to achieve and maintain this status. Only in specific areas where the women's movement already had experience and legitimacy to make proposals to the state, such as in health, sexual violence, and legal reform, was it possible to carry out effective programs.

In the area of health, feminists had a solid base from which to develop and propose government initiatives. NGOs already had legitimacy with the state as they were the first feminist groups to institutionalize; international agencies were in-

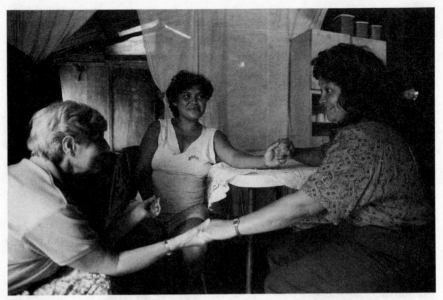

Health issues, which increasingly include AIDS as well as reproductive rights, have long been a central concern of feminist NGOs in Brazil. In São Paulo, counselors provide support for a pregnant woman who is HIV positive.

terested in the issues these NGOs addressed, making it possible to obtain funding and skills to analyze problems and formulate alternatives. At the federal level, the Integrated Program for Women's Health was created, and the right to family planning was incorporated into the Brazilian constitution of 1988. However, since the CNDM's deactivation in 1989, implementation of these programs has been inconsistent.

Women's health policies are still being developed in various states and municipalities. In the city of São Paulo, the PT government (1989–1992) developed city programs on women's health. Most interestingly, services were created to treat women in cases where abortion was legally permitted. In Brazil, abortion is a criminal act except when pregnancy results from rape or when the mother's life is in danger.[37] In practice, even in these cases, the public health service does not perform abortions. The city administration created a legal abortion service to address these cases in 1989. This service had very positive effects for women, many of whom sought out the service for treatment of complications from illegal and clandestine abortions.[38]

Sexual violence against women generated several very concrete and significant initiatives. The incidence of violence against women is alarming, and approximately 70 percent of offenses are committed by husbands, companions, or lov-

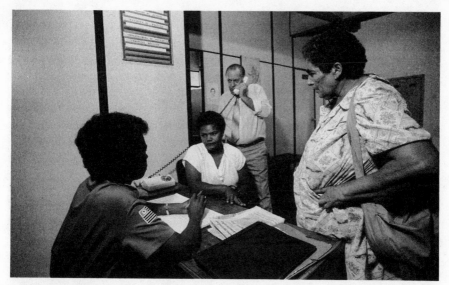

Police stations staffed by women police officers, like this one in São Paulo, respond to complaints by women who are victims of violence. These stations are the result of careful collaboration between the women's movement and the state.

ers.[39] Murderers of women are as a rule absolved from their crime based on arguments about "defending male honor" and the victims' bad conduct. Impunity for violent acts against women has long been a principal theme and a policy priority of the feminist movement. In response to the growing visibility of domestic and sexual violence, pressure from the women's movement, and the inability of traditional agencies to appropriately address the problem, special police stations for women were created in the beginning of 1985. Ten years later, more than one hundred such stations exist in almost all states.

The impact of the police stations has been extremely significant. Everywhere they have been instituted, the number of complaints has grown, and they have made visible the physical, sexual, and emotional aggression women experience.[40] As part of broader policies against gender violence, shelters have also been created for women whose lives are in danger, although these shelters are still limited in number. While this has been an important and visible policy victory for the feminist movement, the stations require ongoing monitoring to prevent them from repeating traditional police practices that fail to recognize violence against women as a crime and encourage impunity.

Finally, the movement's work in the area of legal reform, especially related to the federal constitution of 1988, is also significant. With the firm support of the CNDM, the Brazilian women's movement presented a range of proposals to be incorporated into the text of the constitution. The movement monitored the debates and voting, making its presence felt at each decisive moment, and also initiated several popular amendments supported by thousands of signatures.[41] Women workers were also deeply involved in the constitutional process; rural workers fought for rights already guaranteed to urban workers and joined the latter in their efforts to achieve new rights.

This mobilization process resulted in a new constitution that included provisions on equality between men and women, a chapter on the family that reordered family relations democratically, maternity leave of 120 days, paternity leave of 5 days, and new rights for domestic and rural workers. While abortion was not legalized or decriminalized, neither was the existing legislation made more restrictive, as was advocated by the Catholic church. While Brazilian women have had the majority of their fundamental rights formalized, great efforts are still required to ensure they can exercise these rights through adequate public policies that have real impact on the lives of women.

Issues and Challenges for the Future

One important challenge facing the women's movement is how to better articulate theory and practice, feminist action and academic production. The production of feminist knowledge in Brazil in the last twenty years has followed a thematic course similar to that of the movement's agendas. Until the 1980s, women's studies and gender studies in the Brazilian academic community concentrated on those areas that women's movements had raised in the first half of the twentieth century, such as women and work, women's education, and women's political participation. As the feminist movement increasingly focused on the specificity of women's oppression, grounded in unequal gender power relations, gender studies began to develop new theoretical frameworks for exploring the areas of women's work, education, and political participation.[42]

The issue of public policy and women's relationship to the state became central to feminist scholarship as the movement struggled to define new strategies in the context of political liberalization. During the 1980s, women's studies "nuclei," or centers, were started within some universities and research institutions; this facilitated the creation of working groups on women and gender issues in nearly all of the national postgraduate social science associations. The academic community that was focused on women gradually came closer to the feminist movement, prompting the academic nuclei to organize into networks on the model of feminist groups. While this has been effective in providing scholars working on women's issues with intellectual and moral support, it has been less successful in institutionalizing these themes within the academic mainstream. There are still no graduate courses in the area of women's or gender studies, and undergraduate courses are offered sporadically and seldom incorporated into the regular curriculum. Thus, one of the major challenges confronting the feminist movement is how to ensure the reproduction of feminist production.

Women's political strategies are currently formulated in a number of spheres, including the autonomous movement, unions and professional associations, political parties, NGOs, networks, government organizations, and university research centers. There is a distinct and marked range of levels of institutionalization among these actors. These spheres of activity and advocacy intersect according to political strategies and needs and foster partnerships. The dilemma of reconciling these multiple arenas of feminist activism lies not so much in their capacity for dialogue and partnerships as in their representativeness.

The feminist movement has carefully established practices in order to avoid the representation of all by some, eschewing any type of representational structure by delegation. Priority is given to direct participation, and efforts are made to involve all those interested in participating in a specific initiative. The only representation accepted as legitimate is the representation of ideas. When these ideas materialize into action, involved groups can respond in instances where the need for representation is indispensable to the ideas' recognition and acceptance.

Two debates presently challenging the Brazilian feminist movement illustrate this problem. The first emerges from feminism's relationship with the state. The lack of recognition for the present CNDM by the women's movement is emblematic of a questioning of the representativeness of an official body. The challenge for feminism is to understand its own relation to the state—councils, advisory and coordinating groups, police stations—and propose new forms of organization to incorporate practices consistent with feminist values of broad participation in those arenas.

Another challenge is demonstrated in the preparation for the 1995 United Nations Fourth World Conference on Women, where some women have been invited to "represent" Brazilian feminist positions in a variety of international forums. This has indicated a rupture in the tacit agreement that political dialogue within the national movement is central to both its values and its legitimacy and as such is absolutely indispensable. Neglecting or relegating consultations at the national level to secondary status results in conflict and strain in the movement; these conflicts flourish when issues such as representativeness and institutionalization are not openly discussed. Mechanisms proposed by the movement to address these problems will be closely evaluated in the next decade.

In the current context, conflict within the feminist movement has another complex axis: international cooperation, which seeks to delineate global strategies for dealing with gender issues. Institutionalization and representativeness are also associated with financial resources. There is lingering doubt as to the degree of subordination influencing the actions of women's groups, particularly feminist NGOs, that deal with or receive funding from international agencies to address gender issues. The question is to what extent our agendas, practice, discussion, and exchange are being subordinated to decisions beyond our control. If the institutionalization of feminist groups permits them to negotiate as individuals or in small groups with international agencies, this could compromise the groups' commitment to feminism and even jeopardize the movement's principles of autonomy. Lack of openness about financial resources and projects contributes to mistrust within the movement. Establishing an open dialogue is critical not only to dissipate this kind of mistrust but also to make it possible for an ever more diverse set of women's organizations to understand the mechanisms of international funding and cooperation. In the end, this might serve to foster the development of more democratic forms of international cooperation.

Issues such as abortion, violence against women, and racism have come to challenge the feminist movement and test its capacity to renew ideas, practices, and political alliances. In the case of abortion, just as elsewhere in the world, the question is controversial and very complex. The challenge is to decriminalize a daily practice that involves women, the medical profession, healers, pharmacists, and the police, among others. Rising to this challenge has assumed two directions: one that revolves around the feminist movement, which should examine and renew its strategies to deal with this issue, and the other aimed at society, with the objective of creating new interlocutors and allies.

On balance, over the last two decades feminism or, rather, feminist ideas have been accepted and assimilated into various social and theoretical discourses. The greatest difficulty has been incorporating feminist ideas and values into politics. This is likely to continue to be one of our most significant challenges, particularly if feminism is to continue redefining the very notions of politics and culture without reproducing or mimicking patriarchal forms of "doing politics." These challenges are complex because Brazil is restructuring its democratic institutions in the midst of severe economic and political crises. The movement must build on its diversity in developing broader responses to address these multiple crises and devise more effective ways to improve the real conditions of women's lives.

NOTES

1. This chapter reflects the authors' views about past events, about the relationships established by the feminist movement where women were and are organized, and, in particular, about the challenges that the movement faces today. It does not represent the thinking of all Brazilian feminists on these issues.

This text is based on two meetings. In the first, we agreed to center our analysis on the feminist movement, engaging in a lively discussion evaluating the movement in the 1980s and 1990s. In the second meeting, we worked from separate texts we had developed to produce a first draft of this chapter. While we agreed about the issues most important for the movement today, some differences emerged in our perspectives on the relationship between the feminist and the women's movements and the performance of public policies. Those differences are reflected here.

2. Instituto Brasileiro de Geografia e Estatística (IBGE), *Pesquisa Nacional por Amostragem de Domicílios* (Rio de Janeiro: IBGE, 1990). The IBGE, which conducts the census surveys and other statistical calculations, presents data on the nonwhite population, separating it into "black," "brown," and "yellow" categories. The choice of which of these categories a person is placed in rests with the individual. "Yellows" are those of Asian origin, who represent 1 percent of the total population and are not considered here.

3. V. Soares, "Tempos de Vargas—Tempos da Domesticidade Feminina" (São Paulo: Faculdade de Educação da Universidade de São Paulo, 1993), mimeo.

4. The first known writing by Brazilian women in favor of their own emancipation is N. Floresta Brasileira Augusta, *Women's Rights and the Injustice of Men* (Direitos das Mulheres e Injustica dos Homens), published in 1832. It was presented as a Portuguese adaptation of Mary Wollstonecraft's 1792 *A Vindication of the Rights of Woman*. This volume was republished in 1989, constituting a historical recovery of the origins of feminism in Brazil.

5. Z. Alambert, "A mensageira: Uma contribuição feminista," in *A. Mensageira: Revista Literária Dedicada à Mulher Brasileira* (São Paulo: Imprensa Oficial do Estado/Secreteria Estadual da Cultura, 1987), vol. 1, p. ii. Alambert, now seventy-four years old, has been an activist since 1942. Feminist women in Brazil feel she has a great deal to tell them. *A mensageira*, prepared by Alambert, is a facsimile of nineteenth-century women's writings to which Alambert added an introduction.

6. The achievement of women's suffrage occurred within the context of the 1930 revolution, in which sectors of the armed forces ended the "old republic" and installed a dictatorship under Getúlio Vargas, who remained in power for fifteen years. A process of conservative change was initiated, accompanied by accelerated industrialization. Getúlio Vargas introduced a number of social measures, such as creating a ministry of labor, instituting a minimum wage, and extending universal suffrage, in order to expand his network of support.

7. A. A. Costa, "O feminismo 'feminino' e a esquerda no Brasil," *Caderno do NEIM*, no. 2 (1984).

8. S. Simões, *Deus, Pátria, e Família: As Mulheres no Golpe de 64* (Petropólis: Vozes, 1985).

9. A. A. Costa and C. Sardenberg, "Feminismos e feministas," *Revista Baiana de Enfermagem* 6, no. 2 (1993).

10. M.B.G. Delgado and V. Soares, "O movimento de mulheres na transição democrática" (1993), mimeo.

11. A. Goldberg, "Tudo começou antes de 1975: Idéias inspiradas pelo estudo da gestação de um feminismo 'bom para o Brasil,'" in *Relações Sociais de Sexo X Relações Sociais de Gênero* (São Paulo: Faculdade de Filosofia, Letras, e Ciências Humanas da USP, 1988).

12. A. Oliveira Costa, "É viável o feminismo nos trópicos?" in E. M. Oliveira, org., *Mulheres da Domesticidado à Cidadania* (Brasilia: ANPOCS/CNDM, 1988).

13. Ibid.

14. M. A. Figueiredo, "A evolução do feminismo no Brasil," in A. Costa and C. Sardenberg, eds., *Relatório do I Seminário Nacional o Feminismo no Brasil: Reflexões Teóricas e Perspectivas* (Salvador: NEIM/UFBA, 1988).

15. Large numbers of women, especially feminists, participated in the struggle for amnesty in Brazil. P. Singer, "O feminismo e o feminino," in P. Singer, V. C. Brandt, et al., *O Povo em movimiento, Petropolis* (São Paulo: Editora Vozes, 1980).

16. The PMDB was a continuation of the old MDB, containing various sectors of the democratic opposition; the PDT sought to recover the trajectory of the labor party prior to the 1964 coup; and the PT originated largely from the trade unions and popular movements.

17. V. Soares, "Mas Tiempo para Conversar," in *Cotidiano Mujer* (Montevideo, Uruguay: Colectivo Editorial Mujer, 1993).

18. Costa and Sardenberg, "Feminismos e feministas."

19. Ibid.

20. L. Bairros, "A mulher negra e o feminismo," in A. Costa and C. Sardenberg, eds., *Relatório do I Seminário Nacional o Feminismo no Brasil: Reflexões Teóricas e Perspectivas* (Salvador: NEIM/UFBA, 1988).

21. E. M. Oliveira, "Reflexões a partir do IX Encontro Nacional Feminista," in A. Costa and C. Sardenberg, eds., *Relatório do I Seminário Nacional o Feminismo no Brasil: Reflexões Teóricas e Perspectivas* (Salvador: NEIM/UFBA, 1990); A. B. Motta, "Relações de Genero em Movimentos de Bairro em Salvador" (paper presented at "Encontro de Antropólogos do Norte e Nordeste," Recífe, August 1991), mimeo.

22. V. Vargas, "Entre la esperansa e el desencanto," in *Cotidiano Mujer* (Montevideo, Uruguay: Colectivo Editorial Mujer, 1993).

23. M. C. Paoli, "Movimento socíaís no Brasil—em busca de um estatuto político (prepared for ILDES, 1993), mimeo.

24. S. Alvarez, *Engendering Democracy in Brazil: Women's Movements in Transition Politics* (Princeton: Princeton University Press, 1990).

25. H.I.B. Saffioti, "Movimentos sociais: Face feminina," in N. V. Carvalho, ed., *A Condição Feminina, Revista dos Tribunais* (São Paulo: Vértice, 1988); A. Goldberg, "Feminismo no Brasil contemporâneo: O percurso intelectual de um ideário político," *BIB*, 28 (1989).

26. S. Alvarez, "The Politics of Gender in Latin America" (Ph.D. diss., Yale University, 1986).

27. Saffioti, "Movimentos sociais"; F. Rosemberg, "O Movimento de Mulheres e a Abertura Política no Brasil—O caso da creche," *Cadernos de Pesquisa*, no. 51 (November 1984) (São Paulo: Fundação Carlos Chagas).

28. S. Alvarez, "Politicizing Gender and Engendering Democracy," in A. Stepan, ed., *Democratizing Brazil* (New Haven: Yale University Press, 1990).

29. M.J.F. Nunes Rosado, "Eglise, sexe et pouvoir—les femmes dans le catholicisme au Brésil—le cas des communautés écclésiales de base" (Ph.D. diss., Ecole des Hautes Etudes en Sciences Sociales, 1991).

30. E. S. Lobo et al., "Lutas operárias e lutas das operárias em São Bernardo do Campo," in E. S. Lobo, *A Classe Operaria tem doís sexos—Trabalho, dominação, e resisténcia* (São Paulo: Editora Brasillense e Secretaria Municipal de Ecultura, 1990). Many forms of gender discrimination in the urban labor force are well known: lower salaries, a greater number of women without employment registration, concentration of women in semiskilled or unskilled labor, professional women's ghettos, difficulty accessing promotions and positions

of responsibility, sexual harassment, and lack of control over the use of sanitary facilities. Added to these is a particular kind of violence against women's reproductive rights practiced by many employers who, in the process of selecting or hiring a candidate, ask her to present a laboratory test showing that she is not pregnant or a medical certificate attesting to her sterilization.

31. The Workers Union Central, the largest of the union centrals, approved a resolution in 1993 establishing a minimum quota of 30 percent women to occupy leading posts in the organization. M.B.G. Delgado, "Sindicalismo: Cosa de varones?" *Nueva Sociedade,* no. 110 (November-December 1990).

32. L. Lavinas and P. Cappellin, "Gênero e classe: Mulheres trabalhadoras rurais," in *Mulheres Trabalhadoras Rurais, Participação a Luta Sindical* (Rio de Janeiro: DNTR/CEDI, May 1991), p. 28.

33. While women have increased their political participation in Brazil, only one Black woman has been elected in the past fifteen years.

34. Soares, "Mas Tiempo para Conversar."

35. N. S. Sternbach et al., "Feminism in Latin America—From Bogota to San Bernardo," *Signs—Journal of Women in Culture and Society* 26, no. 17 (1992) (University of Chicago).

36. M. A. Schumaher and E. Vargas, "Lugar no governo: Álibe ou conquista," *Estudos Feministas* 1, no. 2 (Rio de Janeiro, 1993).

37. According to the World Health Organization, approximately 3 million abortions occur in Brazil every year.

38. M. J. Araujo, "Aborto Legal no Hospital do Jabaquara," *Estudos Feministas* 1, no. 2 (1993) (Rio de Janeiro).

39. Americas Watch, *Criminal Injustice: Violence Against Women in Brazil* (New York: Americas Watch, 1991).

40. M. V. Silva, *Violência Contra a Mulher—Quem mete colher* (Rio de Janeiro: Editora Cortez, 1992.)

41. One of these—on abortion legislation—with thirty thousand signatures resulted in a direct confrontation with the Catholic church.

42. M. L. Heilborn, "Antropologia e feminismo," in *Perspectivas Antropológicas da Mulher* 2, no. 1 (1981) (Rio de Janeiro: Zahar Editores).

13

Building Bridges: The Growth of Popular Feminism in Mexico

MARTA LAMAS, ALICIA MARTÍNEZ,

MARÍA LUISA TARRÉS, & ESPERANZA TUÑON

Translated by Ellen Calmus

THE WOMEN'S MOVEMENT in Mexico owes its identity and history to the cultural, political, and social context of the country.[1] The lives of Mexican women are best understood within the context of a history that is the product of two cultures: indigenous and Spanish. The process of achieving independence and forging a modern nation has taken place in the face of persistent problems of racism and a highly skewed distribution of income. Having to confront powerful obstacles, the women's movement has developed particular strengths: Building bridges among very different kinds of women's groups and forming coalitions and alliances have been central to its evolution. An important feature of the movement has been its attention to issues that are broadly significant to Mexican society in addition to gender-specific concerns. For example, the fact that over half the country's population lives in poverty has focused attention in the women's movement on issues of concern to peasant women and the urban poor.

This chapter examines the particular characteristics, evolution, and modes of expression of the Mexican women's movement during the 1970s, 1980s, and 1990s. In each of these decades, the women's movement in Mexico was characterized by new kinds of organizational and class alliances created in response to specific issues. During the 1970s the women's movement in Mexico was largely expressed in consciousness-raising groups constituted mainly of middle-class women and fo-

MEXICO

GENERAL

type of government: Democratic Republic
major ethnic groups: Mestizo (60%); Indigenous (29%); Caucasian (9%)
language(s): Spanish (official); several indigenous languages
religions: Roman Catholic (89%); Protestant (6%)
date of independence: 1823
former colonial power: Spain

DEMOGRAPHICS

population size: 92.4 million
birth rate (*per 1,000 population*): 29
total fertility (*average number of births per woman*): 3.2
contraceptive prevalence (*married women*): 53%
maternal mortality rate (*per 100,000 live births*): 200

WOMEN'S STATUS

date of women's suffrage: 1947 (municipal); 1953 (federal)
economically active population: M 82%   F 30%
female employment (*% of total workforce*): 29
life expectancy   M 69   F 76
school enrollment ratio (*F/100 M*)

primary	94
secondary	92
tertiary	66

literacy   M 90%   F 85%

---

cused on connecting their personal lives and political issues, mostly those related to sexuality. The United Nations World Conference for International Women's Year in 1975 marked the beginnings of cross-class linkages between middle-class and poor women in Mexico and elsewhere in Latin America. This continued to be an important feature of the movement in the 1980s, when feminists and poor women joined forces to create a "popular feminism" that addressed both class and gender inequality. At the same time that women's organizations were developing around the country, a variety of other organizations, including peasant, academic,

*The feminist logo for the United Nations Decade for
Women, 1975–1985, on display during the 1975
Mexico City Conference for International Women's
Year. Valerie Pitts, designer. Copyright © Fund for
the Decade for Women, Inc.*

media, and professional groups, were initiating similar kinds of activities. Though
not highly visible, the women's movement gained strength during this period by
permeating increasingly diverse segments of society. In the 1990s the movement
has consolidated its efforts around the extension of democracy and political participation. Mexico's rapidly changing economy is significantly impacting women's
social and economic status, providing new challenges and opportunities to the
country's women's movement.

The Context: Centralization, a One-Party System, and Machismo

The social and political context in which the Mexican women's movement has developed has shaped its evolution and significance. Mexico is a highly centralized
country both economically and politically. Mexico City dominates much of the
country's political and economic activity as the center of government, finance,
business, and most of academia. Further, the country has been governed by a single party, the Institutional Revolutionary Party, or PRI, since 1929. The PRI's
power is based heavily on patronage; on occasion it has resorted to electoral fraud
and even repression when this power base has been threatened. The Mexican government, dominated by the PRI, has been characterized as a clientilist state, similar to what in some countries is called a party machine. Politicians achieve positions of power through favors they receive from individuals commanding
political and economic power; votes may be delivered or appointed positions offered, and a politician who achieves power within such a system is then obligated
to return these favors. The resulting complex web of personal loyalties, economic
dependencies, and favors owed makes it very difficult to successfully bring about
reform. There have been a number of attempts in recent years to reform the PRI

and the Mexican government, with these efforts gaining urgency as negotiations around the passage of the North American Free Trade Agreement convinced Mexicans that their economic future depended on being able to project an image of a modern democratic country. However, though there have been some notable changes in the areas of taxation, finance, and banking, reforms have proven easier to propose than to implement.

Mexican feminists' organizational efforts have taken place within a political system that is highly resistant to change. They have faced additional difficulties with implementation and enforcement of laws to enhance and protect women's status due to the notorious corruption of Mexico's judicial and law enforcement systems. For example, while feminists working to strengthen rape laws believed that reporting incidents of rape to police would help deter rapists and strengthen demands for legislative change, they also understood that rape victims' fears of going to the police were legitimate. Cases were common in which, instead of offering assistance, police had further abused, and even raped, the victim. This situation of a clientilist, corrupt government initially made feminists wary of working with the government for fear of being "bought" or co-opted as they perceived other groups, such as labor unions, to have been.

Another key element of the Mexican context is the strong tradition of male dominance. There are many theories on the origins of Mexican men's aggressive/defensive masculinity, which may be traced to the violent history of the Spanish conquest. The conquistadors came to conquer rather than to settle and did not initially bring their wives and families. They saw indigenous women as part of the spoils of war, and it is often said that the origin of Mexico's mestizo race was the rape of the indigenous women by the Spanish conquistadors. Mexican men's masculinity may also be a more complex product of the conquest as a whole, combining the attributes of the conquistadors with those of the conquered indigenous groups, which also had a male-dominated society, as demonstrated in the Aztecs' gift to Hernán Cortés of twenty indigenous slave girls. One thing is certain: The conquest left deep scars on Mexico's social fabric that persist to the present.

One of the most pervasive legacies of the conquest to Mexican society is deep-seated racism. Mexico's indigenous groups continue to be discriminated against and marginalized in many ways. They constitute the poorest of the country's poor, its most disenfranchised, and they suffer the highest rates of illiteracy, infant mortality, poverty, and disease. Indigenous women are especially marginalized; with even less access to education, they often speak only their indigenous language and are thereby limited in their ability to participate in public life or communicate with Mexico's Spanish-speaking majority. These women suffer from malnutrition and high rates of mortality in childbirth, and though they are highly skilled in the production of handwoven textiles and other beautiful arts, it has been even more difficult for them than for other Mexican women to receive appropriate compensation for their labor.

It is perhaps indicative of this culture's deeply entrenched ideology of male dominance and male chauvinism that the Mexican terms for this ideology, *machismo,* and for the attitude it produces, *machista,* have been incorporated or translated into many other languages. This tradition of male dominance in Mexico has been reinforced by the powerful influence of the Catholic church. While the effects on women of such church practices as opposition to birth control and a male-only clergy are certainly not confined to Mexico, the influence of the church has been particularly deep in this country. This is due in part to the active role of the church in the conquest of Mexico, which imposed Catholicism on the indigenous Mexicans even as it enslaved them.

Overview: Women's Health, Sexuality, and Cultural Change

In Mexico the term *women's movement* refers not only to the feminist movement but also to all women's organizations that share the perspective that gender is an issue of political and social concern. While Mexican women have mobilized across the entire political spectrum, the women's movement is composed primarily of four groups: middle-class feminists, both within and outside formal political parties; industrial workers and other employees; peasant women; and women from poor urban sectors. Ongoing struggles for women's rights are also carried out by other groups and individuals, among them women in government, mothers of the disappeared, and artists. However, when we speak of the women's movement in Mexico, we are referring to the four organized sectors.

Beginning in the early 1970s, Mexican feminists established a public identity by placing power and politics in the context of daily life. Feminist activism addressed a range of issues, from interpersonal relations to the apparently more anonymous relations found within economic and political structures. Feminists portrayed women's bodies as suffering various forms of cultural and social oppression, as manifested in unsafe abortion, violence against women, and control or repression of women's sexuality. Feminists also introduced the notion that women's daily activities, such as housework, childrearing, and cooking, constituted a productive sphere. Mexican women also began to insist on participating in the debate on national development. They focused on developing mechanisms to enable women to exchange ideas with one another. Such interchange was rare (and still is) for most Mexican women, who tended to be isolated in their homes and on the job. It was necessary for women to identify, articulate, and address their social and individual needs. From the movement's inception, Mexican feminists have organized their efforts primarily around three demands: the right to voluntary maternity (abortion, sex education, access to modern methods of contraception), an end to violence against women, and freedom of sexual choice. However, they have en-

Reproductive rights and sexuality have been at the center of the Mexican feminist movement since its inception. Here, women attend a discussion group on sexuality conducted by the NGO Salud Integral Para la Mujer.

countered difficulties in translating this discourse into the formal political sphere, primarily because their perspective is one of ideological opposition.

During the late 1980s feminists broadened their discussion and demands in order to be more comprehensible to and resonant with the general public. They expressed the importance of minority rights, expanding the idea of democracy beyond that of a representational political system to encompass a broad range of perspectives and ideas. Some prominent women in Mexican politics and culture declared themselves to be feminists. New issues were added to the feminist debate: redefining women's relation to the state, considering and promoting public policies in terms of their impact on women, and establishing quotas for women in government. As a result, feminists are less insistent on autonomy from other social movements and political structures. As the women's movement has gained experience in negotiating and lobbying for change, it has become less fearful of cooptation by the state. It is still limited by the absence of an organized political force capable of making the government respond to women's political initiatives.

Political parties have not yet paid adequate attention to women's demands. Parties' interest in women is limited to electoral promises, and they have not considered issues of gender in designing their broader platforms or strategies. Nevertheless, within the governing party as well as in opposition parties, feminist groups continue to make gender-related demands. However, in order for the women's movement to move its agenda forward, it is critical that the country progress in terms of basic democratic processes.

In contrast to the political arena, women have made significant progress in the cultural sphere. Feminist discourse has been popularized, along with the image of the "liberated woman." The idea of the liberated woman, a woman who thinks for herself and is not dependent on a man, has become part of the country's cultural iconography and has entered the popular imagination variously as a point of reference, a model, or a warning. Cultural expression increasingly questions the *machista* pattern of men as protagonists and women as passive objects and seeks instead to represent women's experience. This includes creative works in the areas of literature, theater, and music as well as an emerging body of feminist art criticism.

Serious debate on feminist thought does not yet exist among Mexico's intellectuals. This is due in part to the absence of a rigorous intellectual discourse within the feminist movement itself. A number of gender-oriented academic centers have stimulated research and publication and have been especially important in helping institutionalize academic programs on women as well as shaping the next generation of feminist academics. However, their credibility within universities and research institutes and their impact on the country's intellectual debate have been limited by the fact that they are still quite new in Mexico. In spite of these limitations, feminist theory influences research and debate in many academic centers.

Feminists have produced numerous publications.[2] Women have found writing and other forms of communication to be effective outlets for many of their ideas. However, even though they publish both in-depth pieces and articles designed to be more accessible, the distribution is largely limited to an already feminist readership.

Women's participation in public life has significantly changed aspects of daily life and some cultural patterns, generating new forms of family relations, neighborhood socializing, workers' consciousness, and political identity. The creation of multiple support networks and ties among feminists, such as women fighting for social justice, government officials, and academics, promotes new ways of thinking about what "feminine" means. This greater involvement and visibility in public life have improved women's self-esteem, increased their capacity for self-expression, improved their ability to manage political resources, and clarified commitment to support other organized groups and to develop leadership skills. These activities have also helped some women redefine their responsibilities in terms of housework and family authority.

Although individual women's lives and consciousness have been transformed, the women's movement has not yet been able to adequately incorporate these changes into a political dialogue. There has not yet been a feminist political initiative capable of involving the whole society. This has meant that contemporary Mexican feminism has yet to deal with some of the goals proposed during the 1970s.

The 1970s: Parallel Paths

The surfacing of Mexican feminism in the 1970s revived memories of an earlier feminist movement, which began after the Mexican Revolution of 1910 and continued into the 1930s.[3] The 1940s and 1950s saw a suffragist movement among Mexican women until they gained the right to vote. During the 1950s and 1960s many women became politically involved in groups inspired by socialist ideology and the history of the Mexican revolution. While these groups were not feminist, they gave women experience in organizing. The new feminism of the 1970s attracted middle-class women who had a college education and an awareness of the feminist discussions taking place in the United States and Europe. Politically these women broadly identified with the Mexican Left.

In Mexico this new feminism did not address the oppression of women bearing the burden of housework and the responsibilities of parenthood. This difference was largely attributable to Mexico's prevailing cultural tradition and skewed social and economic structure, which enable many Mexican women to hire domestic help or turn to the extended family for support. Instead, Mexican feminists organized to resist the strong *machista* cultural tradition. Encouraged by the counter-cultural movement of those years, they focused on identifying and analyzing women's condition through discussing their personal lives. The main form of organization was consciousness-raising groups, which tended to emphasize the link between the personal and the political, especially in the area of sexuality. The central demands that emerged were for the legalization of abortion, stricter penalties for violence against women, and support for rape victims. These small groups proved to be fundamentally important for empowering women and for spreading their ideas among other sectors of society.

For example, in 1974, the year before Mexico hosted the 1975 United Nations World Conference for International Women's Year, these feminist groups undertook an intense series of activities to articulate their principles and promote debate on women's issues in the broader social arena. The international attention generated by the conference compelled the Mexican government to change laws that were discriminatory toward women. As a result, a number of restrictive measures were repealed, such as the law requiring written permission from a woman's husband before an employer could hire her.

Women in government positions at that time and in the ruling political party, the PRI, were important allies in bringing about these reforms, which were a significant step forward. There were few women in government in the early 1970s, and they tended to be relatives of important male politicians. On paper, the reforms were profound; they included a constitutional amendment guaranteeing equality of the sexes, a law giving peasant women the right to own land, and labor laws prohibiting discrimination against women. However, given Mexico's weak judicial system, few of these laws were effectively implemented; twenty years later a substantial gap still exists between legislation and practice. Further, although the Mexican government has ratified the international Convention on the Elimination of All Forms of Discrimination Against Women, it has not yet taken the actions necessary to meet this commitment.

The celebration of International Women's Year in Mexico City in 1975 was an important juncture for the Mexican feminist movement in terms of both the movement's structure and its links to other social movements. Because the organization of the congress was controlled by the government and women belonging to the ruling party, the feminist movement organized a counter congress to the one convened by the United Nations, which contributed to the growth of the Mexican feminist movement. The formation of the Coalition of Feminist Women allowed the women's movement to project a more coherent image and message. The coalition was united by three demands: the right to voluntary maternity (sex education, contraceptives, and abortion), the fight against sexual violence, and freedom of sexual choice. The coalition first publicly articulated these fundamental ideas, around which many feminist groups in Mexico developed.

During the mid-1970s the first draft of a proposed law for voluntary maternity was presented (1976), the first women's studies course was offered (1976), the first feminist publications appeared (1976), a center was created to offer help to rape victims (1977), and a huge number of demonstrations, assemblies, and public declarations were organized, bringing the feminist movement much greater visibility. Significantly, feminist groups also began forming outside the capital. Given the high level of centralization in Mexico, these groups underscored the extent of feminist organizing throughout the country and the impact and relevance of feminist thinking in Mexican society.

The National Front for Women's Rights and Liberation (FNALIDM), formed in 1979, was the first organization to unite feminist groups with labor unions, gay organizations, and leftist political parties. This effort represented the first attempt to broaden the political base of support for feminist concerns. Although this organization was important in building bridges between feminist groups and other social movements and political organizations, its continuation also entailed some costs. As a result of the movement's growing political significance, the feminist groups that had initiated the National Front ceded control of the organization to women from political parties with different agendas. Differences in members' political positions and sexual orientation compounded the difficulties of connecting

*The women's movement, which started largely in the major
cities of Mexico, now includes the organizations and interests
of rural women such as this sheep farmer in Michoacán.*

productively with political parties, resulting in the virtual disintegration of the
National Front by the early 1980s.

The 1970s also saw increased activism among women who, while not necessarily assuming a feminist perspective, organized around issues important to women's lives. These included women from the leftist and antifascist tradition who had organized at the end of World War II to create the National Women's Union. There were women in the government working for legal reforms and mothers of the disappeared demanding that the government be accountable for the fate of their children. Women involved in liberation theology–inspired Christian base communities, along with women in leftist political groups, organized the rural and urban poor, and women industrial workers and workers' wives became involved through labor unions. Peasant women organized around landownership and income-generating projects, and poor urban women fought for housing and urban services. Women in opposition parties tried to get their parties to incorporate a feminist perspective. Lesbians participated in feminist organizations and worked for their own rights as well as collaborating with gay men working for homosexual rights.

Though the diversity among emerging women's organizations demonstrated the broad range of women's concerns and activism in Mexico, this did not constitute a collective will that could be translated into a political force. Each of these social and political initiatives followed parallel paths without meeting in a broader movement and without developing a clear feminist perspective capable of providing a shared framework for the activities of women's groups in this decade. That would not be achieved until the 1980s, when changes in the country's social and

political conditions, combined with the greater maturity of the women's movement, made it possible to form a broad alliance among women.

The 1980s: Joining Forces in the
Women's Movement

The intense feminist activity in 1970s Mexico City spilled into the first years of the
next decade. The Coalition of Feminist Women and the broader-based FNALIDM
sponsored for the second time a proposal for a law for voluntary maternity (1980–
1981) with the support of an opposition party. The Catholic church and the Right
launched a fierce campaign against the proposed law, featuring posters accusing
feminists of murder and depicting dismembered fetuses. Leftist parties, which
had only recently been legalized, were a weak presence in the legislature and unable to effectively support the proposal. Given these limitations, and the governing party's unwillingness to address the proposal, the proposed law was finally ta-
bled, never having been formally discussed in the legislature.

This experience had a number of seemingly contradictory consequences as formal feminist organizations withered and women's influence expanded. Violence
instigated by conservatives intimidated the leftist opposition leaders who had
sponsored the voluntary maternity law. As a result, most political leaders disasso-
ciated themselves from the abortion issue. Both the National Front and the coalition dissolved. Women political activists returned to their parties, where they
tried to incorporate specific women's issues, such as increased penalties for rape
and support for battered women, into party strategies and platforms; such issues
generated less public opposition than abortion rights. Women from diverse organizations of the poor concentrated on integrating a gender perspective into their
many social and economic demands. Thus, paradoxically the fragmentation following the dissolution of the FNALIDM actually generated increased popular
support for the women's movement as feminist organizers relinquished organizational initiative to women from low-income groups. This development helps explain the apparent contradictions of the diminished public visibility of the feminist movement coupled with its broader influence at the beginning of the 1980s.

In the absence of a cohesive national movement, women activists turned to localized activities. They looked toward new political projects and their own survival; some formed support groups, while others created nongovernmental organizations (NGOs) in order to work with poor women. A number of women got
involved in government projects for women and worked on designing new public
policies. Women activists also worked as academics, offering courses on women's
studies, establishing research programs, and teaching at universities. In the media
women worked on creating forums for feminist ideas in print, on radio, and on
television.

A number of Mexico City activists migrated to cities outside the capital, where they joined local feminist groups. Linkages were developed between feminists and women from groups associated with the Catholic church's progressive wing and with leftist organizations working with the poor. This helped open new channels of communication with poor women and incorporate gender concerns into the demands of poor people's movements: the need for public services, housing, basic consumer goods, fair salaries, and access to credit.

A new phenomenon known as popular feminism developed during the 1980s. Between 1980 and 1987 there were ten national conferences of women workers, peasant women, and poor urban women, each attended by approximately five hundred women. In addition, there were innumerable local and regional meetings of low-income women's groups. These events, sponsored by feminist support groups, NGOs, and the feminist sectors of urban poor movements, included discussions of class and gender issues and established specific mechanisms for exchanging experiences. Popular feminism took the feminist demands of the 1970s and combined them with the demands of low-income women. This attempt by middle-class women and women from the poorer sectors to "walk together" was a new phenomenon characterizing the women's movement in the 1980s. The formation of these partnerships was an enormous achievement. The experience of a multiclass movement had previously been unknown in Mexico because of its entrenched social and economic stratification and deep-seated cultural and racial prejudices. The desire to understand and communicate the very different experiences of being women predominated, although the areas of mistrust were not easy to overcome.

In fact, this interaction was not without its difficulties. Political relations between middle-class feminists and low-income women sometimes suffered from problems of communication and differing priorities. In addition to the already difficult processes of identifying a common agenda, there were disputes about funding, control of decisionmaking, and the different value placed on the theoretical concepts of the middle-class feminists versus the experiential knowledge of the low-income women. Many groups working in urban areas among labor and low-income women abruptly dissolved.

Interestingly, this type of conflict among different strands of the women's movement did not emerge in rural areas, perhaps because relations between feminists and peasant women were newer or because the urgency of addressing rural problems outweighed these conflicts. Peasants' long-standing relationships with outside development agents may also have given them experience with negotiating such conflicts. Peasant women also questioned the decisionmaking process of peasant organizations, which had traditionally excluded women and ignored their interests. Since the 1970s political party activists had tried to mobilize peasant women, as had academics and feminist groups since the mid-1980s, but these efforts remained low profile. They were effective in addressing immediate needs while also encouraging members' self-esteem and individual development. Groups composed entirely of peasant women established income-generating activities and social services such as cooperatives, health centers, and mills for grinding corn. This independent organization of women occurred mainly in the poorest and most remote rural areas. In contrast, in areas where agriculture was oriented toward large-scale production, peasant women's concerns tended to be subordinated by the peasant organizations' power structures.

Women in the women's movement were spurred to organize among low-income groups by the economic crisis that affected Mexico in the 1980s. Resulting from a combination of Mexico's difficulties in meeting payments on its foreign debt, a rise in the interest rates charged by U.S. banks, and a drop in the price of petroleum, one of Mexico's most important exports, the economic crisis had brought on a recession, sharp inflation, and a concomitant decline in real wages. The impact on Mexico's poor was exacerbated by sharp cuts in government spending on social services, including health and education. The economic crisis of the 1980s also had major implications for the rural economy and Mexicans living in rural areas. A reduction in urban buying power and a drop in international agricultural prices reduced the profits that could be made from certain crops, thereby resulting in reductions in some kinds of agricultural activity. Seasonal day-labor jobs on which many peasants relied to supplement their low incomes became scarcer. Rural women's activity outside the home was also reduced. When seasonal day-labor jobs were plentiful, women shared them with men. However, when the demand for labor was filled by men, women were no longer hired.

In response to these changing conditions, women's groups began to develop their own discourse, which combined feminism and the perspective of the poor. Although the expanding women's movement still did not adequately address persistent discrimination against Mexico's indigenous peoples, its discourse and actions increasingly reflected attempts to respond to issues rooted in both class and gender. This new political consciousness evolved simultaneously in different areas of the country, fed mostly by women's efforts to advance their values, aspirations, and practices. These explorations were shaped by the individual character of each region, and different discussions took place among industrial workers of central Mexico, women from the *maquiladora* export assembly plants in the north, and women from the agricultural cooperatives in the southeast. What was important was that women from all over the country were beginning to talk about women's issues.

During this period a number of effective and loosely allied networks were created, among them the Network Against Violence Toward Women, the Feminist Peasant Network, and the Network of Popular Educators. These issue- or sector-oriented networks took the place of the earlier and more formal movement structures, such as the Coalition of Feminist Women and the FNALIDM. This new mode of organization made it possible to convene different kinds of women's groups across social, economic, and political lines and to successfully carry out joint activities. The networks were active in coordinating concrete tasks as well as in achieving political alliances or accords. Not having a formal supranational group structure allowed natural leadership to emerge. The effectiveness of these networks may largely be attributed to the fact that they did not institutionalize but maintained their agility in responding to specific needs.

One important function of the networks was promoting awareness and linkages among women across the length and breadth of the country. However incipient and fragmented, these links laid the groundwork for a broad women's movement and reinforced its autonomy from other social and political entities. The networks also facilitated important relationships with organizations and individuals outside the movement, such as academic and professional institutions and public officials. Thus, what started as spontaneous localized struggles became a loosely structured network that forged ties and influence outside its membership.

In the second half of the 1980s opportunities for consolidating the political presence of the women's movement emerged in the enormous popular response to the 1985 earthquake as well as in the extensive citizen mobilization against the electoral fraud of 1988. Following the earthquake that devastated Mexico City in 1985, the whole society mobilized into generous, vital activity whose impact far surpassed the government's insufficient efforts at disaster relief. Citizens independently organized rescue teams to pull people out of collapsed buildings, to provide food and water to stricken neighborhoods, and to help people deal with trauma through organized classes and workshops. The speed and quality of response from an apparently disorganized society were truly striking.

Among those participating in these efforts, groups of low-income women emerged as leaders, and two new contingents of women gained visibility. The first were poor women from the city's downtown who joined the Coordinating Committee of Earthquake Victims and later emerged as key leaders and members of neighborhood associations. The second was the September 19th Garment Workers Union, an association of unemployed garment workers whose factories had been destroyed in the earthquake. The effectiveness of these groups of women in addressing the devastation demonstrated their problemsolving ability and legitimized their organizations. As a result, the government and social and political movements came to recognize these groups' members as legitimate leaders and spokespersons.

From that point on the influence of women's groups on Mexican society was unmistakable, and it became possible to speak of a broad-based women's movement. In 1986 the International Women's Day march was, for the first time, convened by low-income women and industrial workers rather than by feminists; it brought together five thousand women, the largest turnout ever at this event. For some Mexican feminists this represented a significant step forward, demonstrating the influence the feminist perspective had gained within broad social move-

*Effective organizing by women following the 1985 earthquake
in Mexico City helped them gain legitimacy as leaders and
spokespersons for their communities. These medical workers
rest outside a morgue following the quake.*

ments. Other feminist activists resented this development as an invasion and
feared that feminists were losing control over their own agendas. This dynamic remains a central part of the Mexican women's movement.

Broad-based developments were also taking place on the international level. In
1986 a coordinating committee was established to prepare the Fourth Latin American and Caribbean Feminist Conference, to take place in the Mexican city of
Taxco in 1987. In an impressive turnout, more than twenty-five hundred women
attended. Participants included many women from political organizations, activists from low-income movements, mothers of the disappeared, members of peasant organizations and unions, Catholics involved in liberation theology, exile
groups, and many Central Americans involved in the wars and politics of their
countries. The extensive participation by low-income groups contrasted sharply
with the limited presence of the middle-class activists and organizations that had
long been the core of the feminist movement.

The stakes in Taxco were high as participants sought to establish a formal conception of feminism and its political practice. By the end of the conference a document had been compiled that attempted to reconcile the divergent positions of
low-income and middle-class women. It stated that recognizing political and
ideological differences within the movement was necessary both to determine the
movement's direction and to constitute an effective social and political force.

Taking advantage of the presence of large numbers of women in Taxco, the First
National Lesbian Conference and the First Latin American Lesbian Conference

Women rally in Mexico City to support a candidate of the
newly formed Party of Democratic Revolution in 1989.

also took place in 1987. Until then lesbians had been largely invisible in Mexico, though many had participated actively in women's movements without identifying themselves as lesbians. In general Mexico is an extremely homophobic society, and homosexuality is rarely discussed in public. In the absence of a strong gay rights movement in Mexico, most lesbian organizing has taken place within the women's movement, and lesbians are an important sector of the movement. Lesbians organized around gender issues as a step toward claiming their rights to sexual orientation. Among feminists some expressed fear that some heterosexual women would be alienated from the women's movement if lesbian groups gained visibility; this in turn generated resentment from lesbians. While the tension in this dynamic has not been entirely resolved, the groups continue to work together.

In 1987 there was massive popular mobilization and public debate about democracy in anticipation of the national elections to be held in 1988. The effects of the economic crisis had increased public demand for change and provided strong incentives to organize. The recent empowering experience of creating citizens' groups to address the earthquake's devastation had given Mexicans new confidence in the efficacy of independent organizations. For many Mexicans this was the first time it seemed possible to bring about a change in government and to elect a presidential candidate from a party other than the ruling PRI. The potential for change aroused great interest among organized women. In the women's movement the key question was how to incorporate specific women's issues into the electoral agenda.

During this period two new women's organizations emerged. One, intended to mobilize low-income women from a gender perspective, was called the Benita Galeana Coordinating Committee. It was named for one of Mexico's most venerable activists, who, now in her nineties, is still active in organizing peasants, industrial workers, and women. The committee brought together women from thirty-three organizations, including urban groups, unions, NGOs, and political parties. The other organization, Women Fighting for Democracy, involved many prominent women from the country's cultural and political spheres and aimed to bring together women from outside the parties. Both groups subsequently worked to promote the candidacy of women in the political parties as well as joining in efforts to overcome the problem of fraud in Mexican elections.

The 1990s: Creating Public Debate

In the 1990s the political and economic climate of the country has been shaped by the programs of economic adjustment and austerity in public finances implemented by the administration of President Carlos Salinas de Gortari (1988–1994). Salinas, the PRI candidate, was determined the winner of the 1988 election in spite of many people voting for the opposition in response to the economic crisis. The climate of general disapproval deriving from charges of electoral fraud produced such widespread discontent that the new administration was forced to take immediate measures to assert its legitimacy. Programs were quickly implemented to present a more ethical image and to fight corruption. Among these was the National Solidarity Program, which in effect modernized and revived the traditional clientilist model of granting favors in return for political loyalty. The program offers matching funds to community efforts to provide services. It has distributed massive amounts of government funding to poor areas; since prior community organization is required, this funding goes through local leaders. This has served to provide highly focused economic assistance to just those local organizations and leaders most capable of constituting independent or opposition groups. The result has been to mute discontent and to redefine the role of the state. The program has proven to be double edged: While it has opened channels of social involvement, it has also often been used to exert increased political control.

The National Solidarity Program has brought much-needed services to rural areas as well as new challenges to the power base of women's groups. Through this program the government has addressed some of the demands of peasant women and those in popular movements, such as basic urban services in the cities and agricultural credit and production projects in rural areas. In its role as an intermediary, the program has come into competition with local social organizations,

Women Fighting for Democracy organized a march in Mexico City in July 1992 to urge the government to recognize the election of Party of Democratic Revolution candidate Cristobal Arias Solis as governor of Michoacán. The march coincided with the North American Free Trade Agreement talks.

NGOs, and political groups. In the past such organizations served as intermediaries in negotiating with the government on behalf of the poor. While the majority of organized women's groups have taken advantage of some of the resources made available by the program, they have also had to fight to preserve their organizational autonomy and the integrity of their programs.

Widespread efforts under way in recent years to modernize the country have greatly affected peasant women and women workers. Many women workers moved from traditional unionized jobs in the garment industry, food processing, and electronics as well as in universities to newer sectors and services such as banking and communications. Jobs in Mexico have been redefined by the arrival of foreign companies and the adoption of new production processes in Mexican companies. Some factories have improved their working conditions, offering a striking contrast to those prevalent in Mexican industry. Women workers' demands have moved beyond the traditional protectionist view of female employment, which focused on securing maternity leave and prohibiting employers from requiring women to work at night or carry heavy loads. These demands are increasingly perceived as putting women at a disadvantage in competing for jobs, and there is a growing insistence that these demands not be differentiated by gen-

Mexico's changing economy has opened up new work opportunities for women. These women work in an electronic assembly plant in a maquiladora *near the U.S. border in Ciudad Juarez.*

der. If maternity leave is granted to women, men should also receive paternity leave; men as well as women should be protected from having to carry excessively heavy loads. New labor demands are in the areas of women's access to job training, placement in nontraditional positions, participation in unions' negotiations with employers, and a voice in decisionmaking at all levels.

On the negative side peasant women throughout rural Mexico have suffered a number of setbacks in the 1990s. Legislation passed in 1971 had given women legal equality in the distribution of traditional communal farming lands, or *ejidos,* and created the program Agroindustrial Projects for Women. However, it was not until 1975 that the government passed legislation giving women access to farming credit programs, too late for many women farmers to make their land productive. The land distribution program soon ended, and in 1992 these communal lands were opened to market forces. Women are only minimally represented in peasant organizations, where their position has been diluted as these groups focus on defending threatened community rights and family ownership of property, which tends to undermine property rights for women. To replace day-labor jobs lost in the 1980s economic crisis, a growing number of peasant women are becoming migrant farm laborers or industrial workers; others are defending their rights as peasants by organizing their own production projects. Unfortunately, even in changing their labor status, peasant women have made little progress toward resolving their most urgent need: reducing their interminable workday, which would produce profound changes in their lives.

In contrast, the 1990s have broadened the national feminist debate and activities in urban areas. Mexico City feminists worked to reconstitute their organizations following the Sixth National Feminist Conference in 1989. Contrary to expectations, there was a conciliatory and positive attitude among the groups at the conference. Participants created a feminist coordinating committee to serve as a representative public liaison for the movement. A subsequent debate on legalizing abortion in the state of Chiapas in 1990 drew support from all feminist groups. The feminist coordinating committee, however, failed to establish mechanisms of democratic representation; neither it nor unity on the abortion issue was successful in reformulating the terms of feminist political discourse in Mexico.

Organizational progress and unity among many diverse groups have coalesced around addressing sex crimes. A group of feminists proposed to cooperate with Mexico City's Public Attorney's Office to open centers to aid rape victims. Although this initiative was shunned by the broader feminist movement as co-optation by the government, the group continued its work. Participants reasoned that if working with the government could achieve specific feminist goals, perhaps they should not be so apprehensive about co-optation. In general, fear of co-optation had diminished as feminist groups gained experience and became more confident of their identities. Once the first Special Agency for Sex Crimes was opened in 1989, the debate about whether to collaborate with the government reopened. A number of feminists negotiated and cooperated with government agencies such as the Human Rights Commission and the Attorney General's Office, which convened a group to propose reforms in the law on sex crimes.

The unifying effect of the sex crimes issue had further repercussions on the structure and success of the women's movement. Overcoming resistance from their peers, a number of feminist groups worked jointly with a group of women government officials in discussions about sexual violence and the need for monitoring government responses. A feminist congresswoman from an opposition party, Amalia García, did an impressive job of lobbying and alliance building and was able to unite all the parties and thus achieve a complete change in the law in 1991. By addressing an issue on which there was consensus, a new multiparty feminist potential was realized to articulate and advocate positions corresponding to women's interests. Although the feminist movement has not yet identified any other issue with the same unifying force, the experience of successfully working with government agencies has demonstrated the value of collaboration.

New women's groups continued to emerge. In academic centers around the country, women's studies programs were started. Women's centers were opened, offering counseling services on sexuality, support groups for working women, and clinics offering therapy for battered women. Regional groups working on similar programs began to communicate with one another directly. The growing importance of groups in the regions was demonstrated at the Seventh Feminist Conference in 1992, primarily attended by women's groups from the states.

Outside the capital, feminist activity is carried out mostly by young, highly ed-ucated, middle-class women. It has been both strengthened and limited by the common dynamics of personal relationships in small cities, where most people know each other. While it is possible to influence the official power structure through a friend or family member in local government offices, such close ties can also be restrictive. For example, it can be very difficult for women to openly press for abortion rights in the presence of their church and family.

In addition to the growing significance of the regions, the women's movement in the 1990s is characterized by its focus on democracy and electoral participation. The parties, increasingly aware of the value of obtaining votes, are directing more of their campaign strategies toward women voters. But women are now interested in a new role: They want to be candidates. Through the National Convention of Women for Democracy, a number of women committed to women's issues were included in the party lists of candidates for popular representation in the 1991 congressional elections.

The hallmark of the women's movement in the 1990s is the creation of forums for public debate and alliance building among women with differing ideological and party affiliations. Party activists, including for the first time members of the PRI, convened representatives of feminist organizations to define a multiparty political agenda. The women's movement has independently launched an affirm-ative action campaign called Gaining Ground to promote quotas for women in political positions. This campaign has also highlighted discrimination and under-representation of women in a number of other areas. The debate over quotas has been intense. Some feel that mandating more women in Congress will not ensure a feminist perspective in the design of public policies; others believe quotas will constitute a valuable resource for women's empowerment.

Prospects

As the twentieth century comes to a close, Mexico is undergoing internal democ-ratization as well as opening its economic borders with the United States and with the rest of Latin America. These developments present the country with a number of challenges. Mexico must implement real democratic change without violence. It must also become the partner of the economic giants the United States and Canada and define a constructive role as an economic bridge and political buffer between developing and industrialized countries in the hemisphere. Mexican so-ciety, already in great ferment, will surely experience major changes.

Though it is difficult to predict the consequences of this process of economic and social change, it is clear that Mexico's entry into the international market will disrupt old patterns of social behavior. The internationalization of economic ac-tivity promotes the adoption of new lifestyles and consumer models, creating pressure for work to be freed from the traditional restrictions imposed by institutions, legislation, and the family. In this context women will likely face changes in their work and family lives. New kinds of jobs will likely cause dislocation in the family and community. This has already occurred for women migrant workers, women working for the export assembly plants and other transnational companies, and women in high-technology industries. In spite of generally exploitative conditions in the workplace, many women will probably be satisfied with paying jobs that provide independence and social contacts outside the home as well as income.

The new job market's greater employment opportunities for women, especially younger women, may alter relations between the sexes and between the generations, creating profound cultural changes. Maternity and housework may cease to be perceived as women's natural destiny, becoming options to be coordinated with women's jobs. While this may cause a degree of social disruption, it may also lead to reconsideration of assigned gender roles and questioning of male authority. The erosion of traditional patterns will likely bring about new social values, such as autonomy, personal development, and independence, while also weakening some traditional support systems. The prospects are not equally promising for all women since in Mexico and the rest of Latin America the distribution of wealth is more unequal than ever. Poor women find it very difficult to improve their situation because they lack the resources to take advantage of modernization, which paradoxically creates wealth at the same time that it excludes many from that process.

In this process of change emphasis is being placed on extending democracy and on reducing the role of the state in economic and social organization. In Mexico, the process of democratization, which has been agonizingly slow because of the difficulties of reforming such a deeply entrenched system, will most likely accelerate. This will contribute to competition among political parties to gain votes, including women's votes. This competition could favor issues central to the women's movement if women can successfully incorporate their demands into electoral platforms and campaigns.

It will take political will, clarity, and energy for the Mexican women's movement to meet these challenges. The movement will need to become a political force capable of both influencing public policy and party platforms and offering opportunities for more women to get involved. This poses several internal challenges. The movement's different groups will have to recognize both their limitations and their accomplishments and work together to develop a political agenda linking demands from many sectors, broadening these demands, and expressing them in ways that are relevant to society.

To date the women's movement's agenda has developed primarily as the sum of a series of demands, but it has been difficult to set priorities among them. The movement has tended to focus on the most immediate issues. While this makes it possible to rapidly resolve specific problems, it also makes it more difficult to generate lasting programs and organizational structures. The lack of stable and representative organizational structures is a serious impediment to consolidating the women's movement in Mexico. A related problem is representational leadership. Movement leaders tend to rise not through democratic mechanisms of election but through personal charisma. This can seriously confuse issues of representation and voice within the movement and in its public face.

In spite of these difficulties, new channels for women's participation in the movement are being opened. Clearly, the movement's priorities are being reformulated in terms of autonomy and pluralism. Feminists in political parties, realizing that none of the parties treats women's issues seriously, have established alliances with women doing political work outside of party organizations. The high value set on autonomy has led to a number of agreements or accords on specific issues. These experiences have demonstrated the need for a larger number of women to be present when all decisions are made. Feminists have initiated a national campaign for affirmative action, and they are raising the issue of equality. They have taken the political notion of democracy and applied it more broadly, calling for recognition of and respect for difference.

Thus, on the threshold of the turn of the century, Mexican women face the challenge of developing a more structured and better organized movement with a broader capability for influence in a number of areas: lobbying the government as it defines public policy, improving women's economic situation in the public and private spheres, influencing political parties to incorporate feminist perspectives into their platforms and sponsor more women as candidates, making the public more aware of gender issues, and encouraging artists, critics, and intellectuals to include the criticism of sexism in their work. The women's movement's most critical challenge is to work with the majority of Mexican women, who in their isolation suffer poverty and machismo silently, to discover that collective action with other women offers an effective way to address the pressing problems of their daily lives.

NOTES

1. This chapter began with a series of discussions among twenty-one women and men from a broad sample of Mexican women's groups, including urban poor and rural groups, academics, policymakers, and feminist activists. All twenty-one reviewed the writing in process, so that it might represent the most inclusive perspective possible of the women's movement in Mexico.

2. For further reading, see Marta Lamas, "El movimiento feminista en la década de los ochenta," in Enrique de la Garza T., ed., *Crisis y sujetos sociales en México* (Mexico City: UNAM-Porrúa, 1992); Alicia Martínez, *Mujeres mexicanas en cifras* (Mexico City: FLACSO, 1994); María Luisa Tarrés, *La voluntad de ser: Mujeres en los noventa* (Mexico City: El

Colegio de México, 1993); and Esperanza Tuñon, *Las luchas de las mujeres en el cardenismo* (Mexico City: UNAM, 1986).

3. The organization of that time, the Unified Front for Women's Rights, at its peak had a membership of fifty thousand women, according to Lourdes Ruiz de Silva, "Las mujeres y los cargos público en México, 1954–1984" (Undergraduate thesis, UNAM, Mexico, 1986).

PART FOUR

Russia, Europe, and the United States

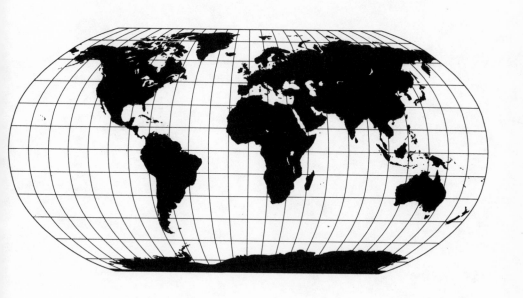

14

Democracy Without Women Is No Democracy: Women's Struggles in Postcommunist Russia

ELIZABETH WATERS

& ANASTASIA POSADSKAYA

WHEN RUSSIANS WENT TO the polls in December 1993, they were asked to choose from a list of parties representing views and programs ranging from nationalist and hard-line communist to proreform and social democratic. Eight percent of the voters cast their ballots for the Women's Party. A decade earlier, both the holding of democratic elections and the existence of a party dedicated to defending the interests of women would have seemed inconceivable outside the realms of science fiction.[1]

From the time of the October Revolution of 1917, the country was ruled by a communist party that tightly controlled every aspect of government and administration and held elections for which its nominees were the sole candidates. Political opposition was illegal, and of women's independent organization there could be no question. Change began in the mid-1980s when the new party secretary, Mikhail Gorbachev, took up a reformist agenda. Extensions of political freedoms were initially modest, designed primarily to give the communist apparatus more legitimacy and effectiveness, but once the principle of extension had been granted,

---

The second section of this chapter is an edited transcript of an interview in June 1994 by Elena Kochkina with Anastasia Posadskaya and a series of self-reflections.

RUSSIA

GENERAL

type of government: Federation
major ethnic groups: Russian (82%); Tatar (3%)
language(s): Russian; Ukrainian
religions: Russian orthodox (25%); nonreligious (60%)

DEMOGRAPHICS

population size: 149.5 million
birth rate (*per 1,000 population*): 15
total fertility (*average number of births per woman*): 1.7
contraceptive prevalence (*married women*): 22%
maternal mortality rate (*per 100,000 live births*): 49

WOMEN'S STATUS

date of women's suffrage: 1917
economically active population*: M 75%   F 60%
female employment (*% of total workforce*)*: 48
life expectancy   M 63   F 74
school enrollment ratio (*F/100 M*)

    primary   *not available*
    secondary   *not available*
    tertiary   *not available*
literacy   M 99%   F 99%

*Data for USSR, 1990

---

it was difficult to draw the line. The Soviet Union lurched turbulently toward democracy, and the communist system (and the Soviet Union) was swept away.

For women, the liberalization of politics since the mid-1980s has not brought straightforward progress. Political representation, notwithstanding the success of the Women's Party, is now far lower than during the communist period. During the 1970s and early 1980s, roughly 33 percent of the deputies to the Supreme Soviet, the highest government body in the USSR, were female, while in the lower level soviet and union organizations the percentage was sometimes 50 or above.[2]

In contrast, the percentage of women deputies returned in the elections of 1991, the first occasion on which procedures were fully democratic, fell to 5.6, and in local soviets the figures were even lower. In many regions of Russia, particularly in the provinces and in rural areas, women have more or less disappeared from politics.[3]

Critics of the communist system have pointed out that the relatively high percentage of female deputies in the USSR was the result of quotas set by the authorities. The disappearance of these token women is held to be no real loss, particularly since the power of the soviets was so minimal, their main function merely to endorse the decisions of the party. However, the reduced visibility of women in politics has been paralleled by other indications of a declining status, most obviously the drop in female participation in the workforce. In 1993 about 70 percent of those officially registered as unemployed were female,[4] which, given the level of hidden female unemployment in Western industrial countries, suggests a very substantial gender imbalance in hiring and firing policies.

The number of women workers was higher in the Soviet Union than in other Western industrialized countries; approximately 90 percent of women of working age were employed or in school. Full employment for all adults of both sexes was one of the ideals of the Russian revolutionaries at the beginning of the twentieth century, and though in the USSR over the years of autocratic one-party rule the original socialist vision faded, a rhetoric of women's emancipation was retained, and certain assumptions about women's right and obligation to work outside the home informed government policy. While women were expected to manage their households and encouraged to have families sufficiently large to maintain a rising birthrate, relatively generous maternity leave and benefits were granted to mothers, and day care was provided for children at nominal cost.

Critics of the communist system have long regarded the idealism of Soviet rhetoric as a mask for exploitation and the Soviet welfare system as an instrument for social control and suppression of individual initiative. In Russia in recent years, since perestroika made wide-scale and open criticism a possibility, the problem has been identified not simply as a gap between ideals and performance, aims and means, but as a flaw in fundamental principles. The target of full female employment and of emancipation for women is, it has been suggested, a misguided one. Politicians from across the political spectrum have omitted equal rights from their list of legitimate and desirable goals. The democrats, the supporters of radical political and economic reforms, share with the conservatives a belief that the years of communist rule instilled in the population an exaggerated allegiance to the collective at the expense of the private and that this weakened the bonds of trust and solidarity between family members and undermined the norms of human dignity and decency without which civilized society cannot survive. Concern about the family cuts across political divides; Left and Right agree that measures to promote its health and stability are indispensable.[5]

Economic necessity coupled with ideology prompted the pre–World War II Soviet Union to employ women in industry, services, education, and health care. Employment did not, however, release women from their domestic roles.

A direct connection between family and financial stability has been taken for granted. Advocates of market reforms hold out the hope that in restructuring the economy along Western lines, they can rescue the country from poverty and backwardness and create the affluence that will make possible the return of women to the home. At the same time the streamlining of the inefficient and backward Soviet economy by the introduction of modern management and technology requires a reduction in the workforce, something that can be achieved by making women redundant. Ideology and economics are indeed in convenient accord. By the late 1980s economists were forecasting that by the next century millions would find themselves unemployed and that of these millions the majority would be women.

Though women at present are overwhelmingly in the majority among the unemployed, the levels of unemployment are relatively low.[6] The present government, despite its commitment to ending intervention in economic life, has had to abandon strict monetarist policies in the face of public anxieties about the impact of inflation on income and savings. During the Soviet era, full employment was the major mechanism for ensuring social security, and high levels of unemployment will therefore be extremely difficult for society to bear unless alternative forms of welfare protection are developed.

However, the discussion in the media during 1992 on a proposed new family law illustrated the extent to which the image of women as guardians of hearth and home has firmly established itself in the public consciousness. The return of women to the home is widely perceived as an ideal worth striving for, even if it is not always realizable. The possible consequences for decisionmaking about female educational and career opportunities are not difficult to envisage.

The Law of the Russian Federation on the Protection of Family, Maternity, Paternity, and Childhood in its draft form sought to restrict the hours worked by mothers with children, an obvious violation of human rights. Similarly, legislation in preparation on preventing the spread of the human immunodeficiency virus (HIV) in the Russian Federation included the compulsory testing of certain social categories, such as prostitutes.[7] This conservatism on the part of Russian politicians and lawmakers requires some explanation. The bitter experience of Soviet repression might be expected to have made Russians particularly sensitive on issues of human rights, but in Russia sexual equality is not counted among human rights. There has also undoubtedly been an element of opposition for the sake of opposition: The very fact that the Soviet regime espoused the principle of women's equality was enough to bring it under suspicion. The picture, however, is a good deal more complex. Russia has telescoped into a few years transformations that in other societies have been dealt with at a slower pace over decades: An empire has been lost, a new economic mechanism adopted, political institutions overturned. The country has not had the benefit of high living standards or social stability or advanced technology that could have helped cushion the population

The negative effects of economic change in Russia are borne disproportionately by women. In 1993, 70 percent of those officially registered as unemployed were female. This woman, unemployed for the first time, visits an employment center in search of work.

from the dislocations that inevitably accompany rapid change. In this context the continuities and hierarchies of the traditional family have had obvious appeal.

The nationalists in particular—though by no means the nationalists alone—have hailed the strong family as a truly Russian institution, one that flourished before the communists seized power and one that should flourish once more now that they have gone. It is true that the Bolsheviks were committed modernizers, and undoubtedly their policies initially promoted the development of new family forms and relationships. In 1917 shortly after the October Revolution, secular marriage and easy divorce were introduced. A 1920 decree legalized hospital abortion. Except for the nineteen years from 1936 to 1955, abortion remained available on demand, and particularly in the towns women used this means to limit their families. But while the Russian revolution and the consolidation of the Soviet regime may have accelerated the fall in the birthrate, the emergence of the nuclear family, and an increasingly urban population, they did not generate these developments. In fact, after a short period of radical legislation in the 1920s, the Communist Party sought to contain and control the processes of change within the family, fearing they might prove politically disruptive. In the 1930s the divorce laws were tightened, abortion and homosexuality were banned, and official ideology designated the family the basic cell of communist society.

The government continued both before and after World War II to maintain a high level of female employment—in the absence of migrant labor and modern technology it had little choice. However, the status of women both at work and at home diverged less from the common Western pattern than was admitted by either the supporters or detractors of the Soviet Union. Soviet women's access to education and the professions was certainly not negligible. Over half the student body was female, hundreds of thousands of women worked as engineers, and over 70 percent of doctors were women. These statistics contrasted quite sharply with other industrial societies, especially in the 1950s, when the model of the nonworking mother held sway. The contrast was less marked from the 1960s onward, when sexual equality became a focus for debate in the West and the status of women in education and employment improved. In the USSR, female labor predominated, as elsewhere, in the less skilled and less-well-paid jobs; women were clustered in light industry and in services or were employed in education and health care—in other words, in jobs that were similar to the work women had previously undertaken in the home. Furthermore, though communist ideology did not disapprove of work for women, it saw domestic roles as crucial to their identity in a way that was not the case for men. Postrevolutionary radicals such as Alexandra Kollontai had looked forward to a socialist future that would socialize housework, a future of eating out, of homes cleaned, and of clothes washed by paid state employees. The Soviet government did open and operate inexpensive canteens and laundries, but their quality and quantity were never sufficient to offer an alternative to the domestic household. In fact, the hours spent on housework did not appreciably fall over the course of the twentieth century partly because labor-saving mechanical devices were in short supply and lack of retail outlets kept the shopping lines long. Housework in the 1960s and 1970s, according to the rather numerous surveys undertaken at that time, took around three to four hours daily over and above time spent looking after children.[8] A few five-day nurseries provided child care for the whole working week, but these were the exceptions; the rule was child care for the length of the working day only. Home and children were both the responsibility of the family, which in practice meant the responsibility of the wife and mother. Fatherhood bore minimal responsibilities, and if some sociologists would have liked husbands to have done more washing up, this was not an issue that aroused strong feeling or was pursued with any sense of urgency, perhaps because sociologists and politicians knew it would meet with resistance.

One of the constraints on policymaking throughout the Soviet era was the strongly traditional views on sex roles held by the population in European Russia as well as in the republics of Central Asia. While generations of Soviets took it for granted that women should work—in the peasant household female labor had always been crucial, and its appropriateness had never been questioned—they continued to view women as fundamentally different from men, suited by their psychology to a specific and separate social place.[9] These entrenched beliefs, which the Soviet regime was unable to alter and for the most part after the 1920s did not try to alter, found a new and unexpected source of reinforcement in the social developments of the post–World War II period. By the mid-1960s over half the Soviet population was living in towns, and this continuing urbanization, coupled with rising living standards and greater leisure opportunities, increased the importance of individualism and private life. As the economic functions of family households tended to decline, consumption and leisure acquired greater prominence, and the chief responsibility for them was assigned to women.

This story is familiar from the history of other Western societies, where it was associated, on the one hand, with the rise of ideals of femininity and domesticity and narrow definitions of women's social roles and, on the other, with the emergence of a women's movement that insisted on a broader definition of women's social roles. It is hardly surprising that in a country in the throes of post-communist upheaval, the desire to reaffirm custom should be more in evidence than the desire to challenge it. While in the long term the social pressures that in Western societies have brought gender stereotypes into question are likely to operate with similar impact and consequences, in the immediate term a women's movement in Russia has little prospect of rapid growth, particularly in the light of its weakness historically.

Before the revolutions of 1917, there were a number of women's organizations campaigning for suffrage and educational reforms. Like all political movements of the time, they were tiny and mainly confined to the privileged classes and to the major cities. Some women, including working-class and peasant women, were attracted to the revolutionary movement, which responded in a small way by celebrating International Women's Day and publishing pamphlets and newspapers targeted specifically at women readers.[10] After the Bolsheviks took power, they set up a "women's department" (*zhenotdel*) responsible for the political education and organization of women. Though the department was never independent, its resources were considerable and its activities numerous. The department did not last long, however, and in 1930, at the time of Joseph Stalin's rise to power, the government decreed the woman question to be solved and women no longer in need of special protection. The Soviet Women's Committee (SWC) established during World War II was a much smaller organization than its predecessor, one of its main duties being to represent the USSR in the international arena at the congresses and commissions that became more frequent after the rise of second-wave feminism.

Much more important for the average Soviet woman than the shadowy committee in Moscow and the often equally shadowy women's clubs at the workplace was the magazine *Rabotnitsa*. It had survived the various twists and turns of Soviet policy and by the 1970s boasted a readership of well over 10 million, making it the country's largest-selling publication. This popularity derived not from the po-

The Soviet government encouraged international meetings and congresses of women rather than seriously addressing issues surrounding their participation in the workforce. Here delegates arrive in Moscow to attend the International Conference on Working Women in 1964.

litical articles each issue was obliged to include but from its relevance to the everyday lives of ordinary women. With far less jargon than usual for the Soviet press, the magazine covered individual women's successes and failures at work, tackled questions of family and morality, and gave advice on personal matters, cooking, and education. In short, *Rabotnitsa* dispensed common sense within the bounds of the politically and socially acceptable. It was not a feminist publication.

The internal opposition movement that began in the USSR in the mid-1960s for the most part ignored the "woman question," emphasizing political freedoms and civil liberties. When in 1979 a small group of Leningrad women published *Woman and Russia,* the first independent attempt to assess the effect of the Soviet system on women, few dissidents took the trouble to notice the event. The authors of *Woman and Russia* received far greater attention from the Soviet authorities; several were called in for interrogation by the KGB and were forced to emigrate.[11]

It was almost ten years before feminism tried to make itself heard again. In 1988 five academic women in Moscow set up the League for Society's Liberation from Stereotypes (LOTOS); in Leningrad, a feminist, Olga Lipovskaya, had begun editing a newspaper for women. In other towns small groups met at factories and at the new political clubs to talk and plan, activities that were no longer automatically "anti-Soviet." In 1990 a coalition, the Independent Women's Democratic Initiative, was launched to facilitate the exchange of information and coordinate campaigning. Glasnost was transforming the country beyond recognition. It was now possible, even customary, to criticize the communist regime, to question its values and the claims it made to have improved the lives of Soviet citizens. The press, untrammeled by censorship for the first time in seventy years, eagerly seized on the shortcomings of Soviet society and the gap between its ideology and reality. The peoples of the USSR were more moral than other peoples, yet prostitution flourished; families were happy, yet the divorce rates were soaring and the children's homes were full. Sexuality, a taboo issue before perestroika, became a media staple. The female bodies of beauty contestants and pinups were regarded as symbols of political liberty and maturity as well as of entrepreneurial opportunity.[12]

The liberalization of the communist regime opened up the possibility of independent political organization by women free of the threat of persecution. But otherwise these were not particularly favorable times for feminist initiative. Public discussions of prostitution, child care, and sex did not raise the dimension of gender equality. Feminism was able to drop the derogatory adjective *bourgeois* with which it had been coupled in the Soviet era, but for most people this was not enough to make it a more attractive ideology. It was associated in the public's mind with "deviant" sexuality. Feminism was understood by Moscow professors as well as provincial newspapers to be a synonym for homosexuality, a subject that liberals as well as conservatives found deeply alien and disturbing. Demands for women's rights and liberation had an old-fashioned, faintly Soviet ring to them, and neither the conservatives nor the democrats had any enthusiasm for them. The causes that mobilized meetings and demonstrations in the late 1980s and early 1990s were politics, nationality, living standards, and the environment. Was the USSR to be a one-party system or a democracy? Should the Union continue to exist in its present form, or should the constituent ethnic groups have their own sovereign states? How could industrial reforms be advanced rapidly without increasing economic hardship and pollution levels?

The collapse of the communist regime after the failed coup of August 1991 was followed by the rapid decline of mass political movements. As the economic situation deteriorated and inflation spiraled, hopes for a brave new democratic future were replaced by disillusionment and increasing alienation from the political process. Individual efforts to make ends meet took precedence over collective efforts to influence the affairs of the nation. The old suspicion of politicians and political organization as so much hot air and wasted time reasserted itself.

Women had been active in the movements of the late 1980s and early 1990s, lobbying, protesting, and sometimes forming separate groups and organizations. Some were politically conservative, like the Chechen Association of Women, which linked national self-identity with the traditional family. Only a few, however, had any ambition to be part of a women's movement. Not having benefited from the optimism and activism of perestroika, the women's movement has had less to lose from the public's declining readiness to participate in politics. Numer-

Delegates, including U.S. delegate Dorothy Hegele, meet at the World Women's Congress on Peace in Moscow, June 1987.

ous seminars and two national conferences of the Independent Women's Forum in Dubna have been held; the women's movement has established a network of contact and coordination.[13] At the local level thousands of women have been involved in small-circulation publishing ventures and in campaigns in their towns and regions for consumer rights, health care, and employment opportunities. At the national level women's organizations have made themselves a permanent feature of political life. The Association of Women Entrepreneurs was one of the organizers, along with the State Committee for Sanitary and Epidemiological Supervision and the Russian Federation Academy of Medicine, of a recent roundtable on "Russian Troubles in the Area of Health and Epidemiology." The Russian Women's League has held job fairs for women in collaboration with the Department of Labor and Employment; the Foundation of Liberal Women, set up at the beginning of 1994 by a number of high-profile women, offers financial and moral support to talented women who are finding it difficult to succeed in a man's world.[14] Evgeniya Debranskaya, director of the Russian Association of Gays, Lesbians, and Bisexuals, has been a prominent voice in the recent debate on government proposals for a program of HIV testing.[15]

Sexual politics is becoming a little more acceptable and respectable. In 1991 the First Independent Women's Forum at Dubna was threatened with cancellation when conference facilities were withdrawn after a newspaper article alleged its participants to be gays and lesbians; now false claims of this sort are less fre-

Delegates to the first congress of Mothers Against Violence gather at the Kremlin in 1990 to demand the army's reorganization.   Included among the mothers are those whose sons died while serving in the Soviet Army in peacetime.

quently made, and claims based on fact excite a less dramatic response.[16] Controversy is still far from over, however. The connections between sexuality and human rights, public morality and social policies, will certainly be fiercely contested in the coming period, and the women's movement is bound to want its say. But the more traditional issues of work and family will probably remain uppermost on the feminist agenda.

The NE ZHDI ("Do Not Wait") manifesto published in 1990 by the Independent Women's Democratic Initiative accorded first priority to women's struggles for economic independence. As the transition to the market economy proceeds, the questions of whether and under what conditions women work are likely to remain of central concern. Whatever misgivings Russian feminists may have about the traditional linking of mothers and children, female employment will continue to be discussed in relation to the family. The number of children born has fallen so rapidly that for the past few years a negative birthrate has been recorded, and alarming increases in illness and death among infants are being reported. Calls for larger families and for women to stay at home to look after them will probably grow louder. But there is no guarantee that they will be heeded. Young women have grown to adulthood in the era of glasnost, postcommunism, and widening opportunities for choice and autonomy in daily life. As time goes by the constituency for the ideas of the women's movement is likely to expand.

Until recently there was no independent Russian women's movement. Its emergence has been the work of small groups and organizations such as LOTOS and the Moscow Center for Gender Studies (MCGS). Anastasia Posadskaya was a founding member of LOTOS in 1988 and has consequently had the opportunity to witness all the stages in the development of the women's movement. As founding director of the MCGS, she is involved in current campaigning and research. In the following interview, she answers questions about the ideas and direction of Russian feminism, the legacy of the communist period, and prospects for the future.

Interview with Anastasia Posadskaya

Q: Does a women's movement exist in Russia?

A: When we talk about social movements, we often have in mind something big; we think of masses of people participating in campaigns and demonstrations. This definition of a movement seems to me to be too narrow and not always helpful in understanding how social change comes about. For me the key criteria are independence from government and an explicit orientation toward certain social goals. Targets and strategies are more important than large numbers. Even a small group of committed citizens can be considered a movement. The Independent Women's Forum is small, but I would say it was part of a movement.

Q: Is the Russian women's movement feminist?

A: I would want to make a distinction between a women's movement and a feminist movement. Any public activity of which women are the subjects is a women's movement. As for a feminist movement, I prefer to speak about *feminisms.* I think that no one group of women or no one woman has the right to label the others as "true" or "not quite true" feminists. For me, feminism implies a specific rejection of the perception that society has a gender-neutral character. Feminism also brings an agenda for change on a global and not just a national level. That is not to deny the diversity of national experience. For example, the emphasis in Russia on independence from the state and from all official political structures is a result of our national experience. During the Soviet period, state and political institutions assumed the right to speak on behalf of women, and this practice has not yet completely disappeared. It was as if politicians, and women, too, came to believe that an independent women's voice did not and could not exist in our country. For

this reason, from the very beginning, we have emphasized self-reliance, independence, and grassroots organization.

Q: When did your own involvement in the Russian women's movement begin?
A: It was in 1988. That year proved to be the beginning of a new life for me. I discovered there were other women who were not afraid to call themselves feminists, and we began to meet as a group. There were Valentina Konstantinova,
a historian; Olga Voronina, a philosopher; Natalia Zakharova, a sociologist;
myself; and, a bit later, another philosopher, Tatiana Klimenkova. We did not
agree on everything, but we shared a hostility to the idea that women occupied a special social place, especially since it was other people who were deciding what that place ought to be. At the end of the 1980s at the time of
perestroika, the conventional wisdom in Russia was that woman's place
should be predominantly at home in the private sphere. We did not want to
have others tell us where we belonged; we wanted to find our own way.

Q: Were the democrats critical of the conventional wisdom?
A: No. The democrats had the same views on woman's place as the conservative
opponents of change. The patriarchal ideas underlying the reform movement worried us. In the group we discussed how we could draw public attention to the absence of women's participation in key decisionmaking and how
we could show that politicians' talk of rescuing the female sex from their
"double burden" might end up trapping women in unemployment and poverty. Finding there were others who had the same reservations about
perestroika was more than a relief. It was exciting, exhilarating even, to feel
we were making a collective challenge to the male perspective. I think this
was crucial in providing momentum for the women's movement in the early
stages.

Q: Did the movement at that time have a name?
A: We called ourselves feminists. We called our organization LOTOS, an abbre-
viation of the Russian for the League for Society's Liberation from Stereotypes. There were arguments for and against labels and names. The official
propaganda of the Soviet era taught that feminists were women who hated
men and children and the family; feminists were unattractive and aggressive.
Labeling ourselves was a way to undermine the negative stereotyping. A
number of women's groups were being set up at that time, and a name would
help us be identified with a particular view on the gender dimension of Russian society. On the other hand, a name would make us more vulnerable to
political persecution. In 1988 the threat from the party machine was still real.
In spite of the danger, we decided to take the plunge. I drafted a manifesto
that declared emancipation of women under socialism to be a myth. Patriar-

chy was far from being dead, the document argued; it was still being reproduced at all levels of society, and gender stereotypes were a barrier to the realization of the personality, for both women and men.

Q: How successful was LOTOS?

A: The interest from the mass media was minimal, except on International
Women's Day, the day the Soviet media traditionally remembered women.
Even then we were mentioned only as exotic specimens—"nowadays we, too,
have our own feminists!" We became very wary of journalists, who always
seemed to manage to distort our views, though Natalia Kraminova and Elena
Khanga from Moscow News were two exceptions to this rule. To our great
surprise we found we were far more interesting to foreign journalists and to
feminist scholars and activists from abroad, who were very ready to offer
support and friendship.

Nevertheless LOTOS was an important stage in the development of the
women's movement. It opened a realm of exciting new possibilities. I may
have been more optimistic than some of the others, but we all felt political
liberalization was creating real opportunities for change. We wanted to make
women's voice heard, to show that we women not only existed but had much
to contribute on our own behalf.

Q: Did LOTOS become an officially recognized organization?

A: LOTOS was one of the so-called informal groups that were numerous in the
early years of perestroika. It was independent of the communist apparatus and
was never formally registered. The women's movement in Russia has never
been much concerned with formal registration. The Center for Gender Studies, the Independent Women's Forum, and the Women's Information Project
were all in existence for many years before they became "legal entities."

Russians are very suspicious of official organizations because of their experiences under the centrally controlled communist system. So in the
postcommunist context it is very important to create organizations that are
open and publicly accountable. The difficulties faced by the Independent
Women's Democratic Initiative, NE ZHDI, is a good illustration of this. It
was set up in the summer of 1990 as a coalition of independent women's organizations, but it never really got off the ground. The problem I think was
that the idea for the initiative came, in fact, from only one group, and the
others that joined were not really committed. The preliminary work of building up a true spirit of cooperation is very important. The Independent
Women's Forum has a much more solid base. A number of groups, including
the Free Association of Feminist Organizations, the Moscow Center for Gender Studies, and Grassroots participated in planning from the very beginning.

Q: What has been the history of the forum?

A: The First Independent Women's Forum was held on March 28–29, 1991, in the
     town of Dubna. It was attended by more than two hundred participants
     from all over the former USSR as well as by twenty-five foreign guests. The
     forum adopted the slogan first formulated by NE ZHDI, "Democracy with-
     out women is no democracy," and its concluding document declared that
     discrimination against women, institutionalized under the Soviet regime,
     was continuing under perestroika. While the forum succeeded in putting the
     independent democratic voice of women on the map, it also highlighted dif-
     ferences between women on questions of organization, differences that have
     still not been entirely resolved. Proposals to set up a new women's organiza-
     tion were rejected by the majority of the delegates. The compromise was the
     Women's Information Network (ZhISET), which assists organizations and
     individual women in establishing contacts and exchanging information. But
     this proved to be not enough. At the Second Independent Women's Forum,
     held, again in Dubna, on November 28–29, 1992, this time with over six hun-
     dred participants, five hundred from Russia and over one hundred from
     abroad, it was decided that the forum itself should become a permanent
     body, loosely structured, though, and without rigid hierarchies, its main ob-
     jective being, as the name suggests, to provide a space for discussion and ini-
     tiative. The second forum took as its slogan, "From Problems to Strategies."
     There were over twenty sessions focusing on a range of issues: women's un-
     employment, political participation, political policy and women, rural
     women, women's health, women and violence, women's position in industry
     and the defense sector, young women, and women in the mass media. Today
     the Independent Women's Forum exists as a network of more than two hun-
     dred organizations and has a coordinating information center.

Q: What is your assessment of the Soviet Women's Committee, the official
     women's organization during the communist period?

A: It is important to make a distinction between the institution and the women
     who work in it. The SWC belonged to the party apparatus. Its purpose was to
     advertise to the world the Soviet achievement in solving the woman question
     and to criticize the noncommunist world for falling short of this standard. Its
     primary purpose was propaganda, though one should note that in the Soviet
     era the term *propaganda* did not have negative connotations. I'm sure that
     many of the women who worked in the SWC were sincere in their efforts to
     better women's lot and were not necessarily always unsuccessful. However, at
     the institutional level the SWC was one of the pseudoindependent,

pseudodemocratic organizations that made up the Soviet system. All new activists had to be screened for political reliability before being recommended for election. Membership in the Communist Party was an obligatory condition for those holding office and served to ensure loyalty and obedience. The organization promoted the interests of the Communist Party rather than those of women. And this has left a bitter legacy: Women do not trust women's organizations. We have the Soviet Women's Committee to thank for some of the difficulties we encounter today in trying to interest women in working together in public campaigns and organizations.

Q: How has the SWC responded to the political changes of the past decade?

A: During the first years of perestroika, the committee engaged in ideological and organizational restructuring of its own. During 1986 and 1987, there was an attempt to revive the system of *zhensovety,* or "women's councils." Thousands of local organizations appeared in a matter of months. Many members of these councils were serious in their attempts to defend women's interests. But the SWC remained bureaucratic and undemocratic in its structure. Its political agenda was out of step with the changing needs of women. More recently the SWC—or, rather, the Union of Russia's Women, as the organization has been called since 1992—has moved closer to Western feminism. Instead of insisting on privileges for women as mothers, it demands equal opportunities with men. It now recognizes that discrimination against women occurs in Russia as well as in other countries and that patriarchy is a pervasive feature of our society. In October 1993 during the parliamentary election campaign, the union went so far as to adopt the slogan "Democracy without women is no democracy." This, you remember, has been a slogan of the independent women's movement since 1990! At first we were less than pleased to see our language coopted. Our organizational and ideological independence has been of central importance to us. But eventually we came to view the metamorphosis of the SWC more positively (though this is not a unanimous view). After all, the more that is said about women's emancipation, the better. We recognized, too, that the union's new terminology and its new willingness to take up issues like violence against women and equal opportunities were in some measure a response to the impression we had made on public opinion.

Q: What part did the Independent Women's Forum take in the elections to the Russian Parliament in December 1993?

A: The forum is not a political party, so it didn't run its own candidates. There was fellow feeling for the Women's Party as well as some criticism of its policies. Most of the members of the forum supported the democratic party,

Yabloko,[17] but there was support for a number of other parties as well. In every case members worked for the adoption of a three-point program: socially responsible policies, support for women candidates, and promotion of equal opportunities. Two seminars for women candidates were held in Moscow, one on political training before the elections and a second afterward to analyze the results and plan for the future.

Q: Has the Women's Forum conducted any campaigns of its own?

A: In 1992 the independent women's movement campaigned against the proposed Law of the Russian Federation on the Protection of Family, Maternity, Paternity, and Childhood. The draft put before the Russian Parliament contained a number of articles that were in violation of women's rights. The law aimed to bring back traditional family values and to promote family upbringing as the predominant form of preschool education and care. Women with children under fourteen years old were to work part time, thirty-five hours a week as opposed to the regular forty-hour week. Raising a family of three or more children was to be considered socially necessary labor, paid at the level of the minimum wage. Finally, and most worrying of all, the draft spoke of the rights of the unborn child in a way that appeared directly to threaten women's reproductive right to abortion. A Western reader would certainly have interpreted this article as a declaration of pro-life sentiment.

Q: How did Parliament respond to the draft?

A: Deputies we approached for their views said they did not think the draft was attempting to undermine abortion rights; it represented, rather, a reaffirmation of the state's commitment to care for pregnant women. They advised us to wait for the debate in Parliament before we voiced criticisms. Initially the draft was not made public, and it was difficult to find out its exact wording. To complicate matters, the Union of Russia's Women, which was privy to the exact wording, had come out in support of the draft.

When the parliamentary debate finally got going, it became clear that, despite the deputies' disclaimers, the law was backed and promoted by the right wing, the so-called Patriots. One of the draft's main advocates, Nikolai Pavlov, who belonged to the right-wing bloc Fatherland, went so far as to say that without a family a person is socially dangerous! The democrats unfortunately were not prepared to take issue with statements of this sort. Neither have they dissociated themselves from the other demographic, economic, and moral arguments advanced in favor of the draft. A demographer, Anatoly Antonov, invited to give his expert opinion to Parliament, stressed that a law promoting family values is essential if population growth is to be resumed and normal reproduction patterns restored. The sociologist Igor Bestuzhev-Lada said that the recognition of child care as remunerative work

Irina Khakamada, general secretary of the Party of Economic Freedom, asks to be recognized at the Duma's opening session in January 1994. The proportion of women in the central government body dropped from roughly 33 percent in the late 1970s to 5.6 percent after the democratic elections of 1991.

is desirable, economically and morally as well as demographically: If women receive some money for housework, they will be happy to give up working outside the home, and the path of economic restructuring will be smoother; if women put more time and energy into the family, it will become healthier and happier. When we put to deputy Gleb Yakunin that the draft law discriminated against women, he dismissed the idea with the rhetorical question "Why do women matter?" Gleb Yakunin is a well-known democrat.

In the current Duma the main advocate of this position, Irina Khakamada, is from the wing of liberal democrats. Khakamada, one of the most visible women deputies and a strong supporter of democratic reforms, promotes the alternative approach to social benefits, suggesting that families (i.e., women) should be paid for looking after their children at the level of minimum wage and arguing that this will reduce official unemployment and ensure better-quality child care.

Q: Did your campaign make any headway?
A: The situation seemed hopeless. The law passed its first hearing in June 1992. There was no public debate, and we were told that at this late stage all efforts to amend or stop it would fail. We felt that however slim our chances were, we had to make our criticisms public. We were at the time in the process of preparing for the Second Independent Women's Forum in Dubna, so we used all the organizational resources we had available to contact the mass

media, lobby the democratic deputies in Parliament, publish through academic channels the shortcomings of the draft, and encourage foreign experts on women's affairs to submit comments. In November the Second Independent Women's Forum issued a critique of the draft. Our efforts had an effect. The controversial articles were eventually either modified or deleted. And then in October 1993 both the draft law and Parliament itself came to an end. The draft law was terminated at its second reading by a barrage of approximately four hundred negative appraisals in the form of letters, faxes, and telegrams. Parliament's end, as is well known, was brought about by tank shells. Our campaign was proof that the women's movement has the capacity, even in unfavorable circumstances and with limited resources, to influence politics. It also made clear how easily things can be changed for the worse if watchdogs are not vigilant.

Q: Have there been any attempts to change the laws on abortion and withdraw the provisions for freely available terminations in the first trimester?

A: Recently abortion was excluded from the basic medical insurance coverage provided by the Ministry of Health. And this was only one of a number of measures taken without consultation with women's organizations. Legislation on medical insurance and family planning as well as a government program on safe motherhood was prepared without any public debate whatsoever. To draw attention to this situation, the Moscow Center for Gender Studies launched a series of roundtable discussions on reproductive rights. The first meeting, held in July 1994, dealt with "The Threat to Abortion Rights in Russia: Myth or Reality" and was attended by feminist scholars, activists of the Independent Women's Forum, journalists, and education and health care professionals. Questions such as the lack of sex education and the low quality and poor supplies of modern contraceptives were addressed. Evidence was presented that demonstrated unequivocally the very real threat to abortion rights in Russia. The session released a statement to this effect, which was circulated to the government, parliament and the media. The timing was right. The U.N. International Conference on Population and Development was in progress in Cairo, and in Russia the pro-life movement was beginning to adopt a higher public profile. It is only to be hoped that the Ministry of Health will become more open and accountable in its policymaking practice and more concerned with the issues of women's health.

Q: How is the Moscow Center for Gender Studies organized, and how broad is the range of its activities?

A: The idea of the center was first disussed by the LOTOS group and became a fact in April 1990. Our intention was to create a research center committed to social change and not just pure science. It has not been easy to keep to this choice. We have been criticized from all sides. Mainstream academics argue that we are doing politics, not research. Some women in the women's movement, on the other hand, say that because the center is under the auspices of the Russian Academy of Sciences, we have forfeited our independence. Political opponents from outside the democratic camp accuse us of having non-Russian roots and importing Western feminist ideology. We have remained firm, despite the criticism. Our aims are firstly to promote feminist perspectives within the independent women's movement, secondly to use our expertise to make the state sensitive to women's concerns, and thirdly to win academic recognition for women's and gender studies. In pursuit of these aims, the center organized a series of seminars on "Women in Politics and Politics for Women" (1990–1991), initiated the association NE ZHDI (1990), and contributed to the organization of the First and Second Independent Women's Forums in Dubna (1991 and 1992). In cooperation with other women's organizations, the center conducted seminars on topics including "How to Run Your Own Business" (1992), "Women, Leadership, Democracy" (1993), "How to Be a Successful Candidate for Office" (1993), "How to Run a Nonprofit Organization" (1994), and "Strategy for the Independent Women's Movement" (1994). The center has also participated in setting the organizational and conceptual parameters of a number of new projects, including the ZhISET (1991); Women's Information Project, Archive, Database, Library (1993); Women's Training Network (1993–1994); three partnership projects with the Network of East-West Women (E-mail communication, Legal Advocacy Committee, Self-Defense Training, 1994); and NIS-USA Consortium of Women's Organizations (1994).[18]

Q: What research is the center doing?
A: Research at the MCGS reflects the interests of the scholars working in it. Topics include analysis of laws and policies from the perspective of gender, the position of women in the emerging labor market, new forms of political participation and leadership for women, theoretical issues of feminism, the image of women in the mass media, an oral history of Russia's women, the gender aspects of emigration from Russia, and the position of women in industry. The MCGS has published three collections of articles in Russian, and a fourth is in preparation. In the fall of 1994 *Women in Russia: New Era in Russian Feminism* was published in the United Kingdom, the first book in English to represent the views of Russian feminists in their own words rather than through the interpretation of Western scholars.

Q: What has been the role of the international women's movement in the development of the Russian women's movement?

A: The Russian women's movement was not—as some of our critics in Russia
      have asserted—initiated or shaped by international feminism or created by
      the funds of Western foundations or the United Nations! In fact, unlike the
      official women's movement of the Soviet era, we did not initially have access
      to the networks of the international women's community. The help of West-
      ern governments and foundations also came at a later stage. Here I do not
      consider the views on East-West dialogues; this is the subject for a separate,
      long exploration.
         There are still obstacles to full-scale participation in the international
      movement. Communication between Russian women and the rest of the
      world is still a problem due to the language barrier and also to financial and
      technological constraints. The international feminist movement and West-
      ern funding bodies have been quite sensitive to our need for help that does
      not have strings attached and leaves our independence intact. Two American
      feminists, Katrina van den Heuvel and Colette Shulman, produced a feminist
      magazine in Russian, *You and We,* which has been widely distributed and has
      helped bridge the gap between East and West. Women's organizations in
      Germany, the United States, Britain, the Netherlands, and Finland as well as
      international funding bodies such as the Ford Foundation, the MacArthur
      Foundation, the British Council, the Global Fund for Women, the European
      Union, and the governments of France, Canada, the Netherlands, the United
      States, and Germany have provided in-kind and financial support for train-
      ing, education, research, and organization. Preparation for the U.N. Fourth
      World Conference on Women, to be held in Beijing, is for us a test of the ex-
      tent to which the obstacles to full-scale participation in the global movement
      have been overcome.

NOTES

1. The parliamentary elections of December 1993 are analyzed in M. Urban, "December
1993 as a Replication of Late-Soviet Electoral Practices," *Post-Soviet Affairs,* no. 2 (1994):127–
158; V. Tolz, "Russian Parliamentary Elections: What Happened and Why," *Radio Free Europe, Russian Research Report,* no. 2 (1994):1–8.

2. For women in politics during the Soviet period, see G. Lapidus, *Women in Soviet Society: Equality, Development, Social Change* (Berkeley and Los Angeles: University of California Press, 1978); G. Browning, *Women and Politics in the USSR: Consciousness Raising and
Soviet Women's Groups* (Brighton: Wheatsheaf, 1987).

3. The impact of perestroika on women's political representation in the USSR is discussed in M. Buckley, ed., *Perestroika and Soviet Women* (Cambridge: Cambridge University Press, 1992).

4. T. W. Karasik, "Facts and Figures Annual," *Russia and Eurasia* (Gulf Breeze: Academic
International Press, 1993), pp. 127–128.

5. According to one of the parliamentary deputies, V. Juskevicius, the "revival of society is only possible if there is a revival of the institution of the family." L. Osheverova, "Current Digest of the Post-Communist Press," *Izvestiya*, March 18, 1992.

6. J. Shapiro, "The Industrial Labor Force," in M. Buckley, ed., *Perestroika and Soviet Women* (Cambridge: Cambridge University Press, 1992), pp. 14–38.

7. V. Ignatov, "Sevodnya," *CDP-SP*, no. 24 (June 16, 1994).

8. Lapidus, *Women in Soviet Society*, pp. 269–278.

9. See B. Engel, *Between the Fields and the City: Women, Work, and Family in Russia, 1861–1914* (Cambridge: Cambridge University Press, 1994), on the peasant family in the early stages of Russian industrialization. The Soviet period is covered in B. Farnsworth and L. Viola, eds., *Russian Peasant Women* (Oxford: Oxford University Press, 1992).

10. For a history of the women's movement in Russia and in the USSR during the 1920s and 1930s, see R. Stites, *The Women's Liberation Movement in Russia* (Princeton: Princeton University Press, 1978). The later Soviet period is dealt with in M. Buckley, *Women and Ideology in the Soviet Union* (New York: Harvester, 1989).

11. *Women and Russia: First Feminist Samizdat* (London: Sheba, 1980).

12. On children's homes, see E. Waters, "Cuckoo Mothers and Apparatchiks: Glasnost and Children's Homes," in M. Buckley, ed., *Perestroika and Soviet Women* (Cambridge: Cambridge University Press, 1992), pp. 123–141; on sexuality, see J. Riordan and I. S. Kon, *Sex and Soviet Society* (London: Pluto Press).

13. *Feminist Review*, no. 39 (1991), includes a section on the women's movement in Russia: two articles by Cynthia Cockburn, "In Listening Mode," pp. 124–126, a personal response to the changing shape of East Europe, and "Democracy Without Women Is No Democracy," a report on the First Independent Women's Forum; an interview with Anastasia Posadskaya, director of the Moscow Center for Gender Studies, pp. 133–140; the NE ZHDI manifesto, pp. 127–132; and the concluding document of the First Independent Women's Forum, pp. 146–148.

14. G. Cherkasov, "Sevodnya," *CDP-SP*, no. 7 (February 15, 1994).

15. Ignatov, "Sevodnya."

16. Cockburn, "Democracy Without Women," p. 145. For recent coverage of lesbianism, see A. Alymin, *Trud*, February 16 and 24, 1994.

17. Four democratic blocs contested the parliamentary elections in December 1993: Russia's Choice, the Party of Russian Unity and Concord, the Russian Movement for Democratic Reforms, and Yabloko. The name *Yabloko*, which means "apple" in Russian, was taken from the initials of the bloc's three leaders, Grigorii Yavlinsky, Yurii Boldyrev, and Vladimir Lukin. The party stood for economic reforms, political freedoms, and an independent, critical stance toward the Yeltsin government.

18. The Archive, Database, Library was funded by a three-year grant from a German feminist organization; the Women's Training Network and the partnership projects have developed in cooperation with women's organizations in Britain and the United States, respectively.

15

Finding a Voice: Women in Postcommunist Central Europe

ELZBIETA MATYNIA

WHEN I FIRST RETURNED to my native—and already virtually "postcommunist"—Poland in the summer of 1989 after an eight-year absence, one of the things that struck me most vividly was that in the new and exuberant public life of the country there was an almost total absence of those capable women who had played such an active and essential role in the clandestine operations of the prodemocratic movements of the 1970s and 1980s. I knew many of them well and had been active along with them, but, like them, I had never defined the crucial problems in terms of gender. The primary objective of every social protest and movement then had been to fight for the political rights of *all* members of society. All other issues had seemed to be of secondary importance; it was felt that these could be dealt with after the final battle for democracy had been won. But now, as I watched the freewheeling debates in the new Parliament and read about all those newly created democratic institutions, I found myself wondering where all the women were.

During the first four years following the collapse of the Berlin Wall, when I frequently visited various countries of the region, I could sense a new kind of tension building up around "the problem of women." On the one hand, the issue of gender, never really discussed in those countries before, has been emerging as a response to the deteriorating legal and economic status of women. On the other hand, there was enormous sociocultural and political pressure coming from both men and women to disregard the issue and even to ridicule those involved in discussions of it.

Polish women in Gdansk join workers in protests at the Lenin Shipyard during the summer of 1980. Women played a central role in the movement that became Solidarity and brought about the end of communist rule.

CZECH REPUBLIC

GENERAL

type of government: Republic
major ethnic groups: Czech (81%); Moravians (13%); Slovaks
language(s): Czech
religions: Atheist; Roman Catholic; Protestant

DEMOGRAPHICS

population size: 10.3 million
birth rate (*per 1,000 population*): 13
total fertility (*average number of births per woman*): 1.9
contraceptive prevalence (*married women*): 69%
maternal mortality rate (*per 100,000 live births*): 14

WOMEN'S STATUS

date of women's suffrage: 1920
economically active population*: M 77%   F 62%
female employment (*% of total workforce*): 47
life expectancy   M 69   F 77
school enrollment ratio (*F/100 M*)*

primary	97
secondary	170
tertiary	73

literacy*   M 99%   F 99%

*Data for Czechoslovakia, 1990

The very concept of gender as we understand it in the "West" is difficult to convey here since in Polish, Czech, Slovak, and Hungarian the word for *gender* has only a narrowly grammatical connotation (i.e., the gender of a given noun) and not a sociocultural one, while the word *sex* has only a narrowly biological connotation. The whole situation is additionally complicated by the very complex attitudes toward feminism in this part of Europe. The very word *feminism* is perceived as a pejorative one, and it is considered political suicide for a woman active in public life to identify herself primarily with women's issues.

SLOVAKIA

GENERAL

type of government: Republic
major ethnic groups: Slovak (87%); Hungarian (10%); Gypsy
language: Slovak (official); Hungarian
religions: Roman Catholic; Protestant; Eastern Orthodox; Uniate

DEMOGRAPHICS

population size: 5.3 million
birth rate (*per 1,000 population*): 15
total fertility (*average number of births per woman*): 2
contraceptive prevalence (*married women*): 77%
maternal mortality rate (*per 100,000 live births*): 14

WOMEN'S STATUS

date of women's suffrage: 1920
economically active population*: M 77%   F 62%
female employment (*% of total workforce*): 43
life expectancy   M 68.6   F 77.2
school enrollment ratio (*F/100 M*)*

primary	97
secondary	170
tertiary	73

literacy*   M 99%   F 99%

*Data for Czechoslovakia, 1990

Despite the seeming similarity between some of the problems faced by women in Western Europe and those faced by women in the postcommunist countries, there are overwhelming differences that, if not fully grasped, present obstacles to communication between women activists of the West and their counterparts in the more western countries of the former Soviet bloc that are considered here: Poland, Hungary, the Czech Republic, and Slovakia. Communication is often more difficult precisely because these differences do not entail issues as striking or dramatic as those of veiling or female circumcision, which women in some postcolo-

POLAND

GENERAL

type of government: Democratic Republic
major ethnic groups: Polish (98%); German; Ukranian; Byelorussian
language(s): Polish
religions: Roman Catholic (94%); Eastern Orthodox; Protestant

DEMOGRAPHICS

population size: 38.4 million
birth rate (*per 1,000 population*): 14
total fertility (*average number of births per woman*): 1.9
contraceptive prevalence (*married women*): 75%
maternal mortality rate (*per 100,000 live births*): 15

WOMEN'S STATUS

date of women's suffrage: 1918
economically active population: M 77%   F 60%
female employment (*% of total workforce*): 46
life expectancy   M 66.8   F 75.5
school enrollment ratio (*F/100 M*)

primary	95
secondary	103
tertiary	127

literacy   M 99%   F 99%

---

nial countries must contend with. The differences arise primarily out of the substantially different experience of women throughout the Soviet bloc during the recent forty-year period of their officially proclaimed equality and all their officially extended "privileges." To understand the dynamic of, and the prospects for, the women's movement in the postcommunist societies, I have found it useful to review the discourse regarding their own position that was initiated just a few years ago by women in Poland, Hungary, and Czechoslovakia.

My choice of these countries is based not just on geographic considerations but on cultural affinities and certain similarities in their historical experience. These include their shared exposure to the world of the Hapsburg Empire (as opposed to

HUNGARY

GENERAL

type of government: Parliamentary democracy
major ethnic groups: Magyar (92%); German (2.5%); Gypsy (3%); Serb; Slovak;
   Romanian
language(s): Hungarian
religions: Roman Catholic (67%); Protestant (25%)
date of independence: 1001 (unification)

DEMOGRAPHICS

population size: 10.3 million
birth rate (*per 1,000 population*): 12
total fertility (*average number of births per woman*): 1.8
contraceptive prevalence (*married women*): 73%
maternal mortality rate (*per 100,000 live births*): 15

WOMEN'S STATUS

date of women's suffrage: 1945
economically active population: M 72%   F 53%
female employment (*% of total workforce*): 45
life expectancy   M 66   F 75
school enrollment ratio (*F/100 M*)
   primary   95
   secondary   98
   tertiary   115
literacy   M 99%   F 98%

---

the Ottoman Empire, which left its mark on the Balkans) and to some democratic values and institutions between the world wars as well as the fact that they were the only countries to generate a succession (every twelve years!) of upheavals against the communist system: the Hungarian October in 1956, the Prague Spring in 1968, and Polish Solidarity in 1980–1981. The experience of these movements has significantly reinforced the already existing cleavage between these three countries of Central Europe and the rest of the postcommunist states. Polish historian Adam Michnik has pointed out that the protest movements in Hungary,

A Hungarian woman carries a machine gun in Budapest during the 1956 revolt against the Soviets.

Czechoslovakia, and Poland shared the goal of broadening national and civil rights, while they differed in the dynamics of their social change.[1] But the experience—however different for each country—of building civil society has certainly contributed to the emergence since 1989 of a greater degree of independent discourse on the situation and role of women than has emerged in other countries of the region.

"Until recently I never divided issues into male and female issues. Now I am noticing that actual women's rights in Poland are being threatened. So women's issues have faced me right here on our own front doorstep, and not just slipped in through the international back door."[2] This confession, made in the fall of 1992 by a physician who was then deputy speaker of the Polish Parliament, Olga Krzyzanowska, reflects an extremely crucial process now—slowly and with a lot of resistance—taking place throughout the female population of East and Central Europe: the process of discovering and acknowledging that there is a problem of women in the first place. With the exception of the former Yugoslavia, where both a women's movement and the introduction of free market mechanisms started well before 1989, this process is conspicuously parallel to the closely monitored and studied process of transition from communism to democracy and a market economy.

Krzyzanowska's statement was made in an interview that was considered courageous in Poland and yet at the same time indicative of a changing attitude among ever-larger groups of women. The process of discovering, acknowledging, and defining women's problems is not an easy one, especially in the context of postcommunist societies undergoing systemic transformation. One of the by-products of this transformation has been the rise of nationalist ideologies in which the rights of the nation as a community are given priority over the rights of the citizen. Women are defined here as bearers of the community's distinctive ethnic lineage and are therefore considered a vital factor in national survival. This logic provided a strong argument for the antiabortion lobby in Hungary; it has taken a more perverse form in the at least partially systematic rape of Muslim women in Bosnia as an instrument of "ethnic cleansing."

Women in East and Central Europe are now beginning to recognize both the constraints they were subjected to in the past and those they are facing now. The scale and the depth of this change in awareness are different in each of the four postcommunist countries I am considering here—Poland, the Czech Republic, Slovakia, and Hungary—but in any case it has already begun to create a hitherto unknown intellectual and political climate around women and the question of women.

My focus on these four countries, as I have already indicated, is not accidental. They are not only perceived by the outside world (with its watchful agencies: the World Bank, the International Monetary Fund, the European Community, and the Council of Europe) as the most stable ones in the region and the most advanced in the transition process, but they are the ones that presented the greatest challenges to totalitarianism over the past forty years and that, to varying degrees, gained practical experience in building dissent, creating alternative social structures, and expanding civil society within the communist order. The best-known outbreaks of freedom provided these societies not only with the memory of a joyous taste of democracy but also with practice in self-organization, which could potentially enhance an emerging movement's chances of success.

So in many ways the situation of women in the four countries is similar; yet on closer inspection one finds that in each country the situation is different. The similarities stem from the shared model of the communist order, which was imposed on the bloc as a whole, its legislation uniformly devised in accordance with ideological principles, its clonelike, Soviet-type institutions structuring the social life of each country in similar ways. The differences arise from the specificity of pre-1945 cultural and political traditions and also from the divergent applications of the Soviet model, known as the countries' different "roads to socialism." The differences were further modified during the last decades by the citizenries' varied experiences and accomplishments in their efforts to create civil societies.

In all four countries, the existing constitutions still guarantee—as they did before 1989—the fundamental rights and freedoms of all, regardless of differences of sex, race, religion, ethnic background, and so on. Yet equality for women never did—and still does not—extend much beyond their participation in employment. If one looks at the numbers, the similarities become especially striking. All four countries show very high employment rates for women (70–90 percent), a striking gender segregation of the labor force, and 20–30 percent lower pay for women than for men. The high participation of women in the labor market results from the needs of postwar industrialization, identical in all four countries; from the priority given to ideological principles; and from the pressure on individual families to supplement the family income.

However, the principle of equal pay, explicit in the legislation of all four countries, was and remains a purely theoretical declaration, and in the context of the market economy gender discrimination, especially in hiring practices, is more pronounced than ever (and is openly expressed in the language of newspaper want ads). Growing unemployment, which results from the restructuring of industries, the closing of Soviet markets, and the shrinking of interbloc trade, affects women more than men, especially in Poland and Slovakia.

Similarities are also evident in the legacy of fairly uniform communist legislation, such as protective labor legislation, child care provisions, and abortion rights. All of these are now endangered because of new economic and political factors. The old structural supports for working women—a system of nurseries and kindergartens, similarly designed in the four countries, overcrowded, and often criticized in the past for causing developmental problems in children—are now collapsing, either closing their doors or drastically raising their fees. (Some of the most vocal political groupings in these countries see this development as help-ful in the new effort to define a woman's role in terms of mother and homemaker.)

Looking at the lives of women in particular, one can observe a pair of striking paradoxes. The first is that for many in politics the most politically rewarding be-havior in the first postcommunist years seemed to be that which focused on eradi-cating all remnants of the previous system, which included, ironically, its own un-fulfilled commitments to human rights in general and to women's rights in particular. The second paradox is that the only spheres of freedom available under communist rule, those provided by the Church in Poland, by the so-called second economy in Hungary, and by the family in Czechoslovakia, have now for women become spheres of constraint.

In all four countries (three before 1993), a quota system had been designed by the Communists to ensure that women's participation in Parliament would be nu-merically high but passive (about 30 percent in all three). Various analyses of the composition of the Polish Parliament show that women had always been selected to demonstrate the thesis that even young, inexperienced nonprofessionals with-out political backing could become members of Parliament (MP). Women were selected in such a way as to represent all these features simultaneously. This is why women, to a greater extent than the male MPs, played the role of *fillers*. They were always a numerical minority, but their influence was even smaller than their num-bers might have suggested.[3]

Since the quota was dropped after 1989, the participation of women has been numerically much smaller: about 8–14 percent in each Parliament. But those women now participating are much more visible in the public life of the country, which is sometimes attributed to their average level of education, which is statisti-cally higher than that of men, and to their considerable legislative and political ex-perience.[4] Yet even among those women visible in public life, it is still the excep-tion rather than the rule when they pay any attention to the mounting problems facing women or act on their behalf. On the contrary, there is a continuing as-sumption among many women policymakers and lawmakers that women's prob-lems are inseparable from the problems facing society as a whole and should not be gendered. One of the reasons for such a widely shared position is the need to avoid resembling either of the two models of the woman activist that have been widely ridiculed: that of the thoroughly discredited official communist "women's representative" (whether in Parliament or in some other high office) and that of the Western feminist, parodied with some success by the communist media as a spoiled, pathetic, professionally unsuccessful activist who, on top of everything else, frequently uses the language—so compromised here—of socialist doctrine.

But in the course of the 1990s, in Warsaw, Budapest, Prague, and Bratislava—places where the political scene is more and more frequently looked upon with disappointment and disgust—one has also been able to detect the reemergence of a public-spirited ethos exemplified more often than not by certain individual women and women's groups in parliaments and beyond. Such an ethos combines the experience and civic commitment of former dissidents (from the democratic opposition of the 1970s and 1980s) with a readiness to address imaginatively the unfamiliar challenges of new political and economic circumstances. These women are beginning to be respected by both the broader public and the political elites either because of—or in spite of—their commitment to women's issues.

In Hungary and Poland it was the fight for the preservation of reproductive rights that helped crystallize such an ethos and bring about a broader recognition of women policymakers. In each of the four countries the new women's initiatives are introducing to political and public life an anticonservative agenda and are working on those issues that are the least rewarding politically. In Poland such women established the Women's Parliamentary Group and successfully competed with men in the autumn 1993 elections to Parliament, increasing their participation from 9 to 13 percent. In Hungary such women MPs created in 1992 the Foundation of the Women of Hungary (MONA), dedicated to women's issues, and organized a national women's roundtable the following year, which for the first time brought together all Hungarian women's organizations, representing the full political spectrum—an initiative unthinkable for the dramatically divided political parties in 1993 Hungary. In Czechoslovakia, a well-known former dissident and member of Charter 77 (the human and civil rights movement founded in 1977 by Václav Havel and others), Jirina Siklova, established in 1992 a gender studies center, lending a badly needed credibility to the budding discourse on the social position of women. After the "Velvet Divorce" of Czechoslovakia in 1993, a group of women in the new country of Slovakia not only launched a journal, *Aspekt,* devoted to "unpopular" women's issues but also flouted the official political line in pointedly disregarding the Czechoslovak breakup by making their journal, though published in Bratislava, a joint Czecho-Slovak initiative.

In its often Sisyphean effort to build and strengthen women's organizations, to communicate their concerns effectively to broader groups of women, and to win sympathizers, readers, members, and activists, the emerging women's movement has downplayed some issues that are regarded as too radical for the general public. Only rarely does one hear women's groups addressing in public the problem of sexual harassment or domestic rape and, almost never, sexual difference.[5] Lesbian women involved in women's groups are choosing, usually for tactical reasons, not to confront the issue and further jeopardize the movement's chances of growing. It is hard enough in some women's groups just to call oneself a feminist; one must struggle to overcome a prejudice against the very word.

The problem of women and race, limited as it is in this part of Europe, is beginning to gain some attention with regard to the Roma women, or Gypsies, especially in the countries with a significant Roma population (Hungary, 5–10 percent, Czech Republic, 4–6 percent, and Slovakia, 4–8 percent). Roma women have their own separate organizations, with only very weak connections to other women's groups.

Finding a Voice

At the end of 1992 one of the first books to articulate the problems of women in postcommunist countries was published as the result of a grassroots effort in Poland. The publication, entitled *Women Have the Floor*,[6] is not a translation from English, German, or French but a collection of original essays by Polish women on what it means to be a woman in Poland. The book documents one of the key preoccupations of most active women in the region after 1989: conducting a debate on the recent past—that is, on the specificity of women's experience under communism and its repercussions for the character of the women's movement in these countries. Similar questions appear in a Hungarian feminist periodical, *Nostemely (Female)*, published irregularly since 1991, and in the Slovak *Aspekt* (since 1993). Such questions are also raised at every conference, seminar, and workshop where women from the region get together, often with their Western counterparts.

There are several reasons one should look closely at these debates. In most of the postcommunist countries, where there are various women's groups but no sizable, organized movement at the national level, the very existence of the debates brings women's issues into better focus. In fact, they are the very first manifestation of women's self-mobilization around women's issues and, in some countries, the only one. In Poland and in Hungary more challenging circumstances (especially antiabortion legislation) mobilized women earlier on. Women's movements in other countries, too, may emerge in response to immediate circumstances, but the character and strategies of all of them will be largely determined by the past or, more precisely, by the outcome of their reflection upon those elements from the past that have shaped the identities of Polish, Hungarian, Czech, or Slovak women.

As I look at the debates in those countries with which I am most familiar, the most frequently raised theme is the complexity of the situation women lived in under communism. The argument most commonly offered throughout the region to explain the absence of women's protest in the past—an argument that primarily reflects the views of women from the intelligentsia—runs as follows: There existed a sense of solidarity between men and women under state socialism since they regarded themselves as equally repressed by the centrally controlled institutional structures of the state; so the energies of every social movement were directed entirely toward activities having the potential to effect systemic change. Therefore, as most women in these countries point out, all other issues—including women's issues—seemed at that time to be of secondary importance.

Now that those first steps have been accomplished, two new goals are in order: democratization and marketization. Are women taking part in advancing them? Are they included in the shaping of the new legal, social, and economic order? How do they regard their situation under the new circumstances? Are they actually involved in addressing their own situation as women? The very state of the women's movement is closely related to how the women in each country are handling these questions.

There is yet another goal formulated immediately after the collapse of the Berlin Wall and intensely pursued ever since by the governments of Poland, Hungary, and the Czech and Slovak republics. It is captured in the popular slogan "Return to Europe!" But given the fact that in the process of democratization and the transition to a market economy virtually no room has been allowed for the participation of women or women's organizations—that, in fact, women's role is being relegated to hearth and home—there has arisen an uncomfortable issue for the governments of the region: that they do not meet the standards of the European Community and the Council of Europe when it comes to equality between men and women, as required in the various documents of these organizations. Women's groups in all four countries are using these instruments more and more (even though some only have the character of recommendations) to argue their case and to initiate discussion on practical ways to realize the constitutional principle of the equality of all citizens without regard to gender.

Czech and Slovak Women After Communism: An Escape from Forced Emancipation

For a Westerner, one of the most puzzling trends in post-1989 Czechoslovakia has been the expressed desire of women to withdraw from the world of work into the world of the household, domesticity, and the family. Several factors underlie this trend, and most of them are related to the way women experienced the communist sociopolitical order. But in the Czech Republic especially, an additional factor is the fact that economic reform was not introduced in the manner of "shock therapy," and has neither caused massive unemployment nor generally lowered the standard of living.

For this retreat into domesticity, the simplest and most frequent explanation offered by Czech women is, "We were overemancipated and still are." This attitude seems to be quite disturbing for many of the women activists from the West who visit fashionable Prague. The energies of Czech and Slovak women activists and intellectuals are directed toward explanations that often tend toward defensiveness (e.g., the argument, which I examine more closely in the following section, that emancipation was not a matter of choice but was imposed from above).

This strong preference for the private sphere in general and the family in partic-ular, as the only realm where Václav Havel's "living in truth" is possible, is further reinforced by the Czechs' and Slovaks' relatively limited experience of civil society in the 1970s and 1980s. After the crackdown on the Prague Spring of 1968, Czecho-slovakia became one of the most repressive regimes in the region, and Charter 77's activities, though well known abroad, were confined to a relatively small circle of courageous intellectuals. The combination of these two elements has made the sit-uation of Czech and Slovak women—since the very beginning of the changes in 1989—quite different from that of the Poles and Hungarians. In Slovakia, which is Catholic and whose population is generally more religious than the faintly Protes-tant Czechs, the focus on family has a less secular explanation. The family was and is the traditional center of spiritual life, offering asylum from the pressures of the official structures to conform. Czechoslovak families also developed successful strategies for accessing the goods, both material and cultural, controlled by the state by placing various family members in different key positions. This very spe-cial role of the family (analyzed by a sociologist from Brno, Ivo Mozny) in playing the game, or cheating the state, in a "redistribution of commodities" further strengthened the family's position in Czechoslovakia.

Through my visits to Prague and Bratislava over the last couple of years I have come to realize that the vast majority of women here do not feel they are in any way worse off than men are. Slovak women told me in the summer of 1994 that most of the problems they face are not specific or exclusive to women but are fam-ily problems caused by the economic transformation and the split of Czechoslo-vakia (unemployment, loss of social services, divided families, the sex trade, and citizenship issues). One Czech participant in the debate on women's issues, Hana Havelkova, observed in 1992 that "nothing has yet happened publicly to show women the importance of their solidarity, their lobbies, and their political repre-sentation, and they do not yet think about it themselves."[7]

The antiabortion legislation that provoked Polish and Hungarian women to or-ganize themselves did not take place in either the Czech or Slovak republic. Abor-tion is still legal, but Czech women have to pay a fee that comes close to their aver-age monthly salary and that thus discriminates against poorer women. The severe restriction on the right to abortion that was attempted by the Christian-Demo-cratic government in Slovakia never materialized. Abortions performed during the first six weeks of pregnancy are free, and those performed during the second six weeks require a relatively small payment. There is yet another serious problem, that of female prostitution, which is not discussed publicly at all in this Catholic country: But it is only a one-hour drive from Bratislava to Vienna, Slovaks do not need visas to get to Austria, and for enterprising women the exchange rate can make such trips very lucrative.

Among the more than thirty women's organizations that one might find (most of them only on paper) in the Czech Republic and a comparable number registered in Slovakia, there are very few that express any interest in actually advancing the position of women. Some of them, relics of the past such as the formerly communist Czech Women's Union and Slovak Women's Union (which still retain considerable property and claim memberships in the hundreds of thousands), have lost all their legitimacy. Every political party has its own women's section, convenient for the leadership in its foreign contacts but not particularly active on the national scene.

In both countries of the former Czechoslovakia, as in Poland and Hungary, there is a strong negative reaction among women to the idea of participation in any large nationwide organization. The image of the *sodruzka,* the communist token woman, is still associated in their minds with such structures and still haunts them. "We are neither *sodruzky* nor feminists. We are women." And they prefer to define themselves, for example, as female intellectuals from Bratislava. This cautious search for self-identity and for a definition of women's position in society has been conducted since 1990 through an ongoing debate and through activities that help facilitate that debate. One item of documentation produced in this effort is the so-called Blue Book, entitled, *Bodies of Bread and Butter: Reconfiguring Women's Lives in the Postcommunist Czech Republic.*[8]

Only relatively recently have projects been developed that actually address the concrete problems of women. One such transitional institution that recognizes both the need for debate and the need to tackle immediate problems is the Meeting Place. Supported partially by the Gender Studies Center, its major activity entails organizing legal and psychological services for elderly women while tapping their memories of the past. Foundation ROSA is mostly preoccupied with organizing help for divorced women, and work has begun on setting up a crisis hotline and resource center for female victims of violence.

The debate brings women together in conferences, seminars, lectures, and publications, and—what is more important—it gradually and constantly extends the number of those engaged in it. The first institutional and inspirational hub of these activities was the Gender Studies Center, founded in 1991 by former dissident Jirina Siklova and situated for its first two years, along with an impressive library of feminist literature, in her own apartment in Prague. The statement of its goals reflects what I call the debate-oriented character of this young movement: "to raise gender consciousness in society: to encourage public discussion, research, writing, publication, and study that re-evaluate the roles, images, and positions of men and women."

In Bratislava a group of women originally associated with the progressive literary monthly *Slovenske Pohlady* (Slovak Views) and prompted by the government decision to close it established their own—this time, female only—quarterly. Its title, *Aspekt,* is discreetly accompanied by the female sign: ♀ . The editorial article of the first issue (1993) states their mission clearly: "The old social roles are falling apart and we have to find our place in the new ones."[9] *Aspekt,* which cultivates the civic ideals of the first prodemocratic and antinationalist movement in post-1989 Slovakia, the Public Against Violence, is trying to disregard the split of Czechoslovakia and has created through a joint editorial board a bridge between the readers in both countries who are interested in women's issues. The group around *Aspekt,* constantly striving to remain as informal as possible, has managed to open a library in Bratislava, which is the starting point for an educational center in gender studies.

The Czech and Slovak Debate: Emancipation from Above

By 1948, argues Jirina Siklova, it was clear to the Czechoslovak Communist Party planners that the women's emancipation movement could serve the ideological objectives of the communist system. These entailed a buildup of heavy industry, especially in Slovakia, and a transfer of the labor force from the countryside to the cities. The party regime argued that the effective emancipation of women depended upon their entering the labor force, which could lead to their economic independence. Therefore, party leaders popularized the "working woman" as a role model throughout the 1950s. Hana Navarova, one of the few Czech sociologists studying women's issues, says in her paper "What Did Socialism Give to Women?" that by the 1960s it was also clear that through this emancipation women were being forced to take on a dual role: working woman and housewife/mother.[10] Moreover, their family obligations were holding them back professionally. In a vicious circle, this disadvantageous position at work would further incline them to retreat to the family.

Around this time, Czechoslovakia experienced a significant drop in population, and the state offered a variety of privileges to women who opted for childbearing. Siklova points out that such privileges were awarded only to women when it was felt they would further the development of socialism. For example, when the cheap labor force needed in the 1950s was an economic priority, the maximum maternity leave was four months; but in the 1970s, when the labor market was saturated, priorities changed, and maternity leave was gradually extended to as much as three years. According to research, the very high rate of female employment (currently 90 percent of all working-age women) is primarily the result of financial necessity and only partially an expression of women's professional aspirations.[11]

In Slovakia, which had traditionally been rural, rapid industrialization over the past forty years created a huge army of workers who still live in villages and cultivate their small plots of land but who commute long distances to work in the cities. At the factories women usually work the early shift, and just as they head back for home, their husbands are starting the second shift, often at the same factory. Helena Wolekova, until June 1992 Slovakia's minister of labor, has characterized this as an even further crippling of the family, in which, in accordance with the

Czechoslovak model, both parents work in any case. These women are doing triple duty: in the factory, on the farm, and in the home. What sort of emancipation is that? she asks.[12] Women "were reduced to a cheap source of labor that could be plugged in anywhere without regard to specific capabilities, prerequisites, or ambitions"—so argue two Slovak women philosophers from the *Aspekt* circle.[13]

As a result of this forced emancipation of women in Czechoslovakia, which can be interpreted either in terms of ideological necessity (for the state) or economic necessity (for families, most of which needed two incomes to survive), there now exists among women a kind of allergic reaction to all forms of public involvement. Today liberation does not mean escaping from domesticity. It means acknowledging the family's recent role as a refuge, a place providing shelter from a paternalistic state that always knew "what was best" for the people. And so today for many Czech women liberation means precisely a return to the family, seen as a space where one's lost dignity can be recovered. In Slovakia the question of who can afford this newfound freedom is answered as follows: businessmen's wives.

The traumatic experience of the crushing of the 1968 Prague Spring introduced another factor into the "centrally planned emancipation" of many women of the Czechoslovak intelligentsia. In order to escape the increased pressures of official ideology, an entire generation of politically active young women turned to the family because the family was the only realm sheltered from state control. In the words of Miroslava Holubova, an English teacher and cofounder of a women's group called New Humanity, "If we had won in '68, I don't think I would have had a family right away. I would have been a *public* person: a journalist, a politician. ... But for me the only choice, psychologically, was emigration or having babies."[14] Alexandra Berkova, a well-known writer and the author of New Humanity's manifesto, argues that women, who came home from work to meet their first priority—creating a protective environment for the family—emerged from the totalitarian system psychologically stronger than men, who were more completely exposed to the system.[15]

These educated and critical women, now in their forties, are in fact excited about the possibilities for reentering a public arena that is no longer monopolized by a repressive state. But for twenty years—as they frankly admit—the family was their safe haven and the only place where they could find fulfillment. They are well aware of the fact that to the outsider they appear to be full of contradictions, with their mixed conservative and progressive ideas about women's roles in a changing society. And they will have to face a still small but growing number of younger women still in university and taking their first gender studies courses whose views are both less accommodating to the home-and-hearth tradition and more resistant to the current situation in which women have no voice.

For the moment such student women are the main constituency for the Bratislava-based *Aspekt*. Run rather cautiously by women scholars and writers who for the most part do not want to be labeled as feminists, the journal presents highly abstract articles, translations, and, much less frequently, materials that deal specifically with women in Slovakia. But since *Aspekt* and its circle are perceived as belonging to the antinationalistic and anti-Meciar opposition, the journal has appeal for a broader group of democratically minded intellectuals and is therefore able to lend legitimacy to university gender studies, which still badly need it at the local level. No matter how elitist the current initiatives by women intellectuals may be, they are breaking new ground and are opening up a space—unthinkable just a few years ago—in which women's issues can be considered at all.

Hungarian Women: Between the Past and the West

An outside observer can notice some similarities between the activities of Hungarian women and those of women in the former Czechoslovakia: What is mobilizing women from various—though still mostly intellectual—circles and bringing them together is their reflection on their former and present situations and how these compare with the experience of Western women. One might reasonably argue that in trying to position themselves vis-à-vis the West and vis-à-vis the past, Hungarian, Czech, and Slovak women are engaged in laying the necessary groundwork for confronting the challenges they will inevitably face as a group.

Hungarians talking to Western feminists try to refute the latter's easy assumptions about the privileges women were granted under communism. Eniko Bollobas, who in 1989 founded a political discussion group called Hungarian Feminists, challenged the widespread stereotype of women from the region during a meeting in Strasbourg in the fall of 1992: "Women are not suffering because of the collapse of Communism, but because of the damage Communism has done to their mentality. This has not yet collapsed."[16]

Like some of the Czech feminists, Bollobas points to a problem that may be the greatest obstacle not only to the emergence of a women's movement but also to the very process of democratization in the postcommunist countries. As individuals, people were not encouraged to develop and experience—much less allowed to exercise—their autonomy, self-reliance, or initiative. Despite such general similarities, certain specificities of Hungarian communism made the experience of women in this country quite different.

The departure from the previous system in 1989 was not as dramatically clearcut and spectacular here as it was in Czechoslovakia. Structural changes in the Hungarian economy had already begun in the late 1960s with the general mixing of the command economy with a free market. By the 1980s the process that led to the emergence of this "second economy" had created the peculiar socioeconomic experiment known as "goulash communism."

The Hungarian Debate: The Goulash Economy
and Women's Triple Burden

By introducing a liberalized economic and employment policy in the mid-1960s, a time of chronic shortages, the Kadar regime established conditions under which people were able to improve their living standards by taking second and even third jobs in their own or other small businesses. This second economy, or "private sector," a sphere of economic activity that was legal but outside of the state monopoly and came to be known as the goulash economy, had a major impact on many areas of production. Between 1960 and 1980 it built more apartments and produced more agricultural goods than did the state sector. For individuals, the second economy provided a sphere of freedom from total state control that was unknown in other socialist countries. It created a climate in which people could learn how to make their own choices, take responsibility for their own decisions, and find a new kind of self-respect. (The only comparable situation existed in the Polish countryside, where the majority of private middle-sized farms were in the hands of peasants and were never nationalized.) This important vehicle for maintaining economic standards and reclaiming some degree of personal autonomy from the state depended heavily upon the support of the family unit and a kind of family self-exploitation. It therefore imposed limitations in other areas, and one of those areas affected women: It forced them to concentrate on their traditional role as homemaker even while working and often being otherwise professionally active at the same time.

The second economy, argues sociologist Olga Toth,[17] required a very specific division of labor within the family, one that reinforced existing assumptions about gender roles. Typically, both husband and wife worked in the first (state-run) economy. Then the wife returned home to assume the domestic responsibilities, while the husband went to his second wage-earning job and often on weekends to a third one. By managing the household, and serving as liaison between the family and the bureaucracies governing housing, health care, schools, and even vacation planning, the wife made it possible for the man to be involved in the second economy, thus benefiting the family. Observers often stress that without this mutual support within the family, the second economy could not have functioned since most single men and women could not have handled such a triple burden: a first job, a second job, and the bureaucratic and household demands of everyday life. Approximately 75 percent of families participated in the second economy in various ways, and in effect, since 1989, they still do. Since the late 1970s, this Hungarian specificity, which sociologist Julia Szalai has described as "symbolizing autonomy, cooperation, and success for men and women who share their efforts within it,"[18] has complicated the already difficult situation of women in Hungary.

Economic necessity underlies the popularity of early marriage in Hungary. As Toth points out, establishing a family offers Hungarians more strategies for survival than does remaining unmarried: special social benefits, a better chance for an apartment, at least two incomes, and the necessary conditions for entering the second economy. Yet juggling the roles of employee, housekeeper, and mother throughout an extremely long working day (including those evening and weekend hours when the husband is at his second or third job) has contributed to a very high rate of emotional and mental disorders among Hungarian women: 37 percent in the most active age group (30 to 59).

Why There Is No Women's Movement in Hungary

On Hungary's present political stage, as in any other postcommunist country, there is a striking absence of women. There is also at the moment only a slim chance for the emergence of a women's movement on the national level. For one thing, since 1989 there has been no radical change in the social and economic status of women. As yet the most serious economic and social problems of the new Hungary are not specifically "women's" problems. Despite growing unemployment, for example, especially outside of Budapest, women are not affected by it to the same extent as men since the biggest reduction in jobs has taken place in heavy industry and mining, where most employees are men. It is expected that a second wave of unemployment will hit light industry (because of the collapse of the Soviet market), service industries, and the public sector (because of cuts in state and local budgets). The victims of these employment cuts will mainly be the women who predominate in these industries.

There are three groups of reasons offered by Hungarian women to explain the absence of a women's movement, and the arguments one hears have been a part of the debate since the late 1980s. The first argument, already mentioned, points to the heritage of the communist past: a paternalistic state that infantilized society and typecast women. The second—true for all countries of the region but often a revelation for Westerners—is that women's issues have not achieved agenda status; on the contrary, since 1989 they have constituted a forbidden agenda. In March 1994, six weeks before the parliamentary elections, women's groups organized a forum for the main political parties and asked them what their policies toward women were. They did not have any. They also had very few women running for Parliament. The situation, argue Hungarians, is a vicious circle: Women do not get into decisionmaking positions if they talk about women's issues, and they are underrepresented in public life precisely because women's issues are not taken seriously. The third argument cites the vulnerability of the existing women's organizations, trapped between the past and the West. For example, there are two organizations of professionally active urban women in Hungary: the Association of Hungarian Women and the Feminist Network. Both of them are perceived as controversial, but for opposite reasons: The association, for its connection with the communist past, and the network, for its links to the West.

The Association of Hungarian Women was established in 1989 as the successor to the Women's Council, which was an official organization backed by the Communist Party. Although it inherited the council's considerable property, the association now emphasizes its nonpartisan orientation. In its brochure published in 1992, it claims to represent the interests of women and families from different walks of life, with the main objective being "the realization of women's social equality and equal rights."

The Feminist Network, established in 1990, is a much smaller, nonbureaucratic, activist-driven organization whose major goal, as stated in its flier, is "to work against all forms of discrimination against women ... [and] to encourage the participation of women in political life." The network's main liability is that its active participants include a few women from the West: Americans and Britons studying or working in Hungary. Additionally, their organization's name, which was deliberately selected to indicate a commitment to a feminist perspective, is widely considered pejorative in Hungary and has a clearly nondomestic, Western connotation. As I learned when attending one of the network's meetings, all of the participants (mostly in their twenties, thirties, and early forties) had originally become interested in feminism through foreign contacts: a trip abroad or a Western visitor.

Recognizing that the perception of the group's activities is constantly damaged by the very word *feminism,* the Feminist Network, which has recently been functioning as a much looser structure, is gradually dropping the discredited label. The new projects it launched in the beginning of 1994 and through which it wants to reach more women are using straightforwardly self-descriptive names: Women for Women Against Domestic Violence (NANE) and Women's House. The former has organized the first telephone hotline in Hungary and counseling in cases of domestic and sexual violence and has plans for organizing a public education campaign on violence, including a training program for professionals such as lawyers, physicians, and members of the police force.

The second project, Women's House, was organized by an initiative known as the Ombudswoman's Office, which is affiliated with the Department of Social Policy at ELTE University. Women's House, which occupies two rooms in an old former building of the Communist Party, is open during evening hours and offers women the free services of a lawyer and a social worker on matters involving divorce laws, custody laws, child support, or the need for lodging in one of Budapest's two shelters for women. There is a visible effort under way in Budapest to play down Western feminist connections and to rely more on domestic or regional collaborations. In establishing the NANE hotline, experienced women from Belgrade's SOS-HOTLINE, who came to Budapest to provide training for eighteen Hungarian hotline volunteers, played an important role.

The problem of foreign interest in women's issues in Hungary has another dimension. As I was frequently reminded during my stay in Hungary, almost all scholarly research on women in Hungary has so far been inspired, financed, and published by foreign institutions or agencies. Although this activity has raised the awareness of women's problems among the cosmopolitan circles of Budapest's women intellectuals (one of them, Maria Adamik, acknowledging that Western women played an important role as facilitators of feminism), many say that outside of academia there seems to be no market for this research on women's issues. Critics point out that it tends to address a Western set of questions, is tailored to fit the programs of international conferences and English-language publications, is not channeled back to Hungary, and therefore has virtually no impact on the way Hungarians perceive women. Those engaged in the Hungarian debate are aware that there is a lack of connection between academia and the "real world." And they recognize yet another cleavage: that between Budapest and the provinces. Both these gaps, while not limited to women's issues, impede in particular the laying of any groundwork for a nationwide women's movement.

Poland: From Debate to Action

When in April 1989 a team of sociologists asked a representative sampling of Poles to choose from a list the one category that best defined their identity, gender came in last place, after (in this order) human being, Pole, parent, and occupation. The survey was conducted at the time of the roundtable negotiations between the Solidarity-rooted opposition and the ruling Communist Party, during which the communist regime was being forced by society to share power. The feeling of solidarity against the system on the part of all citizens was very strong, and in this struggle gender was a negligible social variable.

But today, after more than five years during which women's civil rights have been put into question and even denied, the same survey would probably yield very different results, with gender almost certainly winning a much higher place on the list. The new antiabortion legislation, which went into effect in March 1993, was preceded by four years of escalating protests organized by women. These, together with the additional impetus given to the mobilization of women by the spectacular rise of women's unemployment after 1990, in fact laid the foundation for a new and growing women's movement in Poland.

The relatively long experience of the Solidarity movement of 1980–1981, in which Poles—with the notable participation of Polish women—practiced the self-organization of citizens independently from governmental structures, is an important source of the difference between the state of the women's movement in Poland and that in the other countries of East and Central Europe. Another difference comes from the unusual position the Catholic church has occupied in Polish

Polish textile workers, among twelve thousand townspeople in Żyrardów protesting food shortages in late October 1981, pray at a makeshift altar outside a factory. The church's central role in Polish life and politics has proven to be a challenge to the contemporary women's movement.

political life. According to popular wisdom, as manifested in the parliaments throughout East and Central Europe, the first step toward a successful transformation to democracy must be a radical departure from the communist past. The vacuum left after the collapse of communism in Poland—and after official ideology had vanished—was quickly filled by the Catholic church. The new political correctness that emerged is visible in parliamentary laws (religious instruction in school, antiabortion laws, restitution of church property), in the recently signed concordat with the Vatican, in the media (now obliged to observe "Christian values"), and in public life. The Polish debate on women's issues therefore examines the impact of the church on the past and current role of women.

Feminism made its very first, shy appearance in Poland among university students in the early 1980s, and this is when the debate on women's issues began. Because of its longer history, today's discourse—compared with that in the other countries I am examining here—is much less Western oriented and Western driven and to a much greater degree generated by indigenous questions and problems. It involves women scholars, journalists, and politicians but also a new breed of women activists. The experience of the past is examined and discussed but is only one of the many issues reflected in the debate.

The Polish Debate: Between Motherhood and Motherland

For the last forty-five years, Poles have been as much affected by the Catholic church—the only institutional survivor from the past—as by the institutional framework of "real socialism." The threatened position of the church vis-à-vis the communist regime afforded the church a particularly strong position vis-à-vis Polish society. Its already high moral authority was further strengthened in the early 1970s when the church became an ally of the democratic opposition and provided a base for many oppositional activities. Before 1980 (pre-Solidarity times) and after the imposition of martial law in December 1981, the church provided the only space where Poles could feel a real sense of freedom and dignity, protected from state control, and it was perceived by the majority of the society as the only possible guardian of spiritual values. Among the closely related elements of the dominant value system was the identification of catholicism with Poland, or, to put it another way, the identification of catholicism with the national tradition of struggle for the independence of the motherland.

A specifically Polish religiosity centers around the cult of the Madonna. The content of this folk-type religiosity committed to a Marian tradition—through its iconography, religious festivals, and pilgrimages—celebrates heroic, self-sacrificing women and motherhood in a national context provided by Polish history and romantic patriotic literature. In this literary tradition, the main duties of Polish women are maintaining the family and preserving Poland's national identity, while men (husbands and sons) fight for the *motherland*, conspire against foreign occupiers, and often spend their lives in prison. This form of "managerial matriarchy" (best captured by the ideal of the *Matka Polka*, the "Polish Mother," the still widely revered role model for Polish women) historically provided women not only with dignity and prestige but also with psychological gratification. These could be gained in virtually no other way than through this role of mother and family caretaker.

After 1945—just as in the other countries of the bloc—this traditional model was upset by a massive enlistment of women into the labor market as a result of ideological and economic pressures. Women were urged to assume new roles, becoming workers and building a new social order alongside men. But in October 1956, after the communist state had suffered its first setback with a workers' protest in Poznan, this crudely promoted concept of a "new breed of socialist women" had to be discarded. At the same time, the collectivization of private farms was suspended; the primate of Poland, Cardinal Stefan Wyszynski, was released from internment; and religious instruction was reintroduced into the schools. Since then, the officially promoted model of Polish women has been largely a by-product of the intricate relationship between the Catholic church and the communist state. The socialist model never recovered its original hard-line position, while the conservative model continued to gain visibility, especially during times of relative freedom (Solidarity, 1980–1981), when the Catholic church increased its influence and presence and thus had a greater impact on public affairs.

Issues, Groups, and Projects

There are several dozen women's groups at work in different parts of Poland, which, though functioning at the local level, constitute a thriving network of projects and initiatives dealing with current women's issues, especially the problems of reproductive rights and of women's unemployment.

Reproductive Rights. The year 1989 was critical for the Polish women's movement, less because of the final break with the communist system than because of the abortion bill prepared by a group of Catholic deputies for the last communist Parliament. The first draft of this bill specified a five-year prison term for a woman who had an abortion. This provoked the rapid establishment of numerous new women's organizations. Among the first registered were the Polish Feminists' Association (PFA), and Pro-Femina. Both of these groups are relatively small (50 to 60 members), urban, young, and intelligentsia based. Pro-Femina is devoted almost entirely to the issue of abortion. PFA's core group in Warsaw had already been meeting informally throughout the 1980s, at which time it resembled today's debate-oriented women's movement in the Czech and Slovak republics. Its program has been broader than Pro-Femina's from the beginning, and in the early 1990s it launched branches in several large university cities (Wrocław, Szczecin, Poznan, Gdansk, and Kraków), which have since turned themselves into autonomous groups having one feature in common: that they all openly call themselves feminists.

The Warsaw PFA group has good international contacts and has earned credibility with women in Parliament, with the ombudsperson, and with other women's groups. The group's natural environment is the university community, and members have few contacts with women workers or peasants. Their leaders, Jolanta Plakwicz, Beata Fiszer, and Magdalena Uminska, speak fluent English. Their general interest is political and includes a monitoring of the legislative process to see how the new laws address women's needs and comply with European standards. The concerns of the Kraków group are more oriented toward a cultural feminism. There they organize conferences, discussions, and film festivals and publish the women's periodical *Pelnym Glosem (With a Full Voice)*. The first Polish feminist book of essays, edited by Slawka Walczewska, was the work of the Kraków group. The Polish Feminist Association is a good example of the way in which the new women's groups in Poland are constituting themselves. In the variety of its local forms it represents one model of organization: grassroots, flexible, nonhierarchical, and committed to preserving its own internally democratic self-governance and to expressing the needs and interests of its own members.

les femmes
ne sont pas
des machines
à faire
des enfants

NON!

kobiety
nie są
maszynami
do robienia
dzieci

NIE!

*Gender and reproductive rights issues that had been buried
under communism reemerged with democratization. This car-
toon, printed in Poland—stating "No! We are not machines
for making children!"—publicized an issue faced by women in
many countries.*

The abortion issue and the general feeling of helplessness on the part of society
vis-à-vis its elected representatives have become major catalysts for the most impressive, liberal-oriented social movement in postcommunist Poland: the
"proreferendum movement." Between November 1992 and March 1993, hundreds
of committees established themselves throughout the country to exert pressure on
Parliament to refrain, at the very least, from criminalizing abortion. The committees collected 1.5 million signatures of adult Poles requesting that a referendum be
held to decide whether abortion should be punished. The referendum committees
continue to have a life of their own, even after their movement was effectively dis-
armed by Parliament's decision in the final bill that only the physician performing
an abortion is to be punished and not the woman undergoing it.

The latest parliamentary elections (October 1993) reflected widespread support for the proreferendum movement when its most vocal leader, Barbara Labuda, gained twice as many votes as Wladyslaw Frasyniuk, a legendary figure from the Solidarity period and a very popular politician, who was running in the same district. Labuda, despite many predictions to the contrary, was not hurt by her openly feminist and anticlerical stand. Moreover, the new Parliament has a significantly larger proportion of women representatives (up from 9.1 to 13.4 percent).

Asked whether she thinks there is a women's movement in Poland, Slawka Walczewska, an activist and cofounder of the Foundation of Women in Kraków, says, "We have many groups—but a movement? Women are extremely resistant to any idea of centralization or of furthering the formal structuring of their activities. None of the existing groups is willing to join or submit itself to a larger structure."[19] This insistence on horizontal autonomous structures results not only from the negative reaction to the superhierarchical communist organizations but also from the experience of Solidarity, both during the period of the triumphantly self-governing society tolerated by the regime in 1980–1981 and—after the government crackdown—during the years of rebuilding the union's structures underground. The less centralized the activities, the more successful they were—and the more difficult for the police to disrupt. This is one of the reasons women in Poland prefer very loose networks or, as they put it, just "a directory of groups." "Give me a list of addresses, and if we need to act, we'll contact them," said one of the activists in Kraków. In fact, the main tool facilitating communication between groups is an address directory of all the women's organizations and initiatives, which was recently prepared by the Women's Promotion Center. This is how women organized themselves in the—as they stressed—informal group Women Too in preparation for the local elections in Poland. Their activities for several months (November 1993–May 1994) were focused on searching for the best women candidates and helping them prepare their election campaigns. They ran seminars and published a handbook, *How to Win the Elections,* which includes a special section offering self-help exercises in leadership, public speaking, negotiation and conflict resolution, stress management, and so forth. They also had a hotline for women candidates from outside Warsaw.

And there is still another factor—that of strategy—that Polish women will have to give considerable attention to as they consider what kind of movement could best grow and succeed in Poland. There is still little doubt that any centralized women's movement operating on a national scale would first have to become a strongly anticlerical movement. But given the peculiarity of Polish society—that its vast majority is pro-choice and yet deeply connected to the church—such an anticlerical orientation might jeopardize the very existence of the movement. This was one of the reasons the referendum movement did not succeed: It would have had to turn against the church. And in Poland it is considered too early to take such a risk.

A respect for the individuality of the various groups' programs has not been an obstacle to the occasional creation of issue-oriented coalitions like the one formed in the spring of 1992 by pro-choice groups to promote and lobby for reproductive rights, called the Federation for Women and Family Planning. Among the participants are the Polish Feminists' Association, Pro-Femina, Neutrum, the Women's League, the Young Women's Christian Association, and the Polish Association of Sexologists. The federation, which for tactical reasons avoided the use of the phrase *reproductive rights* in its name, already has a considerable number of achievements to its credit. The women's hotline provides assistance mostly on questions of contraception, rape, violence, and legal matters for women with life-threatening pregnancies. The offices of the Federation and its hotline (which in Polish is called the trustline) are functioning as a major resource center for women and for the media as well. The latter are regularly supplied with information on the relationship between the church's ban on contraception and the increase in the need for abortions, in deaths caused by illegal abortions, in underground clinics, and so on.

Another model of organization is one that has been inherited from the previous system: a somewhat transformed version of the large-scale, centralized organization with a sizable bureaucratic apparatus. This model is represented by two organizations that claim rather large memberships: the Women's League, with thirty-five hundred members, and the Democratic Women's Union, with six thousand members. The Women's League, founded in 1945, was the only women's organization in the People's Republic of Poland. It still retains a considerable part of its property, offices, and staff. The Democratic Women's Union was established in 1990 for the purpose of accommodating those women, previously members of the Communist Party, who did not want to remain a part of the Women's League.

Interestingly, neither of these organizations is excluded from the community of new women's groups in Poland. They are both listed in the roster of existing groups. Despite all the resentments about the communist past and reservations about centralized national organizations, what emerges from the meetings, demonstrations, conferences, and joint publications is a growing recognition of common interests and sense of community and the realization that a major step is being taken—by women—toward the further restoration of civil society in Poland.

Women's Unemployment. The second major problem that has mobilized women in Poland has been the unprecedented rise in unemployment. The collapse of trade with the former Soviet Union, the closure of big and costly state enterprises, the restructuring of certain industries, and the reduction in the number of civil servants all contributed to an unemployment rate in Poland of 15.41 percent at the end of 1993. While women constitute 53.4 percent of the unemployed, in regions that are centers of the textile industry and in some of the large conglomerates women suffer unemployment at a rate that is twice as high as that for men.

The decentralization of the Polish women's groups and their generally local focus encouraged a relatively prompt response to the issue of unemployment. Either
local women's groups created and launched their own special programs to ameliorate the hardships (such as retraining programs), or women activists solicited the
collaboration of other organizations to establish such programs (such as the collaboration in Lodz of the Center for the Advancement of Women with the International Women's Foundation or the Women's Promotion Program, a project of
the Foundation for Democratic Action).

Women are also aware of another reason for the higher rate of female unemployment. It is a result of those still functioning legal regulations that were designed to let the socialist woman take on the double role of mother and worker.
These stipulate, for example, that women have the "exclusive privilege" of taking
paid leave to care for a sick child. These and similar laws, argues Malgorzata
Fuszara, director of the Center for Social and Legal Studies on Women, are detri-
mental to women in today's competitive labor market. They encourage open discrimination against women on the grounds of their lesser productivity. This issue
is particularly distressing since, in the absence of other labor legislation, it is extremely difficult to bring to bear the constitutional principle of the equality of all
citizens without regard to gender. Women's groups not only recognize the discriminatory effect of yesterday's privileges, but through the Parliamentary Wom-
en's Group they are also demanding prompt changes in labor legislation. Also under way is the introduction to the floor of Parliament a bill called the Act on the
Equal Status of Women and Men.

Conclusions, or Is There a Women's Movement in East and Central Europe?

One of the results of the changes in the postcommunist countries is the emergence
of autonomous activities focused on a set of issues that have never been discussed
here before—even by women themselves—and that are related to the problem of
gender equality in a democratic society. At the moment most of these activities are
still in an initial stage of mapping the field: questioning the past and the present
and articulating the problems. But this debate-driven moment is crucial for any
potential movement; it is here that women meet, problems are identified, goals
drafted, organizational structures initiated, and forms of activity considered. The
initial themes of the debate have been prompted by an urgent need on the part of
many women to rethink their situation both as it was in the recent past under state
socialism and as it is now during the process of transition to democracy and a
market economy. An awareness of the many similarities between their respective
efforts, and the very uniqueness of these efforts historically speaking, frequently
brings women from these countries together. Whereas it is still difficult to speak of

women's movements operating on a national level in any of these countries, there are signs of close collaboration among different women's groups in the region. This makes it additionally tempting to see the initiatives of Polish, Czech, Slovak, or Hungarian women as contributing to a significant change in the sociopolitical landscape of the entire region.

Interestingly, recent collaboration on joint projects by women from different East and Central European countries has frequently been facilitated by a new, nonpatronizing breed of Western women's organizations that seek genuine understanding of, and dialogue with, women from the postcommunist countries. Among these is the Network of East-West Women, initiated by women from the United States but now with members in all the postcommunist countries, including Russia, and with joint governance by an international steering committee. A conference on women and the law, organized by the network in early June 1994 in Budapest, helped women conceptualize not only the issues but also the ways in which to address them in each country's legal environments. Other groups most frequently interested in collaboration with East European women come from Germany and the Scandinavian countries. So women's movements are gaining a firm foothold in much of East and Central Europe, stimulating growth and development of civil society. If successful, they may not only get women's issues onto the official agendas of their respective governments and parliaments, but they may also influence the very process of democratization in their societies.

NOTES

1. Adam Michnik, *Letters from Prison and Other Essays* (Berkeley and Los Angeles: University of California Press, 1985), p. 27.

2. Agnieszka Metelska and Ewa Nowakowska, eds., *Gdzie Diabel Nie Moze* (Warsaw: BGW, 1992), p. 145.

3. Renata Siemienska, "Wybierane i Glosujace," in *Kobiety: Dawne i Nowe Role* (Warsaw: Centrum Europejskie Universytetu Warszawskiego, Biuletyn Nr. 1, 1994), p. 27.

4. Ibid., p. 33.

5. An article on lesbian activism in the Czech Republic was written by Susanna Trnka and published in Susanna Trnka, with Laura Busheikin, eds., *Bodies of Bread and Butter: Reconfiguring Women's Lives in the Postcommunist Czech Republic* (Prague: Prague Gender Studies Center, 1993).

6. Slawka Walczewska, ed., *Kobiety Maja Glos* (Kraków: Convivum, 1992).

7. Hana Havelkova, "A Few Prefeminist Thoughts," in Nanette Funk and Magda Mueller, eds., *Gender Politics and Post-Communism: Reflections from Eastern Europe and the Former Soviet Union* (New York: Routledge, 1993), p. 72.

8. Trnka, with Busheikin, *Bodies of Bread and Butter.*

9. Jana Cvikova. "List z Bratislavy: Pokus o Postsocialisticky Feminismus," *Aspekt* (1993):1.

10. Hana Navarova, "Co Dal Socialismus Zenam?" in *Pastaveni Zen w Ceskoslovenske Spolecnosti* (Prague: Czechoslovak Academy of Sciences, 1991).

11. See, for example, the research by Maria Cermakova, "Gender and the Employment of Higher Education Graduates in Czechoslovakia," Prague: Czechoslovak Academy of Sciences, 1992.

12. Interview with Helena Wolekova, Bratislava, summer 1992.

13. Zuzana Kiczkova and Etela Farkasova, "The Emancipation of Women: A Concept That Failed," in N. Funk and M. Mueller, eds., *Gender Politics and Post-Communism: Reflections from Eastern Europe and the Former Soviet Union* (New York: Routledge, 1993), p. 89.

14. Interview with Miroslava Holubova, Prague, summer 1992.

15. Interview with Alexandra Berkova, Prague, summer 1992.

16. Eniko Bollobas, "The Role of Women and the Transition to Democracy in Central and Eastern Europe" (Paper presented at a conference of the Council of Europe, Center for Democracy, Strasbourg, October 1992).

17. Interview with Olga Toth, Budapest, summer 1992. (Toth elaborates her point in an unpublished paper on women and their changing role in the family and society in Hungary.)

18. Julia Szalai, "Some Aspects of the Changing Situation of Women in Hungary," *Signs* (Autumn 1991), p. 161.

19. Interview with Slawka Walczewska, Kraków, August 1993.

16

Extending the Boundaries of Citizenship: Women's Movements of Western Europe

JANE JENSON

WOMEN'S MOVEMENTS IN Western Europe have a long history. At the end of the nineteenth century movements emerged in many countries, claiming women's right to vote, to work for fair wages, and to have some individual autonomy from fathers or husbands. Organizing in separate women-dominated organizations or as part of existing political parties and trade unions, this first wave of the women's movement was not totally different from its second-wave successors. These latter-day women's movements also mobilized and worked in many different ways. A snapshot of the Dutch women's movement in the mid-1980s captures an image of the situation in many Western European countries since 1968, when the women's movement burst out of the New Left, the old Left, and the student movements:

The movement covers an extremely wide range of ideologies and concrete activities. There are political interest and pressure groups—women for peace, women for legal-ized abortion, women against sexual violence, women dependent on public support, and women's groups within political parties and unions. There are counseling, educa-tion and training groups for women seeking radical therapy; groups for women in midlife; crisis hotlines; courses on society (the so-called VOS, or "Women's Orienta-tion to Society" course) for women with only a few years of secondary education. There are cultural groups such as women's cabarets and theaters, women's art galler-ies, women's publishing and printing companies, women's bookstores, women's newspapers and magazines. And there are more general groups and activities: wom-en's houses or cafes, consciousness-raising groups and women's groups in commu-

405

GERMANY

GENERAL

type of government: Federal Democratic Republic
major ethnic groups: German (93%); Turkish (2.5%); and Italian, Greek, Polish less
    than 1% each
language(s): German
religions: Protestant (44%); Catholic (37%)
date of independence: (reunification 1990)

DEMOGRAPHICS

population size: 80.3 million
birth rate (*per 1,000 population*): 11
total fertility rate (*average number of births per woman*): 1.3
contraceptive prevalence rate (*married women*): 75%
maternal mortality rate (*per 100,000 live births*): 8

WOMEN'S STATUS

date of women's suffrage: 1919
economically active population: M 75%   F 41% (*former Federal Republic of Ger-
                                                  many*)
                               M 83%   F 62% (*former German Democratic Repub-
                                                  lic*)
female employment (*% of total workforce*): 39
life expectancy   M 73   F 79
school enrollment ratio (*F/100 M*)

	FRG	GDR
primary	96	94
secondary	100	92
tertiary	72	114 (including evening and correspondence)

literacy   M 99%   F 99%

An Englishwoman sells a newssheet called "Votes for Women" in London in 1907.

FRANCE

GENERAL

type of government: Democratic Republic
major ethnic groups: European and Mediterranean groups: Celtic, Latin, Teutonic,
    Slavic, and Basque; North African and Indochinese minorities
language: French; declining regional dialects
religions: Roman Catholic (90%); Protestant (2%); Jewish (1%); Muslim (1%)
date of independence: 486 (unification)

DEMOGRAPHICS

population size: 57.8 million
birth rate (*per 1,000 population*): 13
total fertility (*average number of births per woman*): 1.8
contraceptive prevalence (*married women*): 80%
maternal mortality rate (*per 100,000 live births*): 13

WOMEN'S STATUS

date of women's suffrage: 1944
economically active population: M 71%   F 45%
female employment (*% of total workforce*): 40
life expectancy   M 74   F 82
school enrollment ratio (*F/100 M*)

primary	94
secondary	106
tertiary	97

literacy   M 99%   F 99%

---

nity centers. Not all of these activities are equally common, but some combination of them can be found *in most Dutch towns.*[1]

The Netherlands was not alone, of course, in generating an active and varied women's movement engaged in a multitude of actions of this sort. In most of the countries of Western Europe 1968 was a year of legendary political turbulence. The political landscape would never be the same. Student movements, New Left political formations, and workers took to the streets in massive demonstrations as well

SWEDEN

GENERAL

type of government: Constitutional Monarchy
major ethnic groups: Swedish (91%); Finnish (3%); Lapps; other European
language(s): Swedish
religions: Lutheran (official; 95%)

DEMOGRAPHICS

population size: 8.6 million
birth rate (*per 1,000 population*): 13
total fertility (*average number of births per woman*): 2.1
contraceptive prevalence (*married women*): 78%
maternal mortality rate (*per 100,000 live births*): 7

WOMEN'S STATUS

date of women's suffrage: 1919
economically active population: M 71%   F 55%
female employment (*% of total workforce*): 45
life expectancy   M 75   F 81
school enrollment ratio (*F/100 M*)
    primary   95
    secondary   109
    tertiary   89
literacy   M 99%   F 99%

---

as organizing huge strikes in factories, schools, and universities. One of the most enduring legacies of this moment of political turbulence was the women's movement. Many women who had been active in the politics of 1968 realized that their situation as women was not being fully addressed in male-dominated politics, even in the exciting new politics of the 1960s.

In France, for example, a small group of women who had met in several leftist groups marched in August 1970 to the Tomb of the Unknown Soldier at the Arc de Triomphe in Paris in order to lay a wreath in honor of the unknown soldier's even more unknown wife. With this action, the women's liberation movement (mouvement de libération de la femme) was baptized by the Parisian press. The

The first wave of women's movements occurred during times of other social upheaval that included the Industrial Revolution, wars, union movements, and the rise of socialism. This poster marks International Women's Day, March 8, 1914.

women, their numbers growing quickly, became even more audacious, demonstrating, for example, in 1970 at a conference organized by *Elle* magazine to celebrate women's supposed progress. At the same time long-running, rambunctious, loud, and large meetings occurred weekly at the Ecole de Beaux Arts. Women were excited by the possibility of debating and discussing feminism, theory, history, and politics. Groups published new magazines and newspapers, special issues of existing leftist publications, and broadsheets. They organized women's centers and shelters for battered women. They petitioned. They studied, insisting that the academic world open its eyes and its doors to the study of women, gender, and patriarchy. Debate raged within leftist groups, parties, and unions over whether women's demands were legitimate and whether they had the right to practice "double militancy," that is, to be active within a mixed formation as well as in separate women's groups.

These were heady days of political mobilization, hard-fought debate, and angry demonstrations as well as a discovery of the bonds of sisterhood. The goal was no less than a complete transformation of gender relations within French society. Of course, alongside these debates were the more "everyday politics" of reforming the abortion law, promoting women to positions of political power, achieving equality in the workplace, and so on. In these actions the post-1968 "revolutionary feminists" joined feminists within the unions and political parties who had long been working to promote women and change their organizations' understanding of the "female condition." The French women's movement was diverse. There were many forms of action, many claims, and much theoretical dispute about how to overturn unequal and oppressive gender relations.[2]

By the late 1970s, however, the movement was much less active and much less visible. It continued to exist, to be sure, but the focus of work had shifted to the quieter tasks of lobbying for and providing programs to support women, whether for protection against sexual violence and sexual harassment or for income equality. It was also necessary to exercise constant vigilance, as legal rights to abortion and access to contraception came under threat from antichoice groups and religious fundamentalists.

France's story is not unique. Indeed, it is possible to treat Western Europe as a unit for purposes of analysis. Its history of economic and political development displays many similarities, and particularly in the postwar years social democratic politics tended to shape the political agenda. Moreover, the second-wave women's movements began to mobilize in most Western European countries at about the same time, with a good deal of communication among them. Many countries followed similar trajectories, and therefore, despite their internal diversity and specific national stories, it is possible to identify some similarities across women's movements.[3]

The first characteristic to note about the second wave of the women's movements of Western Europe is that in no country do they consist of a single ideological tendency, form of organization and action, or group. It is possible to say that all of the movements share a commitment to transformational politics and therefore that their "'agenda' entails nothing less than the reformulation of public life, the educational sphere, the workplace, and the home—that is, a total transformation of society."[4] This acknowledged, however, it is also the case that the movements in each country have varied in the demands made, in their willingness to work with and within other movements and representative organizations, and in the extent to which they have concentrated on winning new state policy or mobilized for cultural change in gender relations. They have also identified different roots of women's oppression and inequality, with some tendencies blaming oppression on women's relationships to men and family situations and with others seeing the source of gender inequalities in the structures and relationships of the economy and politics.

A second notable characteristic is that the women's movements of Western Europe live in political environments in which left-wing parties and unions have long claimed to be able to represent and even emancipate women. Both social democracy and communism are rich in a tradition of identifying women's oppression as part of their struggle and seeking to draw women to support them. Therefore, women's movements have operated in a universe of political discourse and political opportunity that has also long been occupied by left-wing parties, unions, and other progressive actors.

This coexistence has shaped movement politics as well. Indeed, on balance, studies of specific women's movements conclude that the internal characteristics of the movement, including the kinds of actions undertaken, the theoretical approaches developed, and the forms of mobilization chosen *follow from* the balance of political forces in each national setting.[5] For example, in France the origins of revolutionary feminism within leftist groups after 1968 had a great deal to do with the kinds of politics those feminists subsequently pursued, even after they had broken with their revolutionary brothers. First formed in Trotskyist or Maoist groups, revolutionary feminists spent a lot of time seeking theoretical clarity and purity of action as well as being deeply suspicious of other left-wing actors, including feminists in the traditional parties and unions. In Sweden, in contrast, the hegemony of social democracy, as both theory and politics, had different consequences for the life of the women's movement. Any feminism that did not address women's issues within a social democratic discourse was virtually stifled, at the same time that women within the Social Democratic Party and the unions had difficulty explaining why they needed more than the traditional agenda. Social democratic politics at first blush seemed so women friendly (because of the support for women's work and child care) that feminists were compelled to struggle just to explain that even such programs and policies could hide gender inequities in the family and society.[6]

In many countries, then, second-wave movements still face a challenge that forces them to make a decision. The challenge is to identify the limits to traditional left-wing positions "on women" and to push and prod the Left, old and new, toward more feminist stances, problematizing the gender division of labor and men's sexual exploitation of and violence toward women. In doing so, feminists have had to convince their erstwhile allies that the "personal is political." The decision these women's movements face is whether to work with, within, or not at all with political parties and unions. The choice made has considerable consequences for a related decision of whether to address actions toward the state: Legislative change requires allies inside parliamentary institutions, and this often means allowing others to frame issues and accepting policy compromises.

Variation among women's movements follows from the choices made in the face of these decisions. Some wings of some movements opted for autonomous politics, having little contact with traditional parties and unions and spending little time seeking legal change. Here Germany's second-wave women's movement provides one example. It has been dominated by radical feminists who have concentrated their practical action on combating violence against women in local shelters and who frequently refuse to recognize the "feminist" credentials of and work with women who chose to stay inside the union movement or left-wing parties.[7] The Nordic countries provide a contrasting example. There radical feminism has been relatively weak and autonomous action rare. Second-wave feminists have worked within the institutions of the labor movement and the state, making claims for more participation by women and social and economic programs that can contribute to tilting the gender division of labor in a more equitable direction.[8] Yet in even these cases, as in the movements of all other Western European countries, great diversity exists within the movements and in their relations with other political actors.

Given all this, it is not possible to speak of *the* women's movement of Western Europe; there are many. Such variation complicates the task of writing this chapter immensely, to be sure. It also accounts for its form. This chapter is not, nor could it ever be, a detailed overview of the movements in the countries of Western Europe. That task is immense. In this chapter I set a much more modest goal. I argue, first, that despite their diversity, women's movements of the second wave in Western Europe, just as their first-wave sisters, made claims for the completion of the agenda of citizenship that had emerged on the "old continent" after the French Revolution and throughout the nineteenth century. If not all wings of all movements made the same claims, such claims were nonetheless made by at least a part of each country's movement.[9] In doing so, moreover, the movements innovated, extending the notions of citizenship rights to incorporate new territory. Second, and not unrelated to this innovation, I discuss how second-wave movements, even more than their predecessors, mobilized for cultural change. They often used consciousness-raising as a strategy for generating solidarity. Even if they did not,

their practical work and theoretical efforts were directed toward generating a collective identity, or sense of commonality, among women. In doing so, they also
made demands for the democratization of social and political life. This focus followed from the movement's attention to the recognition and acceptance of diversity, whether between genders or around questions of sexual orientation and racial and ethnic difference. It also created a major tension both within the
movement and with its allies over how to address sexual and other differences.[10]
Third, I examine the situation that the movements face at the dawn of the twenty-
first century. In particular I demonstrate the fragility of some victories of the 1970s
and 1980s, as the political terrain tilts toward neoliberalism.

Completing the Agenda of Citizenship

A goodly proportion of almost all of the women's movements that have been active in Western Europe since the late 1960s have directed their actions toward
achieving the promises of liberty, equality, and solidarity embedded in classic understandings of citizenship derived from the French Revolution and extended in
the post-1945 years of building the welfare state. In doing so, these movements
have challenged the state and other important political actors to live up to their
promises to provide "universal rights" to all citizens, and they have done so by
demonstrating the ways in which the promises of citizenship were in practice
based on a model citizen who was masculine. As a result, the promises sometimes
failed to address the needs and situation of women. In making such critiques,
women's movements have rendered visible a set of distinctions within the postwar
state that hindered the full inclusion of women. In such politics, women's movements have also frequently made claims for the right to difference, the right to
have women's needs treated specifically and collectively, thereby allowing them to
achieve categorical equity.[11]

In presenting the citizenship claims of second-wave women's movements in
Western Europe, I make use of the three analytic categories developed in T. H.
Marshall's classic study of citizenship, in which he documents over a period of two
and a half centuries the struggles of different social groups to realize "the claim to
be accepted as full members of the society, that is, as citizens."[12] *Civil rights* provided protection of the right to work and set boundaries around a sphere of individual liberty. Central to the idea of civil rights was the right to make contracts
and to have bodily integrity, that is, to be protected from state interference.[13] *Political rights* gradually extended to incorporate all male citizens, giving them an
equal right to participate in political life. Nonetheless, it soon became clear that
individual freedom and formal equalities needed to be supplemented if full citizenship was to be achieved. *Social rights* were necessary in order to ameliorate ex-
cessive inequalities or the failure of formal rights to generate full membership in

society. Postwar welfare states providing social protections for all citizens incarnated such social rights.

Access to full citizenship rights were very often gendered. It is hardly surprising, therefore, that when second-wave women's movements surged in the late 1960s in all Western European countries, they targeted the unrealized promise of universal citizenship, seeking to eliminate those distinctions among citizens that had limited women's autonomy and disempowered them.

Extending Civil Rights: Sexuality and Equal Opportunities

Even when women carried a passport and were thereby recognized as citizens, for example, of Italy or Germany by other countries, they did not have the same rights as their male compatriots within their own country. For example, married women in many countries did not have the right to confer their citizenship on their foreign husbands, although men could do so for their wives. Nor did mothers necessarily transfer a citizenship to their children. Married women lacked basic legal capacity—to hold a job without their husband's approval, to manage their own financial affairs, to make decisions about their children's affairs—in several countries well into the 1970s.

Women's civil rights were also limited by institutions, such as segmented labor markets, that restricted women's employment opportunities; single-sex educational institutions (especially those leading to elite occupations); and the policy of banks and other institutions that refused to recognize married women as individual economic actors (often requiring that husbands co-sign credit notes, for example). These practices all limited women's possibilities of "freely contracting" as well as reducing women's capacity for achieving economic autonomy. They remained dependent on a male wage or social provision.

Crucial, too, was the absence for women of that basic civil right of bodily integrity upon which autonomy depends. In almost all Western European countries until at least the mid-1970s, women faced barriers to access to contraception and abortion and therefore to control over their own bodies. Achieving full civil rights has been, therefore, a central focus and terrain of struggle for women's movements throughout the last decades.

Almost everywhere in Western Europe the second-wave women's movement announced its arrival by demanding improved access to contraception and the right to end unwanted pregnancies. The struggle to overturn long-standing bans on abortion, in particular, provided an initial occasion for diverse groups and tendencies to focus on a common issue.[14] The forms of action in the politics of abortion reform were multiple. Groups lobbied parliaments for legislative change and sought allies among the parties. They also engaged in more spectacular events, ranging from mass demonstrations to systematic and widely publicized lawbreaking. In the Netherlands, for example, a broadly based single-issue coalition

brought together a wide variety of women's groups, both those organized autonomously and those affiliated with various left-wing parties, to organize demonstrations, lobbying, clinic occupations, and other actions in an effort to gain liberal
legislation guaranteeing women's right to choose.[15] France and Italy also saw
broad coalitions for reform. In 1971, 343 prominent intellectuals, politicians, and
ordinary women published a manifesto acknowledging that they had broken the
law by having an abortion, while a similarly large number of doctors were willing
to do the same.[16] Common also were well-publicized trips to neighboring countries where the law was less harsh.[17]

All of this law-breaking, accompanied by mobilization for legal changes, was
important because it forced into the universe of political discourse a new way of
thinking about women's rights and sexuality. Even where legislation resulted from
compromises, including efforts by many left-wing politicians to achieve social
equality (because richer women had always had better access to abortion services
than poor ones, even when abortion was still illegal), feminists sought to represent
women as individuals, sexually different from men and not defined simply by
family status. When feminists were successful, they gained legislation recognizing
women's right to choose. In other cases, of course, many actors were less willing to
acknowledge and grant legal space for women to choose. Doctors remained the
gatekeepers in those—usually very limited—situations in which women could
have access to abortion.[18]

In mobilizing for new laws on abortion, organizations from the autonomous
wing of the women's movement commonly worked together with feminists within
the union movement and political parties. In large part this could happen because
the latter had been pressuring their organizations to change their positions on
"women's issues." For example, in France one of the two major union centrals, the
Confédération Française Démocratique du Travail (CFDT), as well as the Socialist
and other left-wing parties joined the family planning organization, autonomous
women's groups, and some doctors to form the Mouvement pour la Libérté de
l'Avortement et la Contraception.[19] For the CFDT this was a sign of the influence
of feminism within the union movement.[20] In the process, the Communist Party
was pushed and prodded toward a position that justified abortion less as a response to the needs of poor and working-class women and more as a right of all
women to control their sexuality. In the end, the legislation passed only because
the right-wing liberal government of Valéry Giscard d'Estaing could count on the
full support of the Left parties, the Socialists and the Communists. His own coalition partners voted against the abortion law.

In Italy the story was similar. The Radical Party and the autonomous women's
organizations pressed for legislation recognizing women's right to choose. Obviously opposed by the Christian Democrats, this stance was also rejected by the
major party of the Left, the Communists. Nonetheless, under pressure from femi-

Italian women in Rome march for legal abortion on March 8, 1977, International Women's Day. The placard reads, "If the Pope needed one, abortion would be a sacrament." Abortion rights have been central to virtually all second-wave feminist movements in Western Europe.

Thousands of Italian women march in Rome in February 1976 during a demonstration for equal job opportunities for women, a critical issue in feminist analyses and policy proposals in Western Europe.

nists within the Communist Party as well as to its left, the Communists eventually supported the 1978 liberalization of the abortion law.[21]

In Norway, too, success in obtaining a liberal abortion law depended upon the capacity of feminists within a left-wing party to convince their reluctant colleagues. The Socialist Left Party, which housed a Christian Socialist faction, allowed its members to vote against liberalization in 1975. Three years later, however, feminists within the party had managed to convince the party as a whole to abandon "conscience voting"; all elected members had to vote for the party's public position, even if they disagreed with it. In this way a pro-choice abortion law was passed in 1978.[22]

Nonetheless, the political configuration did not always take this form. The German women's movement had only the weakest of bourgeois feminist wings and was deeply cleaved by conflict between radical, autonomous feminists and those working within mainstream organizations. Indeed, neither recognized a shared political position, and much energy went into maintaining boundaries between stances and forms of "proper action." In this context, the consideration of reform of the abortion law in the mid-1970s was one in which the parties were left relatively free to respond to the constitutional court's rejection of pro-choice legislation and to restrict access to abortion.[23]

In Spain the women's movement had arisen out of the political ferment of post-Franco democratization, generating discussions of women's issues within the mainstream parties of the Left and in autonomous, radical groups. However, an effective alliance of women in the Socialist Party and autonomous groups could never be constructed, in part because the autonomous movement began to decline in importance after the 1982 election of the Socialist government. The abortion law that passed in 1985 was voted by the Socialists, who had an absolute majority in both houses of the legislature, and reflected the compromises made necessary by the constitutional court's rejection of a more liberal law.[24]

In these histories of the struggle for abortion rights, we see the extent to which some women's movements of Western Europe had difficulty redefining the issue as one of basic rights. We also see the importance of joint action by all tendencies within the movement and the necessity of having a wing of the movement with influence within parties and trade unions.

The other area in which women's movements have made major claims for removing distinctions in women's and men's civil rights is in strategies and programs for achieving equality in the labor market. Second-wave feminists, like their sisters who struggled at the beginning of the twentieth century for women's right to engage in paid work, devoted a good deal of attention to the labor market situation of women. In many countries of Western Europe women's labor force participation was rising rapidly by the early 1960s.[25] Nonetheless, women's jobs were often very concentrated in a few sectors and poorly paid. Explanations developed for these enduring patterns identified the role women and their families played in socializing girls to limit their ambitions in school and the labor market, to be sure. But they also pointed to structural patterns of discrimination that made it difficult for women to contract freely and gain access to a full range of employment.

These blockages were located in educational institutions, some of which still did not permit young women to enroll in the programs likely to lead to high-paying and prestigious occupations and most of which channeled girls into programs considered "appropriate" for them. Therefore, while girls were "investing in their human capital" even more than boys—their rate of success in higher education surpassed that of boys—this investment paid off less.[26] Women's movements quickly pressed for opening up more programs to both sexes and developing programs to encourage girls to take up nontraditional training.[27] The second structural blockage identified was in hiring and in wage setting, both of which were accused of being sources of discrimination. Therefore, campaigns for equal opportunity in hiring and for equal pay for work of equal value became a part of movement politics. These struggles were not always easy, and the allies available to activists in the women's movement sometimes evaporated.

In particular, the movement's relationship to the labor movement was often rocky. In countries such as France, where a weak union movement had always sought to protect the working class by raising the minimum wage, it was relatively easy to accept equality politics. Thus, the labor movement welcomed state legislation in 1983 that prohibited discrimination on the basis of sex and that gave responsibility for instituting equality to negotiations between employers and unions. Unfortunately, the subsequent decline in the power of the union movement meant that there was little change in the gender structures of the labor force after the legislation was passed.[28] In countries such as Germany and Britain, the union movement had since the nineteenth century followed a strategy of the "family wage," in which a male worker earned enough to support a nonwaged wife and children. Feminists had to struggle hard to convince unionists that attention needed to turn toward discrimination, especially in hiring. Therefore, employers who also had well-developed employment practices based on the assumption that women's labor force participation was "atypical" (that is, likely to be only part time and discontinuous because of family responsibilities), faced little organized challenge from the unions seeking pay or employment equity.[29] Another pattern emerged in the Nordic countries, where the unions were both strong and officially committed to gender equality. There the dispute was over the institutional mechanisms appropriate to achieving labor force equality. Unions were reluctant to accept state-mandated policy because their general strategic perspective was to seek resolution of wage issues in collective bargaining.[30] Yet as many feminists were quick to point out, it was previous negotiations about how to solve labor shortages and the labor movement's pressure for social programs that had led to the situation in which women were overwhelmingly segregated into part-time work in a very limited number of sectors. Therefore, feminists sought to use the power of the state to force the unions and employers into new ways of addressing gender relations. The eventual result, however, was that equality programs were grafted onto existing collective bargaining and corporatist practices.[31]

Breaking Away: Delinking Social Rights and the Family

The absence of full citizenship was evident with respect to social rights, too. Sometimes women gained access to social programs only through their husbands. Retirement benefits calculated on the basis of workforce participation meant that nonwaged wives lacked individual benefits, which could become a serious problem in case of divorce, for example. But even in those countries or for those benefits that did not discriminate against or ignore married or nonwaged women, it was universally the case that social programs encoded traditional assumptions about the gender division of labor in the family into policies.[32] Even if not every country assumed that "a man in the house" was sufficient reason to terminate women's social benefits (as the United Kingdom did), procedures for setting school hours or providing access to child care often assumed that women could

Simone de Beauvoir authored the seminal two-volume work
Deuxieme sexe *(The Second Sex), published in 1949.*

count on a male wage and were available for child care, although in reality many could not and were not.[33]

When Western European states established institutions recognizing social citizenship rights, they did not problematize traditionally unequal gender relations within the family. Therefore, second-wave feminists in several countries have concentrated on exposing the inequities of power within the family that limit women's ability to achieve full autonomy and equality. Women are particularly well placed for this struggle because they not only are the clients of the welfare state but also work within it. Therefore, their interests in its functioning are multifaceted.

In Britain, for example, second-wave feminists took as their preferred target the system of state welfare, which reproduced in a myriad of ways the dependence of married women on their husbands and single mothers on the state. Thus, an uneasy relationship within Left political formations between women and men emerged around the very achievements of postwar reformism.[34] In the Nordic countries, too, the welfare state was a target of second-wave feminism, with a focus on the extent to which the state substituted its own form of patriarchal power for that of men.[35] Moreover, feminists have sought programs, such as child care, parental leaves, and a reduced working day, that will allow families to renegotiate their gender division of labor, to institute what some Swedish feminists call the "equality contract."[36] Indeed, in these countries the language of equal opportunities was introduced into the realm of social policy in order to shift the agenda in a direction that could take caring work and responsibilities into account.[37]

The result has been a criticism of the operation of the welfare state characterized by calls for decentralization and democratization. Women's movements have sought to empower clients and workers by ensuring that they can participate in program design and delivery. At the same time, however, these movements have stood behind the welfare state, opposing cutbacks and dismantlement. In France, for example, several large strikes by nurses (who are public employees) opposed the effects of budgetary restraint in the public sector, which compressed the wages of nurses, at the same time as they demanded recognition of the professional qualifications of nurses, most of whom are female. Their major claim was based on the feminist analysis that *because* nursing is done by women, it is seen as relatively unskilled, indeed "natural" for women to do. Thus, behind the mobilizing slogan "Ni nonnes, ni bonnes, ni connes" ("We are neither nuns, maids, nor stupid"), these movements became the most important manifestation of feminist politics to be seen in several years.[38] In Sweden, too, women unionists have been visible and militant, attempting to direct the redesign of the Swedish model in ways that will protect the public sector and create new forms of labor relations that do not lower the chances of moving forward on gender equality at work and at home.[39]

Political Rights and Democratization

Effective limits on political participation also existed because of the gap between the formal right to vote and stand for office and the actual and prevalent practices of political organizations that discriminated actively or implicitly against women. Women's movements, especially those wings that struggled within political parties and unions, pressed hard but with varying degrees of success to achieve greater political representation for women in the legislatures, city halls, and governing bodies of parties and unions as well as the corporate channel. The goal was finally to implement women's political rights by effectively opening these central institutions of representation to women and eliminating the discriminatory practices that had so long kept the doors closed.

In almost all Western European countries there have been efforts to feminize the leadership of the trade unions so as both to represent better the reality of a feminizing labor force and alter the unions' agendas.[40] In the Nordic social democratic countries feminists had considerable success, as their numbers rose in the legislative assemblies, the ranks of unions and parties, and the institutions of social democratic corporatism.[41] Elsewhere, however, the experience has been less positive. In France, for example, representative institutions remain a male sanctuary; the percentage of women in Parliament is lower in the 1990s (5.7 percent) than at the time of the Liberation.[42] Feminists pressured François Mitterrand and the Socialist Party throughout the 1970s to institute quotas within the party organization and for election campaigns. They were stymied in both cases, however. Although Parliament passed legislation in 1982 establishing a quota for municipal elections (no more than 75 percent of the candidates on a list could be the same sex), the constitutional court struck down the law as contravening the French Revolution's Declaration of the Rights of Man and the Citizen. Within the Socialist Party women made little headway, too, because the organization was dominated by competition among potential candidates for the presidency; there was little space left for the promotion of goals such as gender equality.[43]

Nonetheless, efforts by feminists to gain access to elected office and organizational position have borne more fruit in some parties than in others. In both France and Germany the Greens have instituted gender parity for candidates, so that only 50 percent of the candidates are men. Moreover, under newly mounting pressure from feminists inside the party as well as outside it, in the 1994 Europarliamentary elections the French Socialist Party presented a list of candidates that was evenly divided by sex.

Here we see that even the citizenship rights that appear most universal have been profoundly differentiated by gender. The second wave of the women's movement has had to continue the struggle to advance the principle that both women and men have the right to participate in democratic governance and to enjoy full democratic rights at all levels. In doing so, moreover, these women's movements have obviously given attention to more than simply the presence of women in representative institutions. Feminists have been in the lead in efforts to alter the ways of doing politics, to make them more democratic, less hierarchical, less leadership focused, and more user friendly. The processes of decisionmaking were as important as outcomes for many groups, which rejected formal leadership tasks, rotated responsibilities among members, and insisted on full discussion. In turn, these practices fed back into the world of mixed political organizations, where parties such as the Greens and even the Communists began to experiment with other models for organizing their internal activities.[44]

Despite these struggles, the agenda for achieving full citizenship remains to be completed. An overview of the citizenship status of Nordic women, whose situation so often served as a bright star in the years of the second-wave movement, concludes:

> After 20 years of equality policies at various levels, women's and men's life patterns have changed but they still differ, and women still have considerably less societal power. Most social clients are women. Most full-time workers—the powerful "indirect citizens" of corporate structures—are men, most voters are women, most representatives are men. Women are the direct participants in an increasing number of citi-

Petra Kelly cofounded West Germany's Green Party in 1979. In several Western European countries, the Greens have been at the forefront of promoting gender parity in party politics.

zen roles, men are either represented indirectly or are those who fill representative posts at least in the majority of cases.[45]

Therefore, women's movements still struggle to overcome the negative consequences of this differentiation.

Claiming Difference

I have demonstrated here that throughout Western Europe since the late 1960s some parts of the women's movement have sought to complete the agenda of citizenship, seeking full rights for women. These claims have often but not exclusively been concerned with promoting equality (economic, social, and political) and individual autonomy. Yet even these demands, seemingly located within and borrowing from the traditional positions of liberal and socialist thought, have had to address the issues of biological, sexual, and gender difference. Even those parts of the women's movement that are most committed to achieving equality in the labor force, politics, or the family have made their claims for equality in the name of a group—women—that can never be identical to men. In other words, the wings of the second-wave women's movement have sometimes stressed the ways in which women are the same as men and deserve identical treatment. But at other times these wings have emphasized the ways in which women are different from men and deserve particularistic treatment.[46] Thus, the same feminists may make claims for quotas in parliamentary institutions because women are citizens just like men and claim abortion rights because women are citizens with different and specific characteristics.[47]

This question of whether to make claims in the name of difference or equality is much more than a theoretical one. It has provoked immense controversy within the women's movements of Western Europe. In Britain and Italy in particular the partisans of a "politics of difference," who emphasize the sexual and psychological distinctiveness of women and men and advocate cultural politics revaluing things feminine, have clashed with those feminists who use an alternative theoretical lens and pursue alternative strategies.[48] Huge public controversy and deep divisions among feminists have been the result, sometimes resulting in the demobilization of the movement as a whole, as happened in France.[49] But this issue is *also* a theoretical one. There has been little agreement within the various women's movements about the basis for difference.

For some, gender differences, and the unequal power relations associated with them, rest upon *social practices* deeply embedded in everyday life and institutional actions. It is these that have created a relationship of inequality out of sexual difference. Logically, then, movement actions must focus on overcoming unequal power relations by eliminating forms of gender discrimination, by changing family practices and cultural expectations about the gender division of labor, and by revaluing the work that women do. Such arguments locate difference in social practices and then call for changes in such practices in order to liberate women.

Yet even among feminists who agree that the inequalities of gender power are socially constructed, there is disagreement about the character of those power relations. If socialist feminists tend to see them rooted in the social relations of capitalism, radical feminists identify patriarchy as fundamental. Yet both socialist feminists and radical feminists, precisely because of their appreciation of the multitudinous ways in which gender inequalities can be socially constructed, have tended to ally with liberal feminists in seeking legislative change. For all three, the law and the state shape patterns of gender power. Moreover, they have been—some more, some less—willing to work with and within organizations that include men, pushing such organizations to expand their agenda to incorporate feminist positions on sexual politics and nonworkplace issues, to be sure.

This said, however, there have also been many groups that have been much more skeptical of the benefits to be gained from addressing the state or cooperating with mixed organizations. Particularly suspicious have been those parts of the women's movement that consider gender difference less a social construction than a biological fact. In several countries there have been strong wings of the women's movement that have claimed that there is an essential, biological difference between the sexes that has major consequences in all aspects of life. From this perspective, women's oppression is less social than psychological, rooted in early childhood and later experiences of sexuality. Such essentialist positions characterize some women's groups within the peace movements of, for ex-

A consciousness-raising advertisement used by the French Ligue du Droit des Femmes.

ample, Germany, the Netherlands, and Britain; these groups emphasize women's more nurturing nature, supposedly derivative of their biological capacity for childbearing.[50] Essentialism has also been important for French and Italian feminists whose analysis stressed the sexual differences between women and men, their differential experience of sexual pleasure, and the consequences for life experience.[51] These groups have developed theoretical positions about the need for women to liberate themselves from the sexual control of men that have led to a politics of not only organizational but also sexual separatism. In some movements lesbianism has been promoted as a political strategy, the only way for women fully to escape the power of men. Everywhere, solidarity and self-help actions have been used as a way of establishing autonomous, women-only spaces.[52]

An area of practice in which these wings, along with radical feminists, have been first into the fray and continue to be the leaders is that of violence against women. It is not surprising that this matter has dominated the practical politics of groups that identify the roots of gender inequality in the sexual exploitation of women by men, whether in the family or the larger society. The logical consequence of such analyses is to focus on the need to end this exploitation, without which efforts to achieve labor force equality, political participation, or well-designed social policies will never achieve their ends. The women's movement has been central to uncovering and publicizing the extent to which women have been victims of sexual violence, especially within the home. Shelters for battered women, self-help medical centers, and large-scale actions to reclaim public spaces for women by increasing their safety have resulted. "Take back the night" campaigns have been organized in several countries. In Germany, for example, shelters and women's centers have been the action of choice for radical feminists.[53] Campaigns to expose the extent of rape and to provide better protection for victims as well as new legislation have been important forms of movement activity in Italy and France, for example.[54] Having taken the lead in publicizing sexual violence and mobilizing, these wings have been recently joined by state feminists and egalitarian feminists in mobilizing for new legislation and better protection of the victims of violence.

An equally important practical focus has been on generating new cultural spaces for women and validating a "female culture." New magazines, publishing houses, entertainers, bookstores, and cultural centers have all been established by groups seeking recognition of women's difference. They have been promoted as forms of cultural expression and places for cultural encounter that are denied women to the extent that "culture," whether high or popular, is considered to be universal and is validated by male-dominated institutions. In these practices, of course, feminists' actions have been similar to those of other oppressed groups (nationalist movements, indigenous peoples, or gays, for example), which have put a great deal of their effort into fostering and promoting a new and celebratory collective identity for a social category previously devalued.

Into the Future

The second wave of the women's movement in Western Europe has a long history. Yet commentators are likely to speculate that it is no more. They claim that the movement achieved many of its goals and that there is no further need for mobilizing women to end their oppression. Women are no longer confined to the realm of the private and the family. In the countries of the European Union (EU), two-thirds of women between the ages of fifteen and forty-nine are in the paid labor force,[55] and in the nonmember Nordic countries the rate of labor force participation is equally high. Contraception is readily available, and in the era of acquired immune deficiency syndrome (AIDS) its use is even more encouraged. Abortion, the sine qua non of women's emancipation for the second wave, is available in at least some circumstances in all Western European countries. Even if single mothers are relatively poor in all countries, social programs have limited the phenomenon of the "feminization of poverty" so prevalent in North America, and in response at least in part to the mobilization of women since the 1960s, access to such social programs no longer implies the same degree of surveillance by the state and its social workers as it once did. Therefore, what is left for the women's movement to do?

In these concluding remarks, I have selected three issues that are very much on the agenda of women's groups in Western Europe in the 1990s. In selecting abortion rights, neoconservatism, and the European Union, I want to focus on new challenges that make mobilized and creative feminism as necessary as ever. Doing this allows me to make it very clear that there is no conclusion to the story I have been telling here. There is only a future of continued struggle to protect gains already made and to move forward on those matters still in need of attention. This future will occur, of course, in economic and political circumstances that are very different from those of the 1960s, in which the second-wave women's movements of Western Europe first emerged.

Despite abortion rights having been central to the earliest actions of second-wave feminism, and despite legislative victories, the 1990s have been marked by a reemergence of antichoice politics that has put the hard-won laws in doubt. Germany provides the most dramatic example. The unification of East and West Germany raised the question of whether the much more liberal law of the German Democratic Republic would be immediately replaced by the limited access to abortion that existed in the Federal Republic. Efforts to do so were blocked, in part because of a successful interparty alliance of elected women. In addition, many activists considered the moment of unification ripe to press forward, to decriminalize abortion, and to make the Federal Republic's legislation more pro-choice by removing restrictions on the circumstances under which abortions were legal. Feminists mobilized behind new legislation, and a much more liberal law was passed in 1992. Nonetheless, an appeal to the constitutional court struck down the new law and in doing so rolled back access even in comparison to West Germany before unification.[56] The intense debate about abortion in these years resulted in a severe blow to pro-choice positions, and German women have even less access to this crucial civil right.

But Germany is not alone in having seen a resurgence of abortion politics. The growing power of religious fundamentalism among Muslims, Protestants, and Catholics in several Western European countries has generated an upsurge in "pro-life" campaigns, which include harassment of women and doctors as well as efforts to change the law. In France, for example, harassment in clinics where abortions were performed led the Socialist government to create a new crime—interfering with legal abortion. This legislation came only after women's groups had mobilized to publicize the problem and to demand action from public prosecutors who were doing nothing in the face of pro-life actions.[57] Right-wing parties have also introduced legislation to eliminate social security coverage of the costs of abortion, and women's groups must remain on the alert against such attacks, which are not likely to end in the current climate of neoliberalism.

The declining support for traditional formulas of social democracy, even among social democratic parties, and the mounting enthusiasm for neoliberalism (including market-driven economic policies and a reduced role for the state) constitute probably the greatest threat to feminist politics. Economic restructuring carried out in the name of improving international competitiveness has taken a form that privileges the market and market relations. As the state retreats from responsibility for overseeing social solidarity and adopts a discourse of deregulation, it becomes very difficult to promote the kinds of state activities that women's movements have identified as central to overcoming women's economic and social inferiorities. Thus, a discourse of equal opportunities and categorial equity does not sit well with a discourse of competitiveness. Even more costly are the practices of retreating from social spending. Claims for child care, for better training, for elder care, for expanded health services, for protecting women's employment in the state sector—all are more likely to fall on deaf ears when the universe of political discourse is organized around the idea that "cutbacks" are needed in order to render a country's economy internationally competitive.

And finally, the declining electoral power of the Left and the rise of new and very right-wing parties have been marked by the return of traditional notions of family, women's role, and the gender division of labor. It is not only the Italian and French Rights, with their populist and even neofascist parties, that display enthusiasm for stay-at-home women and high birthrates. The Conservative Party in Britain has also presided over policies that push responsibility for care back into "the family," which means, of course, the women of the family. In this era of neoliberalism, which has brought both strong forces opposed to feminism and a weakening of traditional allies, the challenge facing women's movements is to identify and work with those political allies that are willing to and capable of developing credible political alternatives, incorporating the empowerment of women as a central and nonnegotiable element of such alternatives.

If women's movements in many countries must combat the negative effects of neoliberalism for their transformatory politics, those of Western Europe face an additional challenge particular to them: The creation of the European Union presents both threats and opportunities for women's movements, which can be ignored only at great risk. The EU has become in many ways a quasi state, and one of its areas of activity has been to promote equality policy, based on Article 119 of the Treaty of Rome, which guarantees equality between women and men. Women's movements can no longer afford, then, to confine their actions to the local or the national level. Important decisions affecting their future are being taken at the European level, and their presence there as women and as movement activists is essential. For movements that have often confined their organizational efforts to local actions and whose resources are limited, the effort required is great.

Despite these difficulties, there are some signs of potential space. The EU has already shown itself ready to support financially the work of women's groups as well as to provide leadership in some policy areas. Regional funds to promote women's economic activity testify to the first, while the leadership that the EU has shown in the areas of equality policy and sexual harassment point to the second. The EU has been a resource for women's movements in member states as they prod their national governments to act. For example, the European Commission funded and worked closely with the major French organization responsible for raising the issue of sexual harassment in France and campaigning for the legislation passed in 1992. The EU also funds working groups and networks bringing together experts, including movement activists, to work on issues touching on gender equality. Moreover, it has been willing to use a broad definition of equality in order to justify its interest in child care, for example, which is not strictly speaking within its mandate.

Nevertheless, the EU remains very much a work in progress. Actors of varying ideological persuasions do not all share the same vision of its future. Some hope to buttress the best of Europe's progressive traditions by implanting them at the European level and pulling laggards toward the highest standards. But others see in the common economic space an opportunity to enshrine market principles at a supranational level, thereby tying the hands of national governments that might try to be "too social." Given that this major conflict about the shape of the future is being fought in the institutions of the EU as well as in member states, women's movements cannot afford to be absent. The existence of the EU provides opportunities for women's movements to act together across Europe and to continue the struggle for a progressive solution to the problems facing women at the dawn of the twenty-first century.

NOTES

1. Martien Briët, Bert Klandermans, and Frederike Kroon, "How Women Became Involved in the Women's Movement of the Netherlands," in Mary F. Katzenstein and Carol Mueller, eds., *The Women's Movements of the United States and Western Europe: Consciousness, Political Opportunity, and Public Policy* (Philadelphia: Temple University Press, 1987), p. 44; emphasis added.

2. On this experience in France, see Claire Duchen, *Feminism in France: From May '68 to Mitterrand* (London: Routledge and Kegan Paul, 1986), Chapters 1–2; and Jane Jenson, "Representations of Difference: The Women's Movement in France," *New Left Review* no. 180 (June 1990).

3. For the history of these various movements, see Mary F. Katzenstein and Carol Mueller, eds., *The Women's Movements of the United States and Western Europe: Consciousness, Political Opportunity, and Public Policy* (Philadelphia: Temple University Press, 1987); and Barbara Nelson and Najma Chowdhury, eds., *Women and Politics Worldwide* (New Haven: Yale University Press, 1994).

4. Mary Fainsod Katzenstein, "Comparing the Women's Movements of the United States and Western Europe: An Overview," in Mary F. Katzenstein and Carol Mueller, eds., *The Women's Movements of the United States and Western Europe: Consciousness, Political Opportunity, and Public Policy* (Philadelphia: Temple University Press, 1987), p. 5.

5. This is the conclusion of almost all the contributors to ibid.; Judith Adler Hellman, *Journeys Among Women: Feminism in Five Italian Cities* (New York: Oxford University Press, 1987); and of Jenson, 1990, for example.

6. Jane Jenson and Rianne Mahon, "Representing Solidarity: Class, Gender, and the Crisis in Social Democratic Sweden," *New Left Review,* no. 201 (1993).

7. Myra Marx Ferree, "Equality and Autonomy: Feminist Politics in the United States and West Germany," in Mary F. Katzenstein and Carol Mueller, eds., *The Women's Movements of the United States and Western Europe: Consciousness, Political Opportunity, and Public Policy* (Philadelphia: Temple University Press, 1987).

8. See Hege Skjeie, "The Uneven Advance of Norwegian Women," *New Left Review,* no. 187 (1991).

9. I am using a broad definition of women's movements and feminism, refusing the exclusionary practice of some groups to banish other activists beyond the feminist pale. On the tendency to do so, Yasmine Ergas, "Feminism of the 1970s," in Françoise Thébaud, ed., *A History of Women in the West: Toward a Cultural Identity in the Twentieth Century* (Cambridge, Mass: Belknap Press, 1994), pp. 532–536. I define as women's movements' politics all the forms of action detailed in the quote by Briët et al., and I include all women who self-identify as feminists. My definition also includes, however, some women who claim to be "postfeminists," as some French women did at the beginning of the women's movement in France, when they banished feminism to the dustbin of history.

10. In this chapter I pay no attention to one major form of action for creating solidarity: the generation of a new intellectual tradition of feminist theory. That part of the project of many movements merits a study of its own. For a discussion, see Seyla Benhabib and Drucilla Cornell, eds., *Feminism as Critique: On the Politics of Gender* (Minneapolis: University of Minnesota Press, 1987).

11. The notion of categorical equity is developed with reference to the Canadian women's movements in Jane Jenson, "Citizenship and Equity: Variations Across Time and Space," in Janet Hiebert, ed., *Political Ethics: A Canadian Perspective* (Toronto: Dundurn Press, 1992).

12. T. H. Marshall, *Class, Citizenship and Social Development: Essays* (Garden City, N.Y.: Anchor Books, 1965), p. 76.

13. This right emerged first in the form of protection from unreasonable search and seizure, of habeas corpus, etc.

14. Karen Beckwith, "Response to Feminism in the Italian Parliament: Divorce, Abortion, and Sexual Violence Legislation," in Mary F. Katzenstein and Carol Mueller, eds., *The Women's Movements of the United States and Western Europe: Consciousness, Political Opportunity, and Public Policy* (Philadelphia: Temple University Press, 1987), pp. 157–158. In Italy the struggle for abortion rights was preceded by one to reform divorce law, which was one of the first actions in which the second-wave women's movement engaged.

15. Monique Leijenaar and Kees Niemöller, "Political Participation of Women: The Netherlands," in Barbara Nelson and Najma Chowdhury, eds., *Women and Politics Worldwide* (New Haven: Yale University Press, 1994), p. 500. The actual law passed in 1980 was quite restrictive, however, despite this mobilization.

16. Christiane Lemke, "Women and Politics: The New Federal Republic of Germany," in Barbara Nelson and Najma Chowdhury, eds., *Women and Politics Worldwide* (New Haven: Yale University Press, 1994), p. 274. Such confessions were also used by prominent German women in the early 1970s.

17. For Italy, see also Yasmine Ergas, "1968–79—Feminism and the Italian Party System," *Comparative Politics* 14, no. 3 (1982); and Beckwith, 1987. For France, see Jane Jenson, "Changing Discourse, Changing Agendas: Political Rights and Reproductive Policies in France," in Mary F. Katzenstein and Carol Mueller, eds., *The Women's Movements of the United States and Western Europe: Consciousness, Political Opportunity, and Public Policy* (Philadelphia: Temple University Press, 1987), pp. 82ff.

18. This coupling of doctors' "right to choose" with very restrictive conditions was the result of West Germany's reform of abortion law in the 1970s. For a discussion of the Norwegian mobilization to move away from the doctor-controlled model, resulting in the 1978 legislation permitting "free abortion" for twelve weeks, see Janneke van der Ros, "The State and Women: A Troubled Relationship in Norway," in Barbara Nelson and Najma Chowdhury, eds., *Women and Politics Worldwide* (New Haven: Yale University Press, 1994), p. 532.

19. MFPF, *D'une révolte à une lutte: 25 ans de l'historie du planning familial* (Paris: Tierce, 1984).

20. Margaret Maruani, *Les Syndicats à l'épreuve de féminisme* (Paris: Syros, 1979).

21. Beckwith, 1987, pp. 158–162.

22. Van der Ros, 1994, pp. 533–534.

23. Ferree, 1987.

24. Maria Teresa Gallego Mendez, "Women's Political Engagement in Spain," in Barbara Nelson and Najma Chowdhury, eds., *Women and Politics Worldwide* (New Haven: Yale University Press, 1994), pp. 667–668.

25. Isabella Bakker, "Women's Employment in Comparative Perspective," in Jane Jenson et al., eds., *The Feminization of the Labour Force* (Oxford: Polity Press: 1988).

26. Margaret Maruani, "The Position of Women in the Labour Market," *Women in Europe* (supplement), no. 36 (1992):30.

27. See, for example, Skjeie, 1991, p. 89, for Norway.

28. Jane Jenson and Mariette Sineau, *François Mitterrand et les Françaises: Un rendez-vous manqué* (Paris: Fondation Nationale de Science Politique, forthcoming), Chapter 7.

29. Mary Ruggie, "Workers' Movements and Women's Interests: The Impact of Labor-State Relations in Britain and Sweden," in Mary F. Katzenstein and Carol Mueller, eds., *The Women's Movements of the United States and Western Europe: Consciousness, Political Opportunity, and Public Policy* (Philadelphia: Temple University Press, 1987), pp. 251ff.

30. E. Haavio-Mannila et al., *Unfinished Democracy: Women in Nordic Politics* (Oxford: Pergamon Press, 1985), pp. 148–149.

31. See Ruggie, 1987, p. 262, for Sweden; and Skjeie, 1991, pp. 87–89, for Norway.

32. See Ann Orloff, "Gender and the Social Rights of Citizenship: The Comparative Analysis of Gender Relations and Welfare States," *American Sociological Review* 58, no. 3 (1993), for an overview and literature review.

33. Laura Balbo, "Crazy Quilts: Rethinking the Welfare State Debate from a Woman's Point of View," in Anne Showstack Sasson, ed., *Women and the State* (London: Hutchison, 1987).

34. Sheila Rowbotham et al., *Beyond the Fragments: Feminism and the Making of Socialism* (London: Islington Community Press, 1979); Jane Jenson, "Both Friend and Foe: Women and State Welfare," in Renate Bridenthal et al., eds., *Becoming Visible: Women in European History* (Boston: Houghton Mifflin, 1989).

35. Anette Borchorst and Birte Siim, "Women and the Advanced Welfare State—a New Kind of Patriarchal Power?" in Anne Showstack Sasson, ed., *Women and the State* (London: Hutchison, 1987).

36. Jenson and Mahon, 1993, p. 91.

37. Skjeie, 1991, p. 90.

38. Danilèle Kergoat, ed., *Les Infirmières et leur coordination, 1988–89* (Paris: Lamarre, 1992), pp. 19–20.

39. Rianne Mahon, "From Solidaristic Wages to Solidaristic Work," in Wallace Clement and Rianne Mahon, eds., *Swedish Social Democracy: A Model in Transition* (Toronto: Canadian Scholars Press, 1994), pp. 304–305.

40. See Bianca Beccalli, "The Modern Women's Movement in Italy," *New Left Review,* no. 204 (1994): 100–103, 107–108, on Italy; Maruani, 1979, on France; Elisabeth Vogelheim, "Women in a Changing Workplace: The Case of the FRG," in Jane Jenson et al., eds., *The Feminism of the Labour Force* (Oxford: Polity Press, 1988), on Germany; and Joyce Gelb, "Social Movement Success: A Comparative Analysis of Feminism in the United States and the United Kingdom," in Mary F. Katzenstein and Carol Mueller, eds., *The Women's Movements of the United States and Western Europe: Consciousness, Political Opportunity, and Public Policy* (Philadelphia: Temple University Press, 1987), on Britain. See also Skjeie, 1991, pp. 93ff, on Norway. While such efforts have been relatively successful, a surprising holdout has been in Norway.

41. Helga-Maria Hernes, *Welfare State and Women Power: Essays in State Feminism* (Oslo: Norwegian University Press, 1987), p. 40.

42. Jenson and Sineau, forthcoming, p. 40.

43. Ibid., Chapter 10.

44. On the Green-feminist link, see Ferree, 1987, p. 179; on the pressures to change the Italian Communist party, see Stephen Hellman, "Feminism and the Model of Militancy in an Italian Communist Federation: Challenges to the Old Style of Politics," in Mary F. Katzenstein and Carol Mueller, eds., *The Women's Movements of the United States and Western Europe: Consciousness, Political Opportunity, and Public Policy* (Philadelphia: Temple University Press, 1987).

45. Hernes, 1987, p. 141.

46. Here I am explicitly following Ergas, 1992, pp. 537ff., and rejecting the usual tendency to argue that wings of the women's movement can be distinguished by their search for equality or difference. These two terms are not true antonyms. The opposite of equality is inequality, while the opposite of difference is identity, or sameness. Therefore, the question becomes, Do women's movements make claims for overcoming inequality in the name of difference or of sameness?

47. See Skjeie, 1991, p. 94. It is interesting to note that Norwegian feminists claim greater access to representative institutions in the name of difference—that women have the right to be represented by women.

48. Beccalli, 1994, pp. 105–106; and Lynne Segal, "Whose Left? Socialism, Feminism, and the Future," *New Left Review,* no. 185 (1991).

49. Jenson, 1990.

50. Ferree, 1987, p. 179; Segal, 1991.

51. Duchen, 1986, Chapter 5; Beccalli, 1994.

52. Ergas, 1994, pp. 541–542.

53. Ferree, 1987, pp. 185ff.

54. Beckwith, 1987; Janine Mossuz-Lavau, *Les Lois de l'amour: Les Politiques de la sexualité en France, 1950–1990* (Paris: Payot, 1991), pp. 192–196.

55. Maruani, 1992, p. 4.

56. Lemke, 1994, pp. 275–276. For women from the former East Germany, the change was obviously very great. But even in the former West Germany, the court's stress on the "rights of the unborn life" and prohibition of coverage by health insurance of even legal abortions done for "social indications" (90 percent of legal abortions) constituted a major new limit on access.

57. Jenson and Sineau, forthcoming, Chapter 9. For example, antiabortion "commandos" who threatened women or invaded clinics were only rarely charged with assault or trespass.

17

Feminism Lives: Building a Multicultural Women's Movement in the United States

LESLIE R. WOLFE & JENNIFER TUCKER

As WE WERE WRITING THIS chapter, two signs of the times caught our eye. First, the annual *Women's History Catalog* from the National Women's History Project arrived containing a wealth of feminist historical materials about women of every race/ethnicity, class, and cultural background for schools and parents. Then, the *New York Times* reported on a 1990s version of a feminist protest "zap action" in which the voice boxes of talking GI Joe soldier dolls were switched with the Barbie fashion dolls', so that *he* says, "Let's go shopping" and *she* says, "Attack! Eat lead, Cobra," to "ridicule gender stereotyping in children's toys," as the *Times* put it. Clearly, feminism lives.

Barely twenty years ago, women's history was unheard of in our schools, and the challenge to sex-role stereotypes was a radical feminist fantasy. Barely twenty years ago, we could read all the feminist newsletters and new books and keep up with all the national organizations. Today, it is difficult to keep up with the bibliographies of feminist writing and the directories of women's groups. And so we write this chapter with a sense of excitement and optimism about the future, as feminists who have been involved in the movement for twenty years as thinkers and activists, policymakers, and as organizers. Our theoretical and historical approach grows from these experiences and those of our sisters in the movement. We begin with the assumption that the women's movement is not what you think it is. In addition to the well-known, predominantly white and middle-class national women's organizations and individual leaders or writers portrayed in the

435

UNITED STATES

GENERAL

type of government: Federal Democratic Republic
major ethnic groups: White/European (83.4%); Black (12.4%); Asian(3.3%); Native
    American (0.8%)
language: English; Spanish spoken by significant minority
religions: Protestant (56%); Roman Catholic (28%); Islam; Judaism
date of independence: 1776
former colonial power: Britain

DEMOGRAPHICS

population size: 256 million
birth rate (*per 1,000 population*): 14
total fertility (*average number of births per woman*): 2.1
contraceptive prevalence (*married women*): 74%
maternal mortality rate (*per 100,000 live births*): 13

WOMEN'S STATUS

date of women's suffrage: 1920 (national)
economically active population: M 77%   F 50%
female employment (*% of total workforce*): 41
life expectancy   M 72   F 79
school enrollment ratio (*F/100 M*)
    primary   95
    secondary   95
    tertiary   110
literacy   M 97%   F 97%

---

press, the women's movement is the many and diverse organizations and activists
described in the following pages. Thus, the movement *is* the rich diversity of feminist activism of women of color,[1] lesbians, low-income women, and women with
disabilities who are and have been organizing for change. The story of the wom-
en's movement in the United States is one of transformation, expansion, and diversification. Though not yet fully achieved, we believe that this vision of a truly

multicultural feminism will continue to characterize this movement in its maturity.

In this chapter, we want to convey the feeling of movement and change and to capture some of the drama of the U.S. women's movement since the 1960s. We also try to show how feminism is embedded in the political, social, and economic trends of its times and how the various branches of the women's movement grew out of women's participation in other progressive and radical movements. We have shaped this history around what we call "explosive moments," defined as events that helped transform women's consciousness and launch them into new levels of activism. This chapter focuses on a few explosive moments that changed the national debate on women's issues, largely by changing federal policy through legislation or judicial decisions and creating new feminist structures. We recognize that individual women in the women's movement have experienced their own explosive moments. In fact, the success of the women's movement is demonstrated by the diverse ways that women of all backgrounds have moved themselves and their communities toward equality and empowerment. Finally, we seek to clarify the significance of race and class analyses as part of all analyses of women's oppression.

An important part of our task has been to envision the next generation of the U.S. women's movement. To do so, we used three strategies to incorporate many women's voices and perspectives into the shaping of this vision. First, we invited six women thinkers and leaders to serve as consultants;[2] then we conducted a national survey of over eight thousand women activists; and finally we convened a meeting on "The Future of the U.S. Women's Movement" on November 18–19, 1993. The survey results provided a rich source of information on the key issues and strategies, leaders and participants, obstacles, and successes and failures of the U.S. women's movement. The meeting brought together a diverse group of feminist activists from throughout the United States to envision the future by defining the trends that will shape this future, the problems that will demand attention, and the strategies, structures, and leaders who will address them. This shared vision shapes the final section of this chapter.

The U.S. Women's Movement, 1960s–1970s

Origins

The women's movement that burst into public consciousness in the late 1960s had its origins in the nineteenth-century struggle for the abolition of slavery, as African American and white women abolitionists who had been denied membership in some organizations and the right to speak in public began to protest the subordination of women and to agitate for women's rights.[3] The first women's rights convention, held at Seneca Falls, New York, July 19–20, 1848, adopted the formal Declaration of Sentiments and Resolutions on the Rights of Women and launched a multi-issue feminist movement. Soon, however, winning the vote for women became the movement's top priority, and it gradually became a women's suffrage movement.[4]

After the vote was won in 1920, the women's movement continued on a smaller scale as suffragists turned their attention to other issues, working for peace, family planning, workers' rights to unionize, and other social reforms.[5] The racial segregation that had characterized the suffrage struggle, and social life in the United States, continued. African American women who had fought for the vote now turned their energies to the fight against racism and segregation through organizations such as the National Association of Colored Women, Black sororities, and the National Council of Negro Women. When African American women sought support from the League of Women Voters and the National Woman's Party for the struggle against racial discrimination at the polls and for antilynching laws, they were told that these were not "women's issues."[6] Separately, white and African American women built strong organizations that survived to support the women's movement that emerged decades later. Women's organizations also existed among Asian immigrant groups, and Latinas and Native American women organized within their own communities.

The radical suffragists of the Congressional Union formed the National Woman's Party, which devoted itself to the passage of an equal rights amendment (ERA) to the Constitution to guarantee women full equality under the law. While the ERA was introduced into every session of Congress beginning in 1923, it was rarely debated and was opposed by organized labor and a majority of women's organizations because it would invalidate the protective labor laws for which they had fought.

World War II transformed the lives of many American women as they moved into jobs previously held by men who now were soldiers. In the racially segregated United States, however, these employment opportunities rarely were open to women of color.[7] After the war, women lost these jobs to returning men, and a new "cult of domesticity" was touted in policy and in the media. Many women, however, rejected these roles and images and created a cadre of labor union activists who articulated demands, which remain on the feminist agenda, for child care, paid maternity leave, and equal pay for comparable work.[8]

Launching the "New" Women's Movement: 1960s–1970s

During the turbulent, idealistic 1960s, profound social change suddenly seemed possible. The government's war on poverty and the African American civil rights movement generated a fervor for justice and social change that inspired activists in other communities of color and advocates for women. The reinvigorated wom-

Members of the National Organization for Women (NOW) display the text of the Equal Rights Amendment, first presented to Congress in 1923, at the 1978 Women's Equality Day celebration at the Statue of Liberty, New York. Ninety-year-old suffragist Isolda Dubic (foreground) joins them.

en's movement developed along two paths: the liberal women's rights movement and the more radical feminist movement for women's liberation. In both contexts, many women struggled to build a multicultural feminist movement. Confronting the demand from men of color and from white women that they had to choose whether racism or sexism was most oppressive, some feminists of color and white feminist theorists began to develop a third way, considering racism and sexism as twin evils and women of color as the experts on their impact.[9]

Like their foremothers working for suffrage, women of color often experienced racism from white women and sexism from men of color. White feminists often assumed that similarities of gender would overcome differences of race and class and sought to recruit women of color into their organizations and their ideology. Many white feminists thought they were being antiracist by attempting to be "color-blind." However, many women of color and others understood this as an insult, recognizing that asking women to deny their differences was ultimately destructive of the unified feminist vision that was their goal.

Explosive Moments: Moving Forward

The women's movement during the 1960s and early 1970s was exciting, invigorating, and transformational for many women. The movement encompassed efforts to attack sex discrimination in law and social policy through legislative and legal means as well as "consciousness-raising" to understand patriarchy and women's subjugation and create strategies to transform society—from government to religion to the family—into an egalitarian one. While the growth of the women's movement was gradual and built on women's experiences in other progressive social movements, several explosive moments helped shape feminism during the 1960s.

In 1961, in response to pressure from women's groups, President John F. Kennedy appointed the first President's Commission on the Status of Women, chaired by former First Lady Eleanor Roosevelt. Largely in response to the commission's recommendations, President Kennedy in 1962 ordered federal government agencies to stop discriminating against women employees. In 1963, Congress passed the Equal Pay Act, requiring employers to pay women and men "equal pay for equal work." The commission's work initiated government action for women's rights over the next fifteen years and served as the model for other official government structures through which feminist advocates could work for legal and policy changes.

Passage of the first federal civil rights law to prohibit sex discrimination in employment soon followed. In 1964, as Congress was debating landmark civil rights legislation to outlaw race discrimination, an elaborate strategy by the National Woman's Party[10] persuaded a conservative member of Congress to propose adding prohibition of sex discrimination in employment. He perceived this partly as a joke and partly as a way to derail the civil rights bill. However, thanks to the strategic efforts of feminist advocates and Representative Martha Griffiths (D.–Mich.), the bill passed.

During this same period, Betty Friedan's 1963 book, *The Feminine Mystique,* articulated widespread discontent among white upper-middle-class homemakers and assured them that this discontent was not a sign of neurotic maladjustment to their "proper role." The fact that the book was a best-seller reflected the hunger among many women for a larger life and helped prepare them to join the National Organization for Women (NOW), the new women's rights organization that Friedan and her colleagues established three years later in June 1966. This explosive moment had begun when many of the women attending the third annual conference of state commissions on the status of women were denied permission to propose resolutions demanding changes in enforcement of the law prohibiting sex discrimination in employment. Their outrage sparked the creation of NOW, which took the women's movement forward into new levels of activism.

The women's liberation movement developed independently and was created by younger women activists in radical social change movements, particularly the Student Nonviolent Coordinating Committee (SNCC) and Students for a Democratic Society (SDS), who began to question the second-class status of women within these movements during the 1960s. The explosive moment for SDS women came at the National Conference for a New Politics in 1967, when a women's caucus attempted to raise women's issues and was met with ridicule and rejection.

During 1967 and 1968, radical women organized women's liberation groups in several cities.[11] While these groups were predominantly composed of young white activists, women of color were also building feminist organizations such as the National Black Feminist Organization, Asian Women United (San Francisco), and Asian Sisters in Action (Boston).[12] Native American women were leaders in the fishing rights struggles of the 1960s, building on a long tradition of indigenous women's activism as political leaders.[13]

The women's liberation groups suffered through a series of conflicts and splits based on ideology, sexual orientation, ethnic and class differences, and structural problems. Feminist theorists developed extensive analyses of the structures of patriarchy, institutionalized sexism, and male supremacy and the links among sexism, racism, heterosexism, and classism. Disputes erupted between New Left women, who held that the nation's political and economic system was responsible for women's problems, and radical feminists, who insisted that male supremacy and patriarchal institutions were the source of women's oppression.[14] Radical feminists also rejected the notion that moving women into equality with men in an inherently unjust system should be the goal of feminism. Instead, they sought to analyze and alter the cause of all forms of inequality—the oppression of women as a class. Lesbian feminists challenged the movement to confront both misogyny

Attorney Florence Kennedy (left) meets La Donna Harris, a Native American activist, during a 1976 conference on minorities.

and homophobia[15] and to recognize their common source in patriarchal structures.

The radical feminists soon became the movement's creative, cutting edge in both theory and practice, developing tactics that would be used for the next two decades. In 1968, New York Radical Women developed consciousness-raising as a strategy for sharing women's personal experiences in order to explore the many ways in which women were oppressed individually and collectively. Thousands of other women around the country also formed consciousness-raising groups.[16] The first "speak-out" where women publicly described their experiences of abortion was organized in 1969 by the radical feminist group Redstockings. The speak-out created a model for raising a range of other issues, including rape, sexual harassment, and incest, which opened up taboo subjects and transformed them into topics for public debate. Radical feminists also conducted public demonstrations and zap actions, such as the headline-grabbing demonstrations outside the Miss America beauty pageant, where undergarments were stuffed into a "freedom trash can" to protest the treatment of women as sex objects.[17] Finally, women's liberation activists launched several publications and a number of feminist books were published,[18] all of which helped build the movement and shape the thinking of activists and of women who were not affiliated with feminist organizations. In short, radical feminism in the United States during this period was earth-shattering and mind-opening for many women; its participants built new worldviews that have influenced American society in ways they could not have conceived.

The Flourishing of the Women's Movement: The 1970s

The women's movement grew rapidly in the late 1960s and into the early 1970s. Its diversity was the hallmark of its success and evidence of its growing influence. The movement needed these many factions, from the radical to the moderate, as feminists were addressing the underlying patriarchal assumptions that shaped society while also seeking to reform discriminatory laws and policies and to inspire individual women to change their own lives. The movement's diversity helped it build a powerful base of theory and tactics that made it strong enough to withstand both its own internal disputes and the virulent opposition that was to come in the 1980s.

In 1969, the media discovered the new feminism and ran stories that ridiculed radical feminists and trivialized the movement as "women's lib." In spite of this image, across the nation women created and joined local feminist groups,[19] filed sex discrimination complaints, launched demonstrations, and, in 1972, created *Ms.*, a new national feminist magazine. While ridicule, trivializing, and distortion continued, the media began to treat at least a portion of the movement as a real social change phenomenon.

Feminism became a mass movement during the summer of 1970, with the August 26 Women's Strike for Equality. Organized by NOW and many other feminist groups, including Women's Strike for Peace, local women's liberation groups, and the Third World Women's Alliance, these marches brought thousands of women into the streets in cities across the country to put forward feminist demands. The strike became the prototype for numerous national marches for women's equality and reproductive rights in succeeding years.

During the 1970s, the women's movement achieved substantial gains in law and public policy, in the creation and expansion of feminist organizations, and in consciousness-raising that moved many radical feminist ideas and demands into the mainstream. In the early to mid-1970s, many feminist groups focused on creating women's rights law and policy at the federal and state levels, beginning with a constitutional guarantee of equality. Congress finally passed the Equal Rights Amendment in 1972, forty-nine years after it had first been introduced. However, to become an amendment to the Constitution, the ERA had to be ratified by two-thirds of state legislatures. From 1972 to 1982, this struggle at the state level consumed much of the energy of national women's organizations. In spite of their extraordinary efforts and the support of 63 percent of the public, the amendment was defeated in June 1982. Feminists had been outmaneuvered by the well-organized and heavily funded conservative "Stop ERA" movement.[20] However, the

Members of Union de Mujeres Americanas support the Equal Rights Amendment at a 1975 rally in New York City.

ERA struggle itself mobilized women nationwide in grassroots organizations; the defeat of the ERA in the legislatures shaped women's determination to run pro-ERA women for political office against men who had opposed the amendment. Thus, the failure of the ERA was itself an explosive moment for women to enter the political arena.

Feminist lobbying and organizing brought about major legislative victories and built a body of federal anti–sex discrimination law and court decisions during the 1970s and into the 1980s.[21] Following earlier laws mandating equal pay and forbidding sex discrimination in employment, the new statutes prohibited sex discrimination in education, in consumer credit, in home mortgage lending, and in nursing and medical schools. Federal programs were created to fund research on rape and domestic violence, to expand the mandate of the U.S. Commission on Civil Rights to study sex as well as race bias and discrimination, and to create model programs to eliminate sex bias in schools and colleges. However, feminist initiatives to address the social and economic bases of women's lower status—women's poverty, comparable worth, child care, and family leave, for example—were far less successful.

Feminist attorneys brought cases to the U.S. Supreme Court in an attempt to persuade the Court to recognize women's right to equal treatment under the law, even without an Equal Rights Amendment. Feminist attorney Ruth Bader Ginsburg argued a series of important cases for the Women's Rights Project of the American Civil Liberties Union that established a body of women's rights case law that generally protected working women's rights; she was appointed to the Supreme Court in 1993. However, it was the Supreme Court's 1973 ruling establishing a woman's right to abortion[22] that became a defining moment both for the women's movement and its opponents.

Feminists had identified the right to abortion in the context of both equality and individual liberty—recognizing that women's rights would be meaningless without control over their reproduction and that women had to have the fundamental right to bodily integrity and autonomy. Women of color who supported the right to choose abortion[23] argued for a broader reproductive rights agenda to address other issues, such as forced sterilization of low-income women of color and their lack of access to reproductive health care. Feminists worked for legalized abortion in a variety of ways: They violated criminal abortion laws,[24] advocated their repeal, lobbied legislatures, and staged demonstrations and speak-outs. As abortion rights became a highly visible issue, broad public support for the old laws diminished.[25]

The 1973 Supreme Court decision in the case of *Roe* v. *Wade* established a woman's right to abortion in the context of the constitutional guarantee of a right of privacy, permitting abortion without restrictions during the first three months of pregnancy.[26] The ruling touched off a powerful backlash among opponents of abortion rights. However, most feminists did not then recognize the extent to which the conservative religious and secular right-wing forces would mobilize against abortion rights.

For the women's movement, the huge National Women's Conference held in Houston, Texas, in 1977 marked a turning point. It was the U.S. government's response[27] to the United Nations' declaration of 1975 as International Women's Year (IWY) and the first women's rights conference sponsored and funded by the federal government. In preparation, conferences to elect delegates had been held in virtually all of the fifty states. The two thousand delegates who gathered to develop a national plan of action were the most diverse group of women's activists ever brought together in the United States. More than one-third were women of color, whose organizing skills ensured inclusion of a forceful statement in the plan about women of color and the combined issues of racism and sexism. Many were lesbian feminist activists, who demanded an end to homophobia in the women's movement and support for lesbian and gay rights. Women came to Houston from every branch of the women's movement, and many came away aware of the need to build a national, multicultural feminist movement.[28]

To a large extent, the IWY conference was another explosive moment for the U.S. women's movement. It helped launch new organizations and brought much of the feminist agenda into the mainstream of government policy and popular discourse. The National Plan of Action addressed the full range of women's issues, including educational equity, reproductive rights and health, political participation, employment discrimination and workplace policies, child care, poverty and welfare reform, and violence against women. This plan helped shape new coalitions and strategies that helped preserve and expand the movement during the antifeminist backlash years to come.

Backlash and Recovery: The 1980s and Early 1990s

By the end of the 1970s, many feminists believed that their inexorable progress toward full equality for women could not be slowed. However, the 1980s brought to fruition a virulent antifeminist reaction that had begun in the 1970s. It marked the low ebb of the women's movement and slowed much of its progress.

Feminist success inevitably engendered antifeminist backlash. Initially focused on the Equal Rights Amendment and the right to abortion, it was expanded by a right-wing social agenda that defines feminism as a destroyer of the traditional, patriarchal family and the American way of life. The Stop ERA movement and the national antiabortion movement, which its promoters called "pro-life," were priorities of the New Right during the 1970s; it also targeted gay and lesbian rights, defining feminism and gay rights as twin evils.[29]

Some feminist achievements of the 1970s were double-edged swords. International Women's Year not only mobilized women's rights activists nationwide; it also mobilized the right-wing opposition. In some states, local antiabortion activists, religious fundamentalists, anti-ERA groups, and members of conservative political and racist groups participated in the statewide women's conferences in preparation for Houston. Eleven states elected delegations in which the majority opposed most feminist goals.[30] The Houston conference also proved to be an effective organizing tool for conservatives, and its repercussions are still being felt. New Right women's groups were founded, most notably Concerned Women for America, and they emerged as key players in creating the National Pro-Family Movement, which attacked feminism and gay rights with equal fervor.

The 1980 election was a turning point for the New Right and a sign of its success, as Ronald Reagan, a supporter and ally, was elected president. The significance of this explosive moment for feminism cannot be overstated. Although feminists had never been satisfied with the government's progress in ensuring equal rights, substantial changes had been made in law and policy during the 1970s. But the Reagan administration's policy agenda reflected overt hostility to women's rights as well as to civil rights for people of color, gay and lesbian rights, and programs to alleviate poverty. The government was transformed by conservative appointees, and the election of a New Right president gave visibility, legitimacy, and credibility to this ideology.

Women and women's rights came under attack. Abortion rights were threatened, educational equity programs were targeted for elimination, and federally funded efforts to confront violence against women were banned from using the word "lesbian" in reports.[31] Antipoverty programs were sharply reduced and in some cases virtually eliminated. These policies were supported by rhetoric that attacked low-income women as "welfare queens," especially women of color, despite the fact that more white women than women of color receive welfare benefits. The New Right's agenda was clarified in its legislative proposals; the Family Protection Act, introduced in 1981 but never enacted, was emblematic. It proposed to repeal the federal law forbidding sex discrimination in education, forbid coeducation in sports and other school activities, deny federal funds to any school using textbooks portraying women in nontraditional roles, repeal federal laws protecting battered wives from their husbands, eliminate funding to programs for victims of rape and battery, ban federally funded legal aid for divorce or abortion counseling, and create tax incentives for husbands whose wives earned *no* money.[32]

At the same time, more subtle antifeminist reaction was portrayed throughout the mass media, suggesting that the women's movement was both dangerous and dead. Stories and images suggested that society had entered a "postfeminist" and "post–civil rights" era in which "equality" had been achieved for capable women

United Auto Worker union members demonstrate their support of a woman's right to choose in 1989.

and men of color. Some even suggested that feminism *caused* women's problems.[33]

One of the legacies of these years was a subtle shift in defining "women's issues." The feminist vision of these issues as a constellation of concerns for ending structures of dominance and advancing women's equality and empowerment began to disappear. It was replaced by a nonfeminist vision of work and family issues that continued to define women primarily through their roles as mothers and wives. Solutions to these so-called work and family conflicts were portrayed as the working woman's problem, especially the working mother's problem. This undermined feminist demands for real transformation in the cultures of the workplace and the home.

Women's Movement Response and Recovery

Despite media assertions to the contrary, the women's movement in the United States was far from dead. Instead, the movement had become more diverse and diffuse, encompassing women's groups organized everywhere—within unions and churches, state legislatures and corporations, universities and school systems. The persistence of the women's movement during the 1980s is largely attributable to these many organizations, and the movement's strength is in the multiplicity of these organizations and structures. They have brought feminism to diverse groups of women and in the process transformed the women's movement. The unreported news of the women's movement during the late 1970s and into the 1980s was the building of feminist women of color organizations and the gradual adoption of feminist agendas by older, more traditional women's organizations.

Throughout the 1970s, existing women's organizations continued to grow and new ones were founded; most have continued to the present.[34] A variety of other regional and national feminist organizations continue to flourish. Many of these focus on particular issues, such as women's health or employment and training. Others brought together feminists from specific ethnic or age groups to address a range of issues. Furthermore, the agendas of women's organizations that had been in existence for several decades became more feminist and their members more active in the women's movement.[35]

While most of the original women's liberation groups disbanded, their ideology and strategies persisted. Many early activists brought their radical feminist agendas to the pro-choice movement, the environmental and antinuclear movements, the gay and lesbian movement, and NOW and other "mainstream" feminist organizations. Organizations such as the Daughters of Bilitis helped inspire other lesbian feminist groups, and organizations such as the National Gay and Lesbian Task Force have recently been led by lesbian feminists. Furthermore, women with disabilities have been in the forefront of the disability rights movement, leading the Disability Rights Education and Defense Fund (DREDF) and the World Institute on Disability, for example, and bringing their feminist consciousness to these agendas.

New groups responded to specific crises in women's lives that exemplified women's oppression, such as rape, battery, poverty, and health care; feminists established battered women's shelters, rape crisis centers, women's health centers, and centers for displaced homemakers nationwide. These groups also formed coalitions that broadened the reach of the women's movement. Many early radical feminists turned to cultural feminism, building women's culture and founding record companies, bookstores, restaurants, art galleries, and publishing houses. Women's spirituality groups created new rituals, and ecofeminists brought feminist analyses to the environmental movement.

During the 1970s and throughout the 1980s, a feminist "establishment" began to evolve in Washington, D.C., to influence public policy and mobilize support for feminist legislative initiatives. In addition to the national membership organizations headquartered in Washington, these groups include feminist legal groups; feminist political action committees, which raise money to support the election of women political candidates; and independent feminist policy research centers that conduct policy-relevant research and advocacy on issues affecting women.[36] Other policy institutes created women's projects, and women organized caucuses within labor unions and government agencies as well. Washington-based feminist groups joined existing coalitions such as the Leadership Conference on Civil Rights and created new ones, such as the National Coalition for Women and

Left to right: Journalist Gloria Steinem, Representatives Bella Abzug and Shirley Chisholm, and Betty Friedan, author of The Feminine Mystique *and a NOW founder, announce the formation of the new National Women's Political Caucus in 1971. The NWPC works to increase the numbers of women candidates for political office.*

Girls in Education. While feminists operating in the federal policy arena were forced to become far more reactive during the 1980s, as the legal and policy gains of the 1970s were attacked by the New Right and its allies in the White House, they continued to work for legislative changes that would support women's organizing in the workplace.

Women's caucuses flourished within virtually every academic and professional association, working to raise the status of women within their disciplines and professions.[37] Women's studies courses on campuses designed to transform the curriculum through a woman-centered, feminist approach grew enormously during the 1970s and 1980s. Feminists of color, often teaching in ethnic studies programs, led the way in building new courses and research on women of color. Academic feminists launched a national women's studies association and a number of journals; women's presses published women's literature and feminist works.[38] Centers for research on women were established on many campuses and were linked with each other and with independent feminist policy centers through the National Council for Research on Women. Women working in philanthropy also began to support programs for women by making both financial and personal contributions to sustain women's organizations in communities nationwide.[39] Through all of these structures and organizations, feminists built an array of strategies and tactics: They staged protests and demonstrations, developed policy and legislative options, conducted scholarly research, published reports and newsletters, built coalitions with other movements, lobbied Congress and the executive branch, filed lawsuits, and built direct service and advocacy programs for women.

Women's organizing at the local and state levels continued and even increased during the 1980s. Many local women's groups in communities of color led the way, creating programs that combined advocacy for systemic change with service programs to meet women's emergency needs—housing, shelter for battered women, advocacy for refugee women, health care, HIV/AIDS prevention and care, and legal services, for example. Statewide coalitions for women's economic justice created models of multicultural feminist leadership by low-income women.[40]

In addition, established national women's organizations took leadership on new issues,[41] new national groups were forming during the late 1980s and into the 1990s, some of which restored the radical vigor of the earlier days of women's liberation, creating its new image for the future. Revolutionary Sisters of Color, for instance, is led by feminists of color, both lesbians and heterosexual women.

As in earlier decades, explosive moments have continued to galvanize women's attention and focus their activism in the 1990s. One such moment brought the issue of sexual harassment and the realities of combined racism and sexism into public debate during the Senate Judiciary Committee's hearing on an African American woman's charges of sexual harassment against an African American male nominee for the Supreme Court. Watching the televised hearings, many women were appalled by the image of the all-white male committee and its apparent failure to comprehend or respect the realities of sexual harassment in the workplace. One outcome was the mobilization of more women candidates for political office. Two televised rape trials of famous men brought the issues of sexual violence against women into American living rooms via television and also made visible the complex web of race and sex biases.

Another Supreme Court ruling allowed state restrictions on the right to abortion and helped launch a new wave of young women's activism to defend the right to abortion they thought was guaranteed. The first national conference by, for, and about young women, called "Feminist Futures,"[42] was held in November 1989, bringing together a diverse group of more than five hundred women in their twenties. Other conferences and more actions followed, and coalitions organized and led largely by young feminists emerged.[43]

The 1980s and early 1990s also marked the expansion of coalitions between feminists and gay and lesbian activists, culminating in the 1992 March on Washington for Gay and Lesbian Rights. After painful splits between lesbian and heterosexual women during the 1970s in radical feminist groups and in NOW, heterosexism in the women's movement is being confronted. NOW has supported

Lesbians participate in the 1973 Gay Pride March in New York. Lesbians have always had an important role in women's movements in the United States.

lesbian rights for over a decade, the American Association of University Women (AAUW) has recognized a lesbian caucus, and the National Women's Studies Association held its first plenary session on lesbian studies in 1988.[44] To a large extent, the survival of "women's culture" has been the accomplishment of lesbian feminists, who have committed their financial and human resources to the perpetuation of woman-identified institutions. Lesbians of color—though leaders in both theory and activism—remain marginalized in all of the movements in which they work.

While the movement to elect profeminist women to public office had begun in the early 1970s,[45] mobilization expanded during the 1980s. Following in the footsteps of Shirley Chisholm—the first African American woman elected to Congress, who mounted a serious campaign for the Democratic nomination for president in 1972—and with pressure from national women's organizations, 1984 Democratic presidential nominee Walter Mondale selected Geraldine Ferraro as his running mate. This generated excitement among many women, despite the ticket's resounding loss to Ronald Reagan. One outcome of this campaign was the birth of the National Political Congress of Black Women to consolidate African American women's political power and to focus their anger at the invisibility and mistreatment of women of color in the campaign for a woman vice-presidential candidate.[46]

A growing number of organizations encouraged women to run for elected office at the local, state, and national levels; raised money for women candidates; conducted training for candidates and elected officials; and publicized women's campaigns.[47] Largely as a result, the 1992 elections brought more women, including women of color, into Congress than in any previous year. Many of these women are outspoken advocates for women's rights, thus increasing the strength of the Congressional Caucus for Women's Issues.

The election of a Democratic president in 1992, who had courted women's votes by supporting many feminist positions, encouraged many activists. Congress quickly passed the Family and Medical Leave Act, and President Bill Clinton signed it into law; he also issued executive orders that repealed a number of the Reagan and Bush administrations' antiabortion policies. Clinton appointed more women, including women of color and lesbians, to important political positions, including many with feminist backgrounds. Overall, the Clinton administration has been more responsive to feminist demands; after twelve years of presidential administrations whose doors were locked to them, feminists now can be assured that their voices will be heard, if not always heeded.

Perhaps the most powerful success of feminism has been in its transformation of public consciousness and rewriting of the public discourse on women's equality. This national consciousness-raising has changed the world; "millions of individual lives have been transformed by feminism, and many young people are very different today because the women's movement existed when they were growing up."[48]

The aspirations and experiences of countless women and men have been transformed; girls and their parents and teachers do not scoff quite so often at the notion of women in the Senate, in sports, and in the space program. Virtually all U.S. magazines and newspapers regularly carry articles about topics that would have been called wild-eyed radical feminist notions two decades ago. These include serious articles about government and corporate sponsorship of child care at the workplace, employers' approaches to balancing work and family, policies and programs to end sexual harassment, woman-centered biomedical research, reproductive rights, lesbian mothers' rights, and the view that violence against women is a crime of misogyny and gender bias, not lust. Furthermore, the increase in the amount of feminist content of many fashion and beauty magazines is astounding,[49] bringing feminist messages to even more women.

Feminist demands, though diluted, have been taken up by unlikely sources, and feminists themselves have entered unlikely spaces. The American Medical Association, for example, has taken up domestic violence and wife abuse as a major issue for the medical profession, and a leading feminist legal scholar sits on the Supreme Court. Throughout the 1980s, public opinion polls revealed this transformation of consciousness; a majority of Americans supported the Equal Rights Amendment, a woman's right to reproductive choice, and even a woman as a presidential candidate. For example, when a leading news weekly magazine conducted a poll in 1986 asking women, "Do you consider yourself a feminist?" 56 percent said yes, and 64 percent of African American women said yes; 71 percent said that the women's movement had improved their lives.[50] By 1989, 85 percent of African-American women and 64 percent of white women were expressing support of "a strong women's movement to push for changes that benefit women";[51] 71 percent of women under forty-five and 60 percent of women over forty-five agreed.

Feminist Futures[52]

As the twenty-first century approaches, we find that the roots of the feminist movement run deep throughout American society and that its seeds are scattered everywhere, as women advocates, service providers, students, writers, and scholars come to the movement from every community and every institution. Some come from a radical feminist ideology, but many do not; some organizations have a strong national presence, but most do not; some are single issue groups; some are built on shared racial or ethnic backgrounds. Some are enthusiastically multicultural, and some are learning how to value and incorporate difference. Some embrace the word *feminism,* while others have adopted new words such as *womanist,* and still others are uncomfortable with any labels. All are clear that they are part of a long and large struggle for women's equality.

The U.S. women's movement faces at least three major challenges over the next decade. First, it will be challenged to address the economic and political changes in the world, including the upsurge in conservative and fundamentalist movements that seek to obliterate women's equality and what they mean for the U.S. women's movement and its relationship with women's movements worldwide. Second, it must become comfortable with the politics of difference and create strength from diversity. And third, it will have to work to strengthen emerging and expanding feminist organizations so that they can pursue strategies to transform the institutions that govern women's lives.

The U.S. women's movement will continue to be shaped by the many perspectives and experiences of the women in the movement: women of color and white women, low-income women and middle/upper-income women, immigrant women, younger and older women, women with disabilities, and heterosexual, lesbian, and bisexual women. Local and national organizations founded and led by feminists of color have broken new ground in shaping feminist agendas, changing women's lives, and advocating for those whose voices have not been heard.

Women activists nationwide are building woman-focused programs to address women's survival needs, such as economic development and employment, child care, violence in the home and streets, health care, homelessness, and HIV/AIDS prevention and care. For women of color in particular, equality for women is both an individual right and a community necessity. Women of color address the impact of both sexism and the decades of oppression and discrimination their communities have faced.

While local groups reach women where they live, national groups can bring their knowledge and struggles to the national policy arena and to the agendas of national feminist organizations. Leaders of national organizations can benefit from new partnerships with local leaders, which will strengthen the movement. Sixty-four percent of the women responding to our survey felt that women's organizations have been most effective at the regional level, while younger women (53 percent) and lower-income women (61 percent) believed that organizations have been most effective at the local level. Only 5 percent of the respondents thought that the movement and its organizations have been most effective at the national level.

Women of color continue to stress the importance of "doing our own work" to define priorities and set agendas, largely through women of color feminist organizations that come with strength and authority. However, when organizations lack financial resources, their ability to expand their feminist activism into a larger arena is limited. National women of color organizations in particular face a lack of financial resources that requires their leaders, though strong, committed, creative, and experienced, to work as volunteers while also holding full-time jobs elsewhere. While volunteer labor is and has always been the backbone of social change movements, including the women's movement, the next stage of development for such organizations is to become permanent, funded, and staffed institutions.

The forward movement of feminism also requires new leadership ideals. Rather than perpetuating hierarchical patterns of top-down leadership, leadership will need to be defined more broadly and distributed more evenly. To maintain their own leadership roles, for example, the large national membership organizations will be expected to work more closely in coalition with other feminist groups and commit resources to supporting their leadership and increasing their visibility. This will contribute to enlarging the image of the movement and its structures in the public eye, as the visibility of a wide range of groups increases.

The leadership of younger women also is essential to a vigorous women's movement, and it can be nurtured through the creation of intergenerational partnerships to pass the leadership to the next generation. While women who came of age in the late 1980s and early 1990s have reaped many of the benefits of the movement's agenda, from abortion rights to women's studies to feminist organizations and media, veteran activists have not found a way to encourage and support the leadership of these women within the movement itself. Rather than simply helping young women appreciate all that has been learned and achieved, today's feminist leaders must also ask young women what they need to continue the revolution. For example, more than half of the young women who responded to our survey listed mentoring as an essential movement strategy.

Solutions to the problems that women will confront—as both their poverty and their vulnerability to male violence continue—require structural and societal changes that only a mass feminist movement of women can bring. Such a mass movement can be fostered only through understanding, reconciliation, respect, and appreciation of difference. For a national movement in a country as racially and ethnically diverse as the United States, differences are not in and of themselves an obstacle to unity. The obstacle is in how difference is addressed. As the women's movement concentrates on confronting the politics of difference, it will move beyond tolerating diversity to valuing, respecting, understanding, and celebrating differentness. To do this, all feminists will need to make a commitment to learning about their sisters' many cultures and sharing their own, learning how and why they sometimes define issues and set priorities differently.

There is no question that feminism and the women's movement have changed the lives of many American women and the institutions that govern their lives. However, the goal of an egalitarian society has not been achieved, and the extent of change varies widely among women based on their social and economic status, race, ethnicity, national origin, geography, class, disability, and sexual orientation. All women do not have the choice of a safe legal abortion when some women cannot afford to pay and others cannot find qualified health providers to perform abortions. While the "glass ceiling" is a real limitation for many working women moving to the top of their professions, the vast majority of working women in the United States remain trapped on the "sticky floor" at the bottom of the economic ladder.

The women's movement's success is often portrayed in terms of both changes in law and policy and the increase in the numbers of women who have entered formerly male-dominated professions. These include women who have gained seats on academic and corporate boards of directors, become corporate vice presidents and chief executive officers, become college professors and presidents, become visible in the media and in sports, created successful businesses, and been elected to state legislatures, Congress, and other political offices. In short, despite feminist ideology to the contrary, success is often measured by the number of women who rise close to the top in a rigidly hierarchical structure.

At the same time, the majority of women in the United States have remained in low-income, low-status jobs with few benefits, little respect, and less security. Increasingly, women and their children have been falling into deeper levels of poverty, even homelessness, and violence against women is pervasive. While issues of violence, economic justice, and opportunity are not new ones for feminist organizations, the movement's success in the future will be measured by how well it changes the lives of women who are the most oppressed, despised, and disadvantaged.

Therefore, in celebrating women at the top, the movement must also hold them accountable to women who are less privileged. Women elected officials will be expected to use their positions to transform the public debate on domestic and foreign policy to move the needs of women and girls from the margins to the center. The women's movement will increasingly define its success in the future by the changes it makes in the lives of women who are relegated to the bottom by society. Adopting this standard will require the movement to reshape its priorities, strategies, and leadership and to return to the vision of a mass movement for institutional change.

In response to the survey question "How has the women's movement changed your life?" most women said that the movement had expanded their job opportunities, made possible more roles for women, and increased their self-esteem and self-confidence. The fact that so many women credit the women's movement for their personal successes suggests that they can be mobilized to work for the kinds of institutional changes that will bring these benefits to other women who have been left behind.

To flourish in the coming years, the women's movement in the United States must increasingly see itself as part of global women's movements. It will increasingly be affected by global changes in government and economic systems and by the way technology links the destinies of people throughout the world in ways that have never existed before. The women's movement in the United States must build stronger partnerships with women's movements globally to confront the worst offenses of sexism and racism, classism and heterosexism—including HIV/AIDS, the lack of sexual and reproductive freedom, and the persistence of violence against women. The majority of survey respondents defined violence against women as the top priority issue for the women's movement in the future; they also pointed to the constellation of economic and workplace equity issues as central to the feminist agenda. These concerns clearly resonate with women worldwide, defining issues of economic justice and freedom from violence, sexual harassment, and restrictions on sexuality, reproductive rights, and health as paramount concerns for the future.

The global reality of U.S. feminism is brought home to the U.S. women's movement through the experiences of immigrant and refugee women who have escaped repression in other countries only to find that they are blamed for many of the social and economic ills of the United States. These are women who are connected worldwide—staying in touch with their families in their countries of origin, sending money, and bringing siblings and parents to join them. Their expertise can help U.S. feminists understand their role in the context of global women's movements, allowing U.S. women to share and learn from the successes and strategies of women's movements worldwide.

Global feminism enables women worldwide to see themselves as a part of a larger movement for change and to acknowledge and accept diversity of perspective, opinion, and priority. Furthermore, a global feminist movement can respond to increased state repression of women, as governments that have lost control over economic systems try to increase control over social and cultural systems, particularly women and families. All governments and cultures devalue women, accept their second-class status, allow the violation of their human rights, and seek to control their lives. These are the patriarchal values that women's movements must confront. The movement must bring women's ideas into society at large and must bring more feminists into the arenas where decisions are made about women's lives. These are the challenges of the feminist future.

NOTES

We are grateful for the assistance of Center for Women Policy Studies staff members Edna Amparo Viruell, Christine Ogu, Belinda Gonzalez, Lois Copeland, Elaine Gram, Jin Lee, and Sarah Begus and of many other feminist thinkers and activists who have consulted with us: Flora Davis, Elvira Valenzuela Crocker, Barbara Smith, Brigid O'Farrell, Aileen Hernandez, Beverly Guy-Sheftall, Julianne Malveaux, LaVerne Morris, Irene Lee, Elaine Kim, Margaret Peake Raymond, Rayna Green, Charlotte Bunch, Irene Natividad, Margaret Gates, and Jean Hardisty. The participants in our November 1993 "Think Tank on the Future of the Women's Movement" inspired us with their vision of our feminist futures. Our colleagues at the Ford Foundation honored us with their faith in our vision and ability—our thanks to June Zeitlin, Lynn Walker, Marcia Smith, Stephen Zwerling, Betsy Campbell, and our program officer, Christina Cuevas, whose support, good humor, and active involvement in this project were invaluable.

1. The term *women of color* is the term of choice for referring to African American, Latina, Native American, and Asian American women; it replaces the term *minority,* which implies a lesser status and value.

2. These consultants were Elvira Valenzuela Crocker, Aileen Hernandez, Beverly Guy-Sheftall, Irene Lee, Elaine Kim, and Margaret Peake Raymond.

3. J. Hole and E. Levine, *Rebirth of Feminism* (New York: Quadrangle Books, 1971); E. Flexner, *Century of Struggle: The Woman's Rights Movement in the United States* (Cambridge, Mass: Harvard University Press, 1975); P. Giddings, *When and Where I Enter: The Impact of Black Women on Race and Sex in America* (New York: William Morrow, 1984).

4. Flexner, *Century of Struggle;* Hole and Levine, *Rebirth of Feminism;* Giddings, *When and Where I Enter;* Grimke, *Letters on the Equality of the Sexes and the Condition of Woman,* rpt. (Boston: Isaac Kanapp, 1970).

5. The many women's organizations involved in these efforts also formed the Woman's Joint Congressional Committee, which the *Ladies Home Journal* called the "most highly organized and powerful lobby ever seen in Washington." J. Freeman, "From Suffrage to Women's Liberation: Feminism in Twentieth Century America," in J. Freeman, ed., *WOMEN: A Feminist Perspective,* 5th ed. (Mountain View, Calif.: Mayfield, 1994).

6. Giddings, *When and Where I Enter.*

7. Many white women moved from home to factory, and some Chinese American and African American women moved from unskilled and domestic work to semiskilled labor

or from segregated to more integrated work settings. Japanese American women, however, were moved to internment camps for the duration of the war, after which they and their families returned to find that their possessions and livelihoods had been taken away.

8. D. S. Cobble, "Recapturing Working Class Feminism: Union Women in the Postwar Era," in J. Meyerowitz, ed., *Not June Cleaver: Women in the Postwar U.S., 1945–1960* (Philadelphia: Temple University Press, 1994).

9. Surprisingly, some of this work was done in a federal government agency, the U.S. Commission on Civil Rights, which established a women's rights program in 1973 to implement its mandate to address sex discrimination as well as race discrimination. The entire focus of the Women's Rights Program's work was on defining the intersection of racism and sexism and confronting its impact on women of color. The spring 1974 issue of the agency's *Civil Rights Digest,* entitled *Sexism and Racism: Feminist Perspectives,* was a landmark that has not been replicated.

10. F. Davis, *Moving the Mountain: The Women's Movement in America Since 1960* (New York: Simon and Schuster, 1991).

11. A. Echols, *Daring to Be BAD: Radical Feminism in America, 1967–1975* (Minneapolis: University of Minnesota Press, 1989); J. Freeman, *The Politics of Women's Liberation: A Case Study of an Emerging Social Movement and Its Relation to the Policy Process* (New York: David McKay, 1975); Hole and Levine, *Rebirth of Feminism.*

12. S. Shah, "Presenting the Blue Goddess: Toward a National Pan-Asian Feminist Agenda," in K. Aguilar, ed., *The State of Asian America* (Boston: South End Press, 1994), p. 148; Asian Women United of California, *Making Waves: An Anthology of Writings by and About Asian American Women* (Boston: Beacon Press, 1989).

13. M. A. Jaimes and T. Halsey, "American Indian Women: At the Center of Indigenous Resistance in Contemporary North America," in M. A. Jaimes, ed., *The State of Native America* (Boston: South End Press, 1992).

14. Echols, *Daring to Be BAD;* C. Bunch, *Passionate Politics: Feminist Theory in Action* (New York: St. Martin's Press, 1987).

15. Bunch, *Passionate Politics;* Echols, *Daring to Be BAD.*

16. Redstockings, eds., *Feminist Revolution* (New York: Random House, 1978).

17. Echols, *Daring to Be BAD.*

18. These publications included *Voice of the Women's Liberation Movement,* from Chicago; the annual New York journal, *Notes* (*Notes from the First Year,* 1968; *Notes from the Second Year,* 1970; and *Notes from the Third Year,* 1971); and the "Florida paper," from Gainesville. Others soon followed, such as *Women: A Journal of Liberation* (Baltimore), *No More Fun and Games: A Journal of Female Liberation* (Boston), *Quest: A Feminist Quarterly* (Washington, D.C.), and *Off Our Backs* (Washington, D.C.).

Books included Kate Millett, *Sexual Politics* (New York: Avon Books, 1971); Shulamith Firestone, *The Dialectic of Sex* (New York: Bantam Books, 1970); Germaine Greer, *The Female Eunuch* (New York: McGraw-Hill, 1970); Cellestine Ware, *Woman Power: The Movement for Women's Liberation* (New York: Tower, 1970); Toni Cade Bambara, *The Black Woman: An Anthology* (New York: New American Library, 1970); and Joyce Ladner, *Tomorrow's Tomorrow: The Black Woman* (Garden City, N.Y.: Doubleday, 1971) as well as such feminist anthologies as Robin Morgan, *Sisterhood Is Powerful* (New York: Vintage Books,

1970); and Anne Koedt, Ellen Levine, and Anita Rapone, *Radical Feminism* (New York: Quadrangle Books, 1973).

19. E. H. Haney, *A Feminist Legacy: The Ethics of Wilma Scott Heide and Company* (Buffalo, N.Y.: Margaret Daughters, 1985).

20. J. Mansbridge, *Why We Lost the ERA* (Chicago: University of Chicago Press, 1986); M. F. Berry, *Why ERA Failed: Politics, Women's Rights, and the Amending Process of the Constitution* (Bloomington: Indiana University Press, 1986).

21. See J. Freeman, "The Revolution for Women in Law and Public Policy," in J. Freeman, ed., *WOMEN: A Feminist Perspective*, 5th ed.(Mountain View, Calif.: Mayfield, 1994).

22. In the 1960s, abortion was a crime in virtually every state, yet at least 1 million illegal abortions were performed each year. L. Lader, *Abortion II: Making the Revolution* (Boston: Beacon Press, 1973).

23. Organizations such as the Mexican American Women's National Association, for example, had adopted a pro-choice position early in its history. Organizations such as the National Black Women's Health Project also linked women's reproductive rights to an expanded agenda for social and economic rights. See J. Brenner, "The Best of Times, the Worst of Times: U.S. Feminism Today," *New Left Review* (July-August 1993): 101–159.

24. Between 1969 and 1973, feminists from the Chicago Women's Liberation Union ran the "Jane" collective, whose members provided counseling and referrals and then, in 1971, began to perform abortions themselves. Davis, *Moving the Mountain.*

25. R. Petchesky, *Abortion and Woman's Choice: The State, Sexuality, and Reproductive Freedom* (Boston: Northeastern University Press, 1984).

26. During the second trimester, the states could regulate abortion to protect a woman's health; once the fetus became viable, states could prohibit abortion, except in cases where the woman's life or health was threatened. L. F. Goldstein, *The Constitutional Rights of Women: Cases in Law and Social Change* (Madison: University of Wisconsin Press, 1988).

27. The fact that the conference was held at all owed much to the leadership and persistence of Representatives Bella Abzug (D.–N.Y.), Patsy Mink (D.–Hawaii), and Margaret Heckler (R.–Mass.).

28. C. Bunch, *Passionate Politics.*

29. B. Adam, *The Rise of a Gay and Lesbian Movement* (Boston: G. K. Hall, 1987).

30. Andrea Dworkin's study of right-wing women offers an explanation for their fervent hostility to feminism and its ideology of liberation and equality for women, suggesting that these women have made a "bargain" to adhere to patriarchal marriage and family in exchange for protection from the outside world and male violence. A. Dworkin, *Right-Wing Women* (New York: G. P. Putnam, 1978). This may explain some of the success of the New Right in mobilizing women, but not all of it.

31. The Women's Educational Equity Act was a particular target. See S. Faludi, *BACKLASH: The Undeclared War Against American Women* (New York: Crown 1991); Brenner, "The Best of Times."

32. Faludi, *BACKLASH.*

33. Ibid.

34. In 1971, NOW and the Women's Equity Action League were joined by the National Women's Political Caucus—the first feminist organization whose goal was political power through election of women to public office. The National Conference of Puerto Rican Women (NaCOPRW), founded in 1972, has local chapters on the mainland and in Puerto

Rico; the National Black Feminist Organization, founded in 1973, held a conference and launched ten local chapters in its first year. The Mexican American Women's National Association (MANA), founded in 1974, and the Organization of Pan Asian American Women, created in 1976, bring Latina, Asian American, and Pacific Islander women's voices into public policy debates. The Black Women's Agenda, founded in 1977, conducts conferences during the Congressional Black Caucus's annual events. OHOYO, a national network of American Indian and Alaska Native Women, held annual conferences in the early 1980s and published resources about and for Native American women. The National Institute of Women of Color was founded in 1981 as a national network of activists, as was the National Coalition of 100 Black Women; the Coalition of Labor Union Women's ethnically diverse national network represents working-class and unionized women.

35. Women's health groups include the National Women's Health Network, the National Black Women's Health Project, and the National Latina Health Organization. Employment and training groups include Federally Employed Women, 9 to 5, and Wider Opportunities for Women. Among those groups focusing on specific age or ethnic groups are the National Political Congress of Black Women, Comisión Femenil, Asian Women United, the Organization of Chinese American Women, the National Network of Asian and Pacific Women, the National Association of Cuban American Women, the National Hispana Leadership Institute, and the Older Women's League. Included in the groups whose agendas and members became more feminist are the Black sororities, the League of Women Voters, the American Association of University Women, the Business and Professional Women's Clubs, the National Council of Negro Women, Women in Communications, the National Association of Negro Business and Professional Women, the North American Indian Women's Association, the Young Women's Christian Association of the United States, and the American Nurses Association.

36. Legal groups in Washington include the National Women's Law Center and the Women's Legal Defense Fund. Feminist legal groups in other cities are part of a national network of feminist lawyers, including Equal Rights Advocates in San Francisco and the NOW Legal Defense and Education Fund in New York. Feminist political action committees include the Women's Campaign Fund, the Democratic EMILY's list, and the Republican WISH list. Among the policy research groups are the Center for Women Policy Studies, the Women's Research and Education Institute, and the Institute for Women's Policy Research.

37. Davis, *Moving the Mountain.*

38. Journals included *Women's Studies, Feminist Studies, Signs: A Journal of Women in Culture and Society,* and *Sage: A Scholarly Journal on Black Women;* and among the presses are the Feminist Press and Kitchen Table: Women of Color Press.

39. These philanthropic groups include Women and Foundations/Corporate Philanthropy, the Ms. Foundation for Women, a variety of local women's funds, and the National Network of Women's Funds

40. The New York Asian Women's Center, now more than ten years old, is a leader in fighting violence against Asian American women, as are newer groups that have become active in the battered women's movement (Manavi in New Jersey and Sneha in Connecticut, for example). Groups such as the Washington Alliance of Korean American Women are both support groups and activists. Shah, "Presenting the Blue Goddess," p. 148.

Similarly, Native American women activists built women's organizations, such as Women of All Red Nations, the White Buffalo Calf Society, the Oglala Women's Society, and the Native American Women's Health and Education Resource Center in Lake Andes, South Dakota, that have confronted violence against women, alcoholism, and the full range of native women's economic and health issues. Women and AIDS advocacy networks have developed nationwide to support women confronting HIV disease and to advocate for woman-focused prevention and care services—e.g., The Positive Woman and the D.C. Women's Council on AIDS in Washington, D.C.; Sisterlove in Atlanta; the New Jersey Women and AIDS Network; and the Women's AIDS Network and Women Organized to Respond to Life-Threatening Disease (WORLD) in California.

41. For example, the National Council of Negro Women, the Women's Division of the Southern Christian Leadership Conference, and the Women's Missionary Society of the African Methodist Episcopal (AME) Church made advocacy for HIV/AIDS prevention and care top priorities for their local branches and chapters; the AAUW adopted educational equity for girls as its top issue.

42. The conference, sponsored by the Center for Women Policy Studies, was shaped by a steering committee of young feminists in their twenties and included plenary panels and workshops that modeled intergenerational partnerships.

43. These new groups include the Women's Health Action Movement, the Women's Action Coalition, the Young Women's Project, and The Third Wave.

44. Brenner, "The Best of Times."

45. In fact, women members of Congress had created the Congresswomen's Caucus in the mid-1970s and expanded it into the Congressional Caucus for Women's Issues, with membership open to nonwomen members of Congress, in the early 1980s.

46. Mondale did not interview any women of color, though several were qualified and available.

47. These organizations include the National Women's Political Caucus, the Center for the American Woman in Politics, Emily's List, the National Political Congress of Black Women, and the Women's Campaign Fund.

48. Bunch, *Passionate Politics*, p. 63.

49. K. Doner, "Women's Magazines: Slouching Toward Feminism," *Social Policy* 23, no. 4 (Summer 1993): 37–44.

50. Davis, *Moving the Mountain*.

51. Brenner, "The Best of Times."

52. We first used the term *feminist futures* as the title of the center's 1989 conference by, for, and about young women in their twenties. The ideas in this section of our chapter reflect many women's perspectives, including the women who responded to our national survey of over eight thousand women activists from the center's database and the feminist activists from throughout the United States who participated in our November 1993 "Think Tank on the Future of the United States Women's Movement." The center will publish a complete report of the "Think Tank" and the survey of U.S. women in 1995.

Selected Bibliography

Agarwal, Bina. *Structures of Patriarchy.* New Delhi: Kali for Women, 1988.

Buckley, M. *Women and Ideology in the Soviet Union.* New York: Harvester, 1989.

Buckley, M., ed. *Perestroika and Soviet Women.* Cambridge: Cambridge University Press, 1992.

Bunch, Charlotte. *Passionate Politics: Feminist Theory in Action.* New York: St. Martins Press, 1987.

Bystydzienski, Jill M. *Women Transforming Politics: Worldwide Strategies for Empowerment.* Bloomington: Indiana University Press, 1992.

Davies, Miranda. *Third World, Second Sex: Women's Struggles and National Liberation.* London: Zed Books, 1986.

Davis, Flora. *Moving the Mountain: The Women's Movement in America Since 1960.* New York: Simon and Schuster, 1991

Faludi, Susan. *Backlash: The Undeclared War Against American Women.* New York: Crown Publishers, 1991.

Freeman, Jo, ed. *Women: A Feminist Perspective.* 5th ed. Mountain View, CA: Mayfield Publishing Company, 1994.

Funk, Nanette, and Magda Mueller, eds. *Gender Politics and Post-Communism: Reflections from Eastern Europe and the Former Soviet Union.* New York: Routledge, 1993.

Honig, Emily, and Gail Hershatter. *Personal Voices: Chinese Women in the 1980s.* Menlo Park, CA: Stanford University Press, 1988.

Jaquette, Jane S., ed. *The Women's Movement in Latin America: Participation and Democracy.* 2d ed. Boulder: Westview Press, 1994.

Jayawardena, Kumari. *Feminism and Nationalism in the Third World.* London: Zed Books, 1986.

Katzenstein, Mary F., and Carol Mueller, eds. *The Women's Movements in the United States and Western Europe: Consciousness, Political Opportunity and Public Policy.* Philadelphia: Temple University Press, 1987.

Kruks, Sonia, Rayna Rapp, and Marilyn B. Young, eds. *Promissory Notes: Women in the Transition to Socialism.* New York: Monthly Review Press, 1989.

Lapidus, G. *Women and Soviet Society: Equality, Development, Social Change.* Berkeley: University of California Press, 1978.

Moghadam, Valentine M., ed. *Identity Politics and Women: Cultural Reassertion and Feminisms in International Perspective.* Boulder: Westview Press, 1994.

Mohanty, Chandra, Ann Russo, and Lourdes Torres, eds. *Third World Women and the Politics of Feminism.* Bloomington and Indianapolis: Indiana University Press, 1991.

Mohanty, Chandra, and Jacqueline Alexander, eds. *Third World Feminism*. London: Basil Blackwell, 1993.

Morgan, Robin. *Sisterhood Is Global: The International Women's Movement Anthology*. Garden City, NY: Anchor Books, 1984.

Nash, June, Helen Safa, and contributors. *Women and Change in Latin America*. South Hadley, MA: Bergin and Garvey Publishers, 1986.

Nelson, Barbara J., and Najma Chowdhury, eds. *Women and Politics Worldwide*. New Haven: Yale University Press, 1994.

Parpart, Jane L., and Kathleen A. Staudt. *Women and the State in Africa*. Boulder and London: Lynne Rienner Publishers, 1989.

Peterson, V. Spike, and Anne Sisson Runyan. *Global Gender Issues*. Boulder: Westview Press, 1993.

Robertson, Claire, and Iris Berger, eds. *Women and Class in Africa*. New York: Holmes and Meier, 1986.

About the Book and Editor

This pathbreaking book provides for the first time an overview of the genesis, growth, gains, and dilemmas of women's movements worldwide. Unlike most of the literature, which focuses on the industrialized Western world, this volume devotes greater attention to the postcolonial states of Asia, Africa, and Latin America. The book challenges the assumptions that feminism can transcend national differences and, conversely, that women's movements are shaped and circumscribed by national levels of development. All the authors reject the notion, proposed by its detractors and champions alike, that feminism is of middle-class origins and Western inspiration. Instead they seek to locate women's movements within the terrain from which they emerge.

Virtually all the authors are from the countries or communities about which they write; the few exceptions are women who have spent lengthy periods studying and living in the region. Most are scholars, often in women's studies, and many are closely associated with the movements they describe. Thus, these writers share a commitment to the substantive concerns as well as the collective processes of women's movements. As a key book for the Fourth World Conference on Women in Beijing, this volume will be essential reading for anyone interested in the global scope and implications of feminism.

Amrita Basu is professor of political science and women's and gender studies at Amherst College. **C. Elizabeth McGrory** works as a consultant on reproductive health and women's rights. She was previously a program officer for women's reproductive health at the MacArthur Foundation and has worked on women's programs in several nongovernmental organizations. She holds degrees in public health and in the international development studies.

About the Contributors

Hussaina Abdullah is a social anthropologist trained in Nigeria and England whose main research areas are labor, governance, and religion in West Africa. She works as an independent researcher and consultant on gender and development issues in Nigeria. She is a member of Women in Nigeria (WIN) and the Association of African Women in Research and Development (AAWORD).

Amrita Basu is professor of political science and women's and gender studies at Amherst College. She is the author of *Two Faces of Protest: Contrasting Modes of Women's Activism in India* (Berkeley: University of California Press and Delhi: Oxford University Press, 1992) and coeditor of the forthcoming *Appropriating Gender: Women's Activism and the Politicization of Religion in South Asia*. She is completing a book on the rise of Hindu nationalism in India.

Cecilia Blondet is the director of the Instituto Estudios Peruanos (Institute of Peruvian Studies), where she has worked as a researcher since 1983. A historian, her research focuses on shantytowns in urban areas and on the social and political participation of women in grassroots organizations. She is the author of a number of books and articles on these topics and is the coauthor of *Diagnosis of the Situation of Women in Peru 1980–1995*, which will be submitted as Peru's country report to the U.N. Fourth World Conference on Women.

Cristina Maria Buarque is a researcher and head of the coordinating group on women's studies at the Institute of Social Research, Joaquim Nabuco Foundation in Recife, Brazil. She is also coordinator of research for the North-Northeast Regional Network of Studies and Research on Women and Gender Relations.

Ana Alice Alcantara Costa is a professor of political science and researcher at the Nucleus of Interdisciplinary Studies on Women at the Federal University of Bahia, Brazil.

Denise Dourado Dora is a Brazilian feminist lawyer and a member of the Nucleus for Juridical Studies and Assistance and of The Latin American Committee for the Defense of Women's Rights.

Alicia Frohmann, a historian, is a professor and researcher at the Latin American Faculty of Social Sciences–Chile (FLACSO) where she coordinates the program on teaching. She has been an active member of the Chilean feminist movement for many years.

Dianne Hubbard is a lawyer at the Legal Assistance Center, a public interest law firm in Windhoek, Namibia, where she does legal research on gender issues. She is also a member of Women's Solidarity, a volunteer group involved in education and counseling around the issue of violence against women.

Islah Jad is a member of the new Women's Studies Program at Birzeit University, where she is on the faculty of the Cultural Studies Program. She is active in a number of women's organizations and alliances, including the Women's Technical Committee and the Women's Affairs Center in Gaza. She has published a number of articles on the evolution of the Palestinian women's movements, and her book on the history of the Palestinian women's movement is forthcoming in Arabic.

Roushan Jahan is a literary scholar, researcher, and activist who has been involved in women's issues since 1973. She is a cofounder and former president of Women for Women and an active member of Mahila Parishad as well as of two international women's networks. She is the author of numerous books and articles on the women's movement and on women in education, employment, and culture, published in Bangladesh and abroad.

Jane Jenson is currently professor of political science at the Universite de Montreal. Author of numerous articles and books on women's movements and politics in Western Europe, she has most recently published *Mitterrand et les Francaises: Un redez-vous manque.* She works with several international research groups on women and politics and serves on the advisory boards of *Signs: A Journal of Women and Culture* and *Social Politics.*

Wanjiku Mukabi Kabira is a lecturer in the Department of Literature at the University of Nairobi, where she specializes in oral tradition, gender, and culture. She is the author of a number of scholarly and literary works, including *The Oral Artist, Celebrating Women's Resistance,* and *The Good Witch of Kiarithaini.* She is also a consultant on gender and development and works with the African Women Communication and Development Network.

Amanda Kemp, a doctoral student at Northwestern University in the United States, is an African American feminist poet. Active in the antiapartheid movement, she is preparing a dissertation on identity politics among Black women in the South African liberation movements.

Radha Kumar is the author of *A History of Doing: An Illustrated Account of Movements for Women's Rights in India, 1800–1990* (1993). She has been active in the Indian women's movement and anticommunal movements and directed The Helsinki Citizens' Assembly, a coalition of groups in East and West Europe that campaigned for the democratic integration of Europe. Currently she is a Fellow at the Institute of War and Peace Studies at Columbia University.

Marta Lamas is a feminist activist who has been involved in the women's movement since the 1970s. She is a founder of Mexico's first rape crisis center, its first prochoice group (GIRE), and its first feminist magazine (*Fem*); she has also been active in forming feminist coalitions since the movement's inception. As an anthropologist she has researched prostitution in Mexico and is currently the director of *Debate Feminista,* an academic journal.

Nozizwe Madlala is currently a member of Parliament in South Africa. She is the former managing secretary of the Transitional Executive Sub Council on the Status of Women and member of the National Steering Committee of the Women's National Coalition. She is the past chair of the Natal Organization of Women, an affiliate of the United Democratic Front that later dissolved to join the African National Congress. During the 1980s she was in and out of detention under the Internal Security Act.

Alicia Martínez has written extensively on women's issues; she is a professor in the master's program in social sciences at the Latin American Faculty of Social Sciences–Mexico (FLACSO) and at the Interdisciplinary Program of Women's Studies at the Colegio de Mexico. She is currently conducting a national study on women and political movements.

Elzbieta Matynia, a sociologist trained at the University of Warsaw, currently teaches at the Graduate Faculty of the New School for Social Research in New York. She is the director of the Graduate Faculty's East and Central Europe Program, which collaborates with scholars in fourteen countries, and is an active member of the Network of East West Women.

Asha Moodley is a Black consciousness activist who strongly believes in its ethic of self-reliance, self-determination, and the empowerment of Black people, particularly Black women. Secretariat head for information and research of the Azanian People's Organization (AZAPO), Moodley is also an editorial member of the feminist journal *Agenda.*

Naihua Zhang is a doctoral candidate in the Department of Sociology at Michigan State University. She worked for a number of years as a journalist in China, writing about women and other social issues, and has actively participated in the contemporary Chinese women's movement. She is a member of the Chinese Society for Women's Studies, a group of overseas Chinese students and scholars advocating studies of women.

Wilhelmina Oduol is a lecturer in social anthropology at the Institute of African Studies at the University of Nairobi, where her teaching, research, and writing focus on gender and development. She is an active member of a number of women's organizations, including the Association of African Women in Research and Development, the African Women Development and Communication Network, and the National Council of Women of Kenya.

Anastasia Posadskaya is the founding director and member of the coordinating committee of the Moscow Center for Gender Studies, Institute for Socio-Economic Population Studies, at the Academy of Sciences of Russia. An economist, she specialized in women's employment under socialism and is currently using oral histories in the project "Retrieving the Voices of Old Russia's Women" as a Special Visitor at the Institute of Advanced Study in Princeton. She was one of the initiators of the Independent Woman's Forum in Russia and a coorganizer of the first and second Independent Woman's Forum in Dubna.

Lilia Quindoza Santiago is associate professor at the University of the Philippines and the editor of the *Diliman Review.* She has done research and written on the history of women's cultural and literary expression in the Philippines and has been active in several nationalist and women's movements and organizations.

Elaine Salo is a South African anthropologist, feminist, and mother. She teaches in the Department of Sociology and Anthropology at the University of the Western Cape. Her current interests include research on cultural interpreations of sexuality, fertility, and reproduction.

Wania Sant'Anna is a historian; assistant director of the Federation of Social Assistance and Educational Organizations (FASE); correspondent for FEMPRESS, a Latin American feminist news service; and director of the Institute for Religious Studies (ISER) in Brazil.

Vera Soares is a physicist at the University of São Paulo, Brazil, and a member of Centro Informacao Mulher (The Women's Information Center) and Elizabeth Lobo consultants.

Colette Solomon conducts social and economic research for the Social Sciences Division of the Multi-Disciplinary Research Center at the University of Namibia. She is also active in the women's movement and a member of the committee convened by the government's Department of Women Affairs to prepare the national report for the U.N. Fourth World Conference on Women.

María Luisa Tarrés is a professor at the Center for Studies in Sociology and the Interdisciplinary Program of Women's Studies at El Colegio de México. Her research has included studies of women involved in conservative social and political movements.

Jennifer Tucker is the vice president of the Center for Women Policy Studies in Washington DC, a feminist policy research and advocacy organization. She directs several center initiatives, including the National Program on Girls and Violence and programs that examine the connections among women's educational opportunities, employment options, economic status, and family roles. She serves on a number of boards for organizations involved with education and women of color.

Esperanza Tuñon teaches in the Department of Political and Social Sciences at the Mexican National University (UNAM), where she is best known for her research on women in the urban popular movement.

Teresa Valdés, a sociologist, is a professor and researcher at FLACSO–Chile, where she coordinates the gender studies area. She was a member of the human rights and political group *Mujeres por la Vida* and has long been a member of the Chilean feminist movement.

Elizabeth Waters has written and published widely on twentieth-century Russian history and society. She taught at the Australian National University from 1984 to 1994 and is currently in Russia researching a book on the family in the 1920s.

Leslie R. Wolfe is president of the Center for Women Policy Studies in Washington DC, a national feminist policy research and advocacy organization founded in 1972. She has worked on numerous government and nongovernment initiatives for gender equality, including the Project on Equal Education Rights, the Women's Education Equity Act Program, and the Women's Rights Program in the U.S. Commission on Civil Rights. She also serves on the boards of a number of educational, children's and women's organizations.

Wu Xu is a doctoral candidate in the Department of Sociology at Utah State University and currently works as an information analyst with the Utah Department of Health. She previously taught at Tianjin Normal University in China, where she was involved in starting women's studies. She is also a member of the Chinese Society for Women's Studies, a group of overseas Chinese students and scholars advocating studies of women.

Photo Credits

Index